War Stories

WAR STORIES
The War Memoir in History and Literature

Edited by
Philip Dwyer

Published by
Berghahn Books
www.berghahnbooks.com

© 2017, 2018 Philip Dwyer
First paperback edition published in 2018

All rights reserved. Except for the quotation of short passages
for the purposes of criticism and review, no part of this book
may be reproduced in any form or by any means, electronic or
mechanical, including photocopying, recording, or any information
storage and retrieval system now known or to be invented,
without written permission of the publisher.

Library of Congress Cataloging-in-Publication Data
A C.I.P. cataloging record is available from the Library of Congress
LCCN: 2016026097
https://lccn.loc.gov/2016026097

British Library Cataloguing in Publication Data
A catalogue record for this book is available from the British Library

ISBN 978-1-78533-307-1 (hardback)
ISBN 978-1-78533-840-3 (paperback)
ISBN 978-1-78533-308-8 (ebook)

Contents

Preface		vii
1.	Making Sense of the Muddle: War Memoirs and the Culture of Remembering *Philip Dwyer*	1
2.	War Memoirs, Witnessing and Silence *Jay Winter*	27
3.	'A Lively School of Writing': George Gleig, Moyle Sherer and the Romantic Military Memoir *Neil Ramsey*	48
4.	'The Tallest Pine in the Political Forest': Race and Slavery in the Confederate Veteran's Memoir, 1866–1915 *Craig A. Warren*	73
5.	British Memoirs and Memories of the Great War *Ian Isherwood*	94
6.	A Cog in the Machine of History? Japanese Memoirs of Total War (1937–45) *Aaron William Moore*	111
7.	Post-Soviet Russian Memoirs of the Second World War *Roger D. Markwick*	143
8.	Reimagining the Yugoslav Partisan Epic *Vesna Drapac*	168
9.	The War That Was Not: 1948 Israeli War Memoirs *Ilan Pappe*	193

10. Remembering the 'Endless' Partition: From Memoirs about
    the 1947 Conflict to the Post-Memoir   208
    Tarun K. Saint

11. 'To Be Made Over': Vietnamese-American Re-education
    Camp Narratives   229
    Subarno Chattarji

12. Memoir Writing as Narrative Therapy: A South African   252
    Border War Veteran's Story
    Gary Baines

13. Pugnacity, Pain and Professionalism: British Combat   277
    Memoirs from Afghanistan, 2006–14
    Joanna Bourke

Index   301

Preface

This book is based on a symposium held in Newcastle, Australia, in 2010. The symposium was part of a project looking at veteran culture and the military memoirs from the Revolutionary and Napoleonic Wars, but it was meant to provide a forum in which researchers working on similar projects for other wars and other time periods could come together and discuss their work. They thereby contribute theoretical or comparative expertise to the study of memory and war memoirs in the modern era. War memoirs can be incredibly popular, as witnessed by the success surrounding Anthony Swofford's *Jarhead*, which of course was made into a Hollywood movie with a heartthrob in the lead role (one critic called it *Full Metal Jacket* light). But it is also a testimony to the impact that memoirs can have on a whole generation and the way they can shape how wars are seen and recalled.

The literature on war memoirs is beginning to come into its own as more and more scholars grapple with the ways in which the experience and memory of war is transmitted from one generation to the next through textual representations, and the ways in which that transmission helps form perceptions of the past. From the outset, papers at the symposium and indeed in this collection have been limited to only those that dealt, if not exclusively then in large part, with memoirs. Part of the rationale was that other textual representations of wars – letters, diaries and journals in particular – were fundamentally different sources from the memoir. Letters home or diaries are, it could be argued, possibly more accurate as historical documents (although not without their own problems) since they are more immediate, more spontaneous. Memoirs, on the other hand, are necessarily subject to the tricks that time and memory can play on the individual attempting to recount events that took place many years, sometimes decades before. Paul Fussel, in his own memoirs of the war in Europe, *Doing Battle: The Making of a Skeptic,* asserted that because memoirs are written after the event, they cannot escape what he calls 'the necessity of fiction'. I would argue this is precisely where war memoirs are useful, for what they might tell the reader about how the wars and the individuals in them are represented, for what they tell us about emotions and experiences, however filtered, and for what they tell us also about the silences. We are hoping that the following collection will engender broader discussions about the types of stories that were and are told, what kinds of representations of the wars dominate a given society, and why particular representations succeed in dominating the public imagination.

The more difficult flip side to that coin is figuring out what kinds of memories were considered unacceptable and were therefore marginalised, excluded or reworked. One of the themes that recurs throughout the following texts is why veterans choose to remember, and to recall their experiences in writing, sometimes with a view to publication but often not. There is a wonderful passage in the novel *Soldiers of Salamis* by Javier Cercas reflecting on a fictional veteran of the Spanish civil war called Miralles: 'He remembers', writes Cercas, 'because, although they [his comrades] died sixty years ago, they're still not dead, precisely because he remembers them. Or perhaps it's not him remembering them, but them clinging to him, so they won't die off entirely'. In between the projections, evasions, myths and outright fantasies, the authors of the following chapters sometimes are also looking for the signs of pain, fear and anxiety in the hope of better understanding the impact war has had on the lives of whole generations of men and women under arms.

This project has taken a long time to realise since its inception all those years ago. It could not have come into being without the support of the Australia Research Council, the School of Humanities and Social Science, and the support of my colleagues at the Centre for the History of Violence at the University of Newcastle in Australia. This book is part of an ongoing research programme that encompasses all aspects of the history of violence in the modern world. It is our hope that this collection will not only be used in the classroom, but will stimulate further study of the war memoir in history.

Can the foot soldier teach anything important about war, merely for having been there? I think not. He can tell war stories.
—Tim O'Brien, *If I Die in a Combat Zone: Box Me Up and Ship Me Home*

All stories are true.
—Chinua Achebe

Chapter 1

Making Sense of the Muddle
War Memoirs and the Culture of Remembering

Philip Dwyer

WRITING TO REMEMBER, WRITING TO FORGET

The early modern autobiography coincided with the rise of the centralising state.[1] It was written by the military and political elite in the service of one European monarchy or another, and was modelled on the wars of the ancients and in particular Caesar's *Gallic Wars*. This began to shift in the seventeenth century when memoir writing was given a significant impetus by the Thirty Years War (1618–48) and the English Civil War (1642–51). Although most memoirs from those protracted and bloody conflicts were written by the gentry or the aristocracy, we see for the first time a surge in 'popular' autobiography, that is, accounts written by junior officers and common soldiers.[2] However, it was not until the war memoir became democratised from the middle of the eighteenth century onwards that the voice of the common soldier, anxious to be part of and a witness to history, was for the first time heard in a meaningful way.[3] The American War of Independence (1775–83), and in particular the French Revolutionary and Napoleonic Wars (1792–1815), gave the memoir a tremendous impetus. Thousands of memoirs were published, in all the major European languages, as individuals realised they had taken part in a momentous historical process and felt the need to testify to what they had lived through.[4] This was especially the case for wars that followed political upheaval, during which individuals realised not only that they were part of history, but also that they had lived through life-transforming personal experiences. Soldiers of all modern wars share this at least in common.[5]

The democratisation of a genre that had once been the reserve of an aristocratic elite overlapped with a number of important cultural developments taking place in Western Europe. Those developments were increased literacy rates; the rise of the novel or the *Bildungsroman*; the transformation in thinking about the place of the individual in society and history; the interest in self-representation that came to fruition in the eighteenth century;[6] the change in status of the common soldier, increasingly socially accepted during the course of the nineteenth century;[7] the evolution in military strategy from small professional armies to massed conscript armies; and the advent of what has been dubbed a 'culture of sensibility' when 'feeling' first came into its own in the literary and philosophical world.[8] With modern armies being made up of citizen soldiers, and with a growing awareness of certain sentiments and sensibilities, the literate, upper classes were far more ready to listen to and read accounts by their social inferiors.[9] The sentiments expressed by common soldiers – generally scenes of horror and destruction described in pathetic terms, but also as we can see in the following chapters, narratives of pain and suffering – were designed not only to elicit a response in the reader, but also to develop and refine the reader's own sentiments and sensibilities. Take the description of the retreat from Moscow in 1812 written by a survivor, Raymond de Montesquiou-Fezensac, who explicitly asks the reader to 'participate in the sentiments ... to share in my admiration of so much courage, and to sympathize with my compassion for so much misfortune'.[10]

With the end of the First World War the genre reached new heights. The generation that fought in the trenches seems to have been educated, literate and 'vigorously literary' in ways that soldiers in other wars were not.[11] Thousands of memoirs have been published by veterans of the Great War from all sides of the conflict, not to mention the number of diaries and the collections of letters.[12] One can also include hundreds of novels inspired by the direct experience of trench warfare, from one of the most famous of them all, Erich Maria Remarque's *All Quiet on the Western Front*, to the lesser known Australian work, Frederic Manning's *The Middle Parts of Fortune* (once described by Hemingway as the 'finest and noblest book of men in war that [he had] ever read'). These novels, especially when based on first-hand experience, are often more powerful and more convincing documents than memoirs.

The Second World War differed again from the First to the extent that the men writing their memoirs were often less literary, and more direct.

This was particularly the case of the Pacific theatre of war where conscripts and civilians alike confronted a particularly brutal enemy in the Japanese imperial soldier, who not only gave no quarter, but also treated his enemy appallingly. Robert Leckie's *Helmet for My Pillow*, published in 1957, and Eugene Bondurant Sledge's *With the Old Breed: At Peleliu and Okinawa*, first published in 1981, both describe how the Japanese would routinely mutilate dead American soldiers and how retaliations would inevitably follow, so that a vicious racialised war ensued in which both sides were guilty of committing atrocities and systematically murdering prisoners. Here too, as with the First World War, the novelised account of the pacific theatre, including in Japan where there was a rich tradition of autobiographical novels, blurred the lines between fact and fiction.[13] In the United States, Norman Mailer's *The Naked and the Dead*, which appeared in 1948, and James Jones's *The Thin Red Line*, published in 1962, have become two of the most recognised novels on the American war in the Pacific. Much like the First World War novel, both play on the incompetence of military high command, as well as questioning the integrity of some of the men they depict.

Vietnam again changed the war memoir mould. Many more memoirs show a tripartite structure of before, during and after as participants testify to the transformative nature of the war.[14] Before Vietnam, there is no life before or after war. With few exceptions, the war narrative usually starts with either recruitment or training, and finishes with the end of the recruit's war. Colonel Noël, for example, declared at the end of his memoirs on the Napoleonic wars that there was no more to tell. 'I have almost nothing to say about the period of peace'.[15] The same could be said for most veterans of most wars. Childhood, peace and the mundane do not elicit a reflex to remember. A new life starts and finishes with time in the services and nothing that happens before and nothing that comes after has any importance in defining the experience that was combat.

There are important exceptions to that rule. Robert Graves and Siegfried Sassoon begin their memoirs detailing their family lives. So too does Remarque's novel *All Quiet on the Western Front*, which can be read as memoir. The opening pages of Ron Kovic's *Born on the Fourth of July* dwell on his life growing up in Massapequa, New York, before joining the United States Marine Corps straight out of high school. On the other hand, Marian Novak's *Lonely Girls with Burning Eyes*, about the life of a military wife who stays at home while her husband is in Vietnam, is really about the post-war experience. On the whole, however, war is considered a rupture to one's 'normal' life, and is therefore generally treated as completely separate from the civilian life led both before and after.

***

The reasons men and women decide to write about their wartime experiences are as varied as the individuals who put pen to paper: to justify individual acts or their participation in a war; to leave something behind for posterity (memoirs are often dedicated to children);[16] as an act of remembrance in which the veteran not only speaks for himself, but in the name of others; to set the record straight; to commemorate fallen comrades; to bear witness; and to express dissatisfaction with the ways in which wars are officially portrayed. For Ron Kovic, writing was a way of 'leaving something of meaning behind, to rise above the darkness and despair'.[17]

Writing can, in other words, be a cathartic experience, a means of better coping with the present, of helping the author understand what they have lived through. It may have got them through a particularly difficult period in their lives, one in which the memories of past hardships and lost comrades have come flooding back to haunt them. This is not always the case though. Sometimes, writing about the past can be a traumatic experience as individuals relive what they had hoped to forget. Regardless of the person's politics or background, regardless of whether they belonged to the oppressors or the oppressed, the reasons people testify in writing are ultimately the same. All put pen to paper in the knowledge that they have lived through, and survived, something extraordinary, that they have been part of a larger historical moment.[18] The memoirist does not, however, set out to write history, but to give a privileged point of view, a personal perspective of what has been witnessed, experienced and suffered. In doing so, the author leaves himself open not only to the gaze of contemporaries, some of whom may have shared similar experiences, but also to the critical gaze of generations to come.[19]

***

The chapters in this collection study diverse aspects of what we now know to be an enormous body of literature comprising tens of thousands of works for the modern period, across languages and cultures. Until quite recently, this body of work was not taken seriously, largely dismissed as unimportant because memoirs were considered notoriously inaccurate and unreliable. Historians consequently approached them in much the same manner as a lawyer questioning an aging witness with a history of perjury.[20] They were all the more critical because the memoir often falls between two worlds, between truth and fiction, between primary and secondary source, between reality and imagination.[21] This scepticism was exacerbated by historians traditionally shying away from the individual as subject, from the 'I' in history, wary of biography as much as autobiography and the memoir.[22]

The advent of alternative approaches to history, in particular oral history, cultural history, memory and the experience of war, has enabled scholars to tackle the war memoir from an entirely different perspective. Of interest now is not what people claim to have occurred, but what the author thinks worth remembering, how an event is remembered, how war memoirs shape 'cultural memory', and the impact they can have on the ways in which a society prefers to remember and celebrate past wars.[23] The individual may recall particular experiences and events in the past, but that past is interpreted through the filter of time and shaped by larger social and political attitudes towards the war. There is, moreover, to paraphrase Jay Winter, a difference between what soldiers write, and what readers do with their words.[24] It is the difference between a veteran's memory of a war and 'cultural memory'.

The literature has thus grown in recent years but there are still vast lacunae. Apart from the two world wars, there are no studies, for example, on war memoirs and the Mexican War of 1846–48, the Crimean War, the Italian and German wars of unification or the Franco-Prussian War of 1870.[25] Nor are there any studies focusing on the wars of colonisation that took place throughout the nineteenth century, not to mention the twentieth-century wars of decolonisation. There is little for the Spanish Civil War – Franco's death and the introduction of democracy saw an outpouring of war memoirs in Spain[26] – nothing for the Korean War and little for Vietnam. Some of the chapters in this book are therefore the first to examine particular wars from the perspective of the memoir. Memoirs by American, British and Australian soldiers who have served in Afghanistan and Iraq have appeared since at least 2001, but we have almost no knowledge of what has been written from the Arab perspective. And, yes, *jihadis* write their memoirs too. There is, subsequently, a need for studies that further place war memoirs in context, that reflect on how memoirs have been used to transmit particular views of war as well as the experience of war itself, and that reflect on the ways in which veterans shape their reminiscences and the ways in which, in turn, veteran memories are shaped by the social and political environment.[27] Scholars are, as is manifest in this collection, increasingly engaging with the ways in which memory and written representations of the past interact, how experiences are transmitted, and how in some instances – think of France, Germany or Yugoslavia in the post-Second World War years, Israel after the 1948 war, or Pakistan and India after Partition – the state, political parties and individuals coalesce to erase from history those who had persecuted and to restore to prominence those who had been proscribed.[28]

WAR, HISTORY AND MEMOIR WRITING

There has always been a certain amount of anxiety surrounding the accuracy or 'authenticity' of memoirs, not only among historians and readers but also especially among veterans writing about their experiences.[29] False memoirs are periodically uncovered, hoaxes written for all sorts of reasons that can discredit the genre.[30] When that happens, the distinction between traditional history and memoir is brought to the fore. History is for the most part written by professionals who have never lived through or experienced the subject matter of their studies. Memoirs are written – the reader assumes – by people who have actually experienced the events they are describing.[31] Some memoirs are published in the hope of influencing future historians, or at the very least in the hope of influencing the way future generations will look back on the author. In the process, memory becomes history, and is transformed into a document later used by historians. The lived experience then is the basis, the source of those documents.

The war memoir is nevertheless a very different animal from history and even from the traditional military autobiography in which generals wrote self-justificatory accounts of campaigns and battles.[32] At its most basic level, the story is told from an entirely different perspective – that of the common soldier or civilian who has little or no control over the events they are caught up in.[33] It is more personal, it is about the experience of war, as well as experiences beyond the battlefield, and can sometimes include accounts of people whose lives are peripheral to, but touched by war. That is why a more encompassing approach to the genre is required, one that does not limit the definition of the war memoir to those only written by combat veterans.[34] Family members, friends and wives have, for example, also written accounts relating the shared experiences of war that are now considered to be part of the war memoir genre.[35] In the modern era, journalists and writers have invariably 'gone to war' to report on what they see.[36] The study of war writing, in other words, no longer needs to be limited to the experience of men in battle, but can encompass a much broader autobiographical tradition where the myriad voices emerging from war should not be treated in opposition to each other but as component parts of a larger story.

The war memoir was predominantly, but never exclusively, a male preoccupation. In the eighteenth century, there were cases of women disguising themselves as men to fight alongside them, and who later left accounts of their adventures.[37] From the mid-nineteenth century onwards, nurses related their wartime experiences and then in the twentieth century there was a shift with women fighting in the front lines.[38] Women drove ambulances on the Western Front during the First World War, trucks and trams on the Home Front during the Second World War, as well as worked in factories, fought on the Eastern Front in their hundreds of thousands, and supported the resistance in Nazi occupied Europe. They necessarily tell of a different experience to that of the male combatant, although invariably subordinate to male myths about war. The nurse, for example, does not normally place herself alongside the male soldier, but rather she tends to place the wounded soldier on a pedestal while she is before it, head bowed, in tribute to his sacrifice.[39] Also, in nurses' descriptions of interacting with non-white populations, women often imitate the predominant, in this case colonial discourses, infantilising colonial troops, revealing the extent to which they had accepted the myths and stereotypes about race they had learnt growing up.[40] As such, nurses' memoirs are complex records of how white women and non-whites interacted. Only a few from the First World War dared question the myths and the treatment received by African and Indian troops.[41]

In a similar vein, few prisoner-of-war (POW) narratives question the prisoner experience as one based on mateship, courage and survival. This is especially the case within popular Australian memory where the nationalist narrative that conforms to the Anzac legend still survives, despite a number of studies pointing to the tensions between POW memoirs, oral testimonies and the Anzac ethos.[42] Narratives of mateship, courage and survival, however, need to be constructed, and can only occur if former POWs are given a voice during and after war. This was clearly not the case in Soviet Russia, where millions of POWs survived the brutal treatment of the Nazis only to be stigmatised by their own, and treated little better than 'enemies of the people'. A not dissimilar experience existed for the few who survived internment during the war in Vietnam.

National myths require veterans to leave out certain experiences. Soldiers are generally silent about the darker side of war we know they must have either been witness to or involved in. Few mention the mistreatment of civilians, let alone the rape of women. Few mention homosexual encounters in the ranks. Few mention desertion or the execution of prisoners, or reprisals against civilian populations as punishment for partisan activity.[43] The absence of anything that might tarnish the reputations of veterans or which might lead to national myths being questioned says as much about the men and women writing their memoirs as about the overpowering obligation to conform to national expectations.[44] It is only in the modern era that the combat veteran will even admit to killing, and in rare instances admit to the pleasure of killing.[45] Most portray themselves as bystanders, victims of war, rather than as perpetrators or actors. A very few saw beauty in war's death and destruction.[46] Realism is expected, but only up to a certain point, and only an accepted kind of realism, usually one that conforms to the dominant national ideal.[47]

* * *

In the nineteenth, more so than in the twentieth century, memoirs were often based on diaries and journals, 'documents' that helped prod the memory of the author, traces of the past that were brought into the present. In the nineteenth century, too, anxious that their memoirs would be accepted as credible, authors often appended supporting documents (letters, maps, official proclamations). The veracity of memoirs occupied a central place among the memoirists themselves. They told the 'truth', because they had been in the thick of it, they had seen what took place, and they had experienced the pain and suffering. All memoirists want to be taken at their word; they aspire to revealing reality through their stories, to let people know what it was like to live through what they have lived through, to tear the veil from the readers' eyes. It is part of the time-held claim to authenticity – distinct from the debates surrounding 'veracity' – that only those who have experienced battle can talk about war.[48] The authenticity associated with the claim that veterans have lived through and experienced the events they describe in their memoirs gives them a moral authority the historian does not possess. From the very start, then, there is a tension between memory and history that can be found in all memoirs.

This is why memoirists often distinguished themselves from novelists, although the distinction with biography and history was far less clear in the eighteenth century, and the distinction with the novel became far less obvious after Vietnam when writing styles tended to blur. And yet we know that by the time veterans return to the past to begin to write about their experiences, the past has already often become mythified, and their own memories have been deformed by the ways in which the war has since been interpreted. In the course of that process reality and fiction can merge as memory plays tricks on the author, something that many memoirists are aware of. Take the preface to Edmund Blunden's *Undertones of War*, published less than ten years after the end of the First World War, in which he writes that:

> memory has her little ways, and by now she has concealed precisely that look, that word, that coincidence of nature without and nature within that I long to

remember. Within the space of even one year, this divinity seems to me to take a perverse pleasure in playing with her votaries; 'you'd like to see this, my friend' (she shows for the second time the veiled but seemingly perfect novocreation of some heart-throbbing scene – she slides it into secrecy) 'wouldn't you?' But I am inclined to think that her playfulness has been growing rather more trying latterly: and perhaps I am gradually becoming colder in my enthusiasm to win a few games.[49]

And yet Blunden persisted, attempting to describe what he called 'the image and the horror of it'. When the veteran is mistaken or asserts something that has never happened, it is not that the author deliberately exaggerates or distorts reality, but rather that the process of writing and of ordering a life into a cohesive narrative inevitably deforms that reality.

An interesting example of this occurred with the publication of the memoirs of John Howard, Prime Minister of Australia from 1996 to 2007, who recounted a story of his first weekend in the Prime Minister's residence in Canberra, The Lodge, to which he claimed he invited the daughter of another former Prime Minister, Robert Menzies, for celebratory drinks. Robert Menzies' daughter publicly rejected the account as 'fanciful' and insisted it be omitted from any future editions. One can assume John Howard wrote the account in good faith, and that it was not a deliberate falsehood. It could have been embellishment or he may simply have convinced himself of the verity of what he was writing.[50] This type of 'fictionalisation' can really only be contradicted or corrected by a third person privy to the scene in question. When the historical record can be corrected, of interest to the historian is why the author has imagined a particular presence or event. Of course, 'fictionalisation' is really part of the memoir-writing process, and is inherent in the construction of style and structure.[51] To that extent, techniques used by memoirists are similar to the devices used by fiction writers to influence the reception of their text, as well as creating the atmosphere necessary to convey thoughts, feelings and atmosphere.

The model for these fictionalisations is not only the novel, however. Other texts, and in the modern period filmic representations – as we see in a number of the chapters here – can influence not only the manner in which the past is recalled and remembered, but the soldier's conception of war, before he or she actually experiences it. There are, in other words, strong links of memory between wars. The Wehrmacht generals of the Second World War had been young officers during the First, and were immersed in a literature (as well as the experience) of war that was brutal and total. The American boy who went to Vietnam was brought up on the memory of the Second World War – transmitted in part through Hollywood movies – and often believed, naively, that like the war in Europe in 1939–45, Vietnam too was a 'good' war. John Wayne is sometimes evoked in American memoirs of the Vietnam War.[52] As Joanna Bourke points out in her chapter, the professionals who went to Iraq have been brought up on war movies and the memory of Vietnam. Anthony Swofford's *Jarhead*, about the Iraq war, is an example of how tropes from one war, in this case Vietnam, can cross over into another.[53] Every young generation of soldiers is influenced not by the experience of war itself, but rather by the 'experience of war' as schoolboy or schoolgirl.[54] This is not to say that all children glamorise war, but that their imaginings of what the next war will be like are firmly rooted in the past, and are therefore largely out of sync with the reality they are likely to face in the next war.

THE POLITICS OF WAR MEMOIRS

If war museums have often been accused of sanitising or glamorising war by their 'heroic' portrayals of death, the same cannot be said for the modern war memoir.[55] It is true that battlefield feats are sometimes glorified, or that scenes of hand-to-hand fighting are embellished, but by the eighteenth century the glory of war was quickly giving way to detailed descriptions of horror that were meant to serve as a judicious lesson for those who followed in the veteran's wake. This was a tradition that dated back to at least the Thirty Years War, when memoirs were in part meant to serve as a warning to others of the dangers of war. If not yet what Samuel Hynes has dubbed 'battlefield gothic', a change in attitude towards war saw a seismic shift with the Romantic movement in Europe at the end of the eighteenth and the beginning of the nineteenth century, and which regarded war, for the first time in history, as 'evil'.[56]

Soldiers do not, on the whole, portray war as noble and uplifting. This may be the case for particular individuals, but it has not been a general trend since the seventeenth century when self-reflection, the expression of an inner life, and the transformative nature of war and combat all begin to make an appearance in the memoirs.[57] From the end of the eighteenth century onwards, one can find all the tropes belonging to the 'modern' war memoir: descriptions of the first time in combat and the feelings associated with the experience, what is commonly referred to as a 'baptism of fire', as though it were a religious rite of passage; the first time one comes across the dead, mutilated or wounded; the horror, the trauma, the obsession with anecdotal detail that stayed with the veteran for years after (what Fussell calls 'irony-assisted recall'[58]); the day-to-day experience of camp or barracks life or in the lull of fighting; interactions with civilians and especially women (sexual conquests are part of the soldier's narrative); impressions of the landscape and the peoples encountered; the bonds of camaraderie; and, inevitably, the disdain for war and its suffering. This latter in particular makes up what is now referred to as the disillusionment narrative, in which war is criticised or at least presented at its worst.[59]

The disillusionment narrative sensationalises the gore of war – extreme violence, detailed descriptions of death, wounding and suffering, mass killings, massacres and atrocities – and includes detailed portrayals not only of the wounded and dead, but of men's bodily movements. *All Quiet on the Western Front* was by no means the first war novel or war memoir to do so, to the point where it was dubbed by right-wing critics the 'lavatory school' of war novels, but the gore of war was clearly present for the first time in novels and memoirs during the 1920s and 1930s.[60] Increasingly, as a shift took place in the way in which war was represented, descriptions of battlefield gothic became not only more common, but more emotionally invested. The twentieth century lifted social taboos that had inhibited earlier forms of writing so that soldiers were able to articulate their thoughts, fears and beliefs in ways they had not been able to in previous generations.

There has, however, been a shift in the way in which war is portrayed in this century. As Joanna Bourke demonstrates in this collection, twenty-first-century war memoirs, written by professional, elite soldiers, eschew the disillusionment narrative, and glorify the blood and guts of war in ways that we have rarely seen in previous generations. This development appears to represent another defining moment in the history of the war memoir. The emotional pleas that can be found in twentieth-century accounts were present, in muted form, in earlier centuries, but really come into their own in the twentieth century. As Jay Winter shows in his chapter, what this says about changing cultural conceptions of the self, about the way soldiers remember wars, and about that which they choose to remain silent, makes for interesting social and cultural insights.[61] There are reasons for the silence. Remembering can be painful, especially when the account touches on deeply traumatic and personal events. Gabriele Köpp, for example, who was repeatedly raped by Russian soldiers in 1945 at the age of 15, did not write of her harrowing experiences, and was only the second German woman to do so, until the age of 80.[62] Köpp would have had to endure the traumatic violence of the rapes, and would have then had to endure the memory of that violence for decades after. For her at least, the act of writing about that violence was a liberating experience. For others, however, memories of war and violence are so traumatic that the only way forward is to forget altogether; they never talk and will never write of their experiences.[63]

HOW TO READ A WAR MEMOIR

Apart from the obvious necessity to disentangle fact from fiction, and to contextualise, how does one then read a war memoir? The chapters in this collection take into consideration the complex processes whereby war experiences are reinterpreted, and will hopefully serve as examples to others. Two of the most important elements historians should take into consideration have to do with the ways in which memory is transmitted. The first is that the memoirist chooses, consciously or otherwise, what to include and what to omit in the light of hindsight or in response to the degree of importance an event has taken on over time. There can be a certain amount of self-censorship involved in this process when individuals omit details they do not want the public to know about, or which do not accord with the official narrative of the war. An example of this is the Israeli memoirs that appeared after the 1948 war, which deliberately failed to mention the forced expulsion and massacre of Palestinians.[64] Instead, they adopted the official narrative that, afraid of the Israel Defense Forces, Palestinians 'ran away'. The reasons veterans adopted this Zionist narrative ranged from support for Israel's international image to a desire to portray Israeli citizens and soldiers positively. By the 1970s and 1980s, however, a number of these memoirs were corrected either in newspaper articles or in new, reprinted editions as a more realistic assessment of the war, largely the result of research conducted by the 'new historians' in Israel, began to reveal details of what had taken place. A shift can, therefore, take place over time from an acceptance of the official narrative to a more critical stance.

The second important element historians need to consider when reading war memoirs is that as a consequence of textual, novelistic, filmic and other media influences on the veteran-author, the line between reality and fiction can become blurred. The memoirist, as narrator, especially in his or her old age, may become incapable of distinguishing between imagined memories and the reality of the past.[65] When this happens, the author-veteran necessarily becomes the vector of a social re-memorisation of the war, the fruit of their own personal experiences, and a version of the war that is projected onto them by the media. The individual's recollections are, moreover, constantly being transformed and reformulated, in the first instance by telling others about his or her experiences, and secondly by absorbing what others have to say about the war. In the telling of the story, the individual then has a tendency to only remember that which has been told or written down.[66] It becomes the reference point for further tellings of the story.

The process of writing a memoir, the transformation of the experiences an individual may have lived through and witnessed, necessarily transforms the events described as they are put on paper.⁶⁷ The overall narrative, for a narrative is constructed in the process of writing, alters the memory and with it the attitudes, behaviours and actions that are the basis for that memory. The act of writing, therefore, transforms what may very well have only been a subjective impression into a 'historical reality' that was not. The act of writing about an anecdote or piece of gossip also transforms it into a fact; it now exists, it is true, because it is on paper. In this manner, memoirists become mythmakers, creating records that not only influence the manner in which readers see the past, but also how historians interpret the past.

For those who have never experienced war or extreme violence at close hand, talking about it is largely an intellectual exercise, a question of imposing structures and themes where none previously existed. Like the authors themselves, we attempt to 'make sense of the muddle', to interpret the images and to place everything in a larger context.⁶⁸ The war memoir is often a one off, a work by a veteran who has no pretentions of writing literature, who is entirely unaccustomed to writing narratives, and who at most may have written reports or letters. This was especially the case for the period before the twentieth century when wars were mostly fought by the semi-literate, who only later found the means to express their thoughts and feelings, or to simply describe their experiences, on paper. If veterans' narratives are published at all, the vast majority go largely unnoticed, and then fall into obscurity only to be brought into the light (again) by scholars. The war memoirs that become 'classics' and that are read across generations more often than not strike a chord in the national myths they have helped shape and colour. They are the Robert Graves, the Siegfried Sassoons and the Michael Herrs.

In this collection of essays we deal specifically with war memoirs – and not letters, diaries and journals – because they are remembered, restructured and filtered by time. That is their value to historians, not as immediate impressions of what has just taken place or been observed, but as a remembrance that has survived and has been shaped and coloured by the passage of time. It is their interpretation, their impressions and their feelings that, as part of the experience of war, make them valuable sources for historians trying to figure out what it was like to live through those times. Memoirs written during the time period under study suffer from what Bourdieu dubbed the 'biographical illusion' (*illusion biographique*), the belief that we are getting a privileged and direct access to the past.⁶⁹ In fact, the best memoirs are those written many years after the event, which does not make them more accurate, but which allows for a certain reflection, and a degree of self-reflection among the authors. This retrospection always assumes a certain discontinuity between youth, the period about which the veteran memoirist is most often writing, and old age.[70] The assumption is that the veteran telling the story of his or her youth is the same person, in spite of the decades that might separate them. It is memory that provides the continuity between youth and old age.

We are only just beginning to understand the ways in which the war memoir is ultimately a product of the veteran author's memory. The subjective experience which is often at the centre of the modern war memoir and which constitutes such a large proportion of the 'experience of war' is only one layer of what is a multilayered, multidimensional text. Other layers and dimensions include questions over the extent to which war and violence have influenced people's behaviours and actions, as well as understanding the impact war and violence can have over long periods of time. Why is it, for example, that the victims of war, mass killings and genocide often express feelings of shame and mortification at surviving,[71] while the perpetrators of those crimes generally feel no remorse? If there is a 'duty to remember', does the voice of the perpetrator deserve to be heard in the same way as the victim?[72]

Any interpretation of the war memoir, any understanding of personal experience in war, has to take into account changing frameworks of meaning. That is, the text has to be read where possible from the contemporary's perspective. The scholar has to understand how it was received at the time, and should place it where possible in the continuum of autobiographical texts relevant to the war under study, but also the wars that preceded it. In other words, historians have to take into account not only the social and political context in which the memoir was written, but those cultural influences that may have sculpted and shaped the veteran's memory leading up to the point in time when pen is put to paper. When all of these factors are taken into account, it may be possible to uncover parallels as well as differences in the experience of war, the emotion of war and violence over longer periods of time, between the early modern and the modern.

It is impossible to guess what forms the war memoir will take in the future, although blogging and online memoirs are now common forms of expression among returned soldiers. Separate work needs to be done on those genres. Increasingly, too, women are seeing front-line combat, at least compared with earlier twentieth-century wars. From the little we know of their memoirs – as can be seen in the chapters by Roger Markwick and Joanna Bourke in this collection – they do not differ terribly from those of the male front-line soldier and appear to continue to perpetuate the male myths of war. Moreover, the nature of the front line and even the act of killing has changed; both can now take place at a distance. Such is the enlisted man or woman who drives to work at a military base in San Diego, spends the shift guiding a drone to a kill site, and then drives home to spend the evening with the family. No matter how bloody or horrible war might be, we can be certain of two things: veterans will continue to write about their experiences, leaving tantalising traces of what it was like to live through war, recalling the sights, the sounds, the smells. And no account, however graphic or accurate, is going to dissuade future generations of young men and women from fighting and dying in other wars.

NOTES

1. Jean Garapon (ed.), *Mémoires d'État et culture politique en France: XVIe–XIXe siècles* (Nantes, 2007), 9–15.
2. Paul Delany, *British Autobiography in the Seventeenth Century* (London, 1969), 109, 118–20; James S. Amelang, 'Vox Populi: Popular Autobiographies as Sources for Early Modern Urban History', *Urban History* 20(1) (1993), 32. Two short accounts by a common soldier and a junior officer from the English Civil War are *The Civil War: The Military Memoirs of Richard Atkyns and John Gwyn*, edited by Peter Young and Norman Tucker (London: Longman, 1967).
3. On memoirs and the American War of Independence, see Robert Lawson-Peebles, 'Style Wars: The Problems of Writing Military Autobiography in the Eighteenth Century', in Alex Vernon (ed.), *Arms and the Self: War, the Military, and Autobiographical Writing* (Kent, 2005), 75–78. There is as yet no systematic study of war memoirs for this period. Vernon claims that Colonel Robert Rogers' *Journals*, published in 1765, is the first 'modern military autobiography'.
4. Damien Zanone, 'Les Mémoires au XIXe siècle: identification d'un genre', in John E. *Jackson*, Juan *Rigoli* and Daniel *Sangsue* (eds), *Etre et se connaître au XIXe siècle: Littératures et sciences humaines* (Geneva, 2006), 119–42; Brigitte Diaz, 'L'histoire en personne: Mémoires et autobiographies dans la première partie du XIXe siècle', *Elseneur,* 17 (2001), 125–42. Neil Ramsey, *The Military Memoir and Romantic Literary Culture, 1780–1835* (Farnham, 2011) lists around two hundred war memoirs published by British soldiers between 1792 and 1835. Over 1,700 titles have appeared in French (Natalie Petiteau, Écrire *la mémoire: mémorialistes de la Révolution et de l'Empire* (Paris, 2012), 184).
5. And where once they may not have had an outlet to express themselves through autobiography, veterans found other means. See, for example, the soldier poets of the Elizabethan era in Adam N. McKeown, *English Mercuries: Soldier Poets in the Age of Shakespeare* (Nashville, 2009).
6. Ralph-Rainer Wuthenow, *Das Erinnerte Ich: Europäische Autobiographie und Selbstdarstellung im 18. Jahrhundert* (Munich, 1974).
7. This necessarily varied from country to country. In France, it was not really until the second half of the nineteenth century that soldiers became socially acceptable. See David M. Hopkin, '*La Ramée*, the Archetypal Soldier, as an

Indicator of Popular Attitudes to the Army in Nineteenth-Century France', *French History* 14 (2000), 115–49; Natalie Petiteau, 'La Restauration face aux vétérans de l'Empire', in Martine Reid, Jean-Yves Mollier and Jean-Claude Yon (eds), *Repenser la Restauration* (Paris, 2005), 33; and Raoul Girardet, *La société militaire de 1815 a nos jours* (Paris, 1998), 20–21, 25–32.

8. David J. Denby, *Sentimental Narrative and the Social Order in France, 1760-1820* (Cambridge, 2006); Yuval Noah Harari, *The Ultimate Experience: Battlefield Revelations and the Making of Modern War Culture, 1450-2000* (Basingstoke, 2008), 135–50.
9. Sarah Knott, 'Sensibility and the American War for Independence', *American Historical Review* 109 (2004), 19–40, here 26.
10. Raymond de Montesquiou-Fezensac, *A Journal of the Russian Campaign of 1812*, trans. by W. Knollys (London, 1852), 183.
11. Paul Fussell, *The Great War and Modern Memory* (New York and London, 1975), 157.
12. Edward G. Lengel, *World War I Memories: An Annotated Bibliography of Personal Accounts Published in English since 1919* (Lanham, 2004) has estimated that over 1,400 memoirs, diaries and letters by soldiers and civilians from all belligerent nations have been published in English since the end of the war. The term 'veteran' is used here in its broadest possible sense to designate a person who has lived through, survived or experienced war, including those not in the military.
13. On the Japanese autobiographical novel, see Edward Fowler, *The Rhetoric of Confession:* shishōsetsu *in Early Twentieth-Century Japanese Fiction* (Berkeley, 1988); and Aaron Moore, *Writing War: Soldiers Record the Japanese Empire* (Cambridge, MA, 2013), 1–2, 35–36, 253–55.
14. Bettina Hoffman, 'On the Battlefield and Home Front: American Women Writing Their Lives on the Vietnam War', in Vernon, *Arms and the Self*, 215.
15. Jean-Nicolas-Auguste Noël, *Souvenirs militaires d'un officier du premier Empire: 1795–1832* (Paris, 1895), 199.
16. See, for example, Geoffrey Mortimer, *Eyewitness Accounts of the Thirty Years War, 1618–48* (Houndmills, 2002), 185–88. Writing to leave a record for posterity is one of the most common and conventional reasons given by veterans and is one that can be found across the centuries.
17. Ron Kovic, *Born on the Fourth of July* (New York, 2005), 17.
18. Philippe Ariès, 'Pourquoi écrit-on des mémoires?', in Noemi Hepp and Jacques Hennequin (eds), *Les valeurs chez les mémorialistes français du XVIIe siècle avant la Fronde* (Paris, 1979), 13–20; Hubert Carrier, '*Pourquoi écrit-on* des Mémoires au XVIIe siècle? L'exemple des mémorialistes de la Fronde', in Madeleine Bertaud and François-Xavier Cuche (eds), *Le genre des mémoires, essai de définition* (Paris, 1995), 137–51.
19. A good historical overview of the memoir is in Yuval Noah Harari, *Renaissance Military Memoirs: War, History, and Identity, 1450–1600* (Woodbridge, 2004), 1–22.
20. Kenneth D. Barkin, 'Autobiography and History', *Societas: A Review of Social History* 6 (1976), 83–108, here 84.

21. Gabriel Motzkin, 'Memoirs, Memory, and Historical Experience', *Science in Context* 7(1) (1994), 103–19.
22. There has been far more research into journals and diaries as ego-documents although here too historians have generally neglected to contextualise them. See, for example, Robert A. Fothergill, *Private Chronicles: A Study of English Diaries* (New York, 1974); Ralph-Rainer Wuthenow, *Europäische Tagebücher. Eigenart, Formen, Entwicklung* (Darmstadt, 1990); Gustav René Hocke, *Europäische Tagebücher aus vier Jahrhunderten. Motive und Anthologie* (Frankfurt am Main, 1991); Steven Rendall, 'On Diaries', *Diacritics* 16(3) (1986), 56–65.
23. Jan Assmann, *Cultural Memory and Early Civilization: Writing, Remembrance, and Political Imagination* (Cambridge, 2011). See also Barbara Walker, 'On Reading Soviet Memoirs: A History of the "Contemporaries" Genre as an Institution of Russian Intelligentsia Culture from the 1790s to the 1970s', *The Russian Review* 59 (2000), 327–52.
24. Jay Winter, *Remembering War: The Great War between Memory and History in the Twentieth Century* (New Haven, 2006), 104.
25. There is a considerable literature on the First and Second World Wars. One can consult Samuel Hynes, *The Soldiers' Tale: Bearing Witness to Modern War* (London, 1997), who examines what he refers to as 'personal narratives'; Fussell, *The Great War and Modern Memory*, partly about war narratives; Fussell, *Wartime: Understanding and Behavior in the Second World War* (New York, 1989); Fussell, *A War Imagined: The First World War and English Culture* (New York, 1991); Ann Linder, *Princes of the Trenches: Narrating the German Experience of the First World War* (Columbia, SC, 1989), although her definition of war narratives encompasses novels and diaries as well as memoirs. On British First World War memoirs, see Paul Edwards, 'British War Memoirs', in Vincent Sherry (ed.), *The Cambridge Companion to the Literature of the First World War* (Cambridge, 2005), 15–33. For a different perspective of the wars, that of the Ottoman and Turkish soldier, see Leila Fawaz, *A Land of Aching Hearts: The Middle East in the Great War* (Cambridge, MA, 2014).
26. Foreign volunteers wrote many more memoirs, and many of these, like George Orwell's *Homage to Catalonia*, provide narratives of the war permeated with political viewpoints, often twisting truths to suit a particular political stance and, if the veteran were a revolutionary, writing with dismay and disillusion. Interestingly, the French novelist Claude Simon declared Orwell's *Homage* was 'fake from the very first sentence' (Anthony Cheal Pugh, 'A Conversation with Claude Simon', *The Review of Contemporary Fiction* 5(1) (1985), http://www.dalkeyarchive.com/a-conversation-with-claude-simon-by-anthony-cheal-pugh/). Simon was inadvertently highlighting the conscious and unconscious pressures writers face when memory confronts the tropes of conventional narrative. See also Franz Borkenau, *The Spanish Cockpit: An Eyewitness Account of the Political and Social Conflicts of the Spanish Civil War* (London, 1937). Valentine Cunningham's *Spanish Front: Writers on the Civil War* (Oxford, 1986) is a good introduction to the array of writings on the wars.

27. One exception to the rule is Edna Lomsky-Feder, 'Life Stories, War and Veterans: On the Social Distribution of Memories', *Ethos* 32(1) (2004), 82–109, which deals specifically with Israeli reminiscences of the Yom Kippur war.
28. For France, see the work by Olivier Wieviorka, *Divided Memory. French Recollections of World War II from the Liberation to the Present* (Stanford, 2012); for Germany, a good summary of the literature is in Hannes Heer and Ruth Wodak, 'Collective Memory, National Narratives and the Politics of the Past – The Discursive Construction of History', in Hannes Heer et al., *The Discursive Construction of History: Remembering the Wehrmacht's War of Annihilation*, trans. from the German by Steven Fligelstone (Basingstoke, 2008), 1–13. For Yugoslavia, see Vesna Drapac, and for the Partition in 1948, Tarun Saint, both in this collection.
29. For a discussion on veracity, see Philippe Carrard, 'From the Outcasts' Point of View: The Memoirs of the French Who Fought for Hitler', *French Historical Studies* 31(3) (2008), 482–86; Carrard, *The French Who Fought for Hitler: Memories from the Outcasts* (Cambridge, 2010), 53–84; and for an earlier period, Harari, *Renaissance Military Memoirs*, 27–42.
30. On this topic, see Susan Rubin Suleiman, 'Do Facts Matter in Holocaust Memoirs?', in Suleiman (ed.), *Crises of Memory and the Second World War* (Cambridge, MA, 2006), 159–77.
31. Motzkin, 'Memoirs, Memory, and Historical Experience', 106.
32. A distinction is made between 'autobiography', a retrospective account of an individual's life, and 'memoir', more akin to a historical account. See, for example, Philippe Lejeune, *Le pacte autobiographique* (Paris, 1996), 14. For an earlier period, Petiteau, Écrire *la mémoire*, 71–79.
33. For a discussion on the distinction between the war memoir and military autobiography, see Alex Vernon, 'The Problem of Genre in War Memoirs and Military Autobiographies', in Vernon, *Arms and the Self*, 17–21.
34. A plea made by Vernon, 'The Problem of Genre in War Memoirs', 2–6.
35. See, for example, Marian Faye Novak, *Lonely Girls with Burning Eyes: A Wife Recalls Her Husband's Journey Home from Vietnam* (Boston, 1991).
36. On the war in Bosnia, for example, see the memoirs of an American on the margins of but a witness to the war by Anthony Loyd, *My War Gone By, I Miss It So* (London, 1999).
37. See, for example, Nadezhda Durova, *The Cavalry Maiden: Journals of a Female Russian Officer in the Napoleonic Wars*, trans. by Mary Fleming Zirin (Bloomington, 1988). These cross-dressers, however, invariably adhered to the conventions of a male-dominated genre (Ann Fabian, *The Unvarnished Truth: Personal Narratives in Nineteenth-Century America* [Berkeley, 2000], 4).
38. Reina Pennington, *Wings, Women, and War: Soviet Airwomen in World War II Combat* (Lawrence, 1997); Anna Krylova, *Soviet Women in Combat: A History of Violence on the Eastern Front* (New York, 2010); Roger D. Markwick and Euridice Charon Cardona, *Soviet Women on the Frontline in the Second World War* (Houndmills, 2012).

39. Margaret H. Darrow, 'French Volunteer Nursing and the Myth of War Experience in World War I', *American Historical Review* 101(1) (1996), 80–106, esp. 100–106.
40. See, for example, Alison S. Fell, 'Colonial Troops in French and British Nursing Memoirs', in Santanu Das (ed.), *Race, Empire and First World War Writing* (Cambridge, 2011), 158–74. There were over 600,000 non-white colonial troops used by the French and the British in the trenches in 1914–18, and yet few historians have turned to the memoirs they left behind to understand their wartime experiences. Christian Koller, 'Representing Otherness: African, Indian, and European Soldiers' Letters and Memoirs', in Das, *Race, Empire and First World War Writing*, 127–42, only touches on this vastly under-researched topic.
41. Thérèse Soulacroix, *Notes de guerre et d'ambulance* (Paris, 1917).
42. See the works of Robin Gerster, *Big-Noting: The Heroic Theme in Australian War Writing* (Carlton, Vic., 1987, revised 1992), esp. 225–36; Joan Beaumont, 'Prisoners-of-War', in Peter Dennis et al. (eds), *The Oxford Companion to Australian Military History* (Melbourne, 1995), 472–81; Stephen Garton, *The Cost of War: Australians Return* (Melbourne, 1996); and Frances de Groen, 'Convicts, Coolies and Colonialism: Reorienting the *Prisoner-of-War* Narrative', *Journal of the Association for the Study of Australian Literature* (2000), 86–94.
43. These are particularly lacking in memoirs of the Eastern Front. See Roger Markwick in this collection as well as Xosé-Manoel Núnez, '"Russland war nicht schuldig": Die Ostfronterfahrung der spanischen Blauen Division in Selbstzeugnissen und Autobiographien, 1943–2004', in Michael Epkenhans, Stig Förster and Karen Hagemann (eds), *Militärische Erinnerungskultur: Soldaten im Spiegel von Biographien, Memoiren und Selbstzeugnissen* (Paderborn, 2006), 246–47.
44. Alistair Thomson, *Anzac Memories: Living with the Legend* (Melbourne, 1994).
45. Joanna Bourke, *An Intimate History of Killing: Face-to-Face Killing in Twentieth-Century Warfare* (London, 1999).
46. Stephen G. Fritz, '"We Are Trying…to Change the Face of the World" – Ideology and Motivation in the Wehrmacht on the Eastern Front: The View from Below', *Journal of Military History* 60(4) (1996), 683–710.
47. Michael Roper, 'Re-remembering the Soldier Hero: The Psychic and Social Construction of Memory in Personal Narratives of the Great War', *History Workshop Journal* 50 (2000), 181–204.
48. For a discussion on authenticity, see Carrard, *The French Who Fought for Hitler*, 25–52; and Subarno Chattarji in this collection.
49. Edmund Blunden, *Undertones of War* (London, 1928), vii.
50. For a discussion of how memories can be falsified, see Elizabeth Loftus and Katherine Ketcham, *The Myth of Repressed Memory: False Memories and Allegations of Sexual Abuse* (New York, 1994).
51. The 'fictionalisation' of memoirs is treated in Geoffrey Mortimer, 'Style and Fictionalisation in Eyewitness Personal Accounts of the Thirty Years War', *German Life and Letters* 54(2) (2001), 97–113.

52. Tobey C. Herzog, *Vietnam War Stories: Innocence Lost* (London, 1992), 16–24. Stanley Kubrick's 1987 film, *Full Metal Jacket*, and the semi-autobiographical novel on which it was based, Gustav Hasford's *The Short-Timers*, both include repeated, albeit sardonic references to John Wayne and the mythical war he represented.
53. Anthony Swofford, *Jarhead: A Marine's Chronicle of the Gulf War and Other Battles* (New York, 2003).
54. Echoing Sebastian Haffner's contention that the root of Nazism was not in the 'front experience' of the First World War, but in the 'war experience of the German schoolboy' (Sebastian Haffner, *Defying Hitler: A Memoir*, trans. by Oliver Pretzel [London, 2002]).
55. Andrew Whitmarsh, '"We Will Remember Them." Memory and Commemoration in War Museums', *Journal of Conservation and Museum Studies* 7 (2001), 11–15; and more recently in the Australian context, Henry Reynolds, *Forgotten War* (Sydney, 2013), 41–42, 224–27.
56. See, for example, the remark in *Memoirs of a Sergeant late of the 43rd Light Infantry, previously to and during the Peninsular War* (London, 1835), 215; Robert Blakeney, *A Boy in the Peninsular War: The Services, Adventures and Experiences of Robert Blakeney* (London, 1899), xi–xii.
57. Harari, *The Ultimate Experience*, 1–27.
58. Fussell, *The Great War and Modern Memory*, 29–35.
59. See Harari, *The Ultimate Experience*, 9–10, 72–76, 261–64, and esp. for the following, 263–82, on which these pages are based.
60. See Modris Eksteins, 'All Quiet on the Western Front and the Fate of a War', *Journal of Contemporary History* 15 (1980), 355–56; Harari, *The Ultimate Experience*, 270–71.
61. See also Joanna Bourke, *The Story of Pain: From Prayer to Painkillers* (Oxford, 2014).
62. Gabriele Köpp, *Warum war ich bloß ein Mädchen? Das Trauma einer Flucht 1945* (Munich, 2010). Before Köpp was the anonymous, *A Woman in Berlin*, published in the 1950s. We now know the author of that memoir to be Marta Hillers, whose identity was revealed in 2003, two years after her death.
63. Take, for example, a woman who told a team gathering information for the truth and reconciliation commission in Peru: 'When I forget, I'm well. Remembering, even now, I just go crazy'. It led Kimberly Theidon, the author of *Intimate Enemies: Violence and Reconciliation in Peru* (Pennsylvania, 2012), to conclude that, 'Forgetting is not simply a strategy of domination employed by the powerful against the weak. Rather, it may be a state that is fervently desired by those who suffer from the afflictions of memory and seek relief from the heavy weight of a painful past'. See the review essay by Klaus Neumann, http://inside.org.au/when-i-forget-im-well-remembering-even-now-i-just-go-crazy/.
64. For this see the chapter by Ilan Pappe in this collection, and Rafi Nets-Zehngut, 'Internal and External Collective Memories of Conflicts: Israel and the 1948

Palestinian Exodus', *International Journal of Conflict and Violence* 6(1) (2012), 126–40, esp. 131–34.
65. See, for example, Alessandro Portelli, 'Uchronic Dreams: Working-Class Memory and Possible Worlds', in Alessandro Portelli, *The Death of Luigi Trastulli and Other Stories* (Albany, NY, 1991), 99–116.
66. Maurice Bloch, 'Mémoire autobiographique et mémoire historique du passé éloigné', *Enquête, anthropologie, histoire, sociologie*, 2 (1995), 59–76, here 74; Winter, *Remembering War*, 4.
67. For this, see Steven E. Kagle and Lorenza Gramegna, 'Rewriting Her Life: Fictionalization and the Use of Fictional Models in Early American Women's Diaries', in Suzanne L. Bunkers and Cynthia A. Huff (eds), *Inscribing the Daily: Critical Essays on Women's Diaries* (Amherst, 1996), 39.
68. The phrase is from Samuel Hynes, 'Personal Narratives and Commemoration', in Jay Winter and Emmanuel Sivan (eds), *War and Remembrance in the Twentieth Century* (Cambridge, 1999), 205–20, here 207.
69. Pierre Bourdieu, 'L'illusion biographique', *Actes de la Recherche en Science Sociale*, lxii/lxiii (1986), 69–72.
70. Motzkin, 'Memoirs, Memory, and Historical Experience', 112.
71. Claudine Kahan, 'La honte du témoin', in Catherine Coquio (ed.), *Parler des camps, penser les génocides* (Paris, 1999), 493-513.
72. On the 'duty to remember', see Suleiman, *Crises of Memory*, 1–11; Coquio, 'Du malentendu', in Coquio, *Parler des camps*, 17–86.

BIBLIOGRAPHY

Memoirs

Blakeney, Robert. *A Boy in the Peninsular War: The Services, Adventures and Experiences of Robert Blakeney*. London: John Murray, 1899.
Blunden, Edmund. *Undertones of War*. London: Cobden-Sanderson, 1928.
Borkenau, Franz. *The Spanish Cockpit: An Eyewitness Account of the Political and Social Conflicts of the Spanish Civil War*. London: Faber and Faber Ltd, 1937.
Durova, Nadezhda. *The Cavalry Maiden: Journals of a Female Russian Officer in the Napoleonic Wars*, trans. by Mary Fleming Zirin. Bloomington: Indiana University Press, 1988.
Haffner, Sebastian. *Defying Hitler: A Memoir*, trans. by Oliver Pretzel. London: Weidenfeld & Nicolson, 2002.
Herzog, Tobey C. *Vietnam War Stories: Innocence Lost*. London: Routledge, 1992.
Köpp, Gabriele. *Warum war ich bloß ein Mädchen? Das Trauma einer Flucht 1945*. Munich: Herbig, 2010.
Kovic, Ron. *Born on the Fourth of July*. New York: Akashic Books, 2005.
Loyd, Anthony. *My War Gone By, I Miss It So*. London: Doubleday, 1999.

Memoirs of a Sergeant late of the 43rd Light Infantry, previously to and during the Peninsular War. London: John Mason, 1835.

Montesquiou-Fezensac, Raymond de. *A Journal of the Russian Campaign of 1812*, trans. by W. Knollys. London: Parker, Furnivall, and Parker, 1852.

Noël, Jean-Nicolas-Auguste. *Souvenirs militaires d'un officier du premier Empire: 1795–1832*. Paris: Berger-Levrault, 1895.

Novak, Marian Faye. *Lonely Girls with Burning Eyes: A Wife Recalls Her Husband's Journey Home from Vietnam*. Boston: Little, Brown, and Co., 1991.

Soulacroix, Thérèse. *Notes de guerre et d'ambulance*. Paris: L. Lethielleux, 1917.

Swofford, Anthony. *Jarhead: A Marine's Chronicle of the Gulf War and Other Battles*. New York: Scribner, 2003.

Secondary Sources

Amelang, James S. 'Vox Populi: Popular Autobiographies as Sources for Early Modern Urban History', *Urban History* 20(1) (1993), 30–42.

Ariès, Philippe. 'Pourquoi écrit-on des mémoires?', in Noemi Hepp and Jacques Hennequin (eds), *Les valeurs chez les mémorialistes français du XVIIe siècle avant la Fronde* (Paris: Klincksieck, 1979), 13–20.

Assmann, Jan. *Cultural Memory and Early Civilization: Writing, Remembrance, and Political Imagination*. Cambridge: Cambridge University Press, 2011.

Barkin, Kenneth D. 'Autobiography and History'. *Societas: A Review of Social History* 6 (1976), 83–108.

Beaumont, Joan. 'Prisoners-of-War', in Peter Dennis et al. (eds), *The Oxford Companion to Australian Military History*. Melbourne: Oxford University Press, 1995, 472–81.

Bloch, Maurice. 'Mémoire autobiographique et mémoire historique du passé éloigné'. *Enquête, anthropologie, histoire, sociologie* 2 (1995), 59–76.

Bourdieu, Pierre. 'L'illusion biographique'. *Actes de la Recherche en Science Sociale* lxii/lxiii (1986), 69–72.

Bourke, Joanna. *An Intimate History of Killing: Face-to-Face Killing in Twentieth-Century Warfare*. London: Granta, 1999.

Bourke, Joanna. *The Story of Pain: From Prayer to Painkillers*. Oxford: Oxford University Press, 2014.

Carrard, Philippe. *The French Who Fought for Hitler: Memories from the Outcasts*. Cambridge: Cambridge University Press, 2010.

Carrard, Philippe. 'From the Outcasts' Point of View: The Memoirs of the French Who Fought for Hitler'. *French Historical Studies* 31(3) (2008), 482–86.

Carrier, Hubert. 'Pourquoi *écrit*-on des Mémoires au XVIIe siècle? L'exemple des mémorialistes de la Fronde', in Madeleine Bertaud and François-Xavier Cuche (eds), *Le genre des mémoires, essai de definition* (Paris: Klincksieck, 1995), 137–51.

Cunningham, Valentine. *Spanish Front: Writers on the Civil War*. Oxford: Oxford University Press, 1986.

Darrow, Margaret H. 'French Volunteer Nursing and the Myth of War Experience in World War I'. *American Historical Review* 101(1) (1996), 80–106.

Delany, Paul. *British Autobiography in the Seventeenth Century*. London: Routledge & Kegan, 1969.

Denby, David J. *Sentimental Narrative and the Social Order in France, 1760–1820*. Cambridge: Cambridge University Press, 2006.

Diaz, Brigitte. 'L'histoire en personne: Mémoires et autobiographies dans la première partie du XIXe siècle'. *Elseneur* 17 (2001), 125–42.

Edwards, Paul. 'British War Memoirs', in Vincent Sherry (ed.), *The Cambridge Companion to the Literature of the First World War* (Cambridge: Cambridge University Press, 2005), 15–33.

Eksteins, Modris. 'All Quiet on the Western Front and the Fate of a War', *Journal of Contemporary History* 15 (1980), 345–66.

Fabian, Ann. *The Unvarnished Truth: Personal Narratives in Nineteenth-Century America*. Berkeley: University of California Press, 2000.

Fawaz, Leila. *A Land of Aching Hearts: The Middle East in the Great War*. Cambridge, MA: Harvard University Press, 2014.

Fell, Alison S. 'Colonial Troops in French and British Nursing Memoirs', in Santanu Das (ed.), *Race, Empire and First World War Writing* (Cambridge: Cambridge University Press, 2011), 158–74.

Fothergill, Robert A. *Private Chronicles: A Study of English Diaries*. New York: Oxford University Press, 1974.

Fowler, Edward. *The Rhetoric of Confession: shishōsetsu in Early Twentieth-Century Japanese Fiction*. Berkeley: University of California Press, 1988.

Fritz, Stephen G. '"We Are Trying...to Change the Face of the World" – Ideology and Motivation in the Wehrmacht on the Eastern Front: The View from Below'. *Journal of Military History* 60(4) (1996), 683–710.

Fussell, Paul. *The Great War and Modern Memory*. New York and London: Oxford University Press, 1975.

Fussell, Paul. *A War Imagined: The First World War and English Culture*. New York: Atheneum, 1991.

Fussell, Paul. *Wartime: Understanding and Behavior in the Second World War*. New York: Oxford University Press, 1989.

Garapon, Jean (ed.). *Mémoires d'État et culture politique en France: XVIe-XIXe siècles*. Nantes: C. Defaut, 2007.

Garton, Stephen. *The Cost of War: Australians Return*. Melbourne: Oxford University Press, 1996.

Gerster, Robin. *Big-Noting: The Heroic Theme in Australian War Writing*. Carlton, Vic.: Melbourne University Press, 1987, revised 1992.

Girardet, Raoul. *La société militaire de 1815 a nos jours*. Paris: Perrin, 1998.

Groen, Frances de. 'Convicts, Coolies and Colonialism: Reorienting the Prisoner-of-War Narrative'. *Australian Literary Studies in the 21st Century*, (2000), 86–94.

Harari, Yuval Noah. *Renaissance Military Memoirs: War, History, and Identity, 1450–1600*. Woodbridge: Boydell, 2004.

Harari, Yuval Noah. *The Ultimate Experience: Battlefield Revelations and the Making of Modern War Culture, 1450–2000*. Basingstoke: Palgrave Macmillan, 2008.

Heer, Hannes, and Ruth Wodak. 'Collective Memory, National Narratives and the Politics of the Past – The Discursive Construction of History', in Hannes Heer et al., *The Discursive Construction of History: Remembering the Wehrmacht's War of Annihilation*, trans. from the German by Steven Fligelstone (Basingstoke: Palgrave Macmillan, 2008), 1–13.

Hocke, Gustav René. *Europäische Tagebücher aus vier Jahrhunderten. Motive und Anthologie*. Frankfurt am Main: Fischer, 1991.

Hoffman, Bettina. 'On the Battlefield and Home Front: American Women Writing Their Lives on the Vietnam War', in Alex Vernon (ed.), *Arms and the Self: War, the Military, and Autobiographical Writing* (Kent: Kent State University Press, 2005), 202–17.

Hopkin, David M. '*La Ramée*, the Archetypal Soldier, as an Indicator of Popular Attitudes to the Army in Nineteenth-Century France'. *French History* 14 (2000), 115–49.

Hynes, Samuel. 'Personal Narratives and Commemoration', in Jay Winter and Emmanuel Sivan (eds), *War and Remembrance in the Twentieth Century* (Cambridge: Cambridge University Press, 1999), 205–20.

Hynes, Samuel. *The Soldiers' Tale: Bearing Witness to Modern War*. London: Pimlico, 1997.

Kagle, Steven E., and Lorenza Gramegna. 'Rewriting Her Life: Fictionalization and the Use of Fictional Models in Early American Women's Diaries', in Suzanne L. Bunkers and Cynthia A. Huff (eds), *Inscribing the Daily: Critical Essays on Women's Diaries*. Amherst: University of Massachusetts Press, 1996, 38–55.

Kahan, Claudine. 'La honte du témoin', in Catherine Coquio (ed.), *Parler des camps, penser les genocides* (Paris: Albin Michel, 1999), 493–513.

Knott, Sarah. 'Sensibility and the American War for Independence'. *American Historical Review* 109 (2004), 19–40.

Koller, Christian. 'Representing Otherness: African, Indian, and European Soldiers' Letters and Memoirs', in Santanu Das (ed.), *Race, Empire and First World War Writing* (Cambridge: Cambridge University Press, 2011), 127–42.

Krylova, Anna. *Soviet Women in Combat: A History of Violence on the Eastern Front*. New York: Cambridge University Press, 2010.

Lawson-Peebles, Robert. 'Style Wars: The Problems of Writing Military Autobiography in the Eighteenth Century', in Alex Vernon (ed.), *Arms and the Self: War, the Military, and Autobiographical Writing* (Kent: Kent State University Press, 2005), 75–78.

Lejeune, Philippe. *Le pacte autobiographique*. Paris: Seuil, 1996.

Lengel, Edward G. *World War I Memories: An Annotated Bibliography of Personal Accounts Published in English since 1919*. Lanham: Scarecrow Press, 2004.

Linder, Ann. *Princes of the Trenches: Narrating the German Experience of the First World War*. Columbia, SC: Camden House, 1989.

Loftus, Elizabeth, and Katherine Ketcham. *The Myth of Repressed Memory: False Memories and Allegations of Sexual Abuse*. New York: St. Martin's Griffin, 1994.

Lomsky-Feder, Edna. 'Life Stories, War and Veterans: On the Social Distribution of Memories'. *Ethos* 32(1) (2004), 82–109.

Markwick, Roger D., and Euridice Charon Cardona. *Soviet Women on the Frontline in the Second World War*. Houndmills: Palgrave Macmillan, 2012.

McKeown, Adam N. *English Mercuries: Soldier Poets in the Age of Shakespeare*. Nashville: Vanderbilt University Press, 2009.

Moore, Aaron. *Writing War: Soldiers Record the Japanese Empire*. Cambridge, MA: Harvard University Press, 2013.

Mortimer, Geoffrey. *Eyewitness Accounts of the Thirty Years War, 1618–48*. Houndmills: Palgrave, 2002.

Mortimer, Geoffrey. 'Style and Fictionalisation in Eyewitness Personal Accounts of the Thirty Years War'. *German Life and Letters* 54(2) (2001), 97–113.

Motzkin, Gabriel. 'Memoirs, Memory, and Historical Experience'. *Science in Context* 7(1) (1994), 103–19.

Nets-Zehngut, Rafi. 'Internal and External Collective Memories of Conflicts: Israel and the 1948 Palestinian Exodus'. *International Journal of Conflict and Violence* 6(1) (2012), 126–40.

Núñez, Xosé-Manoel. '"Russland war nicht schuldig": Die Ostfronterfahrung der spanischen Blauen Division in Selbstzeugnissen und Autobiographien, 1943–2004', in Michael Epkenhans, Stig Förster and Karen Hagemann (eds), *Militärische Erinnerungskultur: Soldaten im Spiegel von Biographien, Memoiren und Selbstzeugnissen* (Paderborn: Schöningh, 2006), 236–67.

Pennington, Reina. *Wings, Women, and War: Soviet Airwomen in World War II Combat*. Lawrence: University Press of Kansas, 1997.

Petiteau, Natalie. Écrire *la mémoire: mémorialistes de la Révolution et de l'Empire*. Paris: les Indes savantes, 2012.

Petiteau, Natalie. 'La Restauration face aux vétérans de l'Empire', in Martine Reid, Jean-Yves Mollier and Jean-Claude Yon (eds), *Repenser la Restauration* (Paris: Nouveau Monde éditions, 2005), 31–43.

Portelli, Alessandro. 'Uchronic Dreams: Working-Class Memory and Possible Worlds', in Alessandro Portelli, *The Death of Luigi Trastulli and Other Stories* (Albany, NY: State University of New York Press, 1991), 99–116.

Pugh, Anthony Cheal. 'A Conversation with Claude Simon', *The Review of Contemporary Fiction* 5(1) (1985), http://www.dalkeyarchive.com/a-conversation-with-claude-simon-by-anthony-cheal-pugh/.

Ramsey, Neil. *The Military Memoir and Romantic Literary Culture, 1780–1835*. Farnham: Ashgate, 2011.

Rendall, Steven. 'On Diaries'. *Diacritics* 16(3) (1986), 56–65.

Reynolds, Henry. *Forgotten War*. Sydney: NewSouth Publishing, 2013.

Roper, Michael. 'Re-remembering the Soldier Hero: The Psychic and Social Construction of Memory in Personal Narratives of the Great War'. *History Workshop Journal* 50 (2000): 181–204.

Suleiman, Susan Rubin (ed.). *Crises of Memory and the Second World War*. Cambridge, MA: Harvard University Press, 2006.

Theidon, Kimberly. *Intimate Enemies: Violence and Reconciliation in Peru*. Pennsylvania: University of Pennsylvania Press, 2012.
Thomson, Alistair. *Anzac Memories: Living with the Legend*. Melbourne: Oxford University Press, 1994.
Vernon, Alex. 'No Genre's Land: The Problem of Genre in War Memoirs and Military Autobiographies', in Alex Vernon (ed.), *Arms and the Self: War, the Military, and Autobiographical Writing* (Kent: Kent State University Press, 2005), 1–39.
Walker, Barbara. 'On Reading Soviet Memoirs: A History of the "Contemporaries" Genre as an Institution of Russian Intelligentsia Culture from the 1790s to the 1970s'. *The Russian Review* 59 (2000), 327–52.
Whitmarsh, Andrew. '"We Will Remember Them." Memory and Commemoration in War Museums'. *Journal of Conservation and Museum Studies* 7 (2001), 11–15.
Wieviorka, Olivier. *Divided Memory. French Recollections of World War II from the Liberation to the Present*. Stanford: Stanford University Press, 2012.
Winter, Jay. *Remembering War: The Great War between Memory and History in the Twentieth Century*. New Haven: Yale University Press, 2006.
Wuthenow, Ralph-Rainer. *Das Erinnerte Ich: Europäische Autobiographie und Selbstdarstellung im 18. Jahrhundert*. Munich: C. H. Beck, 1974.
Wuthenow, Ralph-Rainer. *Europäische Tagebücher. Eigenart, Formen, Entwicklung*. Darmstadt: Wissenschaftliche Buchgesellschaft, 1990.
Young, Peter and Norman Tucker (eds). *The Civil War: The Military Memoirs of Richard Atkyns and John Gwyn*. London: Longmans, 1967.
Zanone, Damien, 'Les Mémoires au XIXe siècle: identification d'un genre', in John E. Jackson, Juan Rigoli and Daniel Sangsue (eds), *Etre et se connaître au XIXe siècle: Littératures et sciences humaines* (Geneva: Éd. Métropolis, 2006), 119–42.

Philip Dwyer is Founding Director of the Centre for the History of Violence at the University of Newcastle in Australia. His primary research interest is eighteenth-century Europe with a particular emphasis on the Napoleonic Empire. He is the author of *Napoleon: The Path to Power, 1769–1799* (Bloomsbury and Yale University Press, 2007), which won the National Biography Award in 2008; and *Citizen Emperor: Napoleon in Power* (Bloomsbury and Yale University Press, 2013). He is also the editor, with Lyndall Ryan, of *Theatres of Violence: Massacre, Mass Killing and Atrocity throughout History* (Berghahn, 2012). As well as writing the third and final volume of his Napoleon biography, he is currently working on a number of projects that include civilians in war during the French Revolutionary and Napoleonic wars, and a history of violence.

Chapter 2

War Memoirs, Witnessing and Silence

Jay Winter

Among the things they carried, in Tim O'Brien's phrase,[1] was silence. This applies equally to those who went through combat and to those who lived to tell the tale. War memoirs have silences built into them, silences we rarely hear or acknowledge. I want to suggest that we should start rectifying this omission. To do so, I want to return to the conceptual tools we use to study remembering and forgetting and to assert that we have been missing something ubiquitous but understudied. We have been missing the fact that silence is a socially constructed space entailing both remembering and forgetting. War memoirs always aim at both, and use silence to accomplish both tasks. That is my first claim.

Secondly, I want to offer some thoughts on how we as historians can approach talking about silence. Here I draw on the performative speech act theory of J.L. Austin. I will outline a theory of performative non-speech acts to describe not – to use the title of Austin's most celebrated gem – how we do things with words, but how we do things with silence. Not all silences are performative, but those that are signifiers, I hold, occupy a central place in the way war stories and war memoirs have been constructed. I hope to show in a number of instances that this is so, and then in conclusion, urge you to listen to the silences in the texts and statements we examine as part of the repertoire of narratives of war.

BELOW THE SURFACE

Let me begin with a wonderful snapshot of the position I wish to leave behind. It is a position locating remembering and forgetting in a double helix, each defining the other. Here is the way the French anthropologist Marc Augé sees it: 'Memory is framed by forgetting in the same way as the contours of the shoreline are framed by the sea'.[2] Augé's elegant formulation of the embrace of memory and forgetting draws upon a long tradition of philosophical and literary reflection. It is time, though, to go beyond it, for the topographical metaphor employed here is clearly incomplete. We need to see the landscape of the shoreline in three dimensions. Doing so enables us to observe a vertical dimension which is dynamic, unstable and at times intrusive. I speak of those deposits below the surface of the water that emerge with the tides or with other environmental changes. In the framework of how we think about memory and forgetting, these hidden shapes cannot simply be ignored because they are concealed at some moments and revealed at others. They must be examined as part of the cartography of recollection and remembrance.

Silences: Liturgical, Political, Essentialist

We call these hidden deposits silence. The composer John Cage said all that needs to be said about the performative nature of silence. It exists in the world, and is defined by the world according to certain arbitrary but powerfully reinforced conventions. Those who first heard his composition *4'33"* in 1952 were stupefied by silence. What Cage did was to invite concertgoers to come together facing a pianist who sits at a piano and does not touch the keyboard for four minutes and thirty-three seconds precisely. Cage showed them, much to their discomfort registered on film, that silence is 'the presence of ambient and unintentional noise rather than the complete absence of sound'.[3] Silence, I hold, is never equivalent to the complete absence of meaning. Here I want to draw attention to focused, directed and purposeful silence, not conceived of as the absence of sound, but as the absence, the deliberate absence, of conventional and socially acceptable verbal or tonal exchanges. In this landscape, silences are meaningful spaces either beyond words or conventionally delimited as left out of what we talk about. Topographically, they are there whether or not they come to the surface; and their re-emergence into our line of sight or hearing can occasion a reiteration of the interdiction on talking about them or the end of the interdiction itself.

My central point is this: we cannot accept the commonplace view that silence is the space of forgetting and speech the realm of remembrance. Instead, I offer the following definition of silence. Silence, I hold, is a socially constructed space in which and about which subjects and words normally used in everyday life are not spoken. The circle around this space is described by groups of people who at one point in time deem it appropriate that there is a difference between the sayable and the unsayable, or the spoken and the unspoken, and that such a distinction can and should be maintained and observed over time. Such people codify and enforce norms that reinforce the injunction against breaking into the inner space of the circle of silence.

Let me add one further distinction at the outset. Some speech acts are performative, in the Austinian sense of the term. That is, they create the condition of which they speak, and therefore are not simply constative, or modes of conveying truth statements.[4] I want to suggest that there are performative non-speech acts, silences that are full of meaning; they obey rules that can be normative and occasionally entail severe punishments for breaking them. Consider three. At an Anglican wedding, the priest asks those who know a reason why the marriage cannot be celebrated to speak now or forever hold their peace. Not speaking conveys the licence to marry. Secondly, to say I love you is to create the condition; not to say I love you conveys something too. Thirdly, to take a recent political instance of someone who broke the rule of silence: the Spanish judge Balthazar Garzon, sitting on Spain's Central Criminal Court, was suspended and indicted for investigating amnestied crimes committed during the Spanish civil war. His argument was that human rights instruments transcended national legislation; for the moment, he lost the argument, because silence was and remains performative. More on this later.

To be sure, not all silences are performative. Some are trivial, but others are not, and it is our business as historians to read between the spoken lines of history to hear them. In Austin's theory of language, there is a clear distinction between 'the performance of an act *in* [not] saying something, as opposed to the performance of an act *of* [not] saying something'[5]. Silences can be illocutionary, matters of action and meaning, or simply matters of empty social space. I am interested in the active uses of silence; my aim is to follow Austin's wonderful study, *How To Do Things With Words*, with some reflections on the less noticed subject of how to do things with silence.

Let me add two more brief points to help bolster my case. The first is that every archive I have ever visited is filled with lacunae, things left out, things weeded out, things destroyed. We all know this to be true, and we do our best to connect the dots, even when some are not there. I hold that we need to do this when we examine the language of war memoirs; we need to hear their silences to hear what they say. Secondly, I want to suggest that we all know that silence is performative since every family's narrative is filled with things occluded or left out. I want to give you just one instance of this, and will change the name of the person for evident reasons. I shall call her Anna Winter, my daughter's name, and can affirm authoritatively that this is not a story about my family. Anna Winter is a distinguished French anthropologist. She was born in 1940, and her father, a minor official at Drancy transit camp, managed to spirit her out of the camp to rural Brittany, which she got to know and love, and on whose family life she is a world's authority. Now in retirement she has decided to write the history of her family. To do so she approached the National Archives in Paris and asked the resident specialist to help her investigate the naturalisation papers of her Russian-born grandfather, who came to France in 1900, as the orphan and only son of Russian tailors. These naturalisation papers are extraordinary – there are 600,000 of them, a gift to families and historians alike. It was easy to find her grandfather, but not easy to take in the fact that the naturalisation records indicated that he had nine brothers and sisters who were also naturalised; Anna had never heard of their existence. And what was more, three of them had children who were swept up in the *Grand Raffle* of July 1942 and were deported to Auschwitz. Not a word of any of these people had ever passed her father's lips.

Knowing about the silence was crushing. Why? Because she realised the possibility – impossible to confirm or reject – that her father paid for her life with the lives of others. She collapsed in the Archives, crushed by the weight of silence. Why did he do it? What possible explanation was there for it? Traumatic memory? A wish to keep enormity from a child who survived when so many did not? We will never know. But what we can say is that family silences – intimate war memoirs – are performative. They create the conditions of family life by shaping the narrative we receive when young about who we are. Silences, I hold, are essential features of these stories.

Now let me turn to the question as to why people choose this cultural practice. In the field of commemoration and remembrance, we can identify at least three impulses underlying the social construction of silence. In the first place, silence is always part of the framing of public understandings of war and violence, since these events always touch on the sacred, and on eternal themes of loss, mourning, sacrifice and redemption. I term these uses of silence 'liturgical silences'. They are clearly linked to fundamental moral problems, described in reflections on theodicy, or the conundrum as to why, if God is all good and omnipotent, evil exists in the world. Such liturgical silences are essential parts of mourning practices in many religious traditions, which create such spaces in their acts of worship, during which not speaking enables those experiencing loss to engage with their grief in their own time and in their own ways. Consider, for example, the paradox that the Hebrew prayer for the dead, the Kaddish, does not mention the word 'death' or 'dying' or 'grief' or 'bereavement', all conditions or states of mind associated with the seven days of grief passed together by families in mourning. The prayer is silent over the critical reality this practice marks. Mourning practices always touch on such matters, since they perform the fragility of life and the limitations of our own understandings of our existence.

There is a celebrated passage in a canonical Hebrew text that speaks directly to this point. The great sage Maimonides reflected in the twelfth century on the phrase from the psalms, 'Lecha dumya tehila', which the rabbis understood as a paean to God meaning, 'To you all praise is as silence'. 'No', the Rambam said, 'the phrase should be reversed to say this': 'To God silence is the greatest praise'. The prophet Elijah said the same, when he challenged the priests of Baal to pray to their gods, and when they did, all they heard was silence. In Mendelsohn's oratorio 'Elijah', the sound of the priests of Baal in their incantation is followed precisely by a thundering silence. The silence of the true God had triumphed; performed silence at the celestial level.

The power of silence in music is a huge theme in and of itself; the War Requiem of Benjamin Britten comes to mind here. So does a secular text with sacred echoes. I refer here to Ravel's Concerto for the left hand, written for Paul Wittgenstein, who lost his right arm in service in the Austrian army. What we hear is the silence of the right hand, or the harmony of the disabled. Of course there is much in the history of religious practice that points to the power, indeed the essential power, of silence to engage in sacred matters. Think about Trappist monks and other orders; think about the Quakers, with their silent framing of the search for the still small voice of conscience, as the King James Version of the Bible puts it. If we return to the Hebrew, the power of silence is even more forcefully present. The phrase 'a still small voice' is again from Elijah; it is 'Kol demama daka', which perhaps less poetically but more accurately should be rendered thus: 'The sound of a thin silence'. If conscience is the sound of a thin silence, then it is arguable that silence is at the heart of all religious thinking, and perhaps most moral thinking as well.

The second impulse behind the social construction of silence addresses problems of social conflict more directly. Here silence is deliberately chosen in order to suspend or truncate open conflict over the meaning and/or justification of violence, either domestic or transnational. The hope here is that the passage of time can lower the temperature of disputes about these events, or even heal the wounds they cause. I term these practices yielding political or strategic silences.

I have already had occasion to note the case of Balthazar Garzon. Here is the context of the controversy surrounding him. In the late 1970s, the forty-year reign of Franco's dictatorship in Spain came to an end peacefully. In short order, a socialist government came to power and proceeded to refashion the country as a dynamic and stable member of the new European order. The price of that transition was the postponement or adjournment *sine die* – that is permanently – of any formal and public inquiry into atrocities committed during and after the civil war of 1936–39. Spain's new democracy chose peace over justice, order over the open investigation of the abundant evidence on atrocities which – like the underwater sand bars to which I have referred – was present but invisible. Not seeing what everyone saw, and not saying what everyone knew, became a strategy accepted by everyone in politics at the time to ensure the success of a peaceful transition to democratic rule.[6] Such accords are matters of negotiation and thus suffer from all the faults of political compromise. With time, their hold over the parties begins to loosen, a new generation comes to power, and though silence is still ordained at the national level as wise and necessary, people start talking, looking, digging, writing and inevitably accusing. And how could it be otherwise when the scale of accusations is monumental? Here it is evident that silence, like memory and forgetting, has a life history, and when new pressures or circumstances emerge, silence can be transformed into its opposite in very rapid order. And it is very hard to shut Pandora's box once it is open; many try, few succeed.

Some transformative moments, moments when silence is shown to be performative, are well known. Heidegger's silence about Nazi crimes, and his complicity in them, echoed similar lacunae in many German discursive fields after 1945. Paul Celan's poetry challenged and perhaps ruptured Heidegger's silence about his Nazi past. More recently, silence about war and violence has been punctured verbally, when victims are invited to come forward and are given a forum ensuring that what they say will be heard. This is evidently the case in South Africa and in numerous other 'truth commissions' established for this purpose.[7]

The third impulse behind strategies of silence arises from considerations of privilege. That is, who has the right to speak about the violent past? One nearly universal answer is to privilege one group of people who pass through an experience and who thereby have the right to speak about it, as against others who were not there, and thereby cannot know and cannot judge. Only those who had been there, so this argument goes, can claim the authority of direct experience required to speak about these matters. This is what I term essentialist silences.

There are many examples of such distinctions. Soldiers frequently speak about their war experiences only to other soldiers. Efrat Ben Ze'ev has studied an annual reunion of the members of a unit in the Israeli army of 1948; these events continue to this day. They share memories, secrets, and silences.[8] In other cases, soldiers express a kind of sexist rejection of the very capacity of women to enter and understand this masculine realm. Others take an essentialist line, in defining experience as internal and ineffable. When I addressed a conference on the First World War at the Royal Military College, Sandhurst, forty years ago, one of the participants, Charles Carrington, who was a noted author and survivor of the Great War, urged me to choose another profession. The reason: 'You will never know the war; only we who were there can know what it was like'. This was said with avuncular kindness, which I both acknowledged and rejected.

Other such strictures are more acerbic. Time and again, patriots ask how civilians can criticise soldiers and the choices they make under fire if they haven't been there. And when the fighting is still unfolding, what right do civilians have to criticise what they do? Then there is the charge that moral issues about the cruelties of war are too easily framed by those who, like most of us, have had the moral luck to avoid extreme or violent situations. And even among those who endured suffering, there were distinctions between those who knew the worst and those who luckily never reached such a point. Primo Levi said that even survivors like him did not know the worst; that knowledge was restricted only to those at the bottom of the world he inhabited in Auschwitz, those who had already become the living dead.[9]

Furthermore, others pose the question as to how we judge those who survived the war and kept secrets about their past? Condemnation is the easy way out for people who live comfortable lives. Shoshana Felman took this tack in considering the puzzle that her colleague and great literary critic Paul de Man had written anti-Semitic prose in a Belgian newspaper in 1940. This unsavoury fact came to light only after de Man's death in 1982. How do we interpret his behaviour? Felman sees his scrupulous scholarship as distinct from his earlier behaviour, and goes further in suggesting that his silence about his own past was a profound philosophical reflection on the terrible difficulty of all moral judgement, including judging those who as young men and women fell into the trap of the fascist temptation.[10] While not sharing this conclusion, I feel Felman's argument does offer a telling riposte to the 'enormous condescension of posterity',[11] or the tendency to look down upon those stuck in predicaments we ourselves might not have resolved in any morally superior or adequate manner.

The problem with this approach to silence is its characteristic essentialism. Few any longer subscribe to the romantic definition of experience as ingested, visceral and objectively present in the lives and minds of only some individuals. According to this view, experience is theirs and theirs alone. In contradistinction, experience is much more fruitfully defined as a set of events whose character changes when there are changes – through age, migration, illness, marriage, religious conversion and so on – in the subject position of the person or group in question.[12]

This anti-essentialism is a line of interpretation very familiar to students of memory in the cognitive and neurosciences. They no longer view the mind or memory as fixed, as in a computer's hard drive, but more as dynamic and unstable, as in a collage. The work of Elizabeth Loftus has deepened our understanding of implanted memories, ones suggested to individuals by outsiders and sometimes by clinicians in therapeutic relationships. The danger of such interventions is evident.[13] If memory changes radically over time, then we must abandon the notion that not only memory but also the right to speak about memory is the property of only a chosen few who claim privileges similar to what Calvin termed 'election'.[14] Relegating the rest of us to silence must be seen as a strategy of control, of cutting off debate, of *ad hominem* assertions of a kind unworthy of serious reflection.

Who has the right to speak, to be sure, is a thorny question, especially in the field of research we examine here. War stories are never uncontested, and over time they change as the people who frame them grow old, move on and pass away. When the victims of violence have the sanction to speak out, as in a court of law or truth commission, then they become the authors not only of their stories but also of their lives. Not speaking can entail accepting someone else's story about what happened to you. Or it may be an assertion of dignity by those who, like rape victims, pass through indignity and refuse to do so verbally again. Once more we can see that silence, or non-speech acts, have rules; the entitlement to speak about war and violence is in no sense universal. Some have the right; others do not. The difference between the two categories is a matter of social and cultural codes, which can and do change over time.

CONSTATIVE SILENCES

Let me return to J. L. Austin's fundamental distinction between factual or constative statements and performative statements. There is clearly a vast range of reference in war memoirs and war stories to silence not as literary device or mode of exclusion or indirection, but as an auditory reality, one conveying the uncanny character of the battlefield. There are the reports of the strange silence when the artillery barrage lifts prior to a major attack. There is the silence etched into place by memories of birdsong suddenly audible, audible because the monstrous anger of the guns, in Wilfred Owen's phrase, was stilled.[15]

There is the silence of the Armistice itself, when the big guns stop firing and soldiers can do simple things like standing up in daylight, a suicidal act moments before. There is the silence of that other kind of closure, on the home front, that silence which followed the receipt of the letter or telegram announcing the death of a loved one. In each case, silence is a parenthesis, a bracketing of what over fifty months had become normal – the sound of artillery fire or the family conversations tiptoeing around the fear that the message may come at any time.

There is one very recent semi-fictional account of war – and aren't all war memoirs semi-fictional? – which brings this point home with a thud. In *To the End of the Land* (2008), David Grossman, the Israeli novelist, has produced an extraordinary novel/memoir, in which his central figure, Ora, returns home to Jerusalem after taking her son to join his unit about to launch an attack on an Arab town on the West Bank. On her return, she fears the footsteps of the group of 'notifiers', those who bring families official notification of the death of their children or husbands or fathers, fears it to the point that she refuses to risk hearing it. The Hebrew title of the novel is *Woman Flees the Notification*. She flees her house so she will not be there to hear the news, and through a kind of magical thinking, senses that if she can't be found, if she can't hear the message, the message won't arrive. She refuses to hear the state's message about the feared fate of her son, who, as she puts it, has been nationalised by the army. What is extraordinary about this account of silence as a refusal to hear is that life imitated art. After completing the first drafts of the novel, Grossman and his wife did indeed get the notification that their son Uri had been killed in Lebanon in 2006.

Another sub-genre of war stories with which we are all familiar concerns silence as a symptom of physical or traumatic injury. I refer to the subject of shell shock and the induced inability to speak. In thousands of cases, either temporarily or over a long period, soldiers lost the ability to speak after battle. Some did so after having been buried alive in the course of an artillery barrage. There are also accounts of the use of electric shock treatment to break the hold of silence on a disabled man. This kind of aversion therapy was controversial, and at times the doctors who used it were subject to criticism from some of their medical colleagues. One such case is that of Julius Wagner-Jauregg in Vienna. No less a figure than Sigmund Freud stood up to testify on behalf of Wagner-Jauregg, a prominent anti-Semite, soon to win the Nobel Prize in medicine. The use of electric shock to break mutism or other forms of paralysis, Freud said, was justifiable since the doctor was trying everything available to him to bring the patient back to his pre-combat self.

We have no memoirs of men who were rendered mute by artillery fire or other horrors of the battlefield, but we do have war memoirs of the men who treated them. And now we have fiction based on those memoirs, in the form of Pat Barker's 'Regeneration' trilogy. Here are war stories about war stories about silence, and about how some doctors tried to break its hold on a man. Mutism was not a literary device or even a metaphor; it was a palpable and appalling reality.

Another area in which we need to attend to silence is that of war stories told in cinema. Here we confront what may be termed technical silence – the silence of film before the talkies. Many war memoirs and fiction found a huge audience in film, and for technical reasons, built into the machinery of the art, film remained silent for the first decade after the war. Even when the talkies came, the men and women who made films put silences into the talkies, and did so naturally, since all of them were trained in cinema before soundtracks were invented.

Silent films told the stories that came out of the war on the silver screen in ways that the talkies rarely could. And yet I would like to suggest a paradox in this predicament imbedded in silent film. The technological limits of silent cinema in the post-1918 decade were, I hold, among its greatest strengths. Being unable to imprint voices on nitrate scrolls, filmmakers had to rely on facial expression, gesture and silence to convey meaning. They had to work indirectly, with musical accompaniment instead of voices. Silent film thus rested on the boundary between constative and performative silence. Silence was built into the medium, at least until 1927, and then interposed within scripts thereafter. That is what I mean by a matter-of-fact or constative silence. But who could miss the performative element in many war stories turned into silent film? During and in the decade after the Great War, film replicated and captured for a very large audience the power of the séance. The message of the séance was roughly this. Those who had lost their sons, their fathers, their husbands could not easily answer the question as to the meaning of the death of their own. Nations do not fight wars; people do, and the notation of serving the nation and dying for it wore very thin among families who asked why their man had to die.

Spiritualism performed this predicament. Families rarely knew the how as well as the why their men had died; the bodies did not come home during or after the war, and half of the men who died in the war had no known graves. Industrial war was a vanishing act; making men die and then disappear. Uncertainty and the lingering hope of a mistake, or a hospital incarceration, or imprisonment in an enemy POW camp kept them wondering for years. Is it surprising that spiritualism flourished at a time when the traditional churches – dead set against spiritualism – had few answers for these people? Coming together in the presence of a medium, usually a woman who could channel the brainwaves of their loved ones, such people tried to still their anguish and to find ways of starting their lives again. The pattern of the message they got through spiritualism was roughly this. The voices of the dead are silent, but their message could be conveyed. It was simply that we are all right. We are with our brothers who died with us. You, the living, can go back to your lives again. And in most cases that is what they did.

To be sure, the cinema harnessed spiritualism for profit. In effect, in grand picture palaces and small ones, dozens of war films were produced in the period 1914–29 that used silence to translate spiritualism into commercial and artistic success. In a kind of trance, in the dark, with or without an organ or piano accompaniment, filmgoers saw the dead return to them, albeit for a moment. When that happened, silence framed the message in a kind of veil that carried emotional and visual force alike. Indeed, in the case of one celebrated film, Abel Gance's 'J'Accuse' (1919), we know from Gance's detailed instructions that when the dead rise from the battlefield and go home to see if their suffering had been justified, he turned the sound off. The orchestra stopped playing. And there is nothing more powerful in film to convey affect than silence. The same was true for the 1916 British propaganda film 'The Battle of the Somme'. When the staged attack happened, when a group of men 'went over the top', the music stopped. The effect, apparently, was devastating.

It was indeed the voices of the dead that were conjured up in these cinematic séances. Consider the paradox, therefore, that when voices were added to feature films after 1927, the effect of calling forth the dead diminished. The reason is that verisimilitude turned into pseudo-realism. And pseudo-realism has been the defining feature of war films ever since. The existential quest of spiritualism turned into existential kitsch. The best instance I know of is the remake of 'J'Accuse' by Gance in 1937; it is appalling. Just comparing those two versions of the same story, one silent and one with hurricanes of sound, leads me to the conclusion that silent film could say things that the talkies could not.

PERFORMATIVE SILENCES

Now for what I term performative silences in commemorative practices and in war memoirs. These silences come in many guises, some more familiar than others. There is the two-minute variety, and all its variants. Commemorative practices always entail an element of silence, since they all touch on the sacred, and as I have tried to suggest, the language of the sacred, whatever its denominational character, always has silences imbedded in it.

Political silences govern what some war memoirs can say. They perform language codes related to inglorious events in a nation's bellicose history. And which nation does not have one or two inglorious moments, and which nation does not draw a veil of silence over them? Turkish leaders, as we all know, continue to deny the Armenian genocide took place. German soldiers' war memoirs have tended to treat the Holocaust as an event about which they knew little and say less. As a rule, Japanese acknowledgement of atrocities committed in China and elsewhere is similarly absent from war memoirs. These are political choices, tacitly accepted by the writers of war memoirs, in order to evade the open discussion of painful or compromising episodes.

Codes of what is sayable about war also involve decorum, tact, taste. We mustn't talk about the war, says John Cleese as the mad hotelier, Basil Fawlty, in the British sitcom *Fawlty Towers*, who then, in a literal fit of absence of mind, goose steps his way all around his appalled German guests. I want to dwell on the issue of codes of decency, of what one does not say or do, since they are clearly generational in character, and at one period rule out rough language deemed inappropriate to describe soldiers at war. Paul Fussell has said much of importance about euphemisms in the language of war,[16] but I would like to extend his argument further by saying that linguistic codes as to what is appropriate are language-specific too. Euphemisms are ways of drawing a veil of indirection or silence over realities deemed for one reason or another to be too harsh or too horrible to say.

Euphemism

My argument is that in the study of war memoirs, we need to attend to what may be termed the manifold use of euphemistic silences. Time and again, accounts are sanitised by using gentle words when harsher or more vulgar words could offend or dismay. War memoirs, I believe, are filled with euphemistic evasions of plain speaking about war. And when these memoirs are translated, then euphemisms multiply. Consider this instance, concerning the original and two translations of Henri Barbusse's 1916 novel/memoir *Le feu*. Barbusse's novel was intended to offer his readers plain speaking about war, and was celebrated as the first time in the midst of war the argot of soldiers replaced the soaring rhetoric of patriotic eye-wash. Here is just one sentence taken from Barbusse's memoir/novel that shows us the ease with which euphemism blunts the punch of the original text.

Herewith Barbusse: 'Honte à la gloire militaire, honte aux armées, honte au métier de soldat, qui change les hommes tour à tour en stupides victimes ou ignoble bourreaux'.[17] And herewith the first 1917 English version of the same passage 'Shame on military glory, shame on armies, shame on the soldier's calling, that changes men by turns into stupid victims or ignoble brutes'.[18] Now compare the words used in this translation with a recent rendering of the novel into English 'Shame on military glory, shame on armies, shame on the soldier's profession, which changes men, some into stupid victims, others into base executioners'.[19] Executioners, not brutes; here is the moral core of Barbusse's argument: war entails both degradation and shared culpability for the mutual slaughter. The men in uniform, Barbusse included, are both victims and executioners, but in 1917 in English at least, this could not be said. Language codes precluded direct translation, and silenced the difficult moral judgement Barbusse offered of what war does to soldiers: it turns them into killers.

I want to offer other instances of ways in which silence is something that happens in war memoirs, something that happens in translations, and something we need to notice in how the canon of war memoirs itself was constructed. Those included were written by those with the social sanction to talk about war.

Women's War Memoirs

Who of us is unaware that one powerful delimiting feature in the construction of the canon of war memoirs is its gender bias? This has not only been acknowledged but justified such essentialism. Both Paul Fussell and Samuel Hynes, the greatest analysts of war literature – and both authors of war memoirs – restrict the genre of war memoir primarily or exclusively to those written by men. Why do they do so? Because they hold that men tell the soldiers' tale – and that that story is singular and gendered. Why? Because the experience of combat is such as to constitute a kind of fraternity, whose masculine character is at the core of the identity both of the tale and of the teller. When women's war memoirs enter the canon, it is through contact with the bodies of men – as nurses, mothers, wives, lovers, occasionally daughters. They are there as second order carriers of the soldiers' tale, that account of war and combat, which is the subject of this meeting.

If we object to essentialist silences on principle, why should we accept this one? Who is to say that Doris Lessing's account of her appallingly disabled father[20] – he certainly was disabled as a father – or Pat Barker's memoirs of her mother's coping with not one but two damaged veterans, one who was Pat's biological father and the other his replacement, are not war memoirs, clearly at the heart of Barker's war fiction?[21] They tell the story of the effects of war in vivid and visceral details and power unmatched perhaps by other memoirs. Since war memoirs are, perforce, always about both the war and the aftermath of war, then the restriction of the canon of war memoirs primarily to those written by men is a recipe for silencing some voices and privileging others.

My point is a simple one. The gender bias in the corpus of war memoirs available to us is one of its defining features. What if Virginia Woolf wrote in *A Room of One's Own* about Robert Graves' sister or Henri Barbusse's sister, or Franz Marc's wife, and what other countless voices we will never hear because what they had to say was gendered out of bounds? Would her point be any the less powerful? Yes, there are notable exceptions: Vera Brittain and Rebecca West and Virginia Woolf herself. It is hardly an accident that we cannot read *Fathers and Daughters* alongside *Fathers and Sons*, and it is still on our research agenda to search out those women whose memoirs of war and its aftermath still lie hidden in family collections and hope chests. But, following Woolf, even if we find them, we won't do more than hear but a few of the silenced voices whose tales were never written down, because conventionally women don't write war memoirs, men do. Silences are imbedded not only in voices that do not speak, but in voices that do not have the right to speak. That is one reason why Pat Barker's work has been so important: she is a silence breaker about gendered codes of writing war memoirs.

Family Silences

I have argued that silence conveys absence, that it means something, rather than simply white noise. A second performative instance of silences as vectors of meaning lies in the way they define many family stories about war. Family constellations change in war and because of war; that is self-evident. But how family members themselves tell that story is not self-evident, and there is frequently silence in the way they do it. There is an extraordinary account of family histories in war which shows how this is so. It is called *The Danger Tree*, written by David Macfarlane,[22] and it tells the story of a Newfoundland family defined by who isn't there. The absences define the presences, and tell us what the family became when individual faces were cut out of the family portrait.

Family history is frequently studied separately from war memoirs, as if the men who went to war did not do so to defend their families, and as if their thoughts were restricted to the men with whom they served. Put this way, we can all agree this is unadulterated rubbish, but it is another and harder step to take to braid together war stories with the stories of the people who read them, and for whose benefit most war stories probably were intended. War memoirs are conversations about war; they are dialogic; they answer questions posed by writers and readers at one point in time. And those readers and conversations are ongoing within families as much as they are whenever old soldiers get together.

WITNESSES MORAL AND IMMORAL

Some of these conversations were carried on in verse. War poetry carries many messages about silence. 'Why spake not they...?' Owen asks of survivors of a particularly intense and ferocious battle in 'Spring Offensive'; he tells of the men who came back mute. In his work we confront some of the stylistics of this material, particularly its spare, simple, sometimes hesitant character, informing his attempt to formalise the idea of silence or the refusal or impossibility to speak about some of the horrors of war.

This leads to the last of the categories of silences I want to address today. This category relates to the task some soldier writers took on to expose and replace lies about war. Euphemisms can be politely true, or they can be profoundly untrue. Dead men fall; but are their bodies adorable? One way to understand the construction of one kind of war memoir is as an effort to break the hegemony of sanitised versions of war produced to control and contain the subject Edmond Wilson termed 'patriotic gore'.[23] There is much in Henri Barbusse's *Le feu* to support an interpretation of this war memoir as an attempt to give voice to those who did not speak of war as noble. Consider as well the plain, straight, unvarnished meaning of Remarque's novel, *All Quiet on the Western Front*, and the irony of the title.[24] Not true under any circumstances, and certainly not true in the case of Paul Bäumer's last day on earth. It was hardly surprising, therefore, that Nazis let mice loose in filmic versions of the book, turning its screening into a 'riot' leading to the banning of the film as a threat to public order. Some war memoirs were written to disturb the public order of patriotic lies about war.

Perhaps one way of understanding the different categories of war memoirs arises from this view of war memoirs as pot shots by veterans over the contested terrain of the 'truth' about war. There were three rough camps in which war memoirs can be placed. There were those that reassured and asserted conventional values: Ernst Jünger's *In Stahlgewittern* is one case in point.[25] There were those written against the grain, in anger at the lies the conventional literature conveyed: *Le feu* is in this camp. And there were those in no man's land between the two, uncertain about where the truth – if there is indeed a truth – lies in accounts of war. In very different ways, Graves' *Goodbye to All That* and Louis-Ferdinand Céline's *Voyage au bout de la nuit* should be placed in this intermediary camp.

Some writers wrote to break the silence, to set the story straight, to take the shine off High Diction, to strip the shit off noble and romantic prose or images of the dead, the mutilated and the terrified as the Fallen, the Stoical and the Heroic. To stop the rot in language itself, battalions of memoirs appeared in response to and after those marched up many a publisher's ramp to present to the public an anodyne, antiseptic or reassuring image of what war is. Here is the way Tim O'Brien has put it: 'A true war story is never moral. It does not instruct, nor encourage virtue, nor suggest models of proper human behavior, nor restrain men from doing the things they have always done. If a story seems moral, do not believe it'.[26] Note the unstated but powerful warning against believing war stories that preceded his own. The anger is in the contemplation of lies already in circulation, lies silencing the truth about the stupidity, arbitrariness and horror of war.

The Israeli philosopher Avishai Margalit has explored in more formal language this terrain of reacting to lies, of telling stories about war in response to other stories.[27] He writes of the moral witness, as someone who has been through a violent, life-threatening experience and who lives to tell the tale. I want to push Margalit's argument a step further and claim that the moral witness, in his usage, only appears when and after the immoral witness speaks or writes or draws a veil of loveliness, in Oliver Wendell Holmes's Victorian language, over battle and carnage and death. Here is Holmes in 1895: 'War, when you are at it, is horrible and dull. It is only when time has passed that you see that its message was divine'. 'Adorable' is the word Holmes used for the self-sacrifice of the men who go to war: that is why its message was divine.[28]

Holmes at least had the virtue of having seen battle with his own eyes. He was less an immoral witness than a romantic dreamer. But what about those many memoirists who write about war from afar, not only in terms of physical distance but in terms of euphemistic elevation of the clash of arms they never saw or never understood or – even worse – understood but hid from their readers by noble prose? What about those who had no idea of what they wrote? Their words are legion, and to some men and women, they had to be answered. These euphemists are the men Henri Barbusse answered in his *Le feu*. Barbusse stood up and said: enough of this crap; let me try to tell you the way it was. Of course, he never got there; no one ever does, but his memoir presented as a kind of truth-telling fiction is precisely of the reactive kind to which I want to draw the reader's attention. To paraphrase Brecht, when you hear a war memoir use the word adorable, or any of the dozens of falsifying equivalents, reach for your knife (or your pen).

It is no accident that the Great War was the moment for an avalanche of moral and immoral witnessing, in Margalit's terminology. The industrialisation of war, the appearance of assembly-line killing as the *non plus ultra* of the artillery war of 1914–18, transformed the nature of combat and what constituted heroism, but it did not transform the cadences of many of those who continued to sing the siren's song of the beauty of war or of its divine purpose. As always, language changes more slowly than do the conditions it attempts to describe and convey.

Consequently, since 1914, this sequence seems to be unavoidable. Over time we move from one discursive register of war as noble at one point in time to another discursive register that responds with a very different kind of message. In a nutshell, that message is that it is very, very difficult to write about war without glorifying it. Fall into that trap, and someone will come along to warn others against doing so. They are the moral witnesses; they are the silence breakers. Most of the comments in this chapter are about memoirs of those who saw combat, but we all know about the Ludendorffs and the Haigs of this world, whose capacity to forget or ignore or distort was boundless. Their optic was telescopic. When we adjust our lens to the life-size, to the intimate history of killing, other words and other silences emerge. It is those words and those silences I think we need to hear today.

CONCLUSION

Let me conclude with a claim that needs qualification, but which perhaps is worth presenting in its boldest form. All war memoirs are performative, since they reinvent experience about war, and by doing so incorporate all the silences – liturgical, political, essentialist – to which I have already referred. The Romanian novelist Herta Müller noted in her Nobel Prize acceptance speech in 2009 that, 'What can't be said can be written. Because writing is a silent act, a labor from the head to the hand. The mouth is skipped over'. My point is in the same vein. When dealing with accounts of war, conventions matter. There are those who obey them, and those who break the rules and break the silence. What can't be said frequently can be written, and it is only by hearing the silences in some texts that we can hear the message of others which follow. As Maurice Blanchot put it many years ago, 'to be silent is also to speak',[29] and to speak of silence as a framework within which to set war memoirs is to open up a conversation that is just about to begin.

These remarks can be reduced to two assertions. The first is this. Silence is destabilising: its presence tells us that something or someone is missing. It embodies discomfort, makes us ill at ease. We strain to hear what or who isn't there. The second is this. The difference between performative silence and constative silence lies in the anger underlying the message. Silence breakers try to transcend the euphemistic glorification of war in accounts that range from the banal to the obscene. Say not soft things as others have said, Owen implores his readers. Silence under these circumstances is complicity in the reign of lies. When the writers of war memoirs or war stories express anger at other war memoirs, they are climbing up a hill others have climbed before. For every time someone tries to say, no, war is not so pretty or clean, he or she is engaged in a Sisyphean effort. The big words keep coming back, and so does the war over how to tell a war story, a war without end if there ever was one.

NOTE

1. Tim O'Brien, *The Things They Carried* (New York, 1990).
2. Marc Augé, *Les formes de l'oubli* (Paris, 1998), 4. 'Les souvenirs sont façonnés par l'oubli comme les contours du rivage sur la mer.'
3. Branden W. Joseph, 'John Cage and the Architecture of Silence', *October* lxxxi (1997), 80–104, at page 85.
4. J.L. Austin, *How To Do Things With Words* (Oxford, 1972), on the social construction of performative speech acts, and the rules governing them, 15ff.
5. Austin, *How To Do Things with Words*, 17.
6. Mary Vincent, 'Breaking the Silence? Memory and Oblivion since the Spanish Civil War', in Efrat Ben-Ze'ev, Ruth Ginio and Jay Winter (eds), *Shadows of War: A Social History of Silence in the Twentieth Century* (Cambridge, 2010), 47–67.

7. Louis Bethlehem, 'Now That All Is Said and Done: Reflections on the Truth and Reconciliation Commission in South Africa', in Ben-Ze'ev, Ginio and Winter, *Shadows of War*, 153–71.
8. Efrat Ben Ze'ev, 'Imposed Silences and Self-Censorship: *Palmach* Soldiers Remember 1948', in Ben-Ze'ev, Ginio and Winter, *Shadows of War*, 181–96.
9. Primo Levi, *Survival in Auschwitz* (New York, 2002), 90.
10. Shoshana Felman, 'Paul de Man's Silence', *Critical Inquiry* xv(4) (1989), 704–44.
11. E.P. Thompson, *The Making of the English Working Class* (London, 1963), 18.
12. Joan W. Scott, 'The Evidence of Experience', *Critical Inquiry* xvii(4) (1991), 773–97.
13. Daniel Schacter, *The Seven Sins of Memory: How the Mind Forgets and Remembers* (Cambridge, MA, 1999), 20–23; Elizabeth Loftus, *Eyewitness Testimony: Psychological Perspectives* (Cambridge, MA, 1979); and Veronica Nourkova, Daniel M. Bernstein and Elizabeth Loftus, 'Biography becomes Autobiography: Distorting the Subjective Past', *American Journal of Psychology* cxvii (1) (2004), 65–80.
14. Jay Winter, *Remembering War: The Great War between History and Memory in the Twentieth Century* (New Haven, 2006), ch. 1.
15. Wilfred Owen, 'Anthem for Doomed Youth', in C. Day Lewis (ed.), *The Collected Poems of Wilfred Owen* (London, 1963), 88.
16. Paul Fussell, *The Great War and Modern Memory* (New York: Oxford University Press, 1975), 10-12ff.
17. Henri Barbusse, *Le feu. Journal d'une escouade.* (Paris: Flammarion, 1916). 214.
18. Barbusse, *Under fire. The story of a squad*, trans. Fitzwater Wray (New York: E.P. Dutton, 1917), 257.
19. Barbusse, *Under fire*, trans. Robin Buss (New York: Penguin, 2003), 286
20. Doris Lessing, *Alfred and Emily* (New York: Harper, 2008).
21. Kennedy Fraser, 'Ghost writer', *The New Yorker*, 17 March 2008, 41-2
22. Alan Macfarlane, *The Danger Tree. Memory, War and the Search for a Family's Past* (Toronto: Macfarlane, Walter & Ross, 1991).
23. Edmund Wilson, *Patriotic Gore. Studies in the Literature of the American Civil War* (New York: Oxford University Press, 1962).
24. Erich Maria Remarque, *All Quiet on the Western Front*, trans. A. W. Wheen (Boston: Little, Brown and Company, 1929).
25. Ernst Jünger, *In Stahlgewittern: aus dem Tagebuch eines Stosstruppführers* (Berlin: E.S. Mittler & Sohn, 1930).
26. O'Brien, *The Things They Carried*, 65.
27. Avishai Margalit, *The Ethics of Memory* (Cambridge, Mass: Harvard University Press, 2002), ch. 5.
28. 'The *Soldier's Faith*', in *Speeches by Oliver Wendell, Jr.* (Boston: Little Brown, 1918), 56, 59.
29. Maurice Blanchot, *The Writing of the Disaster*, trans. Ann Smock (Lincoln, NE: University of Nebraska Press, 1986), 11.

BIBLIOGRAPHY

Memoirs

Barbusse, Henri. *Le feu. Journal d'une escouade.* Paris: Flammarion, 1916.
Barbusse, Henri. *Under fire. The story of a squad,* trans., Fitzwater Wray. New York: E.P. Dutton, 1917.
Barbusse, Henri. *Under fire,* trans. Robin Buss. New York: Penguin, 2003.
Barker, Pat. *The Regeneration Trilogy.* London: Viking, 1996.
Céline, Louis-Ferdinand, *Voyage au bout de la nuit.* Paris: Denoëet Steele, 1932.
Day Lewis, Cecil. *The Collected Poems of Wilfred Owen.* London: Chatto and Windus, 1963.
Graves, Robert, *Goodbye to all that. An Autobiography.* London: Jonathan Cape, 1929.
Grossman, David. *To the End of the Land,* trans. Jessica Cohen. New York: Vintage Books, 2010.
Jünger, Ernst. *In Stahlgewittern: Aus dem Tagebuch eines Stosstruppführers.* Berlin: E.S. Mittler & Sohn, 1930.
Levi, Primo. *Survival in Auschwitz.* New York: Basic Books, 2002.
Remarque, Erich Maria. *All Quiet on the Western Front,* trans. A.W. Wheen. Boston: Little, Brown and Company, 1929.

Secondary Sources

Augé, Marc. *Les formes de l'oubli.* Paris: Payot & Rivages, 1998.
Austin, J.L. *How To Do Things With Words.* Oxford: Oxford University Press, 1972.
Bethlehem, Louis. 'Now That All Is Said and Done: Reflections on the Truth and Reconciliation Commission in South Africa', in Efrat Ben-Ze'ev, Ruth Ginio and Jay Winter (eds), *Shadows of War: A Social History of Silence in the Twentieth Century* (Cambridge: Cambridge University Press, 2010), 153–71.
Ben Ze'ev, Efrat. 'Imposed Silences and Self-Censorship: *Palmach* Soldiers Remember 1948', in Efrat Ben-Ze'ev, Ruth Ginio and Jay Winter (eds), *Shadows of War: A Social History of Silence in the Twentieth Century* (Cambridge: Cambridge University Press, 2010), 181–96.
Blanchot, Maurice, *The Writing of the Disaster,* trans. Ann Smock. Lincoln, Nebraska: University of Nebraska Press, 1986.
Felman, Shoshana. 'Paul de Man's Silence'. *Critical Inquiry* xv(4) (1989), 704–44.
Fraser, Kennedy. 'Ghost writer', *The New Yorker,* 17 March 2008, 41-2.
Fussell, Paul. *The Great War and Modern Memory.* New York: Oxford University Press, 1975.
Holmes, Oliver Wendell, Jr., *Speeches by Oliver Wendell Holmes, Jr.* Boston: Little Brown, 1918.
Joseph, Branden W. 'John Cage and the Architecture of Silence'. *October* lxxxi (1997), 80–104.

Lessing, Doris. *Alfred and Emily*. New York: Harper, 2008.
Loftus, Elizabeth. *Eyewitness Testimony: Psychological Perspective*. Cambridge, MA: Harvard University Press, 1979.
Macfarlane, Alan, *The Danger Tree. Memory, War and the Search for a Family's Past*. Toronto: Macfarlane, Walter & Ross, 1991.
Margalit, Avishai. *The Ethics of Memory*. Cambridge, Mass: Harvard University Press, 2002.
Nourkova, Veronica, Daniel M. Bernstein and Elizabeth Loftus. 'Biography becomes Autobiography: Distorting the Subjective Past'. *American Journal of Psychology* cxvii(1) (2004), 65–80.
Schacter, Daniel. *The Seven Sins of Memory: How the Mind Forgets and Remembers*. Cambridge, MA: Harvard University Press, 1999.
Scott, Joan W. 'The Evidence of Experience'. *Critical Inquiry* xvii (4) (1991), 773–97.
Thompson, E.P. *The Making of the English Working Class*. London: Victor Gollancz, 1963.
Vincent, Mary. 'Breaking the Silence? Memory and Oblivion since the Spanish Civil War', in Efrat Ben-Ze'ev, Ruth Ginio and Jay Winter (eds), *Shadows of War: A Social History of Silence in the Twentieth Century* (Cambridge: Cambridge University Press, 2010), pp. 47–67.
Wilson, Edmund, *Patriotic Gore. Studies in the Literature of the American Civil War*. New York: Oxford University Press, 1962.
Winter, Jay. *Remembering War: The Great War between History and Memory in the Twentieth Century*. New Haven: Yale University Press, 2006.

Jay Winter is the Charles J. Stille Professor of History Emeritus at Yale University, Distinguished Research Professor at Monash University, and a specialist on the First World War and its impact on the twentieth century. His other interests include remembrance of war in the twentieth century, such as memorial and mourning sites, European population decline, the causes and institutions of war, British popular culture in the era of the Great War and the Armenian genocide of 1915. He has edited or co-edited twenty five books and contributed more than 110 book chapters to edited volumes. In 1997, he received an Emmy award for the best documentary series of the year as co-producer and co-writer of *The Great War and the Shaping of the Twentieth Century*, an eight-hour series broadcast on PBS and the BBC, and shown subsequently in twenty-eight countries. He is editor-in-chief of the three-volume *Cambridge History of the First World War*, published in French and in English in 2014, and in Chinese in 2016.

Chapter 3

'A Lively School of Writing'
George Gleig, Moyle Sherer and the Romantic Military Memoir

Neil Ramsey

The genre of the military memoir has come to be regarded by historians and literary critics as a distinct and significant cultural form. Viewed as central to the formation of cultural memories and the commemoration of wars, attention has also been drawn to the ways in which memoirs of war are themselves shaped by cultural narratives, tropes and discourses.[1] Although there have, accordingly, been a number of studies that describe and analyse the generic form of military memoirs, it has only been comparatively recently that attention has been directed towards memoirs from before the two world wars.[2] In his work on the genre, Yuval Noah Harari has not only documented the long development of European military memoirs from the seventeenth century through to the present day, but has also demonstrated that the genre underwent key changes from the late eighteenth to the early nineteenth century. Such changes were, he argues, far more crucial in establishing the genre's modern form than the impact of the world wars. Shaped by the cultural influences of sentimentalism and Romanticism, a new form of military memoir emerged, one that was no longer concerned with impersonal historical narrative but which instead described the personal experience of war and its unique significance for the individual.[3] This earlier period was thus central to the formation of the modern military memoir's view of war as a revelatory or *Bildung* experience, in which the soldier narrates his experience of combat and suffering as a process of personal development leading to forms of enlightenment or disillusionment.[4]

Because he considers these changes over such a long duration, however, Harari is only able to provide a relatively general overview. He thus largely conflates sentimental and Romantic treatments of war. Although agreeing with his analysis of developments in the military memoir during the period, this chapter offers a more fine grained examination of this transformation by arguing that it can partly be understood as a change from a sentimental to a distinctly Romantic form of memoir. In particular, it focuses on the influential changes introduced into the genre at the start of the 1820s by the military memoirs of two junior ranking British officers, Moyle Sherer's *Recollections of the Peninsula* (1823) and George Gleig's *The Subaltern* (1825).[5] By drawing attention to their authorial role, their utilisation of the aesthetic of the picturesque and their affinities with what Anne Frey has recently theorised as the State Romanticism of British literary culture during the late 1820s and 1830s, this chapter shows how they transformed the focus on suffering that characterised sentimental forms of the military memoir.[6] While still viewing war in terms of hardship, they also associated their experience of soldiering with the restorative powers of nature and rustic simplicity. They transformed the painful experience of war by insisting that it provided an unparalleled source of inspiration for the individual soldier. Regarded by contemporaries as having made military writing popular, these two books were central to the establishment of the modern form of the military memoir.[7]

THE SENTIMENTAL MILITARY MEMOIR

As a generic form, the military memoir had become well established in European culture by the seventeenth century. Influenced by classical forms of military memoir, such as Julius Caesar's *Commentaries on the Gallic War*, and by the common practice among early modern soldiers of composing 'accounts of services rendered' for their employers, military memoirs were written by generals, nobles and military officers as histories of campaigns in which they had participated.[8] The genre, however, had little to say about the personal experience of war. Rather, it formed what Tim Travers refers to as a 'narrative campaign style of history' that provided impersonal and chronological narratives of major military campaigns.[9] As *The New and Enlarged Military Dictionary* (1802) explained: '[m]emoirs, in *military literature*' were 'written by persons who had some share in the transactions they relate'. As a genre, however, it should be understood as a 'species of history' resembling Caesar's *Commentaries*.[10] Military memoirs were written with little sense at all that the personal experience of war could, in itself, be worthy of recording for a public audience.

During the latter half of the eighteenth century, however, military memoirs began to focus some of their attention on the military experiences of individuals. This change can largely be attributed to the influence of the culture of sentimentality, which not only prompted public interest in forms of autobiographical writing more generally, but which also introduced new ideas into military theories and training practices that placed increasing value on soldiers' feelings. Sentimentalism emerged out of wide-reaching developments in eighteenth-century moral philosophy, physiology, medicine and literature.[11] Although achieving its height in the age of sensibility of the late eighteenth century, sentimentality had far-reaching effects on the understanding of feeling and personal experience right across British literary culture of the late eighteenth and early nineteenth centuries.[12] With its roots in a 'sensationist psychology' derived from John Locke and in Scottish Enlightenment moral philosophy, concerned with understanding the sociability of human nature, sentimentalism established feelings as the basis of morality and social cohesion.[13] As Adam Smith argued in his *Theory of Moral Sentiments* (1759), by entering imaginatively into another's feelings, by experiencing sympathy or compassion for their suffering, we will feel compelled to take moral action on their behalf. Many forms of writing during the period thus began to use sentimental literary techniques in their efforts to cultivate a reader's sensibilities and moral virtue.[14] Genres that were traditionally concerned solely with factual reportage, such as histories and travel writing, began to record individual feelings and include tales of suffering in order to engage readers in 'more inward and sentimental terms'.[15] The generic boundaries between forms of writing were increasingly eroded by this shared impulse to stimulate readers' emotions by focusing on personal experiences.[16]

Military themes were common in sentimental writing because of the emotional intensity associated with war's suffering.[17] Sentimental writing often confronted its readers with images of war's victims, whether war widows, orphans or broken soldiers. Not only did such writing help render the soldier a more sympathetic figure, but, as Harari argues, sentimental culture also impacted directly upon the military realm by influencing the army's perception of soldiers and its approaches to military training. Eighteenth-century armies functioned according to strict hierarchies that treated the soldier as a cog within a clockwork mechanism.[18] Soldiers were drilled in massed formations and expected to follow their officers' commands as unthinking automatons. Under the influence of sentimental culture, however, the late eighteenth century witnessed a growing concern with the sensibilities and capacities of ordinary individuals, leading to educational reforms across nearly all sectors of society.[19] New approaches to education saw an emphasis placed on the cultivation of soldiers' personal initiative, particularly in relation to the training of soldiers in light regiments tasked with independent missions and supporting roles within the army.[20] Such concerns also intersected with the growing nationalistic emphasis of warfare that saw changes in recruitment practices and far greater interest in the soldiers' personal motivation in defence of the nation.[21]

As the eighteenth century progressed, therefore, military memoirs began to incorporate sentimental elements that offered a sympathetic portrayal of the soldier, even at times focusing in unprecedented detail on the protagonist. The *Journals of Major Robert Rogers* (1765), for example, recorded Rogers' personal exploits with the British Army in America during the Seven Years' War (1757–63).[22] Robert Lawson-Peebles has suggested the *Journals* represents the first modern military memoir because of its insistence upon communicating personal experience, which Lawson-Peebles attributes to the more irregular and independent nature of warfare in America and Rogers' role as a scout.[23] Military memoirs also made increasing use of emotional details that drew upon sentimental techniques for eliciting a reader's sympathies. John Simcoe's *A Journal of the Operations of the Queen's Rangers, from the End of the Year 1777, to the Conclusion of the Late American War* (1789) is almost wholly written in the campaign narrative tradition as an impersonal historical narrative of his regiment's actions during the American Revolutionary War (1775–83).[24] However, Simcoe also interrupts his narrative to draw a very brief, sentimental account of the 'dreadfully mangled and mortally wounded' Lieutenant Rynd and the 'horror' of his painful transportation from the field of battle.[25] A more sustained sentimental approach is apparent in the anonymous *Memoirs of the Late War in Asia* (1788) or James Bristow's *Narrative of the Sufferings of James Bristow, Belonging to the Bengal Artillery, During Ten Years Captivity with Hyder Ally and Tippoo Saheb* (1793), both of which drew upon the generic form of the captivity narrative to offer intimate details of the suffering of British soldiers imprisoned by Indian forces during conflicts in the 1780s.[26] It was observed by the *English Review* that the *Memoirs of the Late War*, having been translated into French, had spread such 'general compassion in France for the gallant but unfortunate sufferers' that the French court was prompted to appeal to the soldiers' captor, 'Tippoo Sualtan', for their release.[27]

By the beginning of the nineteenth century a more thoroughgoing sentimental treatment of warfare was increasingly common. Military memoirs began to resemble the sentimental genres of the suffering traveller, such as captivity narratives, accounts of shipwreck and stories of travel involving hardships and exotic events or locations.[28] A relatively large number of such personal narratives by British officers emerged in the years after Britain entered the Peninsular War (1808–14), fuelled by the enormous interest in the war from across the nation's political spectrum and appealing to those readers, the *London Review* claimed, who will 'sympathise with the sufferings, really severe, which the British soldier endured'.[29] Despite continuing in the campaign narrative tradition, supplementing official accounts with historical narratives of the nation's military campaigns, these memoirs also focused to an unprecedented degree on the experiences and suffering of the protagonist as a traveller with the army. They were composed as travelogues that dwelt on the narrator's personal reactions to the scenery, architecture and customs of the inhabitants. Typically, however, such observations are presented alongside descriptions of the enormous hardships experienced while travelling with the army on campaign. In his *Letters from Portugal and Spain* (1809) Robert Ker Porter stated that although 'your mind would be amused by the surrounding landscape', the conditions of travelling nonetheless ensured 'your body is tormented'.[30] James Ormsby similarly noted, in *An Account of the Operations of the British Army* (1809), that much of his experience 'resembled rather a tour than a campaign', although he also reflected on the 'confusion and misery' that attended the army's march.[31] George Burroughs described his experience of campaigning, in *A Narrative of the Retreat of the British Army from Burgos* (1814), as simply 'months of toil'.[32]

The narrators of these works curiously oscillate between describing major military actions and claiming that they lack any capacity to explain military scenes, that they are a 'newcome' or 'novice' at war, unable to comment on the course of the campaign.[33] The naive or touristic quality of the Peninsular War memoirs even resembles the narratives of Waterloo that appeared in the British press soon after the campaign, such as James Simpson's *A Visit to Flanders, in July, 1815* (1815) and John Scott's *Paris Revisited, in 1815, by Way of Brussels* (1816).[34] Most of these were written by civilians who had travelled to the battlefield at the end of the campaign and who therefore lacked any authority at all as military experts.[35] A private view of war was emerging within and alongside the tradition of the military memoir, a view that could be shared by civilians and soldiers and which was concerned principally with documenting intimate personal details and emotional responses to war. If earlier sentimental military memoirs typically described hardships in the remote realms of America or India, accounts of the Peninsular War and Waterloo placed the suffering traveller within major European wars. War itself was coming to be seen as something inherently exotic or extraordinary, a site foreign to the narrator.[36] Although the tenor of this work remained largely patriotic, its innumerable portrayals of war's suffering could, as Ormsby commented, raise the 'still small voice of humanity' in the observer to deplore the effects of war.[37] The narrator was frequently confronted with forms of suffering not easily assimilable to heroic narratives of the soldier's noble death in battle, incidents such as soldiers dying from exhaustion or officers driven mad by the horrors of their experience, where, as H. Milburne lamented, 'their distempered and horror-struck imaginations [were] perpetually pursuing some dreadful hallucination connected with the casualties of war, famine, and shipwreck'.[38] The eyewitness served in such work as a moral rather than simply a military authority, able to provide a humane perspective on war in which war was coming to be definable as a unique and extraordinary experience of horror and suffering.

Although sentimental eyewitness accounts of war were increasingly common in the British press, they were typically dismissed as an inferior or even problematic version of history. The *Quarterly Review* voiced a common opinion when it suggested that although '[t]he accounts of eyewitnesses are always valuable', they must nonetheless 'always be considered as subordinate to the labours of the professed historian'.[39] Reviewers even expressed their disapproval of the way such accounts detracted attention from events of such importance as the nation's wars. As one reviewer commented in *Quarterly Review*, 'who, for instance, could for a moment tolerate a picture of Waterloo, in which the chief figure was Lieutenant McIntosh of the 79th, or Captain Augustus Polidore Brumme of the Royal Scotch Fusiliers?'[40] By placing himself so firmly at the centre of the narrative, an officer memoirist might be able to elicit the reader's sympathies for his suffering, but he also risked becoming an egotist, his personal narration distorting a proper nationalist perspective on war by confronting the reader with a partial and even 'disgusting' corporeality.[41] A focus on personal bodily suffering primarily lent itself to supporting anti-war sentiments. By the start of the 1820s sentimental portrayals of soldiers' suffering were even at times associated with the renewed radicalism of the post-Waterloo era via such books as the autobiographical *Journal of a Soldier of the Seventy-First* (1819), which was published by its editor, John Howell, in the hope of dispelling young men's enthusiasm for war.[42]

However, the publication of Sherer and Gleig's memoirs in the mid 1820s dramatically altered the form and reception of the genre. These two books decisively transformed the manner in which the genre presented the soldier's personal experience of war. Gleig himself reflected in a later edition of *The Subaltern*:

> I have reason to believe, as large a share of public favour as ever was bestowed upon a narrative of the kind [...] It was one of the first works of its kind which appeared, and to this circumstance, perhaps, may in some measure be attributed the general approbation with which all classes of readers received it.[43]

Both men had served with the British Army on campaign during the Peninsular War and their memoirs in many ways resemble the earlier sentimental records of the conflict. But Sherer and Gleig were also professional authors who were able to establish successful and lasting careers writing for the general public, largely through the success of their memoirs. Gleig was remembered throughout his career as the author of *The Subaltern*. For the *Gentleman's Magazine*, Gleig was even responsible for having 'founded a lively school of writing' with his military memoirs.[44] Although they continued to define war as a foreign and painful experience, inviting the reader to sympathise with the suffering of the soldier, they also drew upon the touristic aesthetic of the picturesque travelogue. They thus presented war as a realm of aesthetic pleasure, an approach that could serve to soften its horrors and disgusting corporeality. Their aestheticisation of war also meant, however, that they were able to discover meaning in suffering as they associated the privations of soldiering at war with the restorative powers of nature and a rejection of idle luxury.

THE MILITARY PICTURESQUE

In utilising the picturesque, Sherer and Gleig were drawing upon an aesthetic mode that was very familiar to the British reading public by the start of the nineteenth century. The picturesque represented an appreciation of nature and landscapes that was aligned with broader developments in eighteenth-century aesthetics, positioning itself in particular against the earlier aesthetic categories of the beautiful and the sublime. In his collection *Three Essays: on Picturesque Beauty; on Picturesque Travel; and on Sketching Landscape* (1792) one of the leading theorists of the concept, William Gilpin, defined picturesque travel by envisioning a 'new object of pursuit for the tourist', namely the pursuit of picturesque scenery, or scenery that could 'please from some quality, capable of being illustrated by painting'.[45] Such scenery was principally identified with the roughness and irregularity of uncultivated regions of Britain, in Wales, Scotland or the Lake District, although the aesthetic was expanded to tours and descriptions of foreign localities such as India or the South of Europe.[46] It was no coincidence that while war with France severely curtailed travel to the continent, the picturesque should have developed as an appreciation of natural British scenery. While legal ownership of the land remained crucial to participation in the British political system, the picturesque could enable any Briton with a cultivated and refined sensibility to form an attachment to the land.[47] Working at a far more human level than the related aesthetic of the sublime, the picturesque served to underpin an imaginative identification with the nation.[48]

In adapting the picturesque to his memoirs, Sherer can be seen as attempting to cultivate his readers' aesthetic appreciation of, even their attachment to, the nation's recent wars. The picturesque had formed an element in earlier sentimental military memoirs, and like these, Sherer's narrative revolves around his travels with the army and touristic observations of the landscapes, architecture and people of Portugal and Spain. Travelling through similar country to Sherer, for example, Ormsby had exclaimed '[t]o a romantic eye delighting in the wildness of nature, the country we proceeded through this day was interesting in the extreme'.[49] There are also moments in such memoirs that record the sublimity and even picturesque quality of scenes of war. Adam Neale described his panoramic view of the British forces at Vimiero as 'a scene, the grandest and most picturesque you can well imagine'.[50] Yet reflections on the picturesque in sentimental memoirs are only ever presented as fleeting, interspersed with more general touristic observations on a region's cities and politics while invariably giving way to historical descriptions of military events or accounts of personal suffering and hardships.

Unlike this earlier work, however, Sherer consistently utilises the picturesque to convey his experience of war. His memoirs progress through a series of detailed and lengthy picturesque descriptions. He claims that he is not trying to provide a 'professional sketch of the campaigns' at all, regarding himself as a 'traveller, and a man of feeling' rather than what he terms a 'scientific soldier'.[51] At times, Sherer even feels that his travels had simply become 'an excursion for pleasure' (84). Relating the army's retreat through Portugal during its campaign of 1809, for example, he recounts:

> We now retraced our steps to Alemtejo. One of our camps, on this short retreat, was formed on ground the most wild and picturesque. Half way between Villa Velha and Niza, the road winds through a deep and narrow valley, inclosed on all sides by rudely-shaped and rocky hills; through it flows a small streamlet, descending from the heights in the rugged channel of a wintry torrent, and faintly marking out its course with a silvery thread of the purest water. Here, at night-fall, after being nearly eighteen hours under arms, we halted: the heights ascend on all sides of this little vale so steep and perpendicular, that it is impossible to preserve any regular formation, and the men were dispersed in groups all up the hills. I and my companions spread our cloaks and kindled our fire upon a rocky ledge, close to the top of that ravine down which the rivulet fell, and thus we overlooked the whole encampment. The short dry brushwood, though it made bad fires, sent forth bright and beauteous flames, and the sudden and magic illumination of this rude and

> warlike scene may be conceived, but, I feel, it is impossible to describe it. The fitful glare which gave to view the groups of soldiers, here only shewing the dark outlines of human figures, and there throwing a fiery light on their arms, their dress, and features, the glow reflected from the stream, and the dark lofty masses of hill and rock in the back ground, formed a picture such as only the genius of a Byron, or a Southey, could convey to the mind of a reader in the language of description. (45–46)

Despite his awareness of war's hardships, recording a fatiguing eighteen-hour march, Sherer's focus here is on the 'wild and picturesque' scenery through which he travelled, the 'rudely-shaped and rocky hills' and the 'rugged channel' of a mountain stream. He not only observes, however, that the army is surrounded by picturesque nature. He equally describes the soldiers' camp, its 'rude and warlike scene' as merging into the 'picture' produced by the scenery, the glow of the soldiers' fires setting the background scene into relief as a 'magic' scene. Although he humbly announces that he does not possess the descriptive genius of Lord Byron or Robert Southey, his reference to the two poets nonetheless underscores the aesthetic qualities of his writing, demonstrating that he possesses the poets' taste for picturesque scenery and their desire to impress the 'mind of a reader' with its wild imagery. He even draws attention to the romance of darkly outlined 'human figures', as though the soldiers were Byronic banditti or corsairs simply augmenting and completing the picturesque scene.

As Sherer develops an account of picturesque pleasure, so his narrative serves to erase the harsher elements that troubled the sentimental depiction of war. John Barrell argues that this is one of the principle effects of the picturesque, that as an exclusively aesthetic viewpoint it 'eliminates all sentimental and moral reflection'.[52] The picturesque, in other words, afforded Sherer a remarkable degree of aesthetic distance from the painful elements that featured so prominently in earlier, sentimental accounts of war. Reviewing Sherer's *Recollections*, the *Eclectic Review* was struck by how successfully the work had brought a picturesque style to his description of war, observing:

> He has an eye for the picturesque; and a march through Spain afforded ample opportunities of gratifying his taste, in the costume, the scenery, and the military spectacle, while his feelings seem to have partaken of the intoxication of romance. We could have fancied that we were at times reading the imaginative descriptions of Geoffrey Crayon, rather than the account of a sanguinary campaign; so much does 'the man of feeling' predominate in these pages, over the 'scientific soldier'.[53]

By imagining war as the picturesque traveller, Sherer was able to find a poetically interesting approach to writing of these details, in which his descriptive writing and 'romantic intoxication' could recontextualise the sentimental contemplation of a 'sanguinary' military campaign in terms of an appealing picturesque aesthetic.

Sherer does not maintain this aesthetic distancing entirely without hesitation. Describing the British Army's retreat to Lisbon in 1810, Sherer feels overwhelmed by the level of destruction he encounters (115). His writing could still inspire a reader's sentimental reflection on war's horrors. When the *United States Literary Gazette* reviewed Sherer's *Recollections* it insisted that it 'helps to do away certain errors, and throw some light upon the folly and wickedness of a love of war, and an admiration of military achievement'. Our appreciation of military 'pomp and glories', the *Gazette* concluded, was because we 'consider [war] in the mass, and not in detail'. Sherer's book and its focus on his personal experiences at war helped to dispel these false glories, allowing the reader to, instead, 'follow the individuals who compose this mass, and observe the feelings which govern them, the deeds upon which they are bent ... suffering which it is terrible to read of, and, perhaps, the violent death towards which many are pressing'.[54]

Yet rather than dwelling upon scenes of destruction, Sherer also announces that they pose a threshold to his account that he simply will not cross, so that rather than detail the destruction he encounters upon the retreat, he simply tells his reader, '[m]y pen altogether fails me' (115). If destruction cannot be accommodated to the picturesque, it fails to enter into his account of war. Elsewhere, Sherer concludes his reveries on the destructive impact of warfare by offering a prayer of thanks that Britain has never witnessed the ravages of modern war. 'Happy are ye, my countrymen', he exclaims, who have 'read only of these things, and are spared such trials!' (188). He views himself as bridging this experiential gap between his peaceful reader and war, yet he similarly strives to spare or protect his readers from the worst of war's horrors. He effectively positions himself as a Romantic author, echoing the approach of a poet like Samuel Taylor Coleridge, for whom the poetic imagination represented the most appropriate means to represent war, to enable it to be properly realised as a felt experience.[55] Describing scenes of war through the familiar and distinctly British aesthetic of the picturesque, Sherer was allowing his reader to cultivate a tasteful appreciation for scenes of war rather than inciting their horror and sympathetic compassion.[56]

Although Gleig never claimed that *The Subaltern* was influenced by Sherer's *Recollections*, it is possible to detect a marked degree of similarity in approach between the two books. It was certainly noted at the time that *The Subaltern* was 'written in the same style as that of "Recollections of the Peninsula"'.[57] Featured originally as a series of articles in *Blackwood's Edinburgh Magazine* in 1825, and published by Blackwood as a separate book later that year, *The Subaltern* resembles Sherer's work in its fundamental departure from the campaign narrative tradition. Gleig is adamant that he is not writing a 'regular memoir of the campaigns of 1813 and 1814' nor, he insists, will he 'intrude upon the province of the historian'.[58] His book provides, instead, a personal account of his experiences at war, one that details his feelings and draws heavily on the kinds of picturesque descriptions of nature and warlike scenes that Sherer had employed. Both books were, moreover, praised because of their capacity to introduce the feelings of the protagonist into the account of war. Reviewers noted that Sherer obtrudes his 'personal identity and feelings' upon the reader, and that Gleig 'compels himself to record not only what he did but what he felt'.[59] Adopting Sherer's picturesque style of writing, Gleig similarly legitimates the authority of a subaltern's perspective as an aesthetic and emotive rather than an inferior historical view of warfare, as he endeavours to explain the experience of soldiering 'to the mind of an ordinary reader' (50).

In his work, Gleig also, however, extends Sherer's picturesque style by insisting that he simply speaks as a professional soldier and that he will limit himself to write only about war. He still frames his experiences through the generic form of the picturesque travelogue, repeatedly drawing attention to the 'glorious' (38), 'romantic' (71) and 'picturesque' (328) scenery he encounters while marching with the army. But he equally insists that he will write something quite distinct from earlier officers' 'Journals' or 'Letters to Friends at Home'. Unlike these earlier memoirists, he is not a 'military tourist' concerned with detailing the character of the land and its people (257). While his memoirs resemble Sherer's account by drawing heavily on picturesque description, Gleig is adamant that he is primarily a witness to war itself (164). Rather than offer his narrative as an account of a campaign or region, Gleig felt free to simply title his work *The Subaltern* and to concentrate on the particular experiences of the individual soldier.[60]

Far more than scenes of nature, Gleig's picturesque eye seeks out scenes of war. When Sherer had first entered the Peninsula, sailing into Lisbon harbour, he remarked upon how the scene 'feasts the eye of a traveller' (3). Gleig, conversely, is clear that his first entry to the Peninsula, during the siege of St Sebastian, was 'to the seat of war' and that it is scenes of war itself that constituted 'the object of our gaze' (23–24). Gleig focuses on cannonades, sieges, fortifications and trenches. It is the assorted materiality and activities of war which Gleig believes 'presented a spectacle in the highest degree interesting and grand, especially to eyes, like my own, to which such spectacles were new' (29). Arriving at St Sebastian he reports: 'I was gazing with much earnestness upon the scene before me, when a shot from the castle drew my attention to ourselves and I found that the enemy were determined not to lose the opportunity, which the calm afforded, of doing as much damage as possible to the ships which lay nearest to them' (29). He underscores the fact that he has encountered an environment that is determined, infused and translated by war; he watches and is watched by soldiers in an environment that is anything but, as Sherer defined it, 'most peaceful, most lovely' (33). He is engaged in a 'situation perhaps as interesting as can well be imagined to the mind of a soldier' (25).

For Gleig, therefore, military bivouacs, formations and battles are not simply features within a picturesque landscape, as they were for Sherer, but are themselves the most aesthetically appealing features of his travels. Although he is enraptured by the scenery he encounters in the South of France, for example, exclaiming that '[t]he country around was more romantic and striking than any which I had yet seen' (282), he nonetheless goes on to insist that the military component surpasses the interest of the landscape. More than simply background figures, the military takes pre-eminence. He delights:

> It would have been altogether as sweet and pastoral a landscape as the imagination can very well picture, but for the remote view of the entrenched camp, which from various points might be obtained, and the nearer glimpse of numerous watch-fires, round which groups of armed men were swarming. To me, however, these were precisely the most interesting objects in the panorama, and those upon which I chiefly delighted to fix my attention. (282–83)

It is war that constitutes the most interesting part of any scene he encounters. Presenting himself as a delighted observer of the 'warlike spectacle' (178), Gleig transformed Sherer's picturesque approach into a 'military picturesque' focused principally on the aesthetic spectacle of war itself.

ROMANTIC AUTHORSHIP AND THE *BILDUNG* OF WAR

By framing the soldier's personal view of war through a picturesque aesthetic, the two books were also able to offer a quite different perspective on war's suffering than sentimental forms of military memoir. Both still suppose that war constitutes a distinct experience, one that is constituted by hardships and privation, but both also insist that the experience of war can be understood as a release from the enervating effects of civilian society.

War, therefore, not only offers a source of aesthetic beauty; it equally provides opportunity for self-cultivation. Earlier memoirs certainly demonstrated a stoical endurance of the suffering that the soldier encountered on campaign. Robert Ker Porter, for example, insisted that the soldier's 'military philosophy' was to steel oneself against war's hardships.[61] Nonetheless, the sentimental mode employs a compassionate view of suffering, in which the narrator typically confronts an individual's suffering as something deplorable. Gleig and Sherer, in contrast, celebrate war's suffering, producing military memoirs that can be identified with the narrative tradition Harari terms the *Bildung*, or revelatory experience of war, in which war's suffering is seen to have a fundamental capacity to mould and instruct the individual.[62]

Where both depart most strikingly from earlier military authors, therefore, is the way they present themselves as authorial figures, aligned not only with the descriptive powers of Romantic poets such as 'Byron and Southey', but equally with the poet's capacity to edify and uplift the reader. Their authorial role was operating in terms of what Barbara Benedict identifies as a new, Romantic conception of authorship, one devoted to the 'creative shaping of social mores'.[63] Although primarily identified with 'Romantic verse', this authority was diffused through the era's writing and is visible in Sherer and Gleig's memoirs. Both were seen to display enormous poetic qualities in their writing, using the picturesque and its associations with taste and virtue to transform the military memoir into something of far more personal and moral significance, with the potential to be read as part of an 'elite literature for the aspiring middle classes'.[64] A fundamentally Romantic expressivity was seen to permeate the 'genius' and 'poetic brilliancy' of Sherer and Gleig's writing,[65] in which the freedom of their aesthetic style of writing on war, where they follow their 'own little personal adventures' rather than writing a regular narrative of the campaign, is reflected in their imagining of the soldier's experience of war as a period of rustic simplicity imbued with feelings and virtues lost to the luxuries of civilian life.[66]

Sherer's experience of campaigning at war, his sense of the fundamental connection between war and the picturesque, is inextricably bound with a Romantic view of nature as a morally pure and authentic realm that stands in contrast to the ennui of civilian existence. As a soldier at war he partakes of the rustic life he encounters among the humble peasants of Spain and Portugal. He thus agrees with Byron that there is 'sweetness in the mountain air, / And life that bloated ease can never hope to share' (223), advising the reader that one need not have 'the genius, or the passion of Rousseau' to enjoy such pleasures (100). He concludes of his experiences in the Peninsula: 'The rude simplicity of this life I found most pleasing. An enthusiastic admirer of nature, I was glad to move and dwell amid her grandest scenes, remote from cities, and unconnected with what is called society. Her mountains, her forests, and, sometimes, her bare and bladeless plains, yielded me a passing home' (42–43).

If earlier memoirists had typically viewed the suffering of war as a misery to be stoically endured, Sherer takes a virtuous pleasure from his privations remote from ordinary society. He describes, for instance, how, during an appalling storm while on the march with the army, he was able to find shelter in a Portuguese peasant woman's cottage. Reflecting on her simple generosity, he declares, 'where, let me ask, was the hotel in England which, in the caprice of sickness, would have satisfied all my wants and wishes?' (78). He concludes of this woman's kindness that 'no sermon on the charities of life could be more instructive'. Even physical dangers of wounding can be instructive, capable of lifting 'a man ... almost above the dignity of his nature' so that 'such moments are more than equal to years of common life' (40). Being a soldier at war enables him to escape the dull comforts of civility to participate in 'the interest of foreign scenes, the animation of daily march, and the careless gaiety of camps' (1).

Gleig, too, views war in contrast to the luxuries of civilian life, emphasising even more strongly that the virtues of war derived not simply from the opportunity to commune with nature, but from being active and useful as an 'enthusiastic lover of the profession of arms' (371). From the opening of his account he relates his excitement at the prospect of attaining experience of war, that it had 'been the most prominent petition in my daily prayers, for nearly twelve months past, not to be kept idling away my youth in the country towns of England, but to be sent, as speedily as possible, where I might have an opportunity of acquiring a practical knowledge of the profession which I had embraced' (4).

In contrast to his idle youth, his time at war stands as a period in which he feels his life was not 'uselessly spent' (373). As does Sherer, Gleig repeatedly draws attention to his enjoyment of the 'rude simplicity' of life on campaign, whether the humble pleasures of the bivouac or the numerous opportunities he found for excursions of shooting, fishing or merely rambling amidst the beautiful scenery (90). Recollecting his first night sleeping under the stars in a military camp, he describes a 'perfect delight' that 'any monarch might envy' and of which he believes, he could never find an equivalent in his civilian life (33–34). Writing in the 1845 edition, he would go so far as to describe the simple, vigorous experience of campaigning as a 'school of piety and true devotion' that far excelled the enervating effects of 'the crowded capital', or even the rustic tutelage of the 'quiet village'.[67]

By insisting upon the virtues of war's privations, Sherer and Gleig were moving away from the tradition of the sentimental military memoir to develop something that can be identified as a distinctly Romantic form. Their development of the military memoir has affinities with what Anne Frey terms the State Romanticism of the late 1820s and 1830s. Frey challenges the belief that Romanticism was waning in these years by suggesting, rather, that authors began to situate their writing in relation to the expanding powers and reach of the British state. Accepting state authority, whether that of the church or navy, authors did not rescind their literary ambitions but increasingly situated their writing in relation to the state. They treated the author as a figure who could help carry state authority into the private arena of reading. This is apparent in the latter writing of Wordsworth and Coleridge, in which they turn to the church as a site for uniting individuals with the nation, or in Sir Walter Scott's emphasis on how the novelist can offer correctives to the impersonality of the law. Notably, too, it is also apparent in Jane Austen's emphasis on the navy as a model for community and professional self-sacrifice, a model for a national identity that transcended Britain's aristocratic heritage.[68] Gleig and Sherer advance a similar Romantic enthusiasm for their wartime experience as officers in the British Army, viewing their time as soldiers as a period of pastoral tranquillity in which they are able to develop their aesthetic and moral sensibilities. By drawing on Britain's familiar terrain of the picturesque and meshing their identity as an officer with the man of feeling and taste, they were able to establish the national significance of the individual officer. They were not only helping their readers more easily imagine war, but in elevating the military officer himself to the role of the author they were further enriching the sublime capacities of the state. As the *Monthly Review* insisted in 1831, *The Subaltern* had come to 'maintain an honourable place in every well regulated library in the empire'.[69]

Sherer and Gleig were thus viewed as legitimate authors in the literary realm rather than egotists producing an inferior history or sentimentalists offering a disturbing portrait of the individual at war. By refashioning the military memoir as a genre concerned with the aesthetics of war, their writing had enabled the soldier's personal feelings to be exhibited in a manner that provided a complimentary view of the nation's wars rather than a grotesque, debateable or even radical counter-history of those wars. Partly, too, their exhibition of the talent and taste of the author can be regarded as an effort to align the soldier with the expanding reading public of the 1820s and 1830s, with its growing sense that gentlemanly 'prestige' was related to an individual's breadth and taste in reading.[70] They were reforming the figure of the military officer as a man of professionalism, virtue and taste.

But they not only focused on the aesthetic appeal of war; they also registered war's capacity to serve as a *Bildung*, as a process of self-discovery and growth. Their aestheticisation of war provided a framework for lifting the suffering of the soldier into a pleasurable and transformative experience. This is not to imply that subsequent military memoirs necessarily adopted a picturesque aesthetic or found soldiering tranquil. What is most significant is that Sherer and Gleig had written of their personal experience of war in ways that went decisively beyond sentimental suffering. Their work inspired the enormously popular tales of military adventure that appeared during the 1830s and which celebrated the intrinsic pleasures and moral value of war's hardships and dangers.[71] War was not only emerging as a definable experience in such work, but had come to be viewed as an experience with unequalled significance for the individual soldier.

NOTES

1. T.G. Ashplant, Graham Dawson and Michael Roper, 'The Politics of War Memory and Commemoration: Contexts, Structures and Dynamics', in T.G. Ashplant, Graham Dawson and Michael Roper (eds), *The Politics of Memory: Commemorating War* (New Brunswick and London, 2004), 3–86; 32–34. On the literary qualities of war memoirs, see Paul Fussell, *The Great War and Modern Memory* (New York and London, 1975), 310–14. Fussell goes so far as to argue that the narrative structure of war memoirs is essentially indistinguishable from first-person novels (310).
2. Studies that focus on soldiers' wartime memoirs from the twentieth century include Fussell, *The Great War and Modern Memory*; Samuel Hynes, *The Soldiers' Tale: Bearing Witness to Modern War* (London, 1997); and Alex Vernon (ed.), *Arms and the Self: War, the Military, and Autobiographical Writing* (Kent, 2005). On contemporary British military memoir, see Rachel Woodwards, '"Not for Queen and Country or Any of that Shit...": Reflections on Citizenship and Military Participation in Contemporary British Soldier Narratives', in Deborah Cowen and Emily Gilbert (eds), *War, Citizenship, Territory* (New York and London, 2008), 363–84.
3. Yuval N. Harari, *The Ultimate Experience: Battlefield Revelations and the Making of Modern War Culture, 1450–2000* (Basingstoke and New York, 2008).
4. Harari, *The Ultimate Experience*, 193–96.
5. Moyle Sherer, *Recollections of the Peninsula*, 2nd ed. (London, 1824); George Gleig, *The Subaltern*, 2nd ed. (Edinburgh and London, 1826).
6. Anne Frey, *British State Romanticism: Authorship, Agency, and Bureaucratic Nationalism* (Stanford, CA, 2010).

7. Harari, *The Ultimate Experience*, 193–96. The present chapter is adapted from my book *The Military Memoir and Romantic Literary Culture*, in which I cover in detail the development of the military memoir during the Romantic era.
8. Yuval N. Harari, 'Military Memoirs: A Historical Overview of the Genre from the Middle Ages to the Late Modern Era', *War in History* 14 (2007), 289–309, 290–95.
9. Tim Travers, 'The Development of British Military Historical Writing and Thought from the Eighteenth Century to the Present', in David A. Charters, Marc Milner and J. Bent Wilson (eds), *Military History and the Military Profession* (London and Westport, CT, 1992), 23–44, 24.
10. Charles James, *A New and Enlarged Military Dictionary, or, Alphabetical Explanation of Technical Terms: Containing, Among Other Matter, a Succinct Account of the Different Systems of Fortification, Tactics, &c. Also the Various French Phrases and Words that Have an Immediate or Relative Connection with the British Service, or May Tend to Give General Information on Military Subjects in Either Language* (London, 1802), [n.p.]. Emphasis in original. The term military memoir was also applied to biographical accounts of eminent generals and admirals. Although focused on a single life, eighteenth-century military biographies were themselves as much a 'species of history' as other military memoirs, typically being composed as a historical narrative of the major public events and achievements of the officers' military career. See, for example, 'Military Memoirs of the late Lieutenant-General John Burgoyne', *The British Military Library; or Journal: Comprehending a Complete Body of Military-Knowledge; and Consisting of Original Communications; with Selections from the Most Approved and Respectable Foreign Military Publications*, 2 vols (London, 1801), ii. 369–75.
11. Major studies on the culture of sentimentalism include G.J. Barker-Benfield, *The Culture of Sensibility: Sex and Society in Eighteenth-Century Britain* (Chicago, 1996); Barbara M. Benedict, *Framing Feeling: Sentiment and Style in English Prose Fiction 1745–1800* (New York, 1994), 1–18; Janet Todd, *Sensibility: An Introduction* (London and New York, 1986); and R.F. Brisenden, *Virtue in Distress: Studies in the Novel of Sentiment from Richardson to Sade* (London, 1974).
12. For an overview of how recent studies have stressed the ongoing significance of sentimentalism throughout the Romantic era, see John Brewer, 'Sentiment and Sensibility', in James Chandler (ed.), *The Cambridge History of English Romantic Literature* (Cambridge, 2009), 21–44; Christopher C. Nagle, *Sexuality and the Culture of Sensibility in the British Romantic Era* (Basingstoke, 2007), 1–17; and Susan Manning, 'Sensibility', in Thomas Keymer and Jon Mee (eds), *The Cambridge Companion to English Literature, 1740–1830* (Cambridge, 2004), 80–99.
13. Michael Bell, *Sentimentalism, Ethics and the Culture of Feeling* (Basingstoke, 2000), 16; Evan Gottlieb, *Feeling British: Sympathy and National Identity in Scottish and English Writing, 1707–1832* (Lewisburg, 2007), 28; Brisenden, *Virtue in Distress*, 22–26.
14. Brewer, 'Sentiment and Sensibility', 29–36; Todd, *Sensibility*, 4.

15. Mark Salber Phillips, *Society and Sentiment: Genres of Historical Writing in Britain, 1740–1820* (Princeton, 2000), 103 and xii. On travel writing and sentimentalism, see Mary Louise Pratt, *Imperial Eyes: Travel Writing and Transculturation*, 2nd ed. (New York, 2008); and Nigel Leask, *Curiosity and the Aesthetics of Travel Writing, 1770–1840: 'From an Antique Land'* (Oxford and New York, 2002).
16. Brewer, 'Sentiment and Sensibility', 33.
17. J. Walter Nelson, 'War and Peace and the British Poets of Sensibility', in Roseanne Runte (ed.), *Studies in Eighteenth-Century Culture* (Wisconsin, 1978), 345–66, 357.
18. Harvie Ferguson, 'The Sublime and the Subliminal: Modern Identities and the Aesthetics of Combat', *Theory, Culture & Society* 21(3) (2004), 1–33, 5.
19. Harari, *The Ultimate Experience*, 165–66.
20. Harari, *The Ultimate Experience*, 166–80.
21. See, for example, Stefan Dudnik and Karen Hagemann, 'Masculinity in Politics and War in the Age of Democratic Revolutions, 1750–1850', in Stefan Dudnik, Karen Hagemann and John Tosh (eds), *Masculinities in Politics and War: Gendering Modern History* (Manchester, 2004), 3–21.
22. Robert Rogers, *Journals of Major Robert Rogers: Containing an Account of the Several Excursions He Made under the Generals Who Commanded Upon the Continent of North America, During the Late War; from Which May be Collected the Most Material Circumstances of Every Campaign Upon That Continent, from the Commencement to the Conclusion of the War* (London, 1765).
23. Robert Lawson-Peebles, 'Style Wars: The Problems of Writing Military Autobiography in the Eighteenth Century', in Vernon, *Arms and the Self*, 61–80, 75.
24. John Simcoe, *A Journal of the Operations of the Queen's Rangers, from the End of the Year 1777, to the Conclusion of the Late American War. By Lieutenant-Colonel Simcoe, Commander of that Corps* (Exeter, 1789).
25. Simcoe, *A Journal of the Operations of the Queen's Rangers*, 118.
26. William Thomson, *Memoirs of the Late War in Asia. With a Narrative of the Imprisonment and Sufferings of Our Officers and Soldiers: By an Officer of Colonel Baillie's Detachment* (London, 1788); James Bristow, *A Narrative of the Sufferings of James Bristow, Belonging to the Bengal Artilley [Sic], During Ten Years Captivity with Hyder Ally and Tippoo Saheb* (London, 1793). See also Sharon Alker, 'The Soldierly Imagination: Narrating Fear in Defoe's *Memoirs of a Cavalier*', *Eighteenth Century Fiction* 19(1–2) (2006–7), 43–68, 68. Alker also proposes that Defoe's fictional *Memoirs of a Cavalier* (1720) operates as a critique of traditional military memoirs and their displacement of war's suffering, suggesting, therefore, that Defoe's work may have opened up a space for these later, more personal military memoirs. She does not, however, consider the broader impact of sentimental writing.
27. *English Review, or an Abstract of English and Foreign Literature* 13 (1789), 238.
28. Carl Thompson, *The Suffering Traveller and the Romantic Imagination* (Oxford, 2007), 13–16.

29. Peter Spence, *The Birth of Romantic Radicalism: War, Popular Politics, and English Radical Reformism, 1800–1815* (Aldershot, 1996), 64–67; *The London Review*, 2(4) (November 1809), 273.
30. Robert Ker Porter, *Letters from Portugal and Spain, Written During the March of the British Troops under Sir John Moore. With a Map of the Route and Appropriate Engravings. By an Officer* (London, 1809), 69.
31. James Wilmot Ormsby, *An Account of the Operations of the British Army, and of the State and Sentiments of the People of Spain and Portugal During the Campaigns of 1808 and 1809*, 2 vols (London, 1809), i. iv and 94.
32. George Frederick Burroughs, *A Narrative of the Retreat of the British Army from Burgos, in a Series of Letters. With an Introductory Sketch of the Campaign of 1812; and Military Character of the Duke of Wellington* (Bristol, 1814), 38.
33. John Edgecombe Daniel, *Journal of an Officer in the Commissariat Department, 1811–1815* (London, 1820), 17; Ormsby, *An Account of the Operations of the British Army*, i. 31.
34. James Simpson, *A Visit to Flanders, in July, 1815, Being Chiefly an Account of the Field of Waterloo, Etc.* (Edinburgh, 1815); and John Scott, *Paris Revisited, in 1815, by Way of Brussels: Including a Walk over the Field of Battle at Waterloo. By John Scott, Author of a Visit to Paris in 1814; and Editor of the Champion, a London Weekly Journal* (London, 1816).
35. Stuart Semmel, 'Reading the Tangible Past: British Tourism, Collecting and Memory after Waterloo', *Representations* 69(9) (2000), 9–37, 3.
36. David Bell suggests that under the influence of Enlightenment philosophers, European intellectual culture at the end of the eighteenth century came to see warfare as an extraordinary event lying outside the boundaries of the ordinary course of society. See David Bell, *The First Total War: Napoleon's Europe and the Birth of Warfare as We Know It* (New York, 2007).
37. Ormsby, *An Account of the Operations of the British Army*, i. 31.
38. Adam Neale, *Letters from Portugal and Spain; Comprising an Account of the Operations of the Armies under Their Excellencies Sir Arthur Wellesley and Sir John Moore, from the Landing of the Troops in Mondego Bay to the Battle at Corunna. Illustrated with Engravings ... From Drawings Made on the Spot* (London, 1809), 305; H. Milburne, *A Narrative of Circumstances Attending the Retreat of the British Army Under the Command of the Late Lieut. Gen. Sir John Moore, K.B. with a Concise Account of the Memorable Battle of Corunna, and Subsequent Embarkation of his Majesty's Troops; and a Few Remarks Connected with these Subjects: in a Letter Addressed to the Right Honourable Lord Viscount Castlereagh, One of His Majesties Principal Secretaries of State, &c. &c.* (London, 1809), 32–36.
39. *Quarterly Review* 2(3) (1809), 204.
40. *Quarterly Review* 2(3) (1809), 180.
41. On the issue of egotism in Romantic era autobiographical writing, see James Treadwell, *Autobiographical Writing and British Literature, 1783–1834* (Oxford, 2005).

42. Thomas, *Journal of a Soldier of the Seventy-First, Highland Light Infantry, from 1806 to 1815. To Which Are Now Added, Selections from the Letters of Corporal Meüller, of the First Regiment of Foot Guards, Describing the Attack on Bergen-Op-Zoom, &c.*, ed. by John Howell, 3rd ed. (Edinburgh, 1822), v.
43. George Gleig, *The Subaltern*, 1845 ed. (Edinburgh and London, 1845), x.
44. *Gentleman's Magazine* 101 (1831), 68.
45. William Gilpin, *Three Essays on Picturesque Beauty; on Picturesque Travel; and on Sketching Landscape: To Which is Added a Poem on Landscape Painting* (Westmead, 1972 [1792]), 3. See also Malcolm Andrews, *The Search for the Picturesque: Landscape Aesthetics and Tourism in Britain, 1760–1800* (Aldershot, 1989).
46. Leask, *Curiosity and the Aesthetics of Travel Writing*, 158.
47. Elizabeth Helsinger, 'Turner and the Representation of England', in W.J.T. Mitchell (ed.), *Landscape and Power* (Chicago, 1994), 103–25, 106.
48. Guglielmo Scaramellini, 'The Picturesque and the Sublime in Nature and the Landscape: Writing and Iconography in the Romantic Voyaging in the Alps', *GeoJournal* 38(1) (1996), 49–57, 53.
49. Ormsby, *An Account of the Operations of the British Army*, i. 35.
50. Neale, *Letters from Portugal and Spain*, 12.
51. Sherer, *Recollections of the Peninsula*, 92. All subsequent references are to this edition and will be given in parentheses in the text.
52. John Barrell, 'Visualising the Division of Labour: William Pyne's Microcosm', in John Barrell (ed.), *The Birth of Pandora and the Division of Knowledge* (Philadelphia, 1992), 89–118, 105.
53. *Eclectic Review* 21 (1824), 146. Geoffrey Crayon is the congenial narrator of Washington Irving's *The Sketch Book of Geoffrey Crayon, Gent.* (1820), a widely acclaimed book in the 1820s that mixed tales of Gothic Romance, such as 'The Legend of Sleepy Hollow', with sketches of rural English life and landscapes.
54. *United States Literary Gazette* 1(17) (1824), 257.
55. Simon Bainbridge, *British Poetry and the Revolutionary and Napoleonic Wars* (Oxford, 2003), 72.
56. Carole Fabricant, 'The Literature of Domestic Tourism and the Public Consumption of Private Property', in Felicity A. Nussbaum and Laura Brown (eds), *The New Eighteenth Century: Theory, Politics, English Literature* (New York and London, 1989), 254–75, 259.
57. *United States Literary Gazette* 3(9) (1826), 333.
58. Gleig, *The Subaltern*, 2nd ed., 64 and 205. All subsequent references are to this edition and will be given in parentheses in the text.
59. *Quarterly Review* 30(59) (1823), 62; *Quarterly Review* 34(68) (1826), 407–8.
60. Margaret Cohen notes that the first novel to take its title simply from the 'reputable profession' of its central protagonist was James Fenimore Cooper's *The Pilot* (1823), which had appeared just prior to the publication of *The Subaltern*. See Margaret Cohen, 'Traveling Genres', *New Literary History* 34 (2003), 481–99, 488.
61. Porter, *Letters from Portugal and Spain*, 76.

62. Harari, *The Ultimate Experience*, 193–96.
63. Barbara M. Benedict, 'Readers, Writers, Reviewers, and the Professionalization of Literature', in Keymer and Mee, *The Cambridge Companion to English Literature*, 3–23, 16.
64. Benedict, 'Readers, Writers, Reviewers', 20.
65. *La Belle Assemblée, or Court and Fashionable Magazine* 2 (1825), 35; *Monthly Review* N.S.1 (1826), 62 and 279.
66. *La Belle Assemblée, or Court and Fashionable Magazine* 2 (1825), 35; *Monthly Review* N.S.1 (1826), 62 and 279.
67. Gleig, *The Subaltern*, 1845 ed., x.
68. Frey, *British State Romanticism*, 1–19. Frey does not consider how the army fits into her model of State Romanticism.
69. *Monthly Review* N.S.3 (1831), 391.
70. Paul Keen (ed.), *Revolutions in Romantic Literature: An Anthology of Print Culture, 1780–1832* (Peterborough, ON, 2004), 18.
71. On the popular appeal of war stories, see Michael Paris, *Warrior Nation: Images of War in British Popular Culture, 1850–2000* (London, 2000).

BIBLIOGRAPHY

Memoirs

Bristow, James. *A Narrative of the Sufferings of James Bristow, Belonging to the Bengal Artilley [Sic], During Ten Years Captivity with Hyder Ally and Tippoo Saheb*. Calcutta printed. Reprinted London: J. Murray, 1793.

Burroughs, George Frederick. *A Narrative of the Retreat of the British Army from Burgos, in a Series of Letters. With an Introductory Sketch of the Campaign of 1812; and Military Character of the Duke of Wellington*. Bristol: Joseph Routh, 1814.

Daniel, John Edgecombe. *Journal of an Officer in the Commissariat Department, 1811–1815*. London: Printed for the author, 1820.

Gilpin William. *Three Essays on Picturesque Beauty; on Picturesque Travel; and on Sketching Landscape: To Which is Added a Poem on Landscape Painting*. Westmead: Gregg, 1972 [1792].

Gleig, George. *The Subaltern*, 2nd ed. Edinburgh: William Blackwood and London: T. Cadell, 1826.

Gleig, George. *The Subaltern*, 1845 ed. Edinburgh and London: William Blackwood and Sons, 1845.

James, Charles. *A New and Enlarged Military Dictionary, or, Alphabetical Explanation of Technical Terms: Containing, Among Other Matter, a Succinct Account of the Different Systems of Fortification, Tactics, &c. Also the Various French Phrases and Words that Have an Immediate or Relative Connection with the British Service, or May Tend to Give General Information on Military Subjects in Either Language*. London: Printed for T. Egerton, Military Library, Whitehall, 1802.

Milburne, H. *A Narrative of Circumstances Attending the Retreat of the British Army Under the Command of the Late Lieut. Gen. Sir John Moore, K.B. with a Concise Account of the Memorable Battle of Corunna, and Subsequent Embarkation of his Majesty's Troops; and a Few Remarks Connected with these Subjects: in a Letter Addressed to the Right Honourable Lord Viscount Castleragh, One of His Majesties Principal Secretaries of State, &c. &c.* London: Printed for T. Egerton, Military Library, Whitehall, 1809.

'Military Memoirs of the late Lieutenant-General John Burgoyne', *The British Military Library; or Journal: Comprehending a Complete Body of Military-Knowledge; and Consisting of Original Communications; with Selections from the Most Approved and Respectable Foreign Military Publications*, 2 vols. London, 1801.

Neale, Adam. *Letters from Portugal and Spain; Comprising an Account of the Operations of the Armies under Their Excellencies Sir Arthur Wellesley and Sir John Moore, from the Landing of the Troops in Mondego Bay to the Battle at Corunna. Illustrated with Engravings ... From Drawings Made on the Spot.* London: Richard Phillips, 1809.

Ormsby, James Wilmot. *An Account of the Operations of the British Army, and of the State and Sentiments of the People of Spain and Portugal During the Campaigns of 1808 and 1809*, 2 vols. London: James Carpenter, 1809.

Porter, Robert Ker. *Letters from Portugal and Spain, Written During the March of the British Troops under Sir John Moore. With a Map of the Route and Appropriate Engravings. By an Officer.* London: Longman & Co., 1809.

Rogers, Robert. *Journals of Major Robert Rogers: Containing an Account of the Several Excursions He Made under the Generals Who Commanded Upon the Continent of North America, During the Late War; from Which May be Collected the Most Material Circumstances of Every Campaign Upon That Continent, from the Commencement to the Conclusion of the War.* London: Printed for the author, and sold by J. Millan, 1765.

Scott, John. *Paris Revisited, in 1815, by Way of Brussels: Including a Walk over the Field of Battle at Waterloo. By John Scott, Author of a Visit to Paris in 1814; and Editor of the Champion, a London Weekly Journal.* London: Printed for Longman, Hurst, Rees, Orme, and Brown, Pasternoster-Row, 1816.

Sherer, Moyle. *Recollections of the Peninsula*, 2nd ed. London: Longman & Co., 1824.

Simcoe, John. *A Journal of the Operations of the Queen's Rangers, from the End of the Year 1777, to the Conclusion of the Late American War. By Lieutenant-Colonel Simcoe, Commander of that Corps.* Exeter: Printed for the author, 1789.

Simpson, James. *A Visit to Flanders, in July, 1815, Being Chiefly an Account of the Field of Waterloo, Etc.* Edinburgh: William Blackwood, 1815.

Thomas. *Journal of a Soldier of the Seventy-First, Highland Light Infantry, from 1806 to 1815. To Which Are Now Added, Selections from the letters of Corporal Meüller, of the First Regiment of Foot Guards, Describing the Attack on Bergen-Op-Zoom, &c.*, ed. by John Howell, 3rd ed. Edinburgh: W. & C. Tait, 1822.

Thomson, William. *Memoirs of the Late War in Asia. With a Narrative of the Imprisonment and Sufferings of Our Officers and Soldiers: By an Officer of Colonel Baillie's Detachment.* London: printed for the author, and sold by J. Murray, 1788.

Secondary Sources

Alker, Sharon. 'The Soldierly Imagination: Narrating Fear in Defoe's *Memoirs of a Cavalier*'. *Eighteenth Century Fiction* 19(1–2) (2006-7), 43–68.

Andrews, Malcolm. *The Search for the Picturesque: Landscape Aesthetics and Tourism in Britain, 1760–1800*. Aldershot: Scolar, 1989.

Ashplant, T.G., Graham Dawson and Michael Roper. 'The Politics of War Memory and Commemoration: Contexts, Structures and Dynamics', in T.G. Ashplant, Graham Dawson and Michael Roper (eds), *The Politics of Memory: Commemorating War* (New Brunswick and London: Transaction Publishers, 2004), 3–86.

Bainbridge, Simon. *British Poetry and the Revolutionary and Napoleonic Wars*. Oxford: Oxford University Press, 2003.

Barker-Benfield, G.J. *The Culture of Sensibility: Sex and Society in Eighteenth-Century Britain*. Chicago: University of Chicago Press, 1996.

Barrell, John. 'Visualising the Division of Labour: William Pyne's Microcosm', in John Barrell (ed.), *The Birth of Pandora and the Division of Knowledge* (Philadelphia: University of Pennsylvania Press, 1992), 89–118.

Bell, David. *The First Total War: Napoleon's Europe and the Birth of Warfare as We Know It*. New York: Houghton Mifflin Company, 2007.

Bell, Michael. *Sentimentalism, Ethics and the Culture of Feeling*. Basingstoke: Palgrave, 2000.

Benedict, Barbara M. *Framing Feeling: Sentiment and Style in English Prose Fiction 1745–1800*. New York: AMS Press, 1994.

Benedict, Barbara M. 'Readers, Writers, Reviewers, and the Professionalization of Literature', in Thomas Keymer and Jon Mee (eds), *The Cambridge Companion to English Literature, 1740–1830* (Cambridge: Cambridge University Press, 2004), 3–23.

Brewer, John. 'Sentiment and Sensibility', in James Chandler (ed.), *The Cambridge History of English Romantic Literature* (Cambridge: Cambridge University Press, 2009), pp. 21–44.

Brisenden, R.F. *Virtue in Distress: Studies in the Novel of Sentiment from Richardson to Sade*. London: Macmillan, 1974.

Cohen, Margaret. 'Traveling Genres'. *New Literary History* 34 (2003), 481–99.

Dudnik, Stefan, and Karen Hagemann. 'Masculinity in Politics and War in the Age of Democratic Revolutions, 1750–1850', in Stefan Dudnik, Karen Hagemann and John Tosh (eds), *Masculinities in Politics and War: Gendering Modern History* (Manchester: Manchester University Press, 2004), 3–21.

Fabricant, Carole. 'The Literature of Domestic Tourism and the Public Consumption of Private Property', in Felicity A. Nussbaum and Laura Brown (eds), *The New Eighteenth Century: Theory, Politics, English Literature* (New York and London: Methuen, 1989), 254–75.

Ferguson, Harvie. 'The Sublime and the Subliminal: Modern Identities and the Aesthetics of Combat'. *Theory, Culture & Society* 21(3) (2004), 1–33.

Frey, Anne. *British State Romanticism: Authorship, Agency, and Bureaucratic Nationalism*. Stanford, CA: Stanford University Press, 2010.

Fussell, Paul. *The Great War and Modern Memory*. New York and London: Oxford University Press, 1975.

Gottlieb, Evan. *Feeling British: Sympathy and National Identity in Scottish and English Writing, 1707–1832*. Lewisburg: Bucknell University Press, 2007.

Harari, Yuval N. 'Military Memoirs: A Historical Overview of the Genre from the Middle Ages to the Late Modern Era'. *War in History* 14 (2007), 289–309.

Harari, Yuval N. *The Ultimate Experience: Battlefield Revelations and the Making of Modern War Culture, 1450–2000*. Basingstoke and New York: Palgrave Macmillan, 2008.

Helsinger, Elizabeth. 'Turner and the Representation of England', in W.J.T. Mitchell (ed.), *Landscape and Power* (Chicago: University of Chicago Press, 1994), 103–25.

Hynes, Samuel. *The Soldiers' Tale: Bearing Witness to Modern War*. London: Pimlico, 1997.

Keen, Paul (ed.). *Revolutions in Romantic Literature: An Anthology of Print Culture, 1780–1832*. Peterborough, ON: Broadview Press, 2004.

Lawson-Peebles, Robert. 'Style Wars: The Problems of Writing Military Autobiography in the Eighteenth Century', in Alex Vernon (ed.), *Arms and the Self: War, the Military, and Autobiographical Writing* (Kent: Kent State University Press, 2005), 61–80.

Leask, Nigel. *Curiosity and the Aesthetics of Travel Writing, 1770–1840: 'From an Antique Land'*. Oxford and New York: Oxford University Press, 2002.

Manning, Susan. 'Sensibility', in Thomas Keymer and Jon Mee (eds), *The Cambridge Companion to English Literature, 1740–1830* (Cambridge: Cambridge University Press, 2004), 80–99.

Nagle, Christopher C. *Sexuality and the Culture of Sensibility in the British Romantic Era*. Basingstoke: Palgrave Macmillan, 2007.

Nelson, J. Walter. 'War and Peace and the British Poets of Sensibility', in Roseanne Runte (ed.), *Studies in Eighteenth-Century Culture* (Wisconsin: University of Wisconsin Press, 1978), 345–66.

Paris, Michael. *Warrior Nation: Images of War in British Popular Culture, 1850–2000*. London: Reaktion Books, 2000.

Phillips, Mark Salber. *Society and Sentiment: Genres of Historical Writing in Britain, 1740–1820*. Princeton: Princeton University Press, 2000.

Pratt, Mary Louise. *Imperial Eyes: Travel Writing and Transculturation*, 2nd ed. New York: Routledge, 2008.

Ramsey, Neil. *The Military Memoir and Romantic Literary Culture, 1785–1835*. Farnham: Ashgate, 2011.

Scaramellini, Guglielmo. 'The Picturesque and the Sublime in Nature and the Landscape: Writing and Iconography in the Romantic Voyaging in the Alps'. *GeoJournal* 38(1) (1996), 49–57.

Semmel, Stuart. 'Reading the Tangible Past: British Tourism, Collecting and Memory after Waterloo'. *Representations* 69(9) (2000), 9–37.

Spence, Peter. *The Birth of Romantic Radicalism: War, Popular Politics, and English Radical Reformism, 1800–1815*. Aldershot: Scolar Press, 1996.

Thompson, Carl. *The Suffering Traveller and the Romantic Imagination*. Oxford: Clarendon Press, 2007.

Todd, Janet. *Sensibility: An Introduction*. London and New York: Methuen, 1986.

Travers, Tim. 'The Development of British Military Historical Writing and Thought from the Eighteenth Century to the Present', in David A. Charters, Marc Milner and J. Bent Wilson (eds), *Military History and the Military Profession* (London and Westport, CT: Praeger, 1992), 23–44.

Treadwell, James. *Autobiographical Writing and British Literature, 1783–1834*. Oxford: Oxford University Press, 2005.

Vernon, Alex (ed.). *Arms and the Self: War, the Military, and Autobiographical Writing*. Kent: Kent State University Press, 2005.

Woodwards, Rachel. '"Not for Queen and Country or Any of that Shit...": Reflections on Citizenship and Military Participation in Contemporary British Soldier Narratives', in Deborah Cowen and Emily Gilbert (eds), *War, Citizenship, Territory* (New York and London: Routledge, 2008), 363–84.

Neil Ramsey is a Lecturer in English Literature at the University of New South Wales, Canberra. He has published on the literary and culture responses to warfare during the eighteenth century and Romantic eras, focusing on the representations of personal experience and the development of modern war literature. He is the author of *The Military Memoir and Romantic Literary Culture, 1780–1835* (Ashgate, 2011) and the editor (with Gillian Russell) of *Tracing War in British Enlightenment and Romantic Culture* (Palgrave, 2015). He is currently completing a monograph on military writing of the Romantic era, the research for which was funded by an Australian Research Council Postdoctoral Fellowship that he held from 2010 to 2013.

Chapter 4

'The Tallest Pine in the Political Forest'
Race and Slavery in the Confederate Veteran's Memoir, 1866–1915

Craig A. Warren

For at least fifty years after 1865, the memoirs of Civil War veterans 'poured from the presses' to crowd American libraries, bookstores and nightstands. A few of these works featured nimble narratives and expressive language. More common were rough, plodding memoirs enlivened only by the famous battles and personalities described therein. It hardly mattered. For decades the public demonstrated an insatiable appetite for northern and southern remembrances of every shape, size and literary style. By the mid twentieth century, however, the audience for these works had dwindled and the remaining readers could be unkind. For example, in his 1973 study of American Civil War literature, *The Unwritten War*, Daniel Aaron bemoaned that late nineteenth-century America 'swarmed with veterans more than ready to reminisce about the most exciting years of their lives'. He dismissed veterans' memoirs as shot through with nostalgia, adventure and, above all else, romance.[1]

Despite the efforts of some historians, today these dusty works continue to be viewed as backwards-looking, frivolous and self-serving texts with little to say about the post-war America in which they came to print. Moreover, commentators usually discuss these remembrances as if all were published at once, rather than at discernibly different points within a half-century span. Even the South, the region that produced the most influential body of soldiers' literature, has largely forgotten this chapter of its literary tradition. In championing the fiction and verse of writers such as William Faulkner, Caroline Gordon, Flannery O'Connor, Margaret Mitchell and Allen Tate, southern scholars and lay readers often forget these writers' complex connection to the memoirs of Confederate veterans. The result is a fundamental misunderstanding of a dynamic but neglected literary genre. By studying how a sampling of southern memoirists addressed race and the memory of slavery, I aim to show how veterans' memoirs performed an important function in America in the late nineteenth and early twentieth centuries. Far from taking refuge in the past, the genre responded to ongoing cultural and political developments with a social vision and voice meant to guide readers of the day.[2]

The reasons for the onetime popularity of Civil War memoirs are many, but a widespread fascination with the war and its still-living participants played an important role. By the turn of the century, Americans had come to revere those who had worn the blue and the grey. More so than wartime politicians, businessmen, workers, journalists, women and children, the figure of the soldier stood tall. Bruce Catton, a pioneer among historians of the conflict, recalled being awestruck by the Union veterans living in his hometown during the early twentieth century. 'The Civil War veterans were men set apart', he remembered of his childhood. 'They were pillars [of] the community; the keepers of its patriotic traditions, the living embodiment, so to speak, of what it most deeply believed about the nation's greatness and high destiny.' Above all, Catton's generation held these men in high regard owing to their military adventures from Pennsylvania to Texas: 'Years ago they had marched thousands of miles to legendary battlefields. [...] And we were in awe of them. Those terrible names out of the history books – Gettysburg, Shiloh, Stone's River, Cold Harbor – came alive through these men. They had *been* there'.[3] Yet if past military service explained these men's popularity among their countrymen, it also gave old soldiers a pulpit from which to deliver social and political messages to readers well into the early 1900s. And the public, in turn, gave them its ear. Who better to offer guidance during that tumultuous period than the nation's proven heroes, men who had sacrificed everything for home, cause and country? Facing new national struggles involving reconstruction, emancipation and black–white race relations, Americans gravitated towards these men's perspective on the late war and new national landscape.

Jubal A. Early, former Lieutenant General in the Confederate army, emerged as one of the first and most determined of soldier-memoirists. A veteran of the campaigns of General Robert E. Lee's Army of Northern Virginia, the irascible Early built an impressive reputation early in the war before late reverses in the Shenandoah Valley turned southern sentiment against him. By the end of the Civil War he was without a command and in a state of personal despair. Following Federal victory in 1865, Early fled first to Mexico and then to Canada, ever mindful of his dented reputation in the South and of the threat of imprisonment by US officials. It was while in Canada that he penned the first remembrance published by any high-ranking officer North or South, *A Memoir of the Last Year of the War for Independence* (1866). A detailed account of Early's campaigns in the Valley during 1864 and 1865, the book also gave the recalcitrant Rebel a way to voice ideas that he and others would in time shape into the Myth of the Lost Cause, a civil religion that extolled southern honour and offered white southerners an 'acceptable rationale for secession and a palatable explanation for southern defeat'.[4]

In the preface to his *Memoir*, Early emphasised a major tenet of the Lost Cause: the idea that the South did *not* go to war to preserve and prolong slavery on American soil. 'During the war slavery was used as a catch-word to arouse the passions of a fanatical mob', he wrote defiantly, 'but the war was not made on our part for slavery'. In making this statement, Early ignored the fact that southern oratory and writing in 1861 had explicitly linked secession to the institution of slavery. He instead argued that the southern states seceded and took up arms only to protect the 'inestimable right of self-government'. As for human bondage, Early insisted that a dissembling Federal government and northern press had misrepresented a natural institution in order to justify the illegal oppression of southern citizens. He assured readers that slavery was a benevolent practice in the antebellum South, inherited from Western traditions and sustained in the interest of order and charity: 'The generation in the Southern States which defended their country in the late war, found amongst them, in a civilized and christianized condition, 4,000,000 of the descendants of those degraded Africans. [...] Reason, common sense, true humanity to the black, as well as safety to the white race, required that the inferior race should be kept in a state of subordination'. Early went so far as to portray slavery as a benign and socially progressive practice: 'The condition of domestic slavery, as it existed in the South, had not only resulted in a great improvement in the moral and physical condition of the negro race, but had furnished a class of laborers as happy and contented as any in the world, if not more so'.[5]

Defeat had done nothing to shake the old warrior's faith in the southern cause, and he warned readers of the disastrous consequences of emancipation. 'The right of self-government has been lost and slavery violently abolished. Four millions of blacks have thus been thrown on their own resources, to starve, to die, and to relapse into barbarism; and inconceivable miseries have been entailed on the white race. [...] The civilized world will find, too late, that its philanthropy has been all false'. Such sentiments would have appealed to southern readers who wanted to believe that the section had neither forfeited its honour nor endured four years of loss and suffering without moral purpose. Early was especially keen on persuading young southerners and future generations of these ideas, lest the outcome of the Civil War convince them that their forebears were immoral, foolish and treasonous in attempting to dissolve the Union. As Gary W. Gallagher has observed, Early maintained a 'passionate interest in how the future would judge the Confederacy', making it 'a mistake to see him as looking only to the past'. His defence of the South's prewar social order, and especially his celebration of Confederate military achievement in the face of long odds, 'earned a receptive hearing across the post-war South'. Beginning with his memoir, Early spent the next twenty-five years – until his death in 1894 – revisiting these themes in print and cementing them in the southern mind.[6]

Early's predictions about the social fallout of emancipation would have touched a nerve among many northern readers as well. White southerners were not alone in worrying about an America in which the institution of slavery and its governing laws no longer limited black autonomy. Racism remained virulent throughout northern society in 1866, and thousands of white men and women – including those who supported emancipation as a way to weaken the Confederacy – now worried about what the future would hold. What conflicts would erupt when thousands of former slaves made their way north to inhabit northern cities, compete for jobs and exercise their newfound suffrage? Admittedly, an examination of northern newspapers in the immediate aftermath of the Civil War reveals a steadfast refusal to reconcile with former Confederates or to give any credence to the South's justifications for secession. For example, a Kansas newspaper editorial in August 1866 argued that just as Americans 'look upon BENEDICT ARNOLD so we look upon the leaders of the Southern rebellion, and just as we hate and execrate his foul name so we abhor and detest DAVIS and LEE and all the other traitors who lured the Southern people from loyalty to rebellion'. But on the subject of race, emancipation and 'negro equality', these same publications betrayed deep anxieties about the future. The Kansas editor could find no better image with which to denigrate northern reconciliationists than that of a West African tribesman. He mockingly suggested that one such politician, from Massachusetts, represented public feeling in the Bay State 'just about as correctly as a naked, filthy and disgusting Hottentot represents the genius and progressive civilization of the age'. In lines such as this one, we can see why a shared racism might lead northern readers to ponder former Confederates' views on the death of slavery and the future of US race relations. Similarly, the *New York Times* may have mocked Early by referring to his memoir as the 'Sentiments of one who can Neither Forget nor Learn Anything', but it tellingly published the entire preface of his book in January 1867 – including his remarks about slavery and the dangers of emancipation. Early had scored the kind of rhetorical 'hit' that he so relished throughout his post-war career as a writer.[7]

Yet less happily for Early, his 1866 preface imbued his analysis of military action in the Valley and outside of Washington, DC with social relevance and anxiety. Those struggles of 1864–65, readers understood, had led inexorably to a Reconstruction era during which socio-political conflicts over emancipation and white supremacy took centre stage. Reflecting on his army's failure to take Washington in July 1864, the general pointed out that his small and exhausted force had nonetheless 'arrived in sight of the dome of the Capitol, and given the Federal authorities a terrible fright'. He urged 'the intelligent reader' to wonder, 'not why I failed to take Washington, but why I had the audacity to approach it as I did'. But such bravado could not mask his disappointment over the outcome of the campaign and the future it foretold. Readers knew that Lincoln and his allies, safe behind the city's defences, had passed the Thirteenth Amendment through Congress six months after Early's troops briefly threatened Washington. Early must have remained sensitive to this fact, and worried that any social upheaval created by emancipation would belie his claim that the Civil War had *not* been fought over the future of slavery.[8]

As it should happen, the emerging Lost Cause benefited unexpectedly from early Union memoirists who also denied the centrality of slavery to the recent war. Ethnic groups had comprised many northern units during the war, perhaps none as famous as the Irish Brigade of the Army of the Potomac, whose regiments consisted of mostly Irish immigrants and men of Irish descent. Recruited to showcase Irish loyalty to the US at a time when nativists often looked down on the Irish as 'un-American', the brigade had displayed bravery, fortitude and grit in such battles as Antietam, Fredericksburg and Gettysburg. The first major Irish Brigade historian, David Power Conyngham, began writing *The Irish Brigade and Its Campaigns* in the autumn of 1865 and published it two years later. A former journalist and Irish Brigade staff member, Conyngham – no less than Early – hoped to influence the historical record before longstanding interpretations of the war hardened. One of his key points, when glorifying Irish-American sacrifices, was to deny the importance of black emancipation to the war effort. 'The Irish soldier did not ask whether the colored race were better off as bondsmen or freedmen', he proclaimed: 'he was not going to fight for an abstract idea'. Conyngham maintained that the Irish troops had instead fought and died in support of their adopted country, protecting the Union and therefore deserving recognition as loyal, full-fledged citizens. Surely racism also factored into why Conyngham and later brigade historians resisted any link between Irish service and emancipation. As 'notorious racists' before, during and after the war, Irish-Americans no doubt chafed at the idea that their husbands, fathers and sons had died in support of black freedom. Irish Brigade memoirists argued otherwise, assuring their fellow Irish that superb service in the recent conflict had improved their standing within white America.[9]

Whether or not Early and other Lost Cause advocates knew of northern Irish memoirs, these and similar texts buoyed aspects of the southern interpretation of the Civil War during the first decade after the conflict. Given the uncertainties of Reconstruction and the murky future of race relations, it was helpful to the white South for northern writers to likewise discuss the war in terms of white rights, white rule and white equality. With the passing years, the anxieties of the public shifted in kind. Readers of Sam R. Watkins' 1882 memoir, *Co. Aytch*, harboured fewer doubts about the future of white supremacy in the post-war South. With the end of Reconstruction and the withdrawal of most Federal troops after 1877, the white South more fully asserted its political control over local and state-wide elections and law making. Serious affronts to white supremacy declined in frequency. And although racial tensions continued, memoirists like Watkins could take a less overt approach to slavery and race relations than those writing in the immediate aftermath of the Civil War. Published nearly twenty years after Early's memoir, the remembrance by Watkins, a Confederate private who served in Company H of the 1st Tennessee, combined wry humour with horror to create one of the most arresting memoirs of the struggle. Following its serialisation in a Tennessee newspaper, the memoir saw publication in book form under the subtitle 'A Side Show of the Big Show'.[10]

Watkins emphasised time and again that he wrote 'only from memory', and took pride in the fact that his work lacked the grand scope and informed perspective found in history books and the memoirs of generals, whom he styled the 'big bugs'. In everyday language, the Tennessean detailed aspects of soldiering that likely offended the sensibilities of some Victorian readers: eyewitness accounts of theft, desertion, poor hygiene, bureaucratic foolishness, grisly battlefield wounds, meaningless death and stony callousness. In one episode, for example, Watkins recalled watching a camp snowball fight interrupted by the shooting of a deserter by firing squad. Shot off a tree stump but still alive, the screaming and powder-burned 'wretch' endured a second failed execution attempt before a third finally put him out of his misery. 'He had no sooner been taken up and carried off to be buried', Watkins reported, 'than the soldiers were throwing snow balls as hard as ever, as if nothing had happened'. Yet Watkins also captured moments of great tenderness and human fellowship – particularly when recalling the untimely deaths of comrades in arms. Reflecting on a friend whose dying lips he kissed goodbye, Watkins expressed something of the faith that sustained him despite the ever-present death of young men: 'I thank God that I am no infidel, and I feel and believe that I will again see Tom Webb. Just as sure and certain, reader, as you are now reading these lines, I will meet him up yonder – I know I will'. The southern novelist Margaret Mitchell celebrated *Co. Aytch* for its honest reporting, emotional depth, and for giving history the intelligent foot soldier's perspective on the Civil War. '[A] better book', she maintained, 'there never was'.[11]

But the subject that Watkins left off the page perhaps best reflected the period during which he published the work, the early 1880s. Whereas Early addressed the subject of slavery head-on, denying its centrality to secession and the southern war effort, Watkins hardly addressed slavery at all. Soldiers North and South populate *Co. Aytch* along with occasional civilians: family members, farmers, widows, doctors, politicians and hucksters. Rarely, however, do readers encounter black men and women, an exception being Uncle Zack and Aunt Daphne, the elderly inhabitants of 'a little old negro hut' whom Watkins encounters near Dalton, Georgia. The narrative portrays the aging pair as black caricatures, with the laundress Daphne talking nonstop and the sleepy, 'baboonish' Zack waking only long enough to amuse Watkins with accounts of his comic-religious dreamscapes. Another episode, one involving black Union troops, is also played for laughs. Late in the memoir, Watkins recalls his unit's return to Dalton to discover that former slaves, freed and armed by northerners, now occupy the area. Rather than lead to a fierce struggle, the reunion is bloodless and occurs without rancour: 'The place was guarded by negro troops. We marched the black rascals out. They were mighty glad to see us, and we were kindly disposed to them'. However, the Confederates soon put the black men to work, telling them: 'Now, boys, we don't want the Yankees to get mad at you, and to blame you; so, just let's get out here on the railroad track, and tear it up, and pile up the crossties, and then pile the iron on top of them, and we'll set the thing a-fire, and when the Yankees come back they will say, "What a bully fight *them nagers* did make"'. The author concluded the chapter by addressing his audience: 'Reader, you should have seen how that old railroad did flop over, and how the darkies did sweat, and how the perfume did fill the atmosphere'.[12]

The twenty-first-century reader may well take offence at scenes like these, in which Watkins' attempts at humour only amplify his racism, but it is worth noting that neither episode portrays African Americans as slaves. Old Zack and Daphne appear to be living free of white ownership and supervision. While the portrait of black soldiers forced into labour by the returning southerners may evoke the memory of slavery, the wartime setting and circumstances stand apart from the antebellum institution. As for the slaves serving the white soldiers in camp and on the march, Watkins refers to them throughout the book merely as 'negroes who were acting as servants'. Indeed, he avoids direct mention of slavery whenever possible and distances himself from the practice of owning and commanding enslaved blacks. In an oft-quoted passage early in the memoir, Watkins recalls that '[a] law was made by the Confederate States Congress [...] allowing every person who owned twenty negroes to go home. It gave us the blues; we wanted twenty negroes'. The soldiers 'raised the howl of "rich man's war, poor man's fight"'. For the casual reader, it would seem that *Co. Aytch* stands as the memoir of one of the poor men of the South, fighting for reasons of patriotism and personal liberty, and only indirectly to protect the property and lifestyle of elitist slave-owners. In fact, Watkins' only use of the word 'slave' is applied to himself and other white men serving under the command of General Braxton Bragg: 'No pack of hounds under the master's lash, or body of penitentiary convicts were ever under greater surveillance. We were tenfold worse than slaves; our morale was a thing of the past'.[13]

Yet the research of Patrick A. Lewis demonstrates that *Co. Aytch* falls short of offering readers a true portrait of Watkins and his fellow soldiers in the 1st Tennessee. Far from being poor, common soldiers with few personal connections to slavery, the regiment 'had among the highest per capita wealth and rates of slave ownership in the rebel Army of Tennessee'. Watkins' personal associations with slavery went deep. Drawing on 1860 census and tax records, Lewis discovered that 'Sam's father, Frederick H. Watkins, owned a total of 109 slaves on two separate Maury County, Tennessee, plots'. Even more striking, Sam enjoyed the service of a personal body servant during the Civil War, a slave named 'Sanker' who is absent from *Co. Aytch* but who appears briefly in a remembrance Watkins wrote for the journal *Confederate Veteran*. Lewis concludes that Watkins seriously minimised the role of slavery – as both a motivation for secession and an active practice in the Confederate army – in an effort to support the Lost Cause interpretation of the war that Early and others perpetuated: 'In *Co. Aytch*, Watkins wrote not only an enduring piece of literature, but also a masterful piece of Confederate memory making'. It is worth asking, however, whether Watkins' omissions reflected cultural currents rather than conscious mythmaking. Caroline E. Janney has rightly observed that, 'overwhelmingly, in the latter half of the nineteenth century, Confederate groups were not concerned with race primarily because they simply assumed white supremacy'. Could not the assumed racism of white readers, both North and South, explain the contents of *Co. Aytch*? Ultimately, there exists a great distance between overlooking slavery and overtly avoiding its mention at every turn. In the case of Watkins, it seems especially difficult to reconcile his wealthy family's investment in slavery with the presentation of himself as a young man sharing the complaint of a 'rich man's war, poor man's fight'. Surely there can be no doubt that the narrative sidesteps slavery during any discussion of soldiers' motivations. When Watkins' comrades fall in battle, he suggests that they do so for ideals within which the defence of slavery played too small a part to be mentioned: 'They died for the faith that each state was a separate sovereign government, as laid down by the Declaration of Independence and the Constitution of our fathers'.[14]

Generations of readers have therefore come away from the memoir believing that slavery had little to do with southerners' reasons for seceding, or with what they thought the war 'was all about'. Watkins' narrative therefore illustrates the power and reach of the Lost Cause. As a 'high private' in the Confederate army, he could have scarcely predicted that his memoir would eventually become one of the most beloved first-hand accounts of the war, familiar first to Civil War 'buffs' and in time to millions of Americans owing to its frequent use by filmmaker Ken Burns in his landmark 1990 PBS documentary, *The Civil War*. Yet no matter how small his intended audience, Watkins adhered to the Lost Cause approach to the 'peculiar institution' even if it distorted or papered over his personal experiences. By doing so, he could extol white personal and sectional sovereignty as both the motivation for the conflict and its most cherished legacy. This is not to say that *Co. Aytch* is a Lost Cause narrative in every respect. In particular, Watkins at times contradicts the reverent, saintly picture of southern soldiers propagated by some Confederate memoirs. The book therefore captures its cultural moment in the early 1880s, a period after which the major tenets of the Lost Cause had taken root in southern memory but before some writers politicised and sanitised every aspect of the Confederate military experience.[15]

It would take years for Watkins' memoir to receive national attention. Yet better-known northern memoirs of the same period did not dramatically depart from his focus on the actions of white soldiers, North and South. One of the most famous examples bore the name of the North's greatest wartime commander, Ulysses S. Grant, the 'Savior of the Union' and eighteenth president of the United States. Grant did not avoid mentioning slavery in the manner of Watkins, and indeed, today commentators often cite a handful of quotations on the subject from his *Personal Memoirs* (1885–86). For example, the concluding section of his memoirs begins with a statement that identifies in no uncertain terms the issue over which millions of Americans went to war between 1861 and 1865: 'The cause of the great War of the Rebellion against the United States will have to be attributed to slavery'. In an earlier and even more oft-used passage, Grant reflected on the defeat of his greatest adversary, Confederate general Robert E. Lee: 'I felt like anything rather than rejoicing at the downfall of a foe who had fought so long and valiantly, and had suffered so much for a cause, though that cause was, I believe, one of the worst for which a people ever fought, and one for which there was the least excuse'.[16] Taken out of context, these statements seem to bolster the perspective that slavery stood central to the war, and that the North stood on the moral side of the conflict. Yet no matter how true such assessments may be, Grant's initial readers would have received a somewhat different message.

To be sure, the commander's famously unadorned style should not be confused with a simplicity of thought and circumstance. Having identified slavery as the cause of the war, Grant went on to explain slavery as contentious less for its immorality than for the fact that the northern populace became unwilling to long endure legal measures, such as the Fugitive Slave Act of 1850, that required ancillary support of a foreign institution. 'Prior to the time of these encroachments', he explained, 'the great majority of the people of the North had no particular quarrel with slavery, so long as they were not forced to have it themselves. But they were not willing to play the role of police for the South in the protection of this particular institution'.[17] Little here reflects on the inhumanity and racism inherent in slavery, and Grant made no suggestion that most northerners championed emancipation. As for his comment about Lee's awful and inexcusable 'cause', it arrives within a paragraph devoid of any discussion of human bondage. Rather, the passages before and after recall Lee's days in 'the old army' before he resigned his US commission and joined the Confederate military. The reader is left with the impression that Grant is writing less about slavery than secession, specifically the attempt to dismantle the United States to which Lee had previously sworn allegiance.

Grant's memoirs would not likely have persuaded most readers in the mid-1880s to view the war as a moral conflict over race and slavery. In fact, Grant takes a rather detached approach to African Americans, often limiting his discussion of bondage to the mentality of white southerners 'who believed in the "divinity" of human slavery' or who benefited from it economically. The devotion of these individuals to the practice, he concluded, led the South into the military conflict to which he awards his serious attention. As for post-war race relations, he explained that, as president, he thought of encouraging freedmen to leave mainland US territory. 'The condition of the colored man within our borders may become a source of anxiety, to say the least', he admitted. While black Americans had the right to 'remain here' if they chose, concerns over racial conflict 'led me to urge the annexation of Santo Domingo during the time I was President of the United States. [...] I took it that the colored people would go there in great numbers, so as to have independent states governed by their own race. They would still be States of the Union, and under the protection of the General Government; but the citizens would be almost wholly colored'.[18] With this as his last word on African Americans, Grant's memoir cannot be said to be racially progressive. (He went on to praise the Civil War for leading, if indirectly, to the suppression of Native Americans in the western territories.) The degree to which Grant's memoir contradicted the Lost Cause, therefore, rested more with his version of the conflict's military leadership and execution than with its approach to race.

Scores of other memoirs by northern veterans likewise cast slavery as a legal and cultural cause of disunity, but stressed secession as the war's great moral question. The concept of Union dominated such accounts, with authors typically stressing post-war reunion. After all, northern veterans seldom wished to admit to sectional division long decades after the war, as it would have sullied the legacy of northern victory. Therefore, by the turn of the century the Lost Cause had made inroads even into the North, finding footholds among those who valued national stability over an unvarnished history of slavery and secession. As David Blight and other historians have argued, by 1900 the twin goals of white supremacism and reconciliation 'locked arms' to deliver the country 'a segregated memory of its Civil War on Southern terms'. Nostalgic southern literature and rhetoric also played a role. Charmed by the romance of an Old South replete with happy slaves and traditional values, many northerners found it increasingly easy to accept the idea that slavery played a secondary role in bringing about the events of 1861–65. Granted, many Americans above the Mason-Dixon Line refused to accept Lost Cause thinking, especially those who had lived through the war itself. The prewar abolitionist Lydia Maria Child wrote that she was 'disgusted' by the '"mush of concession" that has passed current under the name of magnanimity'. 'The tendency to speak of both sides as equally in the right', she complained, '[just] because they both fought bravely, is utterly wrong in principle and demoralizing in its influence'. But Child and likeminded commentators were fighting an uphill battle, especially as international events tended to bolster intersectional cooperation and an enthusiasm for reunion – perhaps none more than the 1898 Spanish-American War. In the wake of that short-lived struggle, the St. Louis *Republic* announced that American sectionalism 'received a staggering blow when war with Spain was declared and volunteers from Dixie crowded to the recruiting camps to enroll themselves under the [US] flag'. A New York publication agreed, concluding that the 'Spanish war and the conciliatory speeches of President [William] McKinley in Georgia have done very much to obliterate [the] feeling of estrangement' between the North and South. While not universal, such support for national reunion draped a mantle over the memory of slavery and the bitterness over emancipation.[19]

One of the most politicised memoirs to emerge from any veteran's pen, the 1903 *Reminiscences of the Civil War*, both reflected and perpetuated such sentiments. Its author, John B. Gordon, was a former Confederate major general, a post-war US senator and the governor of Georgia between 1886 and 1890. As an elite orator and the first president of the United Confederate Veterans (UCV) association, Gordon offered a sanitised version of the Civil War steeped with honour, gallantry and piety. He had no tolerance for accounts of soldierly mischief and misdeeds as remembered by writers like Watkins. In Gordon's hands, the Civil War soldier stood as a timeless paragon of upright morality. For example, he attacked Early's report that the South lost the 1864 Battle of Cedar Creek in part because its hungry troops stopped to plunder captured northern camps. Denying that such plunder occurred, Gordon championed 'the reputation, the honor, the character of Southern soldiers'. Over the space of ten pages, he went to great lengths, by way of citing reports and letters, to 'vindicate these chivalrous and self-sacrificing men' of the 'purest blood'. This example, just one of many, illustrates Gordon's dogged polishing of the past. Readers surely knew enough about human nature to doubt the Georgia politician's spotless portrait of the Confederate soldier, but they nonetheless embraced his memoir for its engaging prose, enthusiastic voice and politically 'generous' spirit.[20]

Gordon's version of the Lost Cause ultimately came to eclipse the version pioneered by Early, who 'clung tenaciously to every element of his antebellum world view'. Gordon agreed that the South had maintained its honour by virtue of military heroism, but he stressed reconciliation with the North and urged the transformation of the South into a region committed to modernisation and industrialisation. Another shift away from earlier Lost Cause rhetoric involved Gordon's views on slavery. 'With white rule and racial control firmly established' in the South, Gordon's version of the Lost Cause could afford to admit to the role that slavery played in secession and the southern war effort. We see this perspective on race and slavery in Gordon's memoir published just a year before his death. '[It] is fair to say that had there been no slavery there would have been no war', he conceded: 'Slavery was undoubtedly the immediate fomenting cause of the woful [sic] American conflict. It was the great political factor around which the passions of the sections had long been gathered – the tallest pine in the political forest around whose top the fiercest lightnings were to blaze and whose trunk was destined to be shivered in the earthquake shocks of war'. But Gordon assured readers that 'slavery was far from being the sole cause of the prolonged conflict', and argued that 'if all living Union soldiers were summoned to the witness-stand, every one of them would testify that it was the preservation of the American Union and not the destruction of Southern slavery that induced him to volunteer at the call of his country'. Lines such as these echoed statements found in Grant's *Personal Memoirs*, one reason why Gordon's publisher advertised that his reminiscences 'are destined to take the place on the Southern side held by General Grant's "Memoirs" on the Northern side'.[21]

Gordon's attention to the motivations of northern soldiers spoke to the fact that he wrote for a national audience, people of all sections whom he hoped to reconcile by narrating a version of the Civil War that heaped glory on soldiers both North and South. Examples of Gordon's focus on shared American military achievements can be found in his chapter devoted to the September 1863 Battle of Chickamauga. Gordon did not himself participate in the north Georgia battle, as his command remained with the Army of Northern Virginia at the time. However, his lifelong familiarity with the location of the battle encouraged him to temporarily break off from his personal memories in order to play the role of national historian. Describing Chickamauga as an 'American battle which surpassed in its ratio of carnage the bloodiest conflicts in history', Gordon celebrated the blood-letting as evidence of the fortitude, manliness and patriotism of white Yankees and Rebels both: 'Judged by percentage in killed and wounded, Chickamauga nearly doubled the sanguinary records of Marengo and Austerlitz; was two and a half times heavier than that sustained by the Duke of Marlborough at Malplaquet; more than double that suffered by the army under Henry of Navarre in the terrific slaughter at Coutras; nearly three times as heavy as the percentage of loss at Solferino and Magenta; five times greater than that of Napoleon at Wagram, and about ten times as heavy as that of Marshal Saxe at Bloody Raucoux'. Gordon swelled with pride in describing the superhuman bravery and sacrifice exhibited by North and South, concluding 'that the courage displayed by both sides was never surpassed in civilized or barbaric warfare; that there is glory enough to satisfy both; that the fighting from first to last was furious; that there was enough precious blood spilt by those charging and recoiling columns in the deadly hand-to-hand collisions on the 19th and 20th of September to immortalize the prowess of American soldiery and make Chickamauga a Mecca through all the ages'.[22]

Gordon's praise for his former enemies can likewise be found in accounts of the battles in which he participated personally, even the 1862 Battle of Antietam during which he suffered five wounds. Far from holding a grudge against the Union soldiers whose bullets pierced his body time and again (one minié ball shattered his face), Gordon lionised both famous and anonymous Yankees on the field. Major General George B. McClellan appears as the 'brilliant' and '[v]igorous' Union commander during the campaign, 'a man of great personal magnetism and vivacious intellect'. The *Reminiscences* also praise an unnamed Union officer who held his troops together, and mounted numerous assaults again Gordon's lines, all in the face of relentless fire. 'I have never been able to ascertain the name of this lion-hearted Union officer', Gordon expressed during a pause in his account: 'His indomitable will and great courage have been equalled on other fields and in both armies; but I do not believe they have ever been surpassed. Just before I fell and was borne unconscious from the field, I saw this undaunted commander attempting to lead his men in another charge'.[23] Moments such as this one set Gordon's narrative apart from most memoirs by Civil War soldiers, even those who worked hard to bury – or at least disguise – old hatred for the enemy.

But such passages fit perfectly with the general's interpretation of the Civil War as the sublime forge from which the United States emerged as a moral and glorious superpower. With his attention fixed on the battlefield instead of the home front, and on the future rather than the past, Gordon argued that later generations would 'see that, under God's providence, every sheet of flame from the blazing rifles of the contending armies, every whizzing shell that tore through the forests at Shiloh and Chancellorsville, every cannon-shot that shook Chickamauga's hills or thundered around the heights of Gettysburg, and all the blood and the tears that were shed are yet to become contributions for the upbuilding of American manhood and for the future defence of American freedom'. Black manhood and freedom, needless to say, went unmentioned. The author also ignored the wartime presence of thousands of slaves who made southern military glory possible by virtue of replacing white men in the roles of labourers, foragers, cooks, messengers and nurses. As with Watkins' slave Sanker, Gordon's wartime body servant Jim has no place in the narrative, despite his help in nursing his master back to health after his wounding at Antietam. Jim's absence represents a calculated choice on Gordon's part, especially considering that, even after Confederate defeat and emancipation, the freedman 'took the Gordon name' and accepted an invitation to live with the family.[24]

The impressive sales of the *Reminiscences* upon publication reflected not only the aging Gordon's enduring popularity, but also the fact that he retained the politician's knack for reading public sentiment. His 'uplifting' message and 'desire to avoid personal and sectional prejudices' helped explain why the book went through several printings in 1903, followed by a special Memorial Edition in 1904 after the general's passing. Although he had preached many of the ideas and lessons found in his memoir while on the lecture circuit in previous years, the popularity of Gordon's book reflected the spirit of national reconciliation associated with the Spanish-American War and the dawn of a new century. A *New York Times* book review published in November 1903 by the history professor (and future US diplomat) William E. Dodd emphasised Gordon's refusal to say that either North or South possessed the moral high ground. Furthermore, Dodd made no mention of Gordon's remarks on the role that slavery played in the conflict; rather, he believed the book's emphasis on 'our reunited country' would prove a useful tonic for 'all those veterans, Union as well as Confederate, who even now strive to keep alive the fire of enmity between the sections'.[25]

A minority of veterans did maintain sectional animosity well into the twentieth century. Forced to reunite with old enemies as countrymen but unwilling to reconcile, some of these men refused to attend or even recognise staged 'reunions' such as the veterans' encampment honouring the fiftieth anniversary of the Battle of Gettysburg in July 1913. Sometimes this perspective appeared in popular print, such as when the editor of *Confederate Veteran* found common ground with old Yankees only when they too rejected reconciliation. He declared: '[The] best soldier-veterans are repulsed by it on each side'. But veterans opposed to reconciliation did not produce bestselling memoirs in the style of Gordon, one reason being that major publishers showed little interest in such perspectives during the years surrounding the war's golden anniversary. As for northern veterans wishing to fight the Lost Cause insistence on minimising or forgetting the role slavery played in the Civil War, success was hard to find. Books like Thomas Wentworth Higginson's *Army Life in a Black Regiment* (1870) and Joseph T. Wilson's *The Black Phalanx* (1887) honoured African American military service and reminded readers that black men had helped defend the Union and win emancipation. But such works could not compete with the deluge of soldiers' remembrances, North and South, that advanced or tolerated the Lost Cause. Finally, as Janney has observed, many white northern veterans likely believed that they had *not* forgotten slavery when celebrating national reunion and ignoring civil rights for blacks: 'White US veterans understood that slavery had caused the internecine war and therefore could celebrate emancipation because it had removed that deadly source of sectional conflict, even if they did not favor civil and political equality for African Americans'. As a result, African Americans 'were forced to continue carving out their own spaces to celebrate emancipation and its promise of equal rights'.[26]

As the memoirs of Early, Watkins and Gordon demonstrate, the evolving political and cultural landscape after 1865 shaped the narratives penned by Confederate veterans. Each man undoubtedly included his own personality and value system in the book he published, but each also reacted to current trends, circumstances and controversies when deciding how to remember slavery and emancipation when writing during the 1860s, 1880s and early 1900s. Far from moving in a straight line from prominence to obscurity, the place of slavery in Confederate memoirs shifted from one direction to the next. Early dismissed the centrality of slavery to the war, even as he defended the morality of the institution and cast emancipation as dangerous to whites and blacks alike. Watkins pushed his personal, familial and community commitments to slavery into the shadows of memory. His aversion to the words 'slave' and 'slavery' revealed his project of representing the Civil War as a contest waged by white Americans concerned above all with personal and sectional liberty. Gordon's sweeping remembrance portrayed the war as proof of American valour and manhood unrivalled throughout the ages. While not avoiding the historical reality of slavery or its role in bringing about the war, he defanged the institution by virtually celebrating its role in the grand story of America's rise on the international stage. Gordon implied that if slavery had contributed to a conflict from which the United States emerged as a unified and forward-looking nation, then it could not be regarded in wholly negative terms. The differing approaches of these men – each a response to changing national or global politics – illustrate why it is important to see the soldier's memoir as a genre that developed over time. Future readers should pay close attention to the publication dates of these works, so as to better contextualise and appreciate the contents of each.

In a larger sense, this brief survey has shown that it is a mistake to regard Civil War veterans as writing self-indulgent, romantic works bereft of social vision and political purpose. Admittedly, hundreds of veterans took up the pen to relive fond memories, honour fallen comrades, dispute one another, glorify themselves and earn money. Yet many of these same men sought to write a national as well as personal history, advancing a specific vision of the past and, by doing so, making political statements about the present. Not every writer possessed the historical vision of Early, or saw himself

– like Gordon – as a champion of American democracy and nationhood. And surely not every veteran, in the fashion of Watkins, willingly suppressed details of his antebellum and wartime experiences in deference to a particular interpretation of the conflict. But on some level, all soldier-memoirists undertook to communicate with an American public hungry for literature to help navigate one of the most tumultuous and momentous periods in US history. It is instructive that the publication and popularity of these narratives lasted at least fifty years after Appomattox, ebbing only with the passing of most Civil War veterans. While these citizen-heroes remained alive and possessed a voice, the public remained fascinated by their unique perspectives on America's past and future. These circumstances inspire a number of questions. To what extent did nineteenth and early twentieth-century readers see veterans as political agents operating independently of national parties, elected officials and commercial interests? What did the passing of an author and his historical moment mean for the future of his memoir, its arguments and its readership? (Later generations engaged many of those same memoirs, but never with the immediacy and historical positioning of the first readers.) How did the war memoirs of nonveterans, particularly those by southern women, function for the same reading public? These questions are not merely academic, considering America's recent wars and its ongoing controversies over race, region and historical memory. By studying the content and reception of Civil War remembrances, we might better confront the intersection of personal memory and US politics in the twenty-first century.

NOTES

1. Daniel Aaron, *The Unwritten War: American Writers and the Civil War* (New York, 1973), 211. Aside from memoirs appearing in book form, thousands of veterans' reflections and reminiscences appeared in newspapers and journals of every stripe and circulation. The most famous collection of such works is the *Century* magazine 'ced*Century* War Series', whose start in 1884 led to a circulation boom for the magazine, from 127,000 to 225,000 in a single year. The series in turn led to the popular *Battles and Leaders of the Civil War* (1887–1888), a four-volume bound collection of illustrated articles culled from the magazine. See Robert Underwood Johnson and Clarence C. Buel (eds), *Battles and Leaders of the Civil War*, 4 vols (New York, 1887–88).
2. For an examination of the relationship between twentieth-century southern writers and the memoirs of Confederate veterans, see Craig A. Warren, *Scars to Prove It: The Civil War Soldier and American Fiction* (Kent, OH, 2009), esp. chs 2 and 3.

3. Bruce Catton, *Waiting for the Morning Train: An American Boyhood* (New York, 1972), 189–90, 190.
4. Jubal A. Early, *A Memoir of the Last Year of the War for Independence in the Confederate States of America, Containing an Account of the Operations of His Commands in the Years 1864 and 1865, by Lieutenant-General Jubal A. Early, of the Provisional Army of the Confederate States* (Toronto, 1866; repr., New Orleans, 1867); Gary W. Gallagher, introduction to *Narrative of the War between the States*, by Jubal Anderson Early (New York, 1989), xxi.
5. Early, *A Memoir of the Last Year of the War*, ix, x, ix.
6. Early, *A Memoir of the Last Year of the War*, x; Gary W. Gallagher, *Lee and His Generals in War and Memory* (Baton Rouge, 1998), 201.
7. 'Candid', *Freedom's Champion* (Atchison, Kansas), 30 August 1866, 30; 'JUBAL A. EARLY.: His Memoir of the Last Year of the War – Sentiments of one who can Neither Forget nor Learn Anything', *New York Times*, 7 January 1867, 1; Gallagher, introduction to Early, *Narrative of the War between the States*, xxiv.
8. Early, *A Memoir of the Last Year of the War*, 50, 51.
9. D.P. Conyngham, *The Irish Brigade and Its Campaigns* (1867; repr., New York, 1994), 5–6; William L. Burton, *Melting Pot Soldiers: The Union's Ethnic Regiments* (Ames, 1988), 152. In the North, Irish-American racism was exacerbated by the fact that the Irish had competed with free blacks for unskilled jobs during the antebellum years.
10. Sam R. Watkins, *'Co. Aytch', Maury Grays, First Tennessee Regiment; or, A Side Show of the Big Show* (Nashville, TN, 1882; repr., New York, 1997). The memoir originally appeared in serialised form in the *Columbia* (Tennessee) *Herald* in 1881–82. Following book publication in 1882, new editions appeared throughout the twentieth century, often under the title *Co. Aytch: A Confederate Memoir of the Civil War*.
11. Watkins, *'Co. Aytch'*, 17, 19, 130–31, 119; Mitchell quoted in Warren, *Scars to Prove It*, 50.
12. Watkins, *'Co. Aytch'*, 136, 225, 225.
13. Watkins, *'Co. Aytch'*, 127, 47, 49.
14. Patrick A. Lewis, 'Co. Aytch 2.0: The Online Life of Confederate Memoirist Sam Watkins' (paper presented at the 127th Annual Meeting of the American Historical Association, 4 January 2013), 2, 6, 6; Patrick A. Lewis, 'High Private: How Sam Watkins' "Sideshow" Obscured the "Big Show" of American History' (paper presented at the Chickamauga and Chattanooga National Military Park Symposium, 'The Face of Battle', 24 April 2010), 22; Caroline E. Janney, *Remembering the Civil War: Reunion and the Limits of Reconciliation* (Chapel Hill, 2013), 275; Watkins, *'Co. Aytch'*, 165.
15. Watkins, *'Co. Aytch'*, 19; *The Civil War*, DVD, directed by Ken Burns (Hollywood, CA, 1990).
16. Ulysses S. Grant, *Personal Memoirs of U.S. Grant*, 2 vols (New York, 1885–86), 2:494, 2:469.
17. Grant, *Personal Memoirs*, 2:495, 2:469.

18. Grant, *Personal Memoirs*, 1:94, 2:498.
19. David W. Blight, *Race and Reunion: The Civil War in American Memory* (Cambridge, MA, 2001), 2; Child quoted in Janney, *Remembering the Civil War*, 246; 'Sectionalism Dead', St. Louis *Republic*, 1898, repr., *Literary Digest* 17 (1898), 765; 'Loyalty and Demagogy', New York *Journal of Commerce*, 1898, repr., *Literary Digest* 17 (1898), 765. For the best analysis of Union as the paramount northern war objective, see Gary W. Gallagher, *The Union War* (Cambridge, MA, 2011). On romantic literature and imagery of the Old South that led many northerners to overcome hostility towards the defeated South, see Nina Silber, *The Romance of Reunion: Northerners and the South, 1865–1900* (Chapel Hill, 1993).
20. John B. Gordon, *Reminiscences of the Civil War* (1903; repr., Baton Rouge, 1993), 363, 364, 363; Stephen Cushman, *Bloody Promenade: Reflections on a Civil War Battle* (Charlottesville, VA, 1999), 173. Charles Scribner's Sons of New York published the first edition in 1903. Following Gordon's death in 1904, Scribner's released a 'Memorial Edition' that included an introduction by former Confederate general Stephen D. Lee and a 'memorial account' by Frances Gordon Smith, Gordon's daughter.
21. Gallagher, *Lee and His Generals*, 203; Gallagher, introduction to Early, *Narrative of the War between the States*, xxiv; Gordon, *Reminiscences of the Civil War*, 18, 19; Advertisement for *Reminiscences of the Civil War* by General John B. Gordon, *New York Times*, 17 October 1903, BR7.
22. Gordon, *Reminiscences of the Civil War*, 199, 199, 210.
23. Gordon, *Reminiscences of the Civil War*, 81, 123, 87–88.
24. Gordon, *Reminiscences of the Civil War*, 464–65; Ralph Lowell Eckert, *John Brown Gordon: Soldier, Southerner, American* (Baton Rouge, 1989), 38 n. 48, 131 n. 9.
25. Ralph Lowell Eckert, introduction to Gordon, *Reminiscences of the Civil War*, xxi, xxii; 'GEN. GORDON.: Prof. Dodd Reviews the Southern Soldier's Reminiscences', *New York Times*, 21 November 1903, BR4.
26. Quoted in Janney, *Remembering the Civil War*, 267; Thomas Wentworth Higginson, *Army Life in a Black Regiment* (Boston, 1870); Joseph T. Wilson, *The Black Phalanx: A History of the Negro Soldiers of the United States in the Wars of 1775, 1812, 1861–1865* (Springfield, MA, 1887); Janney, *Remembering the Civil War*, 290, 267.

BIBLIOGRAPHY

Memoirs

Catton, Bruce. *Waiting for the Morning Train: An American Boyhood*. New York: Doubleday, 1972.

Conyngham, D.P. *The Irish Brigade and Its Campaigns*. 1867; repr., New York: Fordham University Press, 1994.

Early, Jubal A. *A Memoir of the Last Year of the War for Independence in the Confederate States of America, Containing an Account of the Operations of His Commands in the Years 1864 and 1865, by Lieutenant-General Jubal A. Early, of the Provisional Army of the Confederate States.* Toronto: Lovell & Gibson, 1866; repr., New Orleans: Blelock, 1867.

Gordon, John B. *Reminiscences of the Civil War.* 1903; repr., Baton Rouge: Louisiana State University Press, 1993.

Grant, Ulysses S. *Personal Memoirs of U.S. Grant*, 2 vols. New York: Charles L. Webster, 1885–86.

Higginson, Thomas Wentworth. *Army Life in a Black Regiment.* Boston: Fields, Osgood, 1870.

Watkins, Sam R. *'Co. Aytch', Maury Grays, First Tennessee Regiment; or, A Side Show of the Big Show.* Nashville, TN: Cumberland Presbyterian, 1882; repr., New York: Touchstone, 1997.

Wilson, Joseph T. *The Black Phalanx: A History of the Negro Soldiers of the United States in the Wars of 1775, 1812, 1861–1865.* Springfield, MA: Winter, 1887.

Secondary Sources

Aaron, Daniel. *The Unwritten War: American Writers and the Civil War.* New York: Knopf, 1973.

Blight, David W. *Race and Reunion: The Civil War in American Memory.* Cambridge, MA: Harvard University Press, 2001.

Burton, William L. *Melting Pot Soldiers: The Union's Ethnic Regiments.* Ames: Iowa University Press, 1988.

Cushman, Stephen. *Bloody Promenade: Reflections on a Civil War Battle.* Charlottesville, VA: University Press of Virginia, 1999.

Eckert, Ralph Lowell. *John Brown Gordon: Soldier, Southerner, American.* Baton Rouge: Louisiana State University Press, 1989.

Gallagher, Gary W. Introduction to *Narrative of the War between the States*, by Jubal Anderson Early. New York: Da Capo Press, 1989.

Gallagher, Gary W. *Lee and His Generals in War and Memory.* Baton Rouge: Louisiana State University Press, 1998.

Gallagher, Gary W. *The Union War.* Cambridge, MA: Harvard University Press, 2011.

Janney, Caroline E. *Remembering the Civil War: Reunion and the Limits of Reconciliation.* Chapel Hill: University of North Carolina Press, 2013.

Johnson, Robert Underwood, and Clarence C. Buel (eds). *Battles and Leaders of the Civil War*, 4 vols. New York: De Vinne, 1887–88.

Silber, Nina. *The Romance of Reunion: Northerners and the South, 1865–1900.* Chapel Hill: University of North Carolina Press, 1993.

Warren, Craig A. *Scars to Prove It: The Civil War Soldier and American Fiction.* Kent, OH: Kent State University Press, 2009.

Craig A. Warren is Professor and Chair of English at Penn State Erie, The Behrend College. He is the author of *The Rebel Yell: A Cultural History* (University of Alabama Press, 2014) and *Scars To Prove It: The Civil War Soldier and American Fiction* (Kent State University Press, 2009). He is also the founder and editor of the Ambrose Bierce Project, a digital humanities project and electronic journal.

Chapter 5

British Memoirs and Memories of the Great War

Ian Isherwood

When Cyril Falls compiled his annotated bibliography of First World War books in 1930, he did so with a clear purpose.[1] 'The Great War', he wrote 'has resulted in the spilling of floods of ink as well as of blood'.[2] In *War Books* (1930), he provided the reading public with a guide to war literature's good and bad books. Falls sought to distinguish which accounts approached the war in a way that he believed was fair in its accounting of soldiers and their conduct, accurate in representations of the war, and worthy of the sacrifice of the war generation. *War Books* was an attempt to drain the cultural floodplain of sensationalist war books that he believed had broken through the levy of public decency by 1930.

In the ten years since the ending of the First World War, there were hundreds of war books released, enough to cause worry for many veterans about how their war was being remembered in print. Falls was one voice of many. As a former officer in the 36th (Ulster) Division, he had no illusions about the difficulties of the war's conduct and was not naïve towards the horrors faced by men on the battlefield.[3] 'The War was a ghastly experience, and everyone should do all that in him lies to ensure that it is not repeated', he wrote.[4] Despite being a realist to the conditions of the battlefield and the sufferings of soldiers, he objected to the tone of so many war books that had been released by the late 1920s, believing that their sense of balance was distorted, that they represented only the horrors of war to the detriment of the courage, spirit and suffering of the men who fought in it. 'The soldier is represented as a depressed and mournful spectre helplessly wandering about until death brought his miseries to an end.'[5] This was not the spirit of men in the British Army that he witnessed at the front. It was not the war he wanted remembered afterwards.

For historians and literary scholars interested in this most literate of wars, there is a conundrum to understanding how war memoirs fit with our overall perceptions of the war, its history and the lessons gleaned from its conduct by subsequent generations. First World War books are too diverse a collection to tidily summarise, too vast in their interpretations to generalise easily about how the war generation felt towards the seminal violent event of their youth. Though critics like Paul Fussell and Samuel Hynes have written important, if not iconic scholarly surveys of British experiential writing of the First World War, their works only partially cover this vast literature. Their conclusions were drawn mostly from literary elites who have had lasting influence over the war's historiography, but were only a few of the voices that debated the war's meaning in war books.[6] Scholarship over the last twenty years has examined some gaps in our understanding, bringing to the forefront writers whose works do not fit the mould of disillusionment cast by their iconic war poet peers.[7] Yet there is still much work to be done to truly understand how the war generation in Britain remembered the Great War through the books they left behind to commemorate those who fought it.

Rather than repeat the efforts of other scholars or summarise the state of the literary historiography, this chapter will survey the types of war memoirs released in the interwar period and discuss the way that veterans approached writing a war memoir. In the 1920s and 1930s, veterans wrote to remember their experiences, but also to discuss and debate the war's legacy with the wider public through their printed books. 'This book', wrote one author, 'like most books, consists of both facts and opinions', a sentiment shared by most who approached writing non-fiction, reflecting the dual purpose of the memoir to inform but also to interpret historical events for the public.[8]

Memoirs are important historical sources because the war remained a cultural catalyst of social meaning well into the interwar period, its legacy debated and re-evaluated by those who lived through it and wrote of its conduct. Indeed, literature became one of the most powerful components of the culture of memory that emerged from the First World War, where both the facts of serving at the front and the opinions of veterans on the meaning of their suffering became important to how the war was being remembered by the next generation of Britons. A.O. Pollard wrote of his *Fire-Eater: Memoirs of a V.C.* that his opinions were 'intended to point out a lesson that war taught us – that, as a Nation, we can accomplish anything so long as we work together'.[9] Pollard's hope to learn a lesson from the war, that its suffering could teach future generations, was an idealistic sentiment shared by many authors, demonstrating a social obligation by some of those who wrote about the war. Similarly, by understanding something of the composition of war memoirs, a process of reconstructed memories that nearly all authors of this literature engaged, we gain further appreciation for this diverse collection of texts and the ways that authors approached the difficult task of putting their war experiences on paper.

WAR MEMOIRS

War poets, short story authors, novelists and memoirists were published extensively during the war and afterwards, their accounts never far from the public consciousness, and certainly never out of print. By 1930, the British 'war book' had appeared in hundreds of versions spanning the literary genres.[10] The sheer variety of war books present in the literary marketplace ensured that the war was never truly forgotten by British readers; the controversies instigated by war books, especially in the first decades of peace, meant that war literature remained an essential and debated part of the war's changing history. War books became one of the means by which the public would come to understand what the 'experience' of the First World War was like to a generation of Britons who suffered and sacrificed for their country.

One of the most popular genres of the 'war book' for publishers and the reading public was the war memoir. War memoirs are invaluable sources for understanding the experiences of the First World War. In Britain, those experiences were vast and their representations dependent upon the front in which the writer was engaged as well as their specific war-related duties. As such, war memoirs do not reflect one uniform experience, but hundreds, diverse in both the fronts and experiences represented as well as in memoirists' individualistic opinions on the recent war. Though certain canonical war memoirs have come down to us as important voices – Edmund Blunden, Robert Graves, and Vera Brittain most notably in Britain – the war did not have one literary 'memory' but instead hundreds of diverse memories, in print, that together became something of a literary canon of true-to-life war experiences, broad in scope yet representative of a single important fact: that the war itself remained a cultural muse long after the guns fell silent on the western front in 1918.[11]

Similar to war novels, non-fiction war books were released in great abundance.[12] Of non-fiction books published, most were war memoirs, in that they were retrospective recollections in which the war was the most important part of the narrative.[13] The density, breadth and scope of war literature is impressive and expansive: war memoirs came from all fronts in which British forces were deployed and represented diverse experiences of both combatants and non-combatant writers.

The two most significant geographical concentrations of war memoirs depicted fighting on the western front and the war in the Middle East. Of western front authors, there is considerable variation in terms of the types of books released and their tone, although much of this literature depicts similar conditions of battle. There were pacifist authors like Vera Brittain, whose works focus largely on the tragedy of the war and its lasting effects on participants. Robert Graves's iconic *Good-bye to All That* is something of an anomaly: few authors matched his wry talent, the book a mixture of gallows humour, impishness, and reluctant heroism.[14] The vast majority of war memoirists inhabited a middle ground, something akin to the middle-brow – accounts that were vaguely heroic but also ambiguous, if not ambivalent, on the war's greater legacy.[15] Men like Edmund Blunden, Charles Douie, Guy Chapman, Charles Carrington, and R.H. Mottram wrote more measured accounts on the war's conduct and legacy, where they discussed whether there was any greater meaning to come out of the killing in which they had participated.[16] Most of these authors, ultimately, believed the war to be a hard-fought necessity, regrettable or tragic though it was to so many of their generation, whom they both mourned but also sought to memorialise in print. Though there is no uniformity of interpretative recollections of the memoirs of the western front, the books that emerged from that tortured landscape all address issues of fear, deep personal anxieties of battle, and the suffering of men under the command of officers who often felt emotionally threadbare. The destructiveness of the war in the west lent itself to disillusioned voices regardless of whether disenchantment was the author's intention in writing.

Accounts from the Near and Middle East depict a vastly different war, one imperial and waged in distant locales against an enemy hardly understood and only begrudgingly respected. The campaigns in the Dardanelles, Palestine, and Mesopotamia each resulted in their own sub-genres of war literature, all depicting the war against the Ottoman Turks. With the exception of the Dardanelles campaign, these accounts depict a more mobile war than their comrades on the western front, officers and men writing books that can be easily interpreted as part imperial adventure/romance and part battlefield memoir.[17] Notable literature to emerge from the east includes the works of imperial agents T.E. Lawrence, Norman Bray, and Hubert Young, as well as more common accounts of infantry officers like Vivian

Gilbert, Cecil Sommers, and pilot John Tennant.[18] There was a small, but distinctive, literature of those who fought and surrendered at Kut al Amara, accounts of the Kuttites largely about Ottoman captivity, and for some, escape from Anatolia. Much of this literature is heroically framed, the war in the east depicted as a vast 'crusade' that was successfully waged by British and Indian army soldiers.

In the literature of both the eastern 'side shows' as well as the western front, the most common writer was the junior officer. Accounts by men in the ranks were rare compared to their officers whose books dominated post-war publishing catalogues. In part, this was an issue of education and the leisure time to write, but it was also an issue of access to the publishing industry and having the right connections to get a book into the hands of an editor. Former rankers like Frank Richards, William Andrews, and Stephen Graham all had connections to publishing, the latter two being professional writers and the former being recommended by Robert Graves.[19] Both Giles Eyre and Bernard Blaser's accounts had forewords by general officers, the latter securing the endorsement of Field Marshal Allenby, which is indicative of some degree of connection to these figures.[20] John Lucy's book, *There's a Devil in the Drum*, is one of the finest to come out of the war, but he was also an exceptional case: an old contemptible, an Irish Catholic working class soldier who earned a battlefield commission and stayed in the British Army for the rest of his career.[21]

If we look beyond the trench parapet, there were notable memoirs published about experiences that do not necessarily fit the stereotype of the western front subaltern's tale. There were a number of memoirs by female nurses and doctors, some of them from other theatres, such as the extraordinary memoirs of women in the Scottish Women's Hospitals.[22] Novelist Compton Mackenzie, staff officer and intelligence agent during the war, wrote four accounts of his exploits in the Aegean.[23] There were dozens of accounts by Prisoners of War (POW), unique in their perspective, written by men like Jocelyn Hardy, Alan Bott, E.H. Jones, and A.J. Evans.[24] POW books are harrowing accounts of capture, confinement, and escape from camps in both Germany and Turkey.[25] For those who served above the trenches, pilots and gunners in the Royal Flying Corps (RFC) the war memoir was an opportunity to contrast their adventures with those suffering through the mired war of attrition on the ground, a chance to reinvent the heroic and romantic war story of the knightly officer.[26] The war's many different experiences were all in print, creating small sub-genres of war literature that catered to different types of readers.

What does such a diverse collection of war memoirs tell us? Importantly, it denotes a change in war literature that is reflective of the war's global scale and the demands of the war of attrition on the British public. The First World War was different to other wars in which the British Armed Forces had waged and was remembered by a different demographic of author who fought. Instead of professional soldiers, civilian volunteers or conscripts fought the war and served for a short period – a matter of a few years on average – before they then returned to more peaceful lives. Most war writers were temporary soldiers, or temporary gentlemen in the nomenclature of army officers, who were fairly 'unmilitant' beings that looked upon their war experiences as distinctly alien compared to lives lived in peace.[27] Because they were written by citizen-soldiers and corresponding adjuncts in the case of medical aid workers, war memoirs of the First World War are different to accounts by career soldiers; they are works of mostly youthful amateur war-workers who grew into their positions, and had something to write about of the war in which they fought and witnessed, in part because it was so very different to their lives afterwards. The diversity of accounts reflects the many different faces of a total war that desperately required people of different skills to be deployed to theatres across the Empire.

The breadth of the war books catalogue demonstrates that though the British publishing industry was selective in terms of the quality of books it was publishing, the market for war literature was wide enough to allow for accounts that represented a diversity of war recollections. Heroic and patriotic memoirs shared the same publishing market as those written by ardent pacifists; female doctors sold war books along with escaped prisoners, pilots, and shell-shocked subalterns. It demonstrates that the war's lived memory was hardly uniform and was instead malleable in a period when Britons were still adjusting to the dislocation following the war's wake. In many ways, what seemed to matter to authors was that their war experiences were represented in this panorama of published memories, that their war, too, was seen as being important to the lived memory, the personal history, of the Great War.

WAR MEMOIRISTS

After the First World War, the memoir became a means for the public to understand both the conduct and the personal transformation of men and women in war. That transformation was represented in varying degrees depending upon when works were written. Books published during and immediately after the war were largely documentary. They were more matter-of-fact, reporting on the war's conduct without much discussion of its wider significance. Accounts published in the later 1920s were more ruminative. They had some distance from the events witnessed and usually contextualised the war in terms of the author's longer life; books written later in the 1920s considered the war's generational, personal, and social impacts more deeply.

Though there are some obvious limitations to writing about experiences distant in memory, the idea of 'truth' was important to war writers of both periods. It was the truth of the eyewitness, after all, that separated the memoirist from their more imaginative peers writing fiction. This is not to say that truthfulness did not exist in war novels; memoirists were similar to novelists in that they remembered and reimagined their experiences, often struggling to communicate events that appeared to be confusing and difficult to remember with any sense of accuracy. Guy Chapman wrote of war novels in his compilation *Vain Glory*: 'Many so-called works of fiction are direct experience, sometimes quite obviously so, which uses this form for a deliberate reason. None the less, they are truthful – more truthful, I regret to say, than the vast number of unit and formation histories, which are often wholly unreliable'.[28] No doubt, this was an important distinction to make in 1937: great works of fiction had been written by Siegfried Sassoon, Frederic Manning, and R.H. Mottram that were 'truthful' or fair representations of the war that each author had witnessed despite the genre chosen for their expression.[29]

What separated memoirs from novels was not the process of authorship, but the sense of social accountability that came from releasing a non-fiction book. Memoirs depicted the story not only of the author, but also of their comrades and units in battle. Authors of war memoirs were bound by a degree of social restraint, particularly as their books were to be read by other veterans. These feelings were incredibly strong in the interwar period, when the war's legacy was a topic held sacred through public displays of remembrance, and where veterans wrote, published and reviewed war books in the press. Writing a true story did matter to veterans: it is part of the reason they sat down with their letters and diaries to painfully search their memories for specific moments as they wrote.

The writing process brought difficult and traumatic memories to the forefront. To write, authors had to remember what they had lived through and then coherently narrate those memories on the page. The writing process itself was one of resurrecting and reimagining memories that were inherently difficult to put into a linear narrative. Llewelyn Wyn Griffith described in 1931 how the writing process was one akin to excavating the past from the present. Griffith described sitting down to write, the walls of his room falling away and before him lay the battlefield panoramic of Mametz Wood.

Even more, after all these years, this round ring of man-made hell bursts into my vision, elbowing into infinity of distance the wall of my room, dwarfing into nothingness objects we call real. Blue sky above, a band of green trees. And a ploughed graveyard in which living men moved worm-like in and out of sight; three men digging a trench, thigh-deep in the red soil, digging their own graves, as it chanced, for a bursting shell turned their shelter into a tomb. [...] So many things are seen more clearly now that the passing of years have allowed the mud of action to settle at the bottom of the pool of life.[30]

Griffith's war memories passed in and out of time, combining present and past memories into a single narrative framed in many ways by the consequences of war and the unexpected human changes the war's experience gave its survivors. His war memories were clear and distinctive – the three men digging their own graves in radiant sunshine – but also contextualised through the prism of a decade of thoughtful reflection as a survivor; the clarity of the western front, as much as it could become clear, came afterwards in the broader context of a life lived in peace. Writers like Griffith had a keen sense that they were engaging with a concept of lived historical memory even if they were not saying as much.

It was out of disjointed and difficult memories that emerged somewhat formulaic memoirs, bound to lived events, that appeared to many to be shared experiences. Though some writers, most notably Robert Graves, intended their war memories to be part of a larger autobiography in which the war played a prominent part in the writer's emotional maturity, most war memoirists confined their narratives to the war itself, closely following the journey taken from the moment they entered the military to the moment they came home from the war. To some degree, the decision to limit a memoir to the war is revealing: it demonstrates further the differences between wartime and civilian life, as if the war was itself another lifetime that was just too jarring, too different to their civilian experiences to associate closely with them. Especially for men who returned from war to go to university or enter a profession, their peacetime lives were simply anticlimactic compared to what they experienced during the war.[31]

It was not uncommon for writers to preface their books with dedications, forewords and introductions to frame the work to follow and provide some context as to the author's purpose in writing. Dedications were often for comrades or units, a means to pay respects for those whose experiences the book to follow was also about. A poem or fairly universal dedication was common. Thomas Hope Floyd dedicated his book 'To All Ranks of the Second-Fifth Lancashire Fusiliers who fell at Ypres on the Thirty-First of July 1917'.[32] Chapman dedicated his memoir 'To the memory of certain soldiers who have now become a small quantity of Christian dust this faint reanimation and for R.A. Smith', the latter his commanding officer and one of the bravest men under whom he served.[33] Authors were certainly conscious of the fact that their works were not exactly theirs alone; that they had, in a sense, a moral duty to represent fairly what they had lived through with others, a vastly important attribute reflecting the martial virtue of comradeship, something that nearly all writers acknowledged for its powerful bond regardless of their opinions on the war. William Linton Andrews wrote in his introduction: 'For I want very much to tell you about my comrades – great-hearted comrades – many of whom did not come home. They wanted to be remembered, not as pale ghosts, but as honest, suffering soldier lads. Can I make some of them live again? Please God, I will try'.[34]

In addition to defining the purpose of the work to follow, forewords carried with them explanations of compositional methods and disclaimers for lapses in memory. Sometimes, the foreword was used to editorialise on the war's memory, or to discuss other war books in circulation. The purpose of doing so was to differentiate works within a crowded field and to offer an explanation as to why this book was different to so many others.[35]

Memoirs describe transformative moments: the entry to military life, an alien environment with its own language and customs; battle, an experience equally alien with its fear and suffering; the temporal bonds formed in war between comrades, what C.S. Lewis described as the 'love between fellow sufferers'.[36] Nearly all war memoirs begin with the process of civilian transformation, becoming a soldier, where the author recognises that something in their matter has been altered, that they are now forced to survive in an environment completely different from their lives at home. For combat memoirs embarkation and travelling to the front was a particularly important experience, one usually where this transformation was first realised as men moved from the home front slowly towards the battlefield. Plowman began his memoir at Charing Cross Station, 'a sombre, sunless place, crowded with khaki figures thinly interspersed with civilians, mostly women, dressed in sombre colors'.[37] The moment of departure carried with it trepidation as well as hope for the return of men departing, their leaving witnessed by those who appear already in the sombre clothes of mourning. 'The hopes and fears of all are the same', he wrote, 'but they are not shared: each one bears his own'.[38]

Going up the line itself was a dramatic moment, remembered and described often as a jarring and terrifying journey. The landscape became gradually destroyed, the air putrid, and sounds of transportation vehicles mixed with the distant thuds of artillery shells. Blunden described the new officer's transformation as 'trench education', where one's body and mind had to become adjusted to new conditions, smells and the many discomforts of merely living in a dug-out.[39] Part of trench education was, of course, actually learning how to be a soldier, in Blunden's case how to be an officer with any degree of professional competency. Nearly all combat memoirs depicted soldiers going up the line for the first time into a new environment, one so vastly different to what they had expected.

This is not to say that all memoirists were terrified of the idea of battle: Carrington remembered mostly excitement the first time he went to the front, comparing it to getting to bat for the first time in a cricket match, feelings that dissipated after he saw a queue of men blown up by a random shell.[40] In Llewelyn Wyn Griffith's case, there was a physical transformation that mirrored the emotional journey of coming up the line: men shaved their heads and were issued with sheepskins before being driven up to the trenches in London buses.[41] With their shorn heads and fuzzy jerkins, his men went up to meet the cold, wet realities of serving in the trenches. After one night in a wet trench, Griffith was thinking entirely of creature comforts: hot eggs and rashers of bacon, tea and jam, and pipe tobacco, basic but important factors in sustaining any degree of positive morale at the front.[42]

The narrative of transformation brought the civilian soldier into contact with the new landscape of the war. Exposure to fear proved the next step in one's trench education, a moment all memoirists faced, and all had to relay to readers. For infantry, their first moments of fear usually involved shelling, watching on from the trench or trying to make it up the line impotently as seemingly random death was doled out from above. For pilots, fear took another form, usually represented in the death of a friend or comrade burning in a plane or crashing down from the skies either from mechanical failure or battle. For nurses or doctors, negotiating professional lines with feelings of empathy for the suffering of others was a narrative experience akin to being in battle. Seeing the ramifications of battles, even from a distance, came with its own realities of service for those who were treating the broken men who moved through Casualty Clearing Stations. All of these moments were awakenings to the front: they were ruminative moments important to share with readers.

In memoirs the importance of such moments is to demonstrate that the writer had witnessed events that were life-altering, ones that gave them the authority of the witness to combat, to comment on how those experiences, in turn, changed their perceptions of truth. The truth of the 'flesh-witness' was different to that of the journalist or historian: flesh-witnesses use battle as a trial of suffering to demonstrate a sense of transcendence in their memoirs.[43] Transcendence could come from disillusionment, of course, where the author's revelation was one of innocence altered by war. Vera Brittain's *Testament of Youth* was intended to be an 'indictment of civilization', a polemical re-examination of the tragedy of her early life recalled for the purpose of preventing future wars, a product of her deep sense of disillusion with the war she lived through.[44] She was certainly not alone; many other authors felt a sense of disconnect between their pre-war and post-war lives. However, these feelings were complex and changed as writers reconsidered the war's impact. Transcendence could also come from another source, emotional resiliency, depicting suffering as a heroic action, showing fear, pain and hardship to demonstrate trial and determination. Charles Carrington wrote in 1929, 'those who bear the greatest suffering survive, and it is this which supplies the heroic element even in modern war'.[45]

Reacting to the war's longevity and the psychological ramifications of the stresses of service is one of the most important legacies of First World War literature. Guy Chapman described this as 'progressive demoralization', a result of both 'pressure and excitement'.[46] Demoralisation was not the same thing as disillusionment with King or Country, but it reflected a sense of emotional weariness as men and women approached the end of their tethers. Charles Douie entitled his war memoir *The Weary Road*, a largely patriotic account of a hard-fought war on the western front, one that though heroic, still broke down the stamina of men who were lucky enough to survive through its major battles. He wrote of the end of the war: 'But the soldier was too tired to be elated; he was none the less deeply conscious of victory and of the freeing of the world from that menace which he had fought for so long, to defy which so many of his friend had died. On his return home he was still very weary, and those who had little knowledge of the soldier's life, and less insight into his mind, observing his weariness, mistook it for disillusion'.[47] When soldiers returned home and confronted their memories, the weariness was part of their story, the brave emotional resiliency of so many moments forgotten, their tiredness often manifested stoically through silence. Guy Chapman reflected that at the war's end, 'we were very old, very tired, and now very wise'.[48] He was only twenty-nine years old.

* * *

It is impossible to summarise neatly the experiences of different people who witness the same events. In war literature, men and women write of experiences in many ways shared, but interpreted differently, their discordant beliefs part of the lived memory of events assumed to be transformative but rarely understood to be that way without the help of the eyewitness narrator. For Cyril Falls, the 'spilling of floods of ink' after the war had led to much confusion over the war's legacy, its tragedy interpreted in hundreds of ways by citizen-soldiers who returned and wrote their war books.

British First World War memoirs reflect two important facets of the war's history: its global reach and its many different experiences. They also reflect a central historiographical issue: that war memoirs offer colour commentary on history, but are not the same thing as history. Memoirs of the First World War demonstrate the breadth of interpretations of events that proved jarring to many different men and women who recalled their war experiences with similar language, but vastly different ideas as to the war's impact on their lives. They provide a means for understanding how historical events affected real people – how great events witnessed were felt – and how those feelings were later resurrected, reimagined and reconstructed to impart the war's personal stories, in their many forms, to the public.

NOTES

1. Cyril Falls, *War Books* (London, 1930).
2. Falls, *War Books*, vii.
3. Falls was the division historian after the war. See Cyril Falls, *The History of the 36th (Ulster) Division* (Belfast, 1922).
4. Falls, *War Books*, xi.
5. Falls, *War Books*, xi.
6. Paul Fussell, *The Great War and Modern Memory* (Oxford, 1975); Samuel Hynes, *A War Imagined* (London, 1990). See also Hynes, *The Soldiers' Tale* (New York, 1997), chs 2–3.
7. Of literary studies, see Brian Bond, *The Unquiet Western Front* (New York, 2002); Bond, *Survivors of a Kind* (London, 2008); Rosa Maria Bracco, *Merchants of Hope* (Oxford, 1993); Hugh Cecil, *The Flower of Battle* (South Royalton, VT, 1996); Santanu Das, *Touch and Intimacy in First World War Literature* (Cambridge, 2005); Jessica Meyer, 'The Tuition of Manhood: "Sapper's War Stories and the Literature of War"', in M. Hammond and S. Towheed (eds), *Publishing and the First World War: Essays in Book History* (London, 2007), 113–28; Meyer, *Men of War* (London, 2009); Jane Potter, *Girls in Khaki, Boys in Print* (Oxford, 2005); Janet Watson, *Fighting Different Wars* (Cambridge, 2004).
8. John Still, *A Prisoner in Turkey* (London, 1920), vii.
9. A.O. Pollard, *Fire-Eater: Memoirs of a V.C.* (London, 1932), 14.
10. The term 'war book' was one used liberally by the publishing industry to refer to books in which the subject matter depicted the recent war, often fiction as well as non-fiction. For more on commerce and war book publication in the interwar period, see Ian Isherwood, 'British Publishing and Commercial Memories of the First World War', *War in History*, 23(3) (2016), 323–340.

11. See Edmund Blunden, *Undertones of War* (London, 1928); Vera Brittain, *Testament of Youth* (London, 1933); Robert Graves, *Good-bye to All That* (London, 1929).
12. Of bibliographies, Falls's *War Books* remains invaluable, though it only includes entries to 1930. The most comprehensive bibliography of war-related non-fiction is Edward Lengel's excellent *World War I Memories* (Oxford, 2001). See also A.G.S. Enser, *A Subject Bibliography of the First World War: Books in English 1914–1978* (London, 1979).
13. Though the term 'war memoir' can be debated at length, Yuval Noah Harari's pragmatic definition is most useful for this study. He writes that memoirs are 'retrospective attempts by combatants to construct a meaningful narrative of their wars', which differentiates them from other forms of war writing. See Yuval Noah Harari, 'Military Memoirs: A Historical Overview of the Genre from the Middle Ages to the Late Modern Era', *War in History* 14(3) (2007), 290.
14. Jay Winter, *The Great War and the British People* (New York, 2003), 303–4. See also Fussell, *The Great War*, 206; Andrew Rutherford, *The Literature of War: Five Studies in Heroic Virtue* (New York, 1978), 93.
15. For more on the idea of the middlebrow in war literature, see Bracco, *Merchants of Hope*, 10–17.
16. Blunden, *Undertones of War*; Charles Edmunds (Charles Carrington), *A Subaltern's War* (London, 1929); Charles Douie, *The Weary Road* (London, 1929); R.H. Mottram wrote three novels, *The Spanish Farm Trilogy*, in addition to several collections of non-fiction essays/reminiscences after the war.
17. For studies of this literature, see James Kitchen, '"Khaki Crusaders": Crusading Rhetoric and the British Imperial Soldier during the Egypt and Palestine Campaigns, 1916–18', *First World War Studies* 1(2) (2010), 141–60; and Pria Satia, *Spies in Arabia* (Oxford, 2008).
18. T.E. Lawrence, *Revolt in the Desert* (London, 1927) and *The Seven Pillars of Wisdom* (London, 1935); N.N.E. Bray, *Shifting Sands* (London, 1934); Sir Hubert Young, *The Independent Arab* (London, 1933); Vivian Gilbert, *The Romance of the Last Crusade: With Allenby to Jerusalem* (New York, 1924); Cecil Sommers, *Temporary Crusaders* (London, 1919); J.E. Tennant, *In the Clouds Above Baghdad* (London, 1920).
19. Frank Richards, *Old Soldiers Never Die* (London, 1933); Stephen Graham, *A Private in the Guards* (New York, 1919); William Linton Andrews, *Haunting Years: The Commentaries of a War Territorial* (London, 1930).
20. Giles Eyre, *Somme Harvest* (London, 1938); Bernard Blaser, *Kilts Across the Jordan* (London, 1926).
21. John Lucy, *There's a Devil in the Drum* (London, 1938).
22. Marguerite Fedden, *Sister's Quarters, Salonika* (London, 1921); Yvonne Fitzroy, *With the Scottish Nurses in Rumania* (London, 1918); I. Elmslie Hutton, *With a Woman's Unit in Serbia, Salonika, and Sebastopol* (London, 1929); Flora Sandes, *The Autobiography of a Woman Soldier* (London, 1927); Henrietta Tayler, *A*

Scottish Nurse at Work (London, 1920); Julier DeKey Whitsed, *Come to the Cook-House Door! A V.A.D. in Salonika* (London, 1932).
23. Compton Mackenzie, *Aegean Memories* (London, 1939), *Athenian Memories* (London, 1931), *Gallipoli Memories* (London, 1929), *Greek Memories* (London, 1932).
24. J.L. Hardy, *I Escape!* (London, 1927); Alan Bott, *Eastern Nights – And Flights* (Edinburgh, 1919); E.H. Jones, *The Road to En-Dor* (London, 1919); A.J. Evans, *The Escaping Club* (London, 1921).
25. For a summary of this literature, see Ian Isherwood, 'Writing the "Ill-Managed Nursery": British POW Memoirs of the First World War', *First World War Studies* 5(3) (2014), 267–86.
26. See Hynes, *The Soldiers' Tale*, 81–93; see also Ian Isherwood, '"To Fly is More Interesting than to Read about Flying": British R.F.C. Memoirs of the First World War', *War, Literature & the Arts* 26 (2014), 1–20.
27. The descriptive term 'unmilitant individual' was used by Philip Gosse in describing his own involvement in the war. See Philip Gosse, *Memoirs of a Camp Follower* (London, 1934), 11.
28. Guy Chapman, *Vain Glory* (London, 1937), viii.
29. Sassoon's three volumes of fictional autobiography were *Memoirs of a Fox-Hunting Man*, *Memoirs of an Infantry Officer* and *Sherston's Progress*; Frederic Manning, *The Middle Parts of Fortune* (London, 1929); Mottram, *The Spanish Farm Trilogy*.
30. Llewelyn Wyn Griffith, *Up to Mametz and Beyond* (Barnsley, 2010), 110. *Up to Mametz* was originally published by Faber in 1931.
31. Hynes, *The Soldiers' Tale*, 2–3.
32. Thomas Hope Floyd, *At Ypres with Best-Dunkley* (London, 1920), Dedication.
33. Guy Chapman, *A Passionate Prodigality* (London, 1965), Dedication.
34. Andrews, *Haunting Years*, 6–7.
35. Forewords became more important – and more aggressive in their language – in the late 1920s, following the popularity of Erich Remarque's *All Quiet on the Western Front*.
36. C.S. Lewis, *Surprised by Joy* (New York, 1984), 188.
37. Mark VII, *A Subaltern on the Somme* (New York, 1928), 3.
38. Mark VII, *A Subaltern on the Somme*, 3.
39. Edmund Blunden, *Undertones of War* (Garden City, NY, 1929), ch. 2.
40. Edmunds, *A Subaltern's War*, 20, 22.
41. Griffith, *Up to Mametz* (London, 1981), 14–16.
42. Griffith, *Up to Mametz*, 29–30.
43. For more on the concept of the flesh-witness in memoirs, see Yuval Noah Harari, 'Armchairs, Coffee, and Authority: Eye-witnesses and Flesh-witnesses Speak about War, 1100–2000', *The Journal of Military History* 74 (2010), 53–78.
44. Vera Brittain, *Testament of Youth* (New York, 2004), 12.
45. Edmunds, *A Subaltern's War*, 200.
46. Chapman, *Vain Glory*, xi.
47. Douie, *The Weary Road*, 16–17.
48. Chapman, *A Passionate Prodigality*, 273

BIBLIOGRAPHY

Memoirs and Novels

Andrews, William Linton. *Haunting Years: The Commentaries of a War Territorial.* London: Hutchinson, 1930.
Blaser, Bernard. *Kilts Across the Jordan.* London: H.F. & G. Witherby, 1926.
Blunden, Edmund. *Undertones of War.* London: Richard Cobden-Sanderson, 1928.
Blunden, Edmund. *Undertones of War.* Garden City, NY: Doubleday, Doran & Co., 1929.
Bott, Alan. *Eastern Nights – And Flights.* Edinburgh: Blackwood, 1919.
Bray, N.N.E. *Shifting Sands.* London: Unicorn Press, 1934.
Brittain, Vera. *Testament of Youth.* London: Gollancz, 1933.
Brittain, Vera. *Testament of Youth.* New York: Penguin, 2004.
Chapman, Guy. *A Passionate Prodigality.* London: MacGibbon and Kee, 1965.
Chapman, Guy. *Vain Glory.* London: Cassell, 1937.
Douie, Charles. *The Weary Road.* London: John Murray, 1929.
Edmunds, Charles (Charles Carrington). *A Subaltern's War.* London: Peter Davies, 1929.
Evans, A.J. *The Escaping Club.* London: John Lane, 1921.
Eyre, Giles. *Somme Harvest.* London: Jarrolds, 1938.
Falls, Cyril. *The History of the 36th (Ulster) Division.* Belfast: McCaw, Stevenson & Orr, Ltd. The Linenhall Press, 1922.
Falls, Cyril. *War Books.* London: Peter Davies, 1930.
Fedden, Marguerite. *Sister's Quarters, Salonika.* London: Grant Richards, 1921.
Fitzroy, Yvonne. *With the Scottish Nurses in Rumania.* London: John Murray, 1918.
Floyd, Thomas Hope. *At Ypres with Best-Dunkley.* London: John Lane, 1920.
Gilbert, Vivian. *The Romance of the Last Crusade: With Allenby to Jerusalem.* New York: Appleton, 1924.
Gosse, Philip. *Memoirs of a Camp Follower.* London: Cassell & Co., 1934.
Graham, Stephen. *A Private in the Guards.* New York: The Macmillan Company, 1919.
Graves, Robert. *Good-bye to All That.* London: Jonathan Cape, 1929.
Griffith, Wyn, *Up to Mametz.* London: Severn House, 1981.
Griffith, Wyn. *Up to Mametz and Beyond.* Barnsley, South Yorkshire: Pen and Sword, 2010.
Hardy, J.L. *I Escape!* London: John Lane, 1927.
Hutton, I. Elmslie. *With a Woman's Unit in Serbia, Salonika, and Sebastopol.* London: Williams and Norgate, 1929.
Jones, E.H. *The Road to En-Dor.* London: John Lane, 1919.
Lawrence, T.E. *Revolt in the Desert.* London: Jonathan Cape, 1927.
Lawrence, T.E. *The Seven Pillars of Wisdom.* London: Jonathan Cape, 1935.
Lengel, Edward. *World War I Memories.* Oxford: Scarecrow Press, 2001.
Lewis, C.S. *Surprised by Joy.* New York: Harcourt Brace, 1984.

Lucy, John. *There's a Devil in the Drum*. London: Faber & Faber, 1938.
Mackenzie, Compton. *Aegean Memories*. London: Cassell, 1939.
Mackenzie, Compton. *Athenian Memories*. London: Cassell, 1931.
Mackenzie, Compton. *Gallipoli Memories*. London: Cassell, 1929.
Mackenzie, Compton. *Greek Memories*. London: Cassell, 1932.
Manning, Frederic. *The Middle Parts of Fortune*. London: Peter Davies, 1929.
Mark VII. *A Subaltern on the Somme*. New York: E.P. Dutton, 1928.
Mottram, R.H. *The Spanish Farm Trilogy*. London: Chatto and Windus, 1927.
Pollard, A.O. *Fire-Eater: Memoirs of a V.C.* London: Hutchinson, 1932.
Remarque, Erich. *All Quiet on the Western Front*. London: Putnam, 1929.
Richards, Frank. *Old Soldiers Never Die*. London: Faber & Faber, 1933.
Sandes, Flora. *The Autobiography of a Woman Soldier*. London: H.F. & G. Witherby, 1927.
Sassoon, Siegfried. *Memoirs of a Fox-hunting Man*. London: Faber & Faber, 1928.
Sassoon, Siegfried. *Memoirs of an Infantry Officer*. London: Faber & Faber, 1930.
Sasson, Siegfried. *Sherston's Progress*. London: Faber & Faber, 1936.
Sommers, Cecil. *Temporary Crusaders*. London: John Lane, 1919.
Still, John. *A Prisoner in Turkey*. London: John Lane, 1920.
Tayler, Henrietta. *A Scottish Nurse at Work*. London: John Lane, 1920.
Tennant, J.E. *In the Clouds Above Baghdad*. London: Cecil Palmer, 1920.
Whitsed, Julier DeKey. *Come to the Cook-House Door! A V.A.D. in Salonika*. London: Herbert Joseph, 1932.
Young, Sir Hubert. *The Independent Arab*. London: John Murray, 1933.

Secondary Sources

Bond, Brian. *Survivors of a Kind*. London: Continuum Books, 2008.
Bond, Brian. *The Unquiet Western Front*. New York: Oxford University Press, 2002.
Bracco, Rosa Maria. *Merchants of Hope*. Oxford: Berg, 1993.
Cecil, Hugh. *The Flower of Battle*. South Royalton, VT: Steerforth Press, 1996.
Das, Santanu. *Touch and Intimacy in First World War Literature*. Cambridge: Cambridge University Press, 2005.
Enser, A.G.S. *A Subject Bibliography of the First World War: Books in English 1914–1978*. London: Andre Deutsch, 1979.
Fussell, Paul. *The Great War and Modern Memory*. Oxford: Oxford University Press, 1975.
Harari, Yuval Noah. 'Armchairs, Coffee, and Authority: Eye-witnesses and Flesh-witnesses Speak about War, 1100–2000'. *The Journal of Military History* 74 (2010), 53–78.
Harari, Yuval Noah. 'Military Memoirs: A Historical Overview of the Genre from the Middle Ages to the Late Modern Era'. *War in History* 14(3) (2007), 289–309.
Hynes, Samuel. *The Soldiers' Tale*. New York: Viking Penguin, 1997.
Hynes, Samuel. *A War Imagined*. London: Pimlico, 1990.

Isherwood, Ian. 'British Publishing and Commercial Memories of the First World War'. *War in History*, 23(3) (2016), 323–340.

Isherwood, Ian. '"To Fly is More Interesting than to Read about Flying": British R.F.C. Memoirs of the First World War'. *War, Literature & the Arts* 26 (2014), 1–20.

Isherwood, Ian. 'Writing the "Ill-Managed Nursery": British POW Memoirs of the First World War'. *First World War Studies* 5(3) (2014), 267–86.

Kitchen, James. '"Khaki Crusaders": Crusading Rhetoric and the British Imperial Soldier during the Egypt and Palestine Campaigns, 1916–18'. *First World War Studies* 1(2) (2010), 141–60.

Meyer, Jessica. *Men of War*. London: Palgrave Macmillan, 2009.

Meyer, Jessica. 'The Tuition of Manhood: "Sapper's War Stories and the Literature of War"', in M. Hammond and S. Towheed (eds), *Publishing and the First World War: Essays in Book History* (London: Palgrave Macmillan, 2007), 113–28.

Potter, Jane. *Girls in Khaki, Boys in Print*. Oxford: Clarendon Press, 2005.

Rutherford, Andrew. *The Literature of War: Five Studies in Heroic Virtue*. New York: Harper & Row, 1978.

Satia, Pria. *Spies in Arabia*. Oxford: Oxford University Press, 2008.

Watson, Janet. *Fighting Different Wars*. Cambridge: Cambridge University Press, 2004.

Winter, Jay. *The Great War and the British People*. New York: Palgrave, 2003.

Ian Isherwood is a graduate of Gettysburg College, Dartmouth College and the University of Glasgow, where he did his PhD in modern history. He specialises in British history and war studies with an emphasis on the First World War. Isherwood's research interests focus on the experience of war and war memoirs. His articles and book reviews have appeared in *First World War Studies*, *War, Literature and the Arts*, *The Journal of Military History* and *War in History*. Isherwood is the author of *Remembering the Great War: Writing and Publishing the Experiences of WWI* (I.B. Tauris, 2016).

Chapter 6

A Cog in the Machine of History?
Japanese Memoirs of Total War (1937–45)

Aaron William Moore

It is sad to note that we are living in the final days of the generation that experienced World War Two. They are failing not only in health, but also in memory, and so many have committed their views of the past to paper in the form of memoirs. These texts are among the most important raw materials with which historians will write and rewrite the history of the war from this point onward, in a never-ending discussion over how the past should be remembered. This chapter examines the process by which individuals composed memoirs in Japan, whose memoirs 'count' in the country's collective memory, and how the differences in four categories of memoir writing have emerged as important components in constructing a 'Japanese' memory of the conflict.

It is wrong to assume that memoirs are tightly constrained by the conventions of a single genre. Particularly in societies with a 'free', private (for profit, non-government) mass media, the exact manner in which an author is meant to memorialise the past in textual form is open to interpretation. As such, in post-war Japan, after the end of the US occupation in 1952, individuals who had experienced the war exercised agency in determining how to write their memoirs and present them to the public. Nevertheless, in many cases, these transformations in (or, sometimes, conflicts over) memory discourse are conducted not in the for-profit mass media or government offices, but in non-government (NGO), non-profit museums, many of which refer to themselves as 'peace museums' (*heiwa shiryōkan*) or simply part of a 'Peace Movement' (*heiwa undō*). The state, in its centralised, national form, was largely absent from the process of memorialisation until recently, leaving the ground open to multiple initiatives at the level of local government (primarily prefectural, sometimes municipal). Similarly, the mass media has proven a 'fair-weather friend' when it comes to remembering the war, engaging in producing memoirs only when it promises to be profitable. As such, the patchwork of memoirs that have come to constitute the raw materials for past, present and future discussions of how Japan should remember the war have been generated by local state-funded public institutions, the for-profit mass media and a vibrant culture of self-published accounts. With so many sources and institutions, the genre of war memoir writing in Japan is as diverse and ill-defined as it is anywhere else in the world.

This chapter will approach this (admittedly chaotic) collection of documents by closely examining the relationship between social organisation and emerging categories of memoirs and their authors, as well as how social divisions mirror conflicts over historical memory. First, I will argue that memoirs underline the importance of social organisation, whether by local government or voluntary groups, in producing textualised memories of the war. Second, memoirs show changes and shifts regarding whose memories were considered important or, at the very least, *relevant* to the master narrative of the war experience. Third, Japanese memoirs reveal deep divisions in 'collective memory', such as those between soldier and civilian (which sometimes also reflects gender divisions), juvenile and adult, and Japanese and non-Japanese subjects of the imperial state. The production of historical memory in Japan through memoirs is reliant on the emergence of organisations that provide genre tools to individuals who wish to belong to a 'language community'. To the extent that these sub-groups can integrate their narratives into the one that is accepted and understood by post-war society, they become a cog in the machine of that nation's 'historical memory'.

IMPORTANCE OF ORGANISATION

The production of post-war memoirs emerged from social organisations that, in most cases, diverged considerably from those of the wartime era. As such, their impact on the production of these texts must be assessed before analysing memoirs directly. During the war, the state was heavily involved in directing the form and content of any texts claiming to describe the battlefield, either through direct production of propaganda or indirect 'framing' of public discourse through censorship (leading to complex patterns of 'self-censorship' among publishers, editors and authors).[1] Learning to write about past events, then, was a process in which the state exercised guidance, such as the collections of battlefield 'experiences' that approximated memoirs in generic conventions, and were sponsored by military officials.[2] In the post-war era, particularly after the Allied occupation ended in 1952, the state retreated from this role. As I have argued elsewhere, the post-war social organisations supporting the production of memory narratives are remarkably diverse in Japan, primarily because of the state's weak leadership in directing memorial rituals.[3] These organisations then came to represent communities that share political and social values, specific battlefield experiences, and various linguistic and narrative strategies for describing the wartime past.[4]

First, although it never recovered even a modicum of its wartime power, the state was still involved in facilitating the production of memoirs in Japan, but mainly by supporting the spaces that archived relevant wartime records and personal documents. For example, much like official military archives elsewhere in the world, Tokyo's National Institute of Defence Studies (*Bōeishō bōei kenkyūjō*, NIDS) allowed veterans to peruse and photocopy battle diaries, reports, orders and other documents in order to ensure that their memoirs are 'correct'.[5] NIDS also archived unpublished memoirs from the war, which were often not distinguished, in terms of archival organisation, from wartime diaries.[6] The history museums in Chiba (*Rekishi minzoku hakubutsukan*) and Sendai (*Rekishi minzoku shiryōkan*) collect and publish memoirs as part of their mandate to document Japan's modern history; for the war, their display cases have usually focused on domestic issues such as Allied firebombing, rationing and evacuations. However, the majority of activity in the memoir market – particularly self-published accounts – has occurred at the level of local government. Local museums archive and reproduced wartime personal accounts and post-war memoirs as a form of public education. In Tokyo, Sumida, Shinagawa, and Toshima Wards, for example, which experienced heavy firebombing, reprinted diaries and memoirs of children and adolescents who lived through the ordeal. These texts have frequently been featured in museum exhibits, despite the fact that these spaces were not dedicated to the war per se. The Fukushima Prefectural Museum, which included exhibits concerning local archaeological finds to post-war rural tourism, also archived letters, diaries and memoirs that were occasionally published by the museum and sold to schools and libraries, as well as in the museum gift shop. Finally, even small towns such as Kitakami, in Iwate Prefecture, funded local museums that included a small gathering of self-published local accounts of life during the war, and have been woefully under-utilised sources of local history.

Social networks within the 'Peace Movement', most of which have evolved into formalised non-government organisations (NGOs), have been an important group for the generation of textualised 'memory' concerning the wartime experience. First, by running exhibits or establishing permanent museum spaces, they helped to draw in members of the community and encouraged them to share their memories in textual form. These activities were crucial for collecting memoirs that were not 'publishable' or useful for national narratives, but revealed important aspects of the war experience, such as soldiers who secretly articulated anti-war sentiments to their friends on the battlefield.[7] The Tokyo-based Wadatsumi-kai arguably launched the mass publication of personal accounts of the war in 1949 with their collection of documents by 'student soldiers' and, as Fukuma Yoshiaki argued, exerted a powerful influence over the world of writing about the war and 'peace education'.[8] They continue to publish a newsletter today that includes personal documents including memoirs. The 'Grassroots Museum' (Kusa no Ie) in Kōchi also produces a newsletter in which the memoirs of ordinary Japanese are published, including those of Koreans who experienced the war in Japan. Ritsumeikan University's International Peace Center and the Osaka International Peace Museum (AKA 'Peace Osaka') regularly release newsletters and archive local, self-published memoirs of the war years. Newly established museums are even more focused on local experiences, such as Shizuoka's Peace Museum, which emphasises narratives concerning the firebombing of the city. The proximity of the museum, and its staff's close relationship with the local community, also means that they can collect unusual unpublished manuscripts, such as those by women who served the armed forces abroad.[9]

Organisations that mass-produce war memoirs have not been limited to pacifist groups who take a critical view of Japan's imperial past. The Bereaved Families Association (Izokukai) has also helped organise publications that contribute to memoir writing in Japan. The *Iwate Servicemen's War Records* contained several short memoirs, statistics and excerpts from wartime official documents. Although it was sponsored by the prefectural government's social welfare department – which, among other things, oversees benefits for pensioners and veterans – the head editor was a highly placed member of the Bereaved Families Association as well. Yasukuni Shrine's Yūshūkan Museum functioned similar to, for example, Peace Osaka, except that it focuses on patriotic or heroic narratives, including those written by colonial subjects such as the Taiwanese, that take a more positive view of Japan's imperial past. Local government initiatives have adopted a slightly less progressive view of the war, depending on their constituencies and the history of the area. Chiran's Special Attack Pilot Museum ('kamikaze') recognises the wasteful loss of young lives and the futility of the 'kamikaze', but simultaneously valorises their sacrifice. The museum aggressively collected wartime documents, including diaries and letters, as well as memoir literature, both mass-produced and self-published, that it archives in its growing library to the present day.

The mass media, of course, has played an important role – whenever such organisations show an interest (usually on memorial holidays) – in publishing and disseminating the memories of those who lived through the war. Initially, this was driven by the fact that many media figures were actually in the armed forces, either as embedded reporters, propagandists or rank-and-file soldiers. In the early post-war period, intellectuals and writers freed from the army described secret acts of rebellion during the war and unleashed rich descriptions of military incompetence that they had witnessed:

> When I was called up, I didn't know where I was going or what I would do. We just packed up and left from Ujina. I arrived at a boarding house in Hiroshima, which I knew nothing about, and had to pay one yen a night for a bed and some food. It was awful. They had maybe eight beds for twenty people – 'Just sleep anywhere (*tekitō ni neyo*)'. There was no chalk commander [CO for unit transport], and I didn't even know the word. Sometimes this guy Terashita would show up, dressed as a captain, but he wasn't anything – he borrowed his dad's uniform.[10]

After the early post-war criticism gave way to disinterest in the war and dedication to peaceful economic development, mass media publications of war memoirs declined.[11] Memberships in veterans' groups remained high,[12] however, and a tradition of writing 'self-histories' (*jibunshi*)[13] meant that mass media interest did not solely determine the production of these texts. Nevertheless, it was not until the mid-1970s that the Japanese reading public once again became interested in the war. Memorial dates, such as the 40th (1985) and 50th (1995) anniversaries of the surrender prompted media coverage and further publication of memoirs.

Separating the mass media from social organisations, however, is misleading when it comes to the composition and dissemination of war memoirs – they are often closely linked. Yasukuni Shrine has attempted to, in the words of their detractors, 'beautify' (*bika suru*) Japan's imperial past through such publications, but the pacifist interpretation of the war experience has largely determined which sorts of memoirs get published by major commercial presses. This suggests that the Japanese reading public has not been terribly interested in returning to the patriotic or 'moral education' (*dōtoku kyōiku*) of the imperial type – Kobayashi Yoshinori's success in the *manga* world notwithstanding. By contrast, 'Peace Movement' activist and China veteran Azuma Shirō's memoir *My Nanjing Platoon* (1988) and the subsequent *Azuma Shirō Diary* (2001) attracted widespread attention and debate in Japan due to their frank descriptions of combat and battlefield atrocities. In some cases, 'Peace Movement' networks have successfully collaborated with the mass media to generate more texts on war memory that support anti-war sentiment. At the end of 2001, Ritsumeikan University's International Peace Center (Kyoto) and Asahi News (Osaka) shared a museum exhibit on the war to great success.[14] Subsequent to the exhibit, the impressions of attendees were collected into a book and released, including many previously unpublished accounts. The short memoirs included that of an 88-year-old veteran who had been deployed from 1937 to 1945, serving in China, the Soviet border with Manchuria, the Solomons, Guadalcanal and Bougainville, including captivity in Rabaul. He insisted on 'critical self-reflection' (*hansei*), writing: 'I recognise now, more than ever, the responsibility I have to talk about the past accurately, and so I think about how important and meaningful this exhibit is'.[15]

If nothing else, the mass media has contributed to the awareness of the wartime past through simple exposure, and this has encouraged ordinary Japanese to compose memoirs and be part of the discussion.[16] Even after broader public interest faded, those who lived through the war will have already organised into various non-government 'societies' such as veterans' groups (*sen'yūkai*) that enabled horizontal lines of communication, information sharing, and encouraged the composition of personal memoirs. These texts then found a place either in government archives, NGO institutions such as 'peace museums', or (unfortunately for historians) Yasukuni Shrine's museum, which determined the extent to which researchers can gain access to them. As a consequence of these diverse influences, a vast array of memoirs have emerged, but, within this mass of text, important subdivisions should be recognised for the impact they have had on post-war historical memory.

WHO REMEMBERS? THE POLITICS OF MEMOIR PRODUCTION AND PRESERVATION

The composition, publication and preservation of war memoirs reveals not only how certain content is selected for historical memory, but also who is allowed to participate in the process – in other words, whose memories 'count'. Those memories considered 'important' and 'unimportant' have changed throughout post-war history in Japan, corresponding to political and generational shifts. At the end of the Allied occupation of Japan, for example, the memoirs of 'famous people' such as Harada Kumao attracted attention when producing memoirs or 'diaries',[17] in part because the public was still struggling with the culpability of Japan's wartime leadership. However, the focus shifted over the decades to the experiences of 'ordinary Japanese'. Certainly, there were earlier memoirs by less famous figures – usually by servicemen abroad – but the historiographical trajectory has been toward a broader inclusion of the 'ordinary folk' into the narrative of World War Two.[18] 'Ordinary Japanese' is nevertheless a contested group, which also tends to exclude memoirs that touch upon the sensitive subject of empire. Thus, the diversity of memoirs produced in recent decades have exposed deep divisions within the field of historical memory that mirror, in some respects, the social organisations that have archived and published them.

First, the memoirs of soldiers have always been considered critical to the collective memory of the war, and they helped carry over many narrative conventions from the war years. Despite being on the 'losing side' of the war, many Japanese strongly feel that they 'cannot forget the fact that [Japan's post-war] prosperity was built on the sacrifices of countless servicemen who offered their precious lives for the nation'.[19] Veterans' memoirs appeared both in dedicated collections and in monographs over the years. The division between 'fact' and 'fiction' in recalling the war is not always clear, especially in a country that has a rich literary tradition of autobiographical fiction such as the 'I-novel' (*shishōsetsu*).[20] Yoshida Mitsuru's *Requiem for the Battleship Yamato* (1952) borrowed heavily from wartime literary writing styles, even if the account was, strictly speaking, post-war non-fiction. Fiction critical of the war experience still preserved pre-1945 generic conventions. Ōoka Shōhei's *Fires on the Plain* (1951), while much of its specific content is probably fictionalised, was also based heavily on Ōoka's experiences in the Pacific. It relied on various wartime influences for its delivery, including various basic literary devices such as metaphor, synecdoche and symbolism, as does his far more autobiographical *POW Memoir* (1952).[21] The *primus inter pares* may be Shimao Toshio, whose shift from nigh-solipsistic island idylls to pained investigations of post-war survival (from 1946 to 1967) seemed to characterise a personal, but highly literary, investigation of war experience.[22] Japanese authors who described the war have, in other words, recognised the importance of style in its relationship to relating 'truthful' past experiences, even if it often blurred the line between 'fact' and 'fiction'.

These literary interlocutors helped to shape the way in which ordinary veterans penned their memoirs by expanding the parameters of acceptable expression regarding the war. Some veterans undoubtedly were aware of their debts to early pioneers, having read them closely. For those outside of the world of high literature, writing a memoir might not be considered in such sophisticated terms, and thus the influence of, for example, historical memory discourse on their personal accounts may go by unnoticed. As I have described elsewhere,[23] for example, the first stage of 'memory writing' about the war came with the conflict's immediate end. Soldiers abroad began making the transition to being veterans by slowly transforming the language they had used to mobilise for the war effort itself. Kimura Hisao, who would eventually be executed for war crimes in Singapore, expressed the 'injustice' of having to pay for 'Tokyo's crimes'. Nevertheless, while invoking the wartime language of patriotic self-abnegation, he also transitioned into the post-war political reality: 'I won't die as a sacrifice for the Japanese army, but if I perish by covering myself with the crimes of the Japanese people, [in order to save them] from disaster, then I will not be angry. I will die smiling'.[24] After soldiers were repatriated and returned to civilian life, memoir writing quickly began. Some early memoirs stuck tenaciously to an apolitical, military history approach to the war, such as Soemu Toyoda's *The End of the Imperial Navy* (1950). Still, during the repatriation of the majority of Japan's army, veterans would occasionally publish short memoirs in the press that helped broaden discourse on the war. One reason for the shift in language was that wartime opinions were being challenged by veterans' experiences returning to Japan, just as civilians returning from the empire found themselves subjects of discrimination.[25] Iwatani Hiromitsu had so acclimated to life in Japanese-controlled China that when he returned to Japan, he was rudely asked, 'Hey, are you Chinese or Japanese, anyway?'[26] By the early 1950s, some veterans were already penning memoirs that emphasised the cruelty and horror of modern warfare, explicitly calling for pacifism.[27] With time, many veterans adjusted their language to suit Japanese society after 1945, which required a mixture of personal memory, post-war discourse (often pacifist), and wartime records such as field diaries, personal pocket notebooks, letters, and official materials in military archives (such as battle reports). This is how most post-war memoirs were eventually composed.[28]

Veterans combined wartime records with post-war discourse in order to produce memoirs that 'ring true' to the wartime experience, yet would be comprehensible to a post-war audience. First, some unpublished manuscripts so closely approximate wartime discourse that it can be initially difficult to determine when they were composed (and also arguably made them difficult to publish).[29] Indeed, titles can be deceiving: these 'rewritten' wartime personal accounts are alternately called 'memoirs' (*kaisōroku, kaikoroku*), 'notebooks' (*shuki*) or even 'diaries' (*nikki*, effectively memoir-diary hybrid), all of which could be mass published, self-published or simply shared in Xerox form with family and friends. This is because there is rarely a neat division between a 'diary' and a 'memoir' where veterans' accounts are concerned. For the authors, it is more important that the account be 'true', which may not be tied to a specific genre or time of composition. There are, of course, uninterrupted, seamless post-war narratives that we most easily recognise as 'memoirs', but they are sometimes the product of later engagement with wartime diaries and notebooks (other times they are written purely from memory). It is currently possible to directly examine how veterans' 'commentaries' on wartime personal documents, using post-war language, generate 'memoirs' in both published and manuscript form. The diary of Noguchi Fumio, a sailor and later author of fiction, is an 'interrupted' memoir, in that the account still neatly divides wartime record and post-war reflection, without any attempt to fuse them into a single coherent narrative:

> Friday, 29 June [1944]
>
> Morning, lecture by the unit commander, then weeding the cabbage patch. From 2 pm on the main marching grounds, the Tokyo Music School staff and female students held an R&R concert for the troops. [Various musicians] appeared, and the girls played a violin concerto.
>
> [Post-war notes] These outdoor concerts were for all of the naval officers and men. We knelt on the ground and listened, but in a crowd of thousands, I wonder how many were avidly paying attention to the music. It's a bit rude, but the performers picked the wrong audience, as soldiers leave a lot to be desired when it comes to taste in music. As soldiers, they were serious from beginning to end, but that wasn't due to any discriminating sensibility. [...] In the end, they clapped loudly for Asano Chizuko's solo, but that wasn't because of her foreign language lead performance – it was when they heard her sing 'The Flower of Patriotism' in Japanese. I was exactly the same way.[30]

I have shown elsewhere how post-war additions were added to wartime personal records in Kogura Isamu's unpublished manuscript by 'rewriting' his battlefield pocket notebook into a 'diary', using information gleaned from newspapers, military archives and the memoirs of his friends.[31] It is tempting, therefore, to consider veterans' memoirs as primarily influenced by 'collective memory' after 1945.

The tenacity of wartime discourse, however, shows us how important the language of the battlefield was for veterans, because this was how they first learned to describe combat, and they continued to use this language with their fellow veterans in order to create a 'language community'.[32] Despite the growing dominance of post-war memory discourse, then, many of these texts still utilise wartime professional military language, even when written purely from memory. In his memoir, Senta Rinnosuke described action against the Chinese Nationalists in Shanxi Province in a manner almost identical to a wartime field diary:

> Late in the evening of 8 November [1937] our unit installed our mortars and field artillery in Neiling, then proceeding to Ren County at 4 am the next day. It was then decided to attack Ren, so the 52nd Platoon's full strength, supported by cannon, was ordered to attack from the northwest, with the 2nd Battalion emplaced at Wuqiu as a reserve ... This day's battle did not involve all of our units, but it was the first time I had ever seen a battle. In the future, it would influence my élan. The men fought stoically. It was a good fight that gave me confidence in war.[33]

Thus, while there were significant changes in genre and style for war accounts after 1945, old styles, conventions and tropes proved resilient, particularly when these seemed to give the authors personal satisfaction. Special Attack Pilot Hamazono Shigeyoshi took pride in how his military discipline allowed him to work 'two or three times harder' than the average person, and how he was 'in seventy years, never ill'. Nevertheless, the mark of Japanese anti-war sentiment, which was so characteristic of politics after 1945, is present even here:

> So, in the end, we reached the extreme limits of humanity with the organisation of the Special Attack units. It is sad. In any 'dare to die' brigade, there's always some thread of hope [for survival], but not for them. They were all good men. They were full of hopes and dreams. My friends will never return. Only in my memories, in unexpected times and contexts, do they visit me. [...] If they had lived they would be grandparents, holding their grandchildren high and enjoying their golden years. As for me, as well, I had fourteen bullets from a Grumman fighter rip through my body. I was burned as well. This was so painful it felt like the world was coming apart. For four days I was deaf, and ten days blind. My face was deformed by it. There was nothing good about it at all. But, putting aside the moral quandaries, I don't regret, in the passion of youth, risking my life to battle the enemy. Surviving it was the highest form of good fortune ...[34]

Although the initial post-war memoirs focused on pain, victimisation and suffering – and, indeed, those tropes are ubiquitous and enduring in all Japanese war memoirs, especially those by civilians – others eventually felt free to break away from such sad narratives, so not all veterans' stories would reflect the brutality of battle, homesickness or loss. Sugehara Kihachirō's description of life at war in the Pacific often sounded like an exotic adventure – even pleasant:

> On the seashore there was a row of the natives' bamboo houses. The men and women were naked, walking around with just a single loincloth. Everyone here was Papuan, who were a race rumoured to be cannibalistic, and there were no others. [...] Life on these solitary Pacific islands was much better than I expected. Under the shade of the coastal palm trees, I would gaze on the stars through the leaves, and was rendered speechless. [...] At the time, we wanted for nothing.[35]

While many in Japan were gradually accepting a 'victim' narrative for the war, in which civilians were led down a 'dark path' by duplicitous and reckless military leaders, veterans continued to recapitulate wartime tales of heroism, male bonding, adventurism and amusement. Everyone in Japan had to acclimate to a new manner of speaking and writing that reflected the dramatic changes occurring in politics, culture and society,[36] but for veterans this was a greater challenge. As their lives changed in the post-war era, for the most part so too did their writing. These changes allowed veterans an opportunity to bring new perspectives to remembering the past that they had experienced directly. Professional writers certainly provided a broader set of linguistic tools, but veterans worked within a very wide (and changing) range of genres, styles and forms to record their war experiences, sometimes electing to continue with the language they had known from the war.

While veterans struggled to transform a language adapted for the battlefield for an audience eager to move on, civilians were quickly able to separate from the wartime past. Civilian memoirs have become increasingly important throughout post-war Japan, in part because they are far more accessible to a general audience. A greater number of Japanese civilians survived the war than soldiers, for many obvious reasons including the higher ratio of civilians to servicemen and their comparative safety on the home front. In addition to having a larger base of informants, civilian memoirs are also free from military jargon and are located in familiar settings. Post-war desires to cast the Japanese people as 'victims' of the war, rather than supporters of imperialism, are also a factor in why civilian suffering has become the dominant narrative through which Japanese people remember the past.

Memories of privations, missing family members and everyone 'doing their best' are common across civilian narratives. Certain details are curiously widespread in these memoirs as well, such as the strict conformity of dress at the end of the war: 'Men, whether young or old, all wore the national defence colours of the "citizen's uniform" (*kokuminfuku*) and wrapped cloth gaiters, women all donned white aprons (*monpe*) and bonnets'.[37] Initially, immediate post-war diaries showed the tenacity of wartime discourse, epitomised in the countless quotidian descriptions of enduring hardship in Hachiya Michihiko's *Hiroshima Diary*. Samuel Yamashita's translations of wartime documents reveal a persistence in the rhetoric of perseverance and patriotism in civilian diaries: Yoshizawa Hisako, who was openly critical of the country's military and political leadership, still concluded her 15 August 1945 diary entry by writing that the 'true nature of a people is apparent when they lose a war, rather than when they win, and the day has arrived when we should reveal Japan's greatness'.[38] As with soldiers, the narrative strategies of literature have been important in expanding the restricted language of the wartime era. In texts on the atomic bombings, Hara Tamiki's 'Summer Flower' (1947), Ibuse Masuji's *The Crazy Iris* (1951) and Ota Yōko's *Fireflies* (1953) all used a literary style to approach the subject of atomic bombing, rather than address it through overtly personal memoirs or 'factual' reporting. Nagai Takashi's *Bells of Nagasaki* (1946) was not merely a personal memoir, but a reflection on the city's experience of the bombing, as well as its theological and political implications. The literature surrounding firebombing shares a similar preoccupation with lyrical descriptions that push the boundaries between strict 'record' and fictionalised representations of the past. The compelling literary tradition is only one factor, however, in why ordinary Japanese were inspired to write memoirs of the civilian experience; another reason behind their proliferation is that they are arguably the most 'representative' of the general population. For example, in contrast to veterans' accounts, the civilian memoirs tend to make greater reference to the religious institutions and beliefs that suffused daily life for most Japanese. Watanabe Kōhei explicitly thanked 'the gods and buddhas' for saving his life from the Tokyo firebombing. Describing how he saw his best friend, as well as the friend's daughter and grandson, burned to death at the side of the road, he reflected: 'Why had they not come to my home sooner? See them like this, I wept, shouting in a loud voice, and could only pray that their souls could find rest. [...] No man can know his own fate'.[39]

It is important to avoid focusing exclusively, however, on civilian suffering, and attempt to understand different, critical issues such as how post-war Japanese politics were affected by the war's impact on future voters and, perhaps most importantly, why the Japanese public supported the war effort. When Allied firebombing began to raze large sections of Shizuoka, Endō Naoe remembers fleeing with her mother to the nearby hills. Despite the fact that the city was being burned to the ground, after witnessing a B-29 fall in flames, she heard her mother triumphantly shout 'Banzai!'[40] With the benefit of hindsight, civilian memoirs generate narratives that have more internal coherency than veterans' stories, reflecting the 'lessons learned' after many years of reflection. Murai Akira recalled how his parents forced one of his brothers to withdraw from a cadet academy so that all of their sons were not in the armed forces, and reflected, 'I have three children now, and two sons, and I'm really glad that I don't have to have that experience myself'.[41] It would also be misleading to suggest that the 'victim' narrative adopted in many Japanese civilian memoirs totally obscures public support for the war effort and the injustices of the empire. Indeed, even in a collection of memoirs about the atomic bombing of Nagasaki, survivors can speak frankly of their experiences in areas under Japanese control, such as the Wang Jingwei regime on the mainland: 'After graduation, [Chinese youth] studied Japanese and entered the workforce. This was the path that the sons of the Chinese upper class followed. (The best students studied in Japanese universities.) Everything the Chinese did was under control of the Japanese'.[42] Thus, in addition to acknowledging the fact that not all civilian memoirs fall under the category of 'victim narratives', it is also important to recognise that not all 'civilians' were living in Japan – in effect, these memoirists see that the 'civilian experience' must also include the history of the empire.[43]

The memoirs of ordinary Japanese also reveal widespread reservations about the war effort, even while serving the state mobilisation campaigns, and thus they show us how effective the propaganda was in tying family to the state.[44] Kameda (nee Kanemaru) Kiyoko was a 'dormitory mother' (*ryōbo*) for evacuated children from Tokyo. In writing up her reminiscences, she chose to structure her experiences of 'serving the nation' around the figure of her mother, who died from illness at the end of the war. When she decided to quit her current post to 'take care of the children', her own mother replied, 'This is an important job at this critical time so, if you can be even a little useful, this is your calling (*tenshuku*) – think of it as if you're shipping off for war (*shussei*)'. As her mother grew dangerously ill, however, Kameda recalled having many thoughts and feelings that would brand her a 'traitor' (*hikokumin*), including her belief that Japan was losing the war. Instead of Japan's surrender or occupation by the Allies, Kameda concludes her account with the death of her mother: 'As soon as I was asleep, mom suddenly said, "Kiyo, you're away, I'm so lonely"'. Feeling her head, Kiyoko realised her mother was running a fever and rushed out to find ice but, failing to do so, she returned to discover that her mother's heart had stopped.

> I shouted, 'Mom! Mom!' and rubbed her body, but she didn't move, so I slumped down by her body and wept loudly. [...] Mom took a lonely last breath in a room all by herself. As I was returning from [town], in the end I was not able to be by her side. (Mom, I'm sorry, I don't know why I went back. I may have hastened my mother's death.) [...] The day before mom had told me to throw myself into my work for the nation [instead of looking after her ...], but in the morning she told me she was lonely without me. Mom – I can say it now – more than [winning] the war or [serving] the nation I wanted you to be alive. I have to tell the truth.[45]

Despite the fact that Kameda ultimately felt that her mother's life was more important than Japan's success in the war, it is telling that these feelings, to the extent that she was aware of them *during* the war, did not interfere with her 'fulfilling her duty'. Civilian memoirs expose, then, the terrifying effectiveness of state-led social organisation, when loved ones were perishing and the state was failing in even its most basic responsibilities towards Japan's citizens.

In a third major category of recent memoirs, the recollections of those who experienced the war during childhood or adolescence have recently emerged as key informants in the construction of collective war memory. Like soldiers and adult civilians, young people initially used wartime language to attempt their transition to a new peacetime reality through the medium of the diary. Evacuated teenager Yoshihara Yukiko, upon hearing of the Allies' plans to execute Japan's military leadership, wrote:

> From here on out, many bad things may happen, but in order to continue to defend this country, they must be endured, our position regained, and the enemy wiped out. If we continued on like this, no resistance would be possible, we'd all be 'nuked', and the Japanese people would cease to exist. So, in order to make the great Japanese Empire first in the world, we must endure anything. I think that, if our science was advanced, this sort of tragedy wouldn't have happened, and I feel a terrible regret. From here on out, I will apply myself whole-heartedly to scientific research, and make Japan a country that won't be inferior to any other in science.

Yukiko's diary reveals, however, how quickly young people adjusted to the new order in Japan; less than one month later, she described how 'exciting' learning English was, wondered at 'what sort of faces Americans might have', and remarked at how other young people found learning English 'fun'.[46] Memoir writing by wartime youth emerged much later, and more slowly, than those by soldiers and even civilians, for reasons that are not yet entirely clear (but probably not limited to generational factors). Because young people are better 'victims' than adults (and certainly soldiers), recalling childhood and youth during the war often gets funnelled into a myopic narrative that focuses purely on suffering and the horrors of Allied strategic bombing. 'The town was a sea of flame', recalled Endō Ryūza, who was a fourteen-year-old boy in Shizuoka at the time, 'it was illuminated by fires, and there were flashes of the massive B-29s, which looked like demons'.[47] Superficially, they seem to be limited to tales of woe, but these accounts traverse an uneasy space between one-dimensional suffering and more complex expressions, such as resentment over 'lost youth' (*ushinawareta seishun*). Admittedly, most, if not all, memoirs contain a surfeit of content on the way in which the author suffered from wartime privations, such as a lack of fuel during the winter, having to forage for food and being forced to spend long periods away from parents; nevertheless, more complex issues such as class, education, gender and the rural–urban divide often reveal themselves to the diligent reader. As Takano Akimichi wrote, describing his evacuation experience, 'On a quiet night, you would hear the train whistle, and [think that] hopping on that train you could go home to Tokyo and see your parents, but you were completely broke'.[48] Teenagers forced to work in war industries noted who was able to buy tickets to go home on the holidays, and who had to stay in the dormitories, wrapped up in state-issued winter coats and eating drab cafeteria food. Memoirs of childhood and youth during World War Two have revealed a world within the war that was almost totally separate from that created by the adults around them. Fushimi Chizuko, after discovering the diary she kept as a ten-year-old evacuee, described in detail the terror she and other girls suffered under the tyranny of a bully whom they dubbed 'the Queen'.

> A society of children left in that abnormal situation created a 'twisted' world. What I am trying to stress is that, it isn't important who 'the Queen' was, or who was being bullied. That is the 'fear' present in a naturally arising society of children. I also think it is a reflection of the twisted society of adults at that time. The 'twist' here is World War Two. The war, in many forms, left a deep imprint on the people of that era.[49]

As the generation who lived through the war as adults passes away, or finds wartime memories are failing, the voice of 'lost youth' necessarily becomes dominant (until, of course, this generation succumbs to time as well). What the memoirs of young people show us is that their experience of the war was determined by their *understanding* of it, which was necessarily impeded by their incomplete development. Their world is therefore radically different from that of adults who lived through the war, and their accounts provide important details on food, entertainment and social relations that adults did not consider 'relevant' to a personal war record.

Finally, in a discussion of 'who remembers', it would be negligent to overlook the memoirs by non-Japanese people who experienced the war as serving members of the country's vast, multi-ethnic imperial institutions. By the time Allied strategic bombing campaigns started in earnest in November 1944, the Japanese people were in fact a minority within a vast and diverse empire, and even major cities in the home islands contained thousands of non-Japanese imperial subjects, but these individuals' memoirs are only recently becoming part of the collective story. First, the open discussion of sensitive topics such as 'comfort women' (*ianfu*) has prompted some Japanese to include descriptions of colonial subjects and victims of aggression into their memoirs.[50] More importantly, however, interest in the subjects' experiences, in their own words, has produced valuable memoirs in recent years. Taiwanese soldiers and nurses who served in the Japanese armed forces, for example, began writing memoirs in earnest in the 1980s, moving away from the war generation's critiques of Japan.[51] In some cases, the recollections of those who lived under imperialism can be controversial, including Taiwanese who want to view the Japanese period (1895–1945) positively.[52] Most of these memoirs are not published in Japanese, and some are sponsored by the Republic of China's government in Taiwan – especially since the rise of the Democratic Progressive Party and its pro-independence platform. Indeed, the complexities of post-war Taiwanese identity politics inevitably colour these accounts.[53] Xiao Jinhai, who was a volunteer (Ch. *zhiyuanbing*, Jp. *shiganhei*) for an anti-aircraft unit, recalled the fervour with which many young Taiwanese signed up to serve the empire. While at first the Japanese military feared desertion and treachery would arise in Taiwanese units, from 1941 the governor-general of Taiwan began recruiting 'patriotic youth' for 'volunteer training'.

> At the beginning of the recruitment, many Taiwanese youth feared they wouldn't be taken, and began writing blood oaths (Ch. *xueshu*, Jp. *kessho*) expressing their intent to volunteer for the armed forces. This environment was very intense. I read about it in the news, and then went to borrow a knife from the neighbours. That night, in secret, I cut my finger and used the blood to write 'Seven Lives for the Nation' (Ch. *qisheng baoguo*, Jp. *shichishō hōkoku*) (meaning I'd give seven [reincarnated] lives for the nation, which was a phrase I'd heard a lot in school). [...] My parents did not outwardly have any reaction because of the atmosphere of the time, but I think secretly they were worried because they didn't receive any Japanese education. When I think on it now, the education system the Japanese built was very effective. We were 'drugged' (*mazui*) by the Japanese, and I was no different.[54]

Other Taiwanese recall being more ambivalent about the benefits of empire. Wu Jinchuan was a peripatetic young woman who received a university education in Japan and took pride in sending for newly published books from America, 'so that I would always be ahead of the Japanese in critical texts'. Describing the Japanese surrender, and return of Taiwan to mainland China in 1945, Wu reinforced the link between Taiwan and mainland China: 'Half a century had passed since the island was taken from the Manchu Qing in 1895, and our Taiwanese brothers made many sacrifices during these years. In the end, however, we preserved the foundations of Chinese culture in Taiwan, and were returned to the embrace of our fatherland'.[55] Taiwanese accounts that discuss the benefits of empire are sold in Yasukuni's museum shop, showing how quickly these narratives are embraced by the right in Japan, but to associate those narratives with pro-imperialist views is a facile and false equivalency. In their proper (Taiwanese) context, these sorts of memoirs are rather arguments against union with the People's Republic of China, indications of Taiwan's unique history, and often politicised critiques of the Chinese Nationalist Party. In the end, Taiwanese memoirs of the imperial period have consistently engaged, consciously or not, with the complexities of post-war identity politics.

It was in iconic cities such as Nagasaki where Japan's largest domestic minority, Koreans, first made it clear that their memories were important to Japan's national remembrance. Korean memoirs have more assertively embraced the 'victim' narrative of being unwilling pawns in the machinations of the empire. As one Korean recalled, 'Where I lived, even in the Korean countryside, everywhere the mobilisation plans were carried out, and any man younger than 22 was conscripted, and any man older than that taken for labour. Gradually, all the men in the village disappeared'.[56] Koreans who served in the Japanese armed forces have a great number of ironic, and sad, tales to recount. One veteran described Korean soldiers' capture by Soviet forces in 1945:

> One afternoon we were resting when a Soviet officer was passing by on horseback. Immediately he began shouting something, took out a pistol from his belt, and, looking over the wounded POWs, fired two shots. Sitting next to Hirone was a Korean soldier named 'Kunimoto'.[57] The bullets pierced his chest and he fell to the ground covered in blood. He was from the same hometown [in Korea] as Hirone, and they used to tell stories about this nostalgic place. We weren't sure, but a subordinate of this officer might have been killed by a Japanese soldier, and this was some sort of revenge. Hirone said, 'Until this time, I had not felt the horror of what it meant to lose a war and become a prisoner'.[58]

Due in part to post-war Korean nationalism and the rise of the Mindan, Japan's largest domestic organisation in support of resident Koreans' rights, these memoirs are greatly concerned with the 'minority experience' within war, and Koreans' 'double victimisation'. Also, possibly as a consequence of being influenced by foreign discourses of multiculturalism, even Japanese memoirs have come to speak against the public's ignorance of former imperial subjects' suffering in Japan. Still, even before such narratives became vogue in Japan during the 1980s, the empire was not completely absent.[59] The atomic bomb-themed graphic novel, *Barefoot Gen* (serialised from 1973), included a Korean character surnamed Pak, who was forcibly brought to Japan with his father. Before the iconic *Gen*, Ishimure Michiko's *Chrysanthemums and Nagasaki* (1968) also highlighted the contradiction inherent in the Korean case: on the one hand, the Koreans shared with Japanese residents the experience of aerial bombardment but, on the other hand, they were treated, even in death, as second class citizens:

> After the atomic bomb fell, the bodies of the Koreans were the last ones to be collected. [...] The eyeballs in their heads were devoured by the crows. The crows came from all directions to eat the eyes. You might think, Oh! The bodies are moving! They're moving! But this was due to the maggots. [...] There were 17, 18 year old Korean girls, part of the 'Do or Die Units' (*teishintai*), who were brought to Japan. I remember one, with that thing hanging outside her vagina, from inside her uterus, walking. Naked. She probably died right away. [...] The Korean girls of the atomic bomb. I don't think anyone helped them.[60]

In this sense, these stories are similar to non-white Americans' descriptions of their difficulties during World War Two, simultaneously fighting both the enemies of America and discrimination at home – although Koreans in Japan do not have any 'victory' to which they can lay claim.[61] As such, the nuances and contradictions in Taiwanese accounts, alongside the resentful ironies of Korean narratives, must be included in the overall examination of the 'Japanese' experience of World War Two. Otherwise, we are at risk of reifying the teleological narrative of the post-war nation-state, which emphasises the persistence of a purely 'Japanese' community even through the vicissitudes of the modern imperial period.

COMMUNITIES, NARRATIVES AND RESPONSIBILITY

The network of NGO social organisations, the state and the mass media have generated a cornucopia of memoirs on the World War Two experience.

Within social organisations alone, divisions between peace museums and veterans' groups, and furthermore divisions within those divisions, demonstrate the ongoing importance of community structure in determining the content of collective memory. Although there are thousands of memoirs about the war years, as outlined above, there are arguably four important categories to bear in mind when approaching this seemingly inchoate mass of text, namely: memoirs by veterans, civilians, juveniles and non-Japanese imperial subjects (although accounts in this final category are regrettably few in number). The act of creating categories of memoir-writing subjects requires justification, however, because it necessarily excludes other narratives. There are two good reasons for emphasising these specific differences: the way that they structure responses to historical memory issues, and the impact they have had on the continuance of wartime discourse in descriptions of the past.

First, the division between soldiers and civilians, Japanese and non-Japanese, juvenile and adult are crucial because they were exposed to categorically different wartime experiences. This ultimately bears on their views of vituperative post-war debates such as those over 'war responsibility'. Combat veterans have been forced to acknowledge their direct participation in wars of aggression, even 'war crimes' and 'atrocities' – in some cases they understood this as part of the rigorous process of 'critical self-reflection' (*hansei*) that they learned in the barracks. In the midst of debates over the emperor's 'war crimes', Watanabe Kiyo, a former sailor, reflected on the relationship between politics, memory and responsibility:

> I was betrayed by the emperor. Tricked. But I think that being fooled is my weakness. [...] What was betrayed was how I [allowed] myself to believe in the emperor in *that way*. It wasn't the actual emperor – I was betrayed by the false image of the emperor that I had embraced inside of myself. So, you might say that I betrayed myself. I fooled myself.[62]

Adult civilians who lived through the war must understand their complicity in more nuanced ways, including the support they gave to (what one might call 'fascist') social organisations that underpinned the state's mobilisation campaigns, such as the Women's National Defence Association (*Kokubō fujinkai*).[63] Former imperial subjects who served the state (including, as Tomiyama Ichirō argued, Okinawans), will agonise over their status both as victims of imperialism and active participants in the creation of a 'Japanese' modernity that included total war.[64] Even more perplexing are memoirs of those who endured the war as juveniles. Should they hold themselves accountable for embracing wartime belligerence and ultra-nationalism, or completely absolve themselves of the need for 'critical self-reflection' and other acts of self-examination simply because they had not yet reached their eighteenth birthday by 1945? For those who have only vague memories and scanty records of wartime childhood, it will be difficult to determine how far the war influenced their views, and how much of their memoirs are simply empty reproductions of post-war memory discourse. While a working class veteran and a university-educated veteran will have radically different ways of expressing themselves in writing, they will both face, in their memoirs, similar questions of 'responsibility', but will do so in a manner radically different from children who were evacuated to the countryside.

Second, these categories, crude as they may be, expose important divisions in the persistence of wartime discourse in post-war memoirs. For most civilians, juvenile or adult, the ability to (re)create textualised memory in a manner that suits post-war discourse appears to be much easier than it was for veterans. Those who were trained to be soldiers had to imbibe a rich and specialised vocabulary for describing battlefield experience. Diaries, in particular, and reportage were a staple of soldiers' reading materials during the war. Soldiers consumed these texts while experiencing the war itself and, in some cases, writing about it in their personal documents. As I have argued elsewhere, this imbued wartime rhetoric with multiple claims to truthful representation, and consequently the language was difficult for veterans to surrender in the post-war period. Civilians were unaccustomed to writing about war to begin with, and were exposed over a longer period of time in the post-war era to professional writers describing, for example, the bombing of Japan's major cities. The gradual development of a 'victim narrative', in which the Japanese people were the unwitting pawns in a game played by military and political elites, may also explain why those writing civilian memoirs are more likely to compose texts that mirror one another in style and content.

Troublesome memoirs written by those who experienced the war as combat soldiers, children and non-Japanese subjects are therefore perhaps the most important 'monkey wrench' in the gears of any monolithic narrative about the 'Japanese experience of World War Two'. This does not mean, however, that we must continually divide narratives until we reach the ultimate atomisation of history to the individual subject, or text; these divisions should rather encourage broader transnational comparisons within these categories. How do Taiwanese and Korean memoirs of fighting for Japan compare with those by African American servicemen during World War Two or, for that matter, Japanese Americans? Is there a transnational history of childhood and youth during times of total war? How are veterans' narratives received in different national contexts, and what explains these differences? The future study of memoir writing need not be transnational simply to serve academic fashion, however. Comparison of these accounts reveals what is fundamentally 'ethnic' about a Korean's experience of serving the Japanese empire, or which aspects of childhood, specifically, shape later memory of the war. Only the comparative approach, particularly between the European and Asia-Pacific theatre, will expose what was truly global about the 'World War', as well as the textual practices involved in its memorialisation. This will help eschew the construction of a purely 'Japanese' memory of the war in favour of one that elevates individual narratives above being simple cogs in the machine of a national(ised) war memory.

NOTES

1. Jonathan E. Abel, *Redacted: The Archives of Censorship in Transwar Japan* (Berkeley, 2015). Also see Lee Pennington, *Casualties of History: Wounded Japanese Servicemen and the Second World War* (Ithaca, 2015), 163–194.
2. For example, see the collection of soldiers' stories in the National Institute of Defense Studies [NIDS]: Shina: Daitōa sensō nisshi kaisōroku 102–104: Kankō keibi shireikan [Hankou / Hankow Security Command], *Koe naki sensen heitan monogatari* [Barracks Tales from a Front Line without Voices]. Launched on 9 February 1942, the author(s) continued composing the collection of battlefield reflections into 1958.
3. Aaron William Moore, 'Pluralism and the Problem with Collective Memory: Japanese Peace and War Museums in a Comparative Context', in Nicholas Martin, Pierre Purseigle and Tim Haughton (eds), *Aftermath: Legacies and Memories of War in Europe, 1918–1945–1989* (Farnham, 2013), 61–84.
4. On Siberian captives and their communities, for example, see Andrew Barshay, *The Gods Left First: The Captivity and Repatriation of Japanese POWs in Northeast Asia, 1945-1956.* (Berkeley, 2013), and Sherzod Muminov, 'Eleven Winters of Discontent: The Siberian Internment and the Making of the New Japan, 1945–1956', PhD Diss. (Cambridge, 2016).
5. For more on this collection, see Midori Kawashima, 'The Records of the Former Japanese Army Concerning the Japanese Occupation of the Philippines', *Journal of Southeast Asian Studies* 27(1) (1996), 124–31.
6. NIDS does have a category entitled *Bunko: kaisōroku*, which is dedicated to memoirs, but in the archival areas dedicated to army or naval forces, China or Pacific theatre, it is clear that memoirs and diaries, personal and official documents are mixed. For the war in China, the relevant collection is entitled 'China: Diary and Memoir Records' (*Shina: nisshi kaisōroku*), which encompasses 244 documents from multiple genres. For example, folders 35–37 are Kinoshita

Yū's China battlefront diaries from 1 March 1941 to 2 January 1944, but folder 38 is Kurose Heiichi's memoir of the 133rd Infantry Regiment's attack on Hengyang in 1944.
7. The author's brother had apparently said, on the battlefield, 'This is one place I'll never visit again'. Takamatsu heiwa kinen shiryōkan [Takamatsu City Peace Prayer Museum]: Anonymous, 'Sensō aishi' [The War, a History of Sadness], 1985. The brother was deeply upset about being drafted, because he had only just been married. He never returned home. This document was composed based on a speech given at the Takamatsu Civic Center, before the museum was established, during which 'everyone cried'.
8. See the introduction to Fukuma Yoshiaki, *'Sensō taiken' no sengoshi: Sedai, kyōyō, ideorogī* [A Post-war History of 'War Experience': Generation, Education and Ideology] (Tokyo, 1990).
9. Shizuoka heiwa shiryōkan [Shizuoka Peace Museum]: B1-0368: This folder contains the poetry and diaries of a Japanese nurse who was imprisoned on the Philippines after the war's end.
10. See the conversation between Ōya Sōichi, Yokoyama Ryūichi, Nakayama Yoshihide, Ibuse Masaji and Ima Hidemi entitled 'Bunshi jūgun' [Writers off to War], *Nihon hyōron* (September 1950).
11. Takahashi Saburō, *Senkimono wo yomu: Sensō taiken to sengo Nihon shakai* [Reading War Narratives: Wartime Experience and Post-war Japanese Society] (Kyoto, 1988).
12. Takahashi Yoshinori, 'Senyūkai wo tsukuru hitobito' [The Men Who Make Veterans' Groups], in Kyōdō kenkyū (ed.), *Sen'yūkai* [Veterans' Groups] (Tokyo, 2005).
13. Gerald Figal, 'How to *jibunshi*: Making and Marketing Self-histories of Shōwa among the Masses in Post-war Japan', *The Journal of Asian Studies* 55(4) (1996), 902–33.
14. In addition to Ritsumeikan's museum, Wadatsumi-kai (for fallen student soldiers, Nihon senbotsu gakusei kinenkai) and the Iwate Prefecture Rural Culture Preservation Society (Iwate-ken nōson bunka kondankai) all participated in organising the event. These three organisations have independently published memoirs over the decades.
15. Working Group for the Exhibit, *'Heiwa no seiki he' watashi no messēji: 'Isho / ihinten' wo mite* [My Message for the Age of Peace: Looking at 'Objects and Texts Left Behind'] (Osaka, 2002), 45.
16. The mass media's ability to stir up controversy may to some degree explain the growth of memoir and diary publications beginning in the 1970s, as this was the beginning of the debate over Japanese 'massacres' in China. Bob Tadashi Wakabayashi, 'The Nanking 100-Man Killing Contest: War Guilt amid Fabricated Illusions, 1971–1975', *Journal of Japanese Studies* 26(2) (2000), 307–40.
17. A brief account, in English, on memoirs of note up to 1951 is offered in Nobutaka Ike, 'Japanese Memoirs – Reflections of the Recent Past', *Pacific Affairs* 24(2) (1951), 185–90.

18. One of the earliest, and most famous, oral histories of Japanese soldiers abroad was Kanki Haruo's controversial *Sankō: Nihonjin no Chūgoku ni okeru sensō hanzai no kokuhaku* [The 'Three Alls': The War Crimes and Confessions of Japanese in China] (Tokyo, 1957). Donald Gillin and Charles Etter also described some early post-war memoirs by Japanese who served in China both during and after war, which were unusual accounts for the time: Gillin and Etter, 'Staying On: Japanese Soldiers and Civilians in China, 1945–1949', *The Journal of Asian Studies* 42(3) (1983), 497–518.
19. Hamada Shōtarō, Introduction, *Iwate-ken kyōshi shōhei no kiroku* [Records of Local Servicemen in Iwate Prefecture] (Morioka, 1978). Hamada was the head of the Iwate Prefecture Bereaved Families Association (*izokukai*), but the publication was sponsored by the prefecture's Social Welfare Department.
20. For a detailed discussion of the *shishōsetsu*, see Edward Fowler, *The Rhetoric of Confession:* Shishōsetsu *in Early Twentieth Century Japanese Fiction* (Berkeley, 1988).
21. Japanese authors' mixture of life-writing and fiction is ubiquitous and widely recognised. David Stahl's study of Ōoka also combines biography (even psychoanalysis) with the critical examination of his literature: *The Burdens of Survival:* Ōoka *Shōhei's Writings on the Pacific War* (Honolulu, 2003). Also see Keiko McDonald, 'Ooka's Examination of the Self in *A POW's Memoirs*', *The Journal of the Association of Teachers of Japanese* 21(1) (1987), 15–36.
22. Philip Gabriel, 'The Alphabet of Trauma: Shimao Toshio and the Narrative of Dreams', *Journal of the Association of Teachers of Japanese* 30(2) (1996), 23–54.
23. Aaron William Moore, 'The Problem of Changing Language Communities: Veterans and Memory Writing in China, Taiwan, and Japan', *Modern Asian Studies* 45(2) (2011), 399–429.
24. Kimura Hisao, notes written in the margins of a philosophy textbook, in Wadatsumi-kai (ed.), *Heiwa e no isho / ihinten: Senbotsu seinen to no taiwa* (Tokyo, 2002), 27 [probably in early 1946]. The textbook was *Tetsugaku tsūron* (Tokyo, 1933), by Tanabe Hajime, a founder of the Kyoto School of philosophy; this is comparable, in some respects, to a pacifist German POW writing in a philosophical text by Martin Heidegger.
25. Lori Watt, *When Empire Comes Home: Repatriation and Reintegration in Post-war Japan* (Cambridge, MA: 2010).
26. Iwatani Hiromitsu, 'Shūsenji Chūgoku de no omoide' [Memories of Ending the War in China], in Fukushima kenritsu hakubutsukan [Fukushima Prefectural Museum] (ed.), *Senjika no Fukushima* [Fukushima in Wartime] (Aizu-Wakamatsu, 1996), 25.
27. NIDS: Shina: Daitōa sensō nisshi kaisōbun 38: Hirose Heiichi, 'Kasugai to jūken: Kōyō [Hengyang] kōryaku to hohei dai-133 rentai' [Bayonets and the Ties that Bind: The 133rd and the Attack on Hengyang], introduction.
28. For an interesting example of an incomplete memoir 'in progress', see NIDS: Rikkū nisshi kaisōroku 28: Ikeda Masahiro, 'Shuki' [Notebook Diary], which appears to have been composed after his repatriation, but while the war was still ongoing. Compare this to the more famous published diary by Azuma

Shirō, *Azuma Shirō nikki* [Azuma Shirō's Diary] (Kumamoto, 2001), which was also written after his return from China, but before 1945.

29. The fusion of reportage and field diary writing that I describe in my other work persisted into the post-war memoirs (especially if the authors were former officers): Takamatsu heiwa kinenkan: Suruga Hisahiro, *Kairin sakusen: Aru kaishikan no kiroku* [The Battle for Guilin: A Lower-Echelon Officer's Record] (Takamatsu, 1973). NIDS: Shina: Daitōa sensō nisshi kaisōbun 50: Kobayashi Hiro, 'Kō hoku-nan [Jiang bei-nan] senmetsu sakusengo gunki' [A War Record Following the Battle of Annihilation in the North and South Yangtze River Region], 9 May 1943 to 10 May 1944. Written as a diary, the language, including referring to fallen servicemen as 'revered hero-spirits' who 'find eternal rest', is anachronistic for a memoir, but this document shows evidence of being heavily edited and rewritten for coherency and readability. Some documents appear to be recopied wartime records, however, such as NIDS: Shina: Daitōa sensō nisshi kaisōbun 62: Shimane Masaji, 'Ichigō sakusen dai-11-gun no tōshi' [Commanding Forces of the 11th Army during the Ichigo Offensive], 24 March 1944 to 15 September 1944.

30. Noguchi Fumio, *Kaigun nikki: Saikakyūhei no kiroku* [A Navy Diary: Records of a Sailor of the Lowest Rank] (Tokyo, 1982), 226.

31. See Aaron William Moore, 'The Chimera of Privacy: Reading Self-Discipline in Japanese Diaries from the Second World War (1937–1945)', *The Journal of Asian Studies* 68(1) (2009), 165–98.

32. The term 'language community' refers to Ludwig Wittgenstein's refutation of the 'private language' argument, as featured in his later philosophy (*Philosophical Investigations*). I explain my use of this term in Moore, 'The Problem of Changing Language Communities'.

33. Hamada, 116.

34. Hamazono Shigeyoshi, *Suiheisen: Soromon kara Okinawa tokkō made reisen / kanbō tajōin no kiroku* [Ocean Horizon: A Naval Zero Pilot's Record: From the Solomons to the Okinawa Kamikaze] (Chiran, 1998), 72.

35. Hamada, 975.

36. John W. Dower, *Embracing Defeat: Japan in the Wake of World War Two* (New York, 1999).

37. Kinga Setsuko, 'Ane ni okuru taikenki' [A Memoir for My Elder Sister], in Sumida-ku [Sumida Ward Government] (ed.), *Kataritsugō heiwa e no negai: Tōkyō daikūshū Sumida taiken kirokushū* [Let the Story Continue, A Wish for Peace: A Collection of Records on the Great Tokyo Firebombing Campaign in Sumida Ward] (Tokyo, 1995), 168–175.

38. Yoshizawa Hisako, 'Diary', in Samuel Yamashita (ed.), *Leaves from an Autumn of Emergencies: Selections from the Wartime Diaries of Ordinary Japanese* (Honolulu, 2005), 218.

39. Watanabe Kōhei, 'Tasukatta yorokobi wo shinbutsu ni kansha' [I Thank the Gods and Buddhas for the Joy of Survival], in Sumida-ku, *Kataritsugō*, 267.

40. Endō Naoe, 'Tansu ya ningyō wo hitome mite', 20.

41. Murai Akira, 'Fubo no kunō' [The Mental Anguish of the Parents], in Fukushima kenritsu hakubutsukan [Fukushima Prefectural Museum] (ed.), *Senjika no Fukushima* [Fukushima in Wartime] (Aizu-Wakamatsu, 1996), 37–38. Opposition to conscription in Japan has existed from the very beginning of the institution: Stephen Vlastos, 'Opposition Movements in Early Meiji', in Marius B. Jansen (ed.), *The Cambridge History of Japan*, 6 vols (Cambridge, 1988), v. 370–71.
42. Tanaka Junko, 'Watashi no senchū, sengo' [My War, My Post-war], in Higuchi Mieko and Yokota Fusako (eds.), *Ano hi, ano toki: Hibakusha taikenki* [That Day, That Hour: Memoirs of the Atomic Bomb Victims], 7th ed. (Nagasaki, 1996), 406.
43. See especially Lori Watt's new book on the subject of 'returnees' (*hikiagesha*) from Japan's former empire: Watt, *When Empire Comes Home: Repatriation and Reintegration in Post-war Japan* (Cambridge, MA, 2009).
44. Barak Kushner, *The Thought War: Japanese Imperial Propaganda* (Honolulu, 2006).
45. Kameda Kiyoko, 'Watashi to kodomo-tachi' [The Children and I], in Toshima kuritsu kyōdo shiryōkan [Toshima Ward Local History Museum] (ed.), *Toshima-ku no shūdan gakudō sokai shiryōshū (1): Nikki, shokan-hen I – Jishū kokumin gakkō* [Toshima Ward Student Group Evacuation Document Collection (1): Diaries, Correspondence I – The Jishū State School] (Tokyo, 1990), 92, 134.
46. Yoshihara Yukiko, 'Nikki' [Diary], 15 August, 4 September 1945, in Toshima kuritsu kyōdo shiryōkan [Toshima Ward Local History Museum] (ed.), *Toshima-ku no shūdan gakudō sokai shiryōshū (3): Nikki, shokan-hen III – Nagasaki dai-2 kokumin gakkō (sono 1)* [Toshima Ward Student Group Evacuation Document Collection (3): Diaries, Correspondence II – Nagasaki #2 State School (Part 1)] (Tokyo, 1992), 146, 153–54.
47. Endō Ryūza, 'B-29 chōryō' [Invasion of the B-29s], in Shizuoka heiwa shiryōkan wo tsukuru-kai [Society to Create a Shizuoka Peace Museum], *Shizuoka-shi kūshū taikenga*, 16.
48. Takano Akimichi, 'Gakudō sokai kaikoroku' [A Memoir of Student Evacuations], in Toshima kuritsu kyōdo shiryōkan [Toshima Ward Local History Museum], *Toshima-ku no shūdan gakudō sokai shiryōshū (1)*, 138.
49. Fushimi Chizuko, '10-nin no sekai' [A World of Ten People], in Toshima kuritsu kyōdo shiryōkan [Toshima Ward Local History Museum] (ed.), *Toshima-ku no shūdan gakudō sokai shiryōshū (2): Nikki, shokan-hen II – Nagasaki dai-5 kokumin gakkō (sono 1)* [Toshima Ward Student Group Evacuation Document Collection (2): Diaries, Correspondence II – Nagasaki #5 State School (Part 1)] (Tokyo, 1991), 122.
50. Inoue Yoshio, *Jūgun ianfu datta anata he* [To You, a Former Comfort Woman] (Kyoto, 1993).
51. Hui-yu Caroline Ts'ai (ed.), *Zouguo liangge shidai de ren: Taiji Ribenbing* [Those Who Walked through Two Eras: Taiwanese Soldiers in the Japanese Army] (Taipei, 1997). Not all of these publications take a critical view of the empire: see H. Chen, *Taiwanjin jūgun kangofu tsuisōki* [Memories of a Taiwanese Military

Nurse] (Tokyo, 2002). Still, the presence of sex workers of various ethnicities was hardly a secret during the war, so the larger question is why they suddenly disappeared after 1945. See the materials in Kurahashi Masanao's work, such as *Jūgun ianfu mondai no rekishiteki kenkyū: Baishunfu-kei to seitekidorei-kei* [Historical Research on the Comfort Women Question: The Sex Worker Model and the Sex Slave Model] (Tokyo, 1994).

52. Positive views of Japanese imperialism are sometimes correlated with calls for Taiwanese independence from mainland China, as in Wang Yude, *'Shōwa' wo ikita Taiwan seinen* [A Taiwanese Youth Living in Shōwa Japan] (Tokyo, 2011). This publisher, Sōshisha, has produced other 'pro-Japanese' (*shin-Nichi*) publications by former colonial subjects, which has led to some criticism. See also Kim Wan-so, *Shin-Nichi-ha no tame no benmei* [A Defence for the Pro-Japan Faction] (Tokyo, 2002).

53. In English publications, Allen Chun and Leo T.S. Ching have outlined the complexity in Taiwanese identity particularly well: Allen Chun, 'From Nationalism to Nationalizing: Cultural Imagination and State Formation in Post-war Taiwan', *The Australian Journal of Chinese Affairs* 31 (1994), 49–69; Allen Chun, 'Fuck Chineseness: On the Ambiguities of Ethnicity as Culture as Identity', *boundary 2* 23(2) (1996), 111–38; Leo T.S. Ching, 'Give Me Japan and Nothing Else! Postcoloniality, Identity, and the Traces of Colonialism', *South Atlantic Quarterly* 99(4) (2000), 763–88; and, especially, Leo T.S. Ching, *Becoming 'Japanese': Colonial Taiwan and the Politics of Identity Formation* (Berkeley, 2001).

54. 'Xiao Jinhai xiansheng fangwen jilu' [A Record of Interviews with Xiao Jinhai], conducted by Caroline Hui-yu Ts'ai from 8 August to 21 September 1996, edited by Wu Lingqing, in Ts'ai, *Zouguo liangge shidai de ren*, 94. Although this is described as an oral history interview, it is presented as a memoir. It is unknown from the publication the extent to which the interviewers have structured the narrative for Xiao.

55. Wu Dashao et al. (eds), *Riju shiqi Taiwanren fu dalu jingyan* [Taiwanese Experiences in Mainland China during the Japanese Occupation] (Taipei, 1994), 132, 135.

56. Hiroshima-ken Chōsenjin hibakusha kyōgikai (ed.), *Shiroi chogori no hibakusha* [The Atomic Bomb Victims Who Wore White *Chogori*], reprinted in Cho T'agi, 'Zainichi chōsenjin / Kankokujin hibakusha' [Korean Victims of the Atomic Bomb], in Li Chong-yang and Kim Yong-gwŏn (eds), *Zainichi Chōsen / Kankokujin* [Koreans in Japan], 2nd ed. (Tokyo, 1986), 157.

57. During the later period of occupation, colonial authorities put pressure on Koreans to adopt Japanese names (*sōshi kaimei*). For a summary of assimilation policies regarding Korea and Taiwan, see Wan-yao Chou, 'The *Kōminka* Movement in Taiwan and Korea: Comparisons and Interpretations', in Peter Duus, Ramon H. Myers and Mark R. Peattie (eds), *The Japanese Wartime Empire, 1931–1945* (Princeton, 1966), 40–70.

58. Hayashi Eidai, *Wasurerareta Chōsenjin kōgun heishi: Shiberia dassōki* [The Forgotten Korean Soldiers of the Imperial Army: A Record of Fleeing Siberia] (Fukuoka,

1996), 67. Utsumi Aiko, *Chōsenjin 'kōgun' heishi-tachi no sensō* [World War Two Korean Soldiers in the 'Imperial Army'] (Tokyo, 1991); and Higuchi Yūichi, *Kōgun heishi ni sareta Chōsenjin* [Koreans Turned into Imperial Soldiers] (Tokyo, 1991). Utsumi, who lived through the war as a small child, has been very active in promoting the textualisation of Korean memories in Japan.
59. As early as 1977, Kim Kwang-yŏl found Japanese 'trainers' for Korean forced labourers (*kyōsei renkō*) who freely offered interviews and memoirs of their experiences: Kim, *Ashi de mita Chifuku: Chōsenjin tankō rōdō no kiroku*, [Seeing Chikuhō on Foot: Records of Korean Coal Labour] (Tokyo, 2004), 269–70.
60. Ishimure Michiko, *Kiku to Nagasaki* [Chrysanthemums and Nagasaki] (1968), reprinted in Shinshū Ōtani-ha, *Hikaku / hisen no negai ni ikiru* [Living the Wish for Anti-Nuclear, Anti-War Pacifism] (Nagasaki, 2001), 5.
61. Ronald Takaki, *Double Victory: A Multicultural History of Americans in World War II* (New York, 1995).
62. Quoted in Fukuma Yoshiaki, *Sensō taiken' no sengoshi*, 212. Emphasis is Watanabe's.
63. Fujii Tadatoshi, *Kokubō fujinkai* [The National Women's Defence League] (Tokyo, 1985).
64. Tomiyama Ichirō, *Senjō no kioku* [Memory of the Battlefield] (Tokyo, 1995).

BIBLIOGRAPHY

Memoirs and Diaries

Aiko, Utsumi. *Chōsenjin 'kōgun' heishi-tachi no sensō* [World War Two Korean Soldiers in the 'Imperial Army']. Tokyo: Iwanami shoten, 1991.

Akimichi, Takano. 'Gakudō sokai kaikoroku' [A Memoir of Student Evacuations], in Toshima kuritsu kyōdo shiryōkan [Toshima Ward Local History Museum] (ed.), *Toshima-ku no shūdan gakudō sokai shiryōshū (1): Nikki, shokan-hen I – Jishū kokumin gakkō* [Toshima Ward Student Group Evacuation Document Collection (1): Diaries, Correspondence I – The Jishū State School] (Tokyo: Toshima-ku kyōiku iinkai, 1990), pp. 137–141.

Akira, Murai. 'Fubo no kunō' [The Mental Anguish of the Parents], in Fukushima kenritsu hakubutsukan [Fukushima Prefectural Museum] (ed.), *Senjika no Fukushima* [Fukushima in Wartime] (Aizu-Wakamatsu: Self-published, 1996), pp. 37–38.

Azuma, Shirō. *Wa ga Nankin puratōn* [My Nanjing Platoon]. Tokyo: Kiyoki Shoten, 1996.

Azuma, Shirō. *Azuma Shirō nikki* [Azuma Shirō's Diary]. Kumamoto: Kumamoto shuppan bunkakai, 2001.

Chen, H. *Taiwanjin jūgun kangofu tsuisōki* [Memories of a Taiwanese Military Nurse]. Tokyo: Tendensha, 2002.

Chizuko, Fushimi. '10-nin no sekai' [A World of Ten People], in Toshima kuritsu kyōdo shiryōkan [Toshima Ward Local History Museum] (ed.), *Toshima-ku no shūdan gakudō sokai shiryōshū (2): Nikki, shokan-hen II – Nagasaki dai-5 kokumin gakkō (sono 1)* [Toshima Ward Student Group Evacuation Document Collection (2): Diaries, Correspondence II – Nagasaki #5 State School (Part 1)] (Tokyo: Toshima-ku kyōiku iinkai, 13 March 1991), pp. 117–124.

Dashao, Wu et al. (eds). *Riju shiqi Taiwanren fu dalu jingyan* [Taiwanese Experiences in Mainland China during the Japanese Occupation]. Taipei: Zhongyang yanjiuyuan, Jindaishi yanjiusuo, 30 June 1994.

Eidai, Hayashi. *Wasurerareta Chōsenjin kōgun heishi: Shiberia dassōki* [The Forgotten Korean Soldiers of the Imperial Army: A Record of Fleeing Siberia]. Fukuoka: Azusashoin, 1996.

Fumio, Noguchi. *Kaigun nikki: Saikakyūhei no kiroku* [A Navy Diary: Records of a Sailor of the Lowest Rank]. Tokyo: Bungei shunju, 1982.

Hachiya, Michihiko. *Hiroshima Diary: The Journal of a Japanese Physician*, trans. Warner Wells. Chapel Hill: University of North Carolina Press, 1995.

Haruo, Kanki. *Sankō: Nihonjin no Chūgoku ni okeru sensō hanzai no kokuhaku* [The 'Three Alls': The War Crimes and Confessions of Japanese in China]. Tokyo: Kōbunsha, 1957.

Hiromitsu, Iwatani. 'Shūsenji Chūgoku de no omoide' [Memories of Ending the War in China], in Fukushima kenritsu hakubutsukan [Fukushima Prefectural Museum] (ed.), *Senjika no Fukushima* [Fukushima in Wartime] (Aizu-Wakamatsu: Self-published, 1996), p. 25.

Hisahiro, Suruga. *Kairin sakusen: Aru kaishikan no kiroku* [The Battle for Guilin: A Lower-Echelon Officer's Record]. Takamatsu: Self-published, 1973.

Hisako, Yoshizawa. 'Diary', in Samuel Yamashita (ed.), *Leaves from an Autumn of Emergencies: Selections from the Wartime Diaries of Ordinary Japanese* (Honolulu: University of Hawaii Press, 2005), pp. 191–220.

Ichirō, Tomiyama. *Senjō no kioku* [Memory of the Battlefield]. Tokyo: Nihon Keizai hyōronsha, 1995.

Junko, Tanaka. 'Watashi no senchū, sengo' [My War, My Post-war], in Higuchi Mieko and Yokota Fusako (eds), *Ano hi, ano toki: Hibakusha taikenki* [That Day, That Hour: Memoirs of the Atomic Bomb Victims], 7th ed. (Nagasaki: Kyū-Nagasaki kenritsu Nagasaki kōtō jogakkō 42-kaisei, 1996), pp. 102–104.

Kimura, Hisao, notes written in the margins of a philosophy textbook, in Wadatsumi-kai (ed.), *Heiwa e no isho / ihinten: Senbotsu seinen to no taiwa* [A Testament to Peace / Exhibit: A Dialogue with War Youth Who Have Perished]. Tokyo: Self-published, 2002, p. 27.

Hamazono, Shigeyoshi. *Suiheisen: Soromon kara Okinawa tokkō made reisen / kanbō tajōin no kiroku* [Ocean Horizon: A Naval Zero Pilot's Record: From the Solomons to the Okinawa Kamikaze]. Chiran: Chiran tokkō heiwa kaikan, 1998.

Kiyoko, Kameda. 'Watashi to kodomo-tachi' [The Children and I], in Toshima kuritsu kyōdo shiryōkan [Toshima Ward Local History Museum] (ed.), *Toshima-ku no shūdan gakudō sokai shiryōshū (1): Nikki, shokan-hen I – Jishū kokumin gakkō*

[Toshima Ward Student Group Evacuation Document Collection (1): Diaries, Correspondence I – The Jishū State School] (TokyoToshima-ku kyōiku iinkai, 1990), pp. 91–136.

Kōhei, Watanabe. 'Tasukatta yorokobi wo shinbutsu ni kansha' [I Thank the Gods and Buddhas for the Joy of Survival], in Sumida-ku [Sumida Ward Government] (ed.), *Kataritsugō heiwa e no negai: Tōkyō daikūshū Sumida taiken kirokushū* [Let the Story Continue, A Wish for Peace: A Collection of Records on the Great Tokyo Firebombing Campaign in Sumida Ward] (Tokyo: Self-published, 1995), pp. 266–269.

Michiko, Ishimure. *Kiku to Nagasaki* [Chrysanthemums and Nagasaki]. 1968. Reprinted in Shinshū Ōtani-ha, *Hikaku / hisen no negai ni ikiru* [Living the Wish for Anti-Nuclear, Anti-War Pacifism] (Nagasaki: Self-published, 2001), pp. 5–10.

Nagai, Takashi. *The Bells of Nagasaki*, trans. William Johnston. Tokyo: Kodansha International, 1984.

Naoe, Endō. 'Tansu ya ningyō wo hitome mite' [With a Single Glance at the Doll and the Dresser], in Shizuoka heiwa shiryōkan wo tsukuru-kai [Society to Create a Shizuoka Peace Museum] (ed.), *Shizuoka-shi kūshū taikenga: Kūshūka / ikinuita watashi* [Portraits of the Shizuoka Air Raids: I Survived under Bombing], 3rd ed. (Shizuoka, Self-published, 2003), p. 20.

Ooka, Shōhei. *Fires on the Plain*, trans. Ivan Morris. Boston: Tuttle Publishing, 2001.

Ryūza, Endō. 'B-29 chōryō' [Invasion of the B-29s], in Shizuoka heiwa shiryōkan wo tsukuru-kai [Society to Create a Shizuoka Peace Museum] (ed.), *Shizuoka-shi kūshū taikenga: Kūshūka / ikinuita watashi* [Portraits of the Shizuoka Air Raids: I Survived under Bombing], 3rd ed. (Shizuoka: Self-published, 2003), p. 16.

Saburō, Takahashi. *Senkimono wo yomu: Sensō taiken to sengō Nihon shakai* [Reading War Narratives: Wartime Experience and Post-war Japanese Society]. Kyoto: Akademia shuppankai, 1988.

Setsuko, Kinga. 'Ane ni okuru taikenki' [A Memoir for My Elder Sister], in Sumida-ku [Sumida Ward Government] (ed.), *Kataritsugō heiwa e no negai: Tōkyō daikūshū Sumida taiken kirokushū* [Let the Story Continue, A Wish for Peace: A Collection of Records on the Great Tokyo Firebombing Campaign in Sumida Ward] (Tokyo: Self-published, 1995), pp. 168–175.

Shōtarō, Hamada. *Iwate-ken kyōshi shōhei no kiroku* [Records of Local Servicemen in Iwate Prefecture]. Morioka: Iwate Prefecture Society for the Records of Local Servicemen, 1978.

Tadatoshi, Fujii. *Kokubō fujinkai* [The National Women's Defence League]. Tokyo: Iwanami shoten, 1985.

T'agi, Cho. 'Zainichi chōsenjin / Kankokujin hibakusha' [Korean Victims of the Atomic Bomb], in Li Chong-yang and Kim Yong-gwŏn (eds), *Zainichi Chōsen / Kankokujin* [Koreans in Japan], 2nd ed. (Tokyo: Sanichi shobō, 1986).

Toyoda, Soemu. *Saigo no teikoku kaigun*. Tokyo: Seikai no Nihonsha, 1950.

Ts'ai, Hui-yu Caroline (ed.). *Zouguo liangge shidai de ren: Taiji Ribenbing* [Those Who Walked through Two Eras: Taiwanese Soldiers in the Japanese Army]. Taipei: Zhongyang yanjiuyuan Taiwan-shi yanjiusuo choubeichu, 1997.

Wan-so, Kim. *Shin-Nichi-ha no tame no benmei* [A Defence for the Pro-Japan Faction]. Tokyo: Sōshisha, 2002.

Yoshiaki, Fukuma. *'Sensō taiken' no sengoshi: Sedai, kyōyō, ideorogī* [A Post-war History of 'War Experience': Generation, Education, and Ideology]. Tokyo: Daigaku Shuppankai, 1990.

Yoshida Mitsuru. *Requiem for the Battleship Yamato*, trans. Richard H. Minear. Annapolis: Naval Institute Press, 1985.

Yoshinori, Takahashi. 'Senyūkai wo tsukuru hitobito' [The Men Who Make Veterans' Groups], in Kyōdō kenkyū (ed.), *Sen'yūkai* [Veterans' Groups] (Tokyo: Impakuto shuppankai, 2005).

Yoshio, Inoue. *Jūgun ianfu datta anata he* [To You, a Former Comfort Woman]. Kyoto: Kamogawa shuppan, 1993.

Yude, Wang. *'Shōwa' wo ikita Taiwan seinen* [A Taiwanese Youth Living in Shōwa Japan]. Tokyo: Sōshisha, 2011.

Yūichi, Higuchi. *Kōgun heishi ni sareta Chōsenjin* [Koreans Turned into Imperial Soldiers]. Tokyo: Shakai hyōronsha, 1991.

Yukiko, Yoshihara. 'Nikki' [Diary], 15 August, 4 September 1945, in Toshima kuritsu kyōdo shiryōkan [Toshima Ward Local History Museum] (ed.), *Toshima-ku no shūdan gakudō sokai shiryōshū (3): Nikki, shokan-hen III – Nagasaki dai-2 kokumin gakkō (sono 1)* [Toshima Ward Student Group Evacuation Document Collection (3): Diaries, Correspondence II – Nagasaki #2 State School (Part 1)] (Tokyo: Toshima-ku kyōiku iinkai, 1992), pp. 5-156.

Secondary Sources

Abel, Jonathan E. *Redacted: The Archives of Censorship in Transwar Japan.* Berkeley: University of California Press, 2015.

Barshay, Andrew. *The Gods Left First: The Captivity and Repatriation of Japanese POWs in Northeast Asia, 1945–1956.* Berkeley: University of California Press, 2013.

Ching, Leo T.S. *Becoming 'Japanese': Colonial Taiwan and the Politics of Identity Formation.* Berkeley: University of California Press, 2001.

Ching, Leo T.S. 'Give Me Japan and Nothing Else! Postcoloniality, Identity, and the Traces of Colonialism'. *South Atlantic Quarterly* 99(4) (2000), 763–88.

Chou, Wan-yao. 'The *Kōminka* Movement in Taiwan and Korea: Comparisons and Interpretations', in Peter Duus, Ramon H. Myers and Mark R. Peattie (eds), *The Japanese Wartime Empire, 1931–1945* (Princeton: Princeton University Press, 1966), 40–70.

Chun, Allen. 'From Nationalism to Nationalizing: Cultural Imagination and State Formation in Post-war Taiwan'. *The Australian Journal of Chinese Affairs* 31 (1994), 49–69.

Chun, Allen. 'Fuck Chineseness: On the Ambiguities of Ethnicity as Culture as Identity'. *boundary 2* 23(2) (1996), 111–38.

Dower, John W. *Embracing Defeat: Japan in the Wake of World War Two.* New York: W.W. Norton & Company, 1999.

Figal, Gerald. 'How to *jibunshi*: Making and Marketing Self-histories of Shōwa among the Masses in Post-war Japan'. *The Journal of Asian Studies* 55(4) (1996), 902–33.

Fukuma, Yoshiaki. '*Sensō taiken' no sengoshi: sedai, kyōyō, ideorogī* [The Post-war History of 'War Experience': Generation, Education, Ideology]. Tokyo: Chūō kōron shinsha, 2009.

Fowler, Edward. *The Rhetoric of Confession:* Shishōsetsu *in Early Twentieth Century Japanese Fiction.* Berkeley: University of California Press, 1988.

Gabriel, Philip. 'The Alphabet of Trauma: Shimao Toshio and the Narrative of Dreams'. *Journal of the Association of Teachers of Japanese* 30(2) (1996), 23–54.

Gillin, Donald, and Charles Etter. 'Staying On: Japanese Soldiers and Civilians in China, 1945–1949'. *The Journal of Asian Studies* 42(3) (1983), 497–518.

Ike, Nobutaka. 'Japanese Memoirs – Reflections of the Recent Past'. *Pacific Affairs* 24(2) (1951), 185–90.

Kawashima, Midori. 'The Records of the Former Japanese Army Concerning the Japanese Occupation of the Philippines'. *Journal of Southeast Asian Studies* 27(1) (1996), 124–31.

Kim, Kwang-yŏl. *Ashi de mita Chikuhō: Chōsenjin tankō rōdō no kiroku* [Seeing Chikuhō on Foot: Records of Korean Coal Labour]. Tokyo: Akashi shoten, 2004.

Kushner, Barak. *The Thought War: Japanese Imperial Propaganda.* Honolulu, HI: University of Hawai'i Press, 2006.

Masanao, Kurahashi. *Jūgun ianfu mondai no rekishiteki kenkyū: Baishunfu-kei to sei-tekidorei-kei* [Historical Research on the Comfort Women Question: The Sex Worker Model and the Sex Slave Model]. Tokyo: Kyōei shobō, 1994.

McDonald, Keiko. 'Ooka's Examination of the Self in *A POW's Memoirs*'. *The Journal of the Association of Teachers of Japanese* 21(1) (1987), 15–36.

Moore, Aaron William. 'The Chimera of Privacy: Reading Self-Discipline in Japanese Diaries from the Second World War (1937–1945)'. *The Journal of Asian Studies* 68(1) (2009), 165–98.

Moore, Aaron William. 'Pluralism and the Problem with Collective Memory: Japanese Peace and War Museums in a Comparative Context', in Nicholas Martin, Pierre Purseigle and Tim Haughton (eds), *Aftermath: Legacies and Memories of War in Europe, 1918–1945–1989* (Farnham: Ashgate, 2013), 61–84.

Moore, Aaron William. 'The Problem of Changing Language Communities: Veterans and Memory Writing in China, Taiwan, and Japan'. *Modern Asian Studies* 45(2) (2011), 399–429.

Muminov, Sherzod. 'Eleven Winters of Discontent: The Siberian Internment and the Making of the New Japan, 1945–1956', PhD Diss. (Cambridge, 2016).

Pennington, Lee. *Casualties of History: Wounded Japanese Servicemen and the Second World War.* Ithaca: Cornell University Press, 2015.

Stahl, David. *The Burdens of Survival: Ōoka Shōhei's Writings on the Pacific War.* Honolulu: University of Hawaii Press, 2003.

Takaki, Ronald. *Double Victory: A Multicultural History of Americans in World War II*. New York: Little, Brown, and Company, 1995.
Vlastos, Stephen. 'Opposition Movements in Early Meiji', in Marius B. Jansen (ed.), *The Cambridge History of Japan*, 6 vols (Cambridge: Cambridge University Press, 1988), v. 367–431.
Wakabayashi, Bob Tadashi. 'The Nanking 100-Man Killing Contest: War Guilt amid Fabricated Illusions, 1971–1975'. *Journal of Japanese Studies* 26(2) (2000), 307–40.
Watt, Lori. *When Empire Comes Home: Repatriation and Reintegration in Post-war Japan*. Cambridge, MA: Harvard University Asia Center, 2009.

Aaron William Moore is Senior Lecturer in East Asian History in the School of Arts, Languages and Cultures at the University of Manchester. His research focuses on social and cultural history during the Second World War, which takes him into Chinese, Japanese, Russian, British and American archives. He is the author of *Writing War: Soldiers Record the Japanese Empire* (Cambridge, MA, 2013). His second book, *Bombing the City: Civilian Narratives of the Air War on Britain and Japan*, is forthcoming from Cambridge University Press. He was awarded, with Peter Cave, a three-year grant from the Arts & Humanities Research Council (from 2012 to 2015) to analyse the diaries and memoirs of children and adolescents in imperial Japan.

Chapter 7

Post-Soviet Russian Memoirs of the Second World War

Roger D. Markwick

It is a surprising feature of memory: events and encounters, experiences and losses are not all recalled in chronological order. Out of the darkness of a distant, seemingly long-forgotten past can suddenly emerge apparently disconnected associations, pictures and traces of experiences, often accompanied by vague images and feelings. It requires considerable effort to give real definition to these images and feelings.

– Dmitry Lomonosov, *Zapiski ryadovo radista*

Memoirs hover between fact and fiction. While not histories, they purport to tell the truth about the past as the author experienced it. As such, for better or worse, they are often the raw material of historical writing. But memoirs, like memory itself, individual and collective, are notoriously fickle when it comes to precision about the past, seemingly more so when it comes to military history. War memoirs, it has rightly been said, should be treated with caution as historical sources.[1] Nevertheless, the life and death struggles that are the stuff of military memoirs intensify the subjectivities that shape individual recollection about events, past or present. Moreover, as Lorina Repina has argued, the vital issue in relation to memory, and by extension written memoirs, is not so much historical accuracy as the fact that 'individual memory' is at once 'social memory'; accordingly, written recollections are 'structured by language, education, and collectively shared ideas and experience'. In short, memoirs 'simultaneously comprise both personal identity and the fabric of the surrounding society'.[2] In the case of military memoirs, they are so intimately connected with the fate, not just of individuals but also of nations, states, peoples and classes, that they are necessarily fraught with larger political and social implications. Notwithstanding the question of its factual accuracy, the innate value of the memoir genre derives precisely from its 'duality' [*dvoistvennost*']: 'simultaneously creative work and historical source', as Russian literary analyst N.E. Rozhkova has eloquently argued. In this light, it is precisely the authorial 'I' of the military memoir that gives it such purchase as a historical source for the 'psychology of war': 'specific and real facts seemingly pass through the psyche's mental and emotional filter' endowing war memoirs with the powerful 'characteristic of authenticity' [*momentum dostovernosti*].[3]

Nowhere has war, historical memory, and therefore military memoirs, been more fraught than in the Soviet Union and its Russian successor state. For this reason, the inherent scholarly distrust of memoirs as historical sources has been particularly magnified in relation to Soviet memoirs of the Eastern Front in the Second World War. The life and death struggles over history that characterised Stalin's Soviet Union in the 1930s were followed by a titanic struggle on the Eastern Front for the very existence of the Soviet state and its peoples: the 'Great Patriotic War', as *Pravda* declared it. The saga of the Red Army's 'Victory' over fascism, at the unsaid cost of 27 million Soviet dead, half of all victims of the Second World War, immediately became so pivotal to the legitimacy of Stalin's state that it demanded draconian control over the history of the war and its remembrance. While the Khrushchev 'thaw' witnessed a brief relaxation of controls, strict censorship was soon reinstated in the Brezhnev years when the 'Great Patriotic War, 1941–45' displaced the 1917 'Great October Revolution' as the founding myth of the Soviet state.[4] The intense, patriotic conservatism associated with the war was not only orchestrated from above by the Brezhnevite party-state; it was embraced and encouraged from below by war veterans and their associations, who celebrated 'Victory Day', first declared a public holiday on 9 May 1965.[5] The state-sanctified depiction of the war, embodied in massive historical works and numerous, even more massive memorials, prohibited any challenge to the hegemonic, heroic-patriotic narrative of the war.[6] This narrative was celebrated in hundreds of veterans' memoirs, publication of which first began during the Khrushchev 'thaw', proliferating in the Brezhnev period and climaxing in Putin's Russia with the sixtieth anniversary of the victory, in May 2005.[7] But only with the onset of Gorbachev's *perestroika* was state censorship abolished, opening the way for memoirs that could at least stray from the stereotypical heroic narrative of the Patriotic War. Notwithstanding the resurgence in Putin's post-Soviet

Russia of the Patriotic War as the key legitimating state narrative,[8] and the publication of numerous memoirs that celebrate it,[9] a thin stream of memoirs have appeared which cast that narrative in a less glorious light.

This chapter looks at a selection of post-Soviet Russian memoirs, authored not only by male but also by female soldiers and junior officers, that usually boast they are 'uncut' [*bez kupiur*]. Unlike their Soviet precursors, they are refreshingly frank about wartime experiences. Two hitherto taboo issues are particularly focused on here: Soviet prisoners of war (POWs) and sexual harassment of and liaisons with Red Army women by male soldiers. Explosive as such issues have been in Russia since the war, nevertheless, as will become evident, on the whole even memoirs that address or confess to such taboos still remain largely aligned with the Russian state's celebration of the Patriotic War victory. Such close alignment in these memoirs with the Russian patriotic master narrative of the war confirms the hegemonic power of this narrative both in official discourse and in popular memory.[10]

* * *

Perestroika began with high hopes for the renewal and reinvigoration of the Soviet system, in good part by lifting the lid on the Soviet past; it ended with its downfall. A crucial ingredient in its fall was the tarnishing of the 'bronzed saga' of the Great Patriotic War.[11] In the course of perestroika, the Patriotic War became one of the most contentious elements of the debates that erupted in 1987 about the notorious 'blank spots' in and outright 'falsification' of Soviet history, principally the crimes of Stalin; and in the case of the war, his personal responsibility for the catastrophic reverses of 1941–42.[12]

The crisis in official and private memory of the Patriotic War was registered at a round table of historians and novelists that convened in Moscow in December 1987 to discuss 'fact and documentary evidence' in relation to the war. Censorship and falsification of war memoirs, even those by the most illustrious military leaders such as Marshal Georgy Zhukov, had been a crucial obstacle to truth, the roundtable lamented. Written according to an authorised formula, devoid of any intellectual or emotional content, thousands of memoirs were 'gathering dust' in bookshops. Censorship had gutted their credibility.[13]

While the shortcomings of the marshals' memoirs were being taken to task at the roundtable, so too was the dearth of ordinary soldiers' memoirs. Yelena Rzhevskaya, a Red Army interpreter famed for safeguarding Hitler's jaw bone as evidence of his suicide, a story she first told in the literary magazine *Znamya* in 1965, lamented the lack of a 'dedicated almanac of soldiers' memoirs': 'that we could be so unforgivably indifferent to our own history!'[14] Likewise, the writer and war invalid Vyacheslav Kondrat'yev expressed regret that famed war correspondent Konstantin Simonov's 1960 call for the establishment of a centre to archive and publish ordinary 'soldiers' memoirs' had gone unheeded.[15] In this regard, Kondrat'yev expressed particular angst about popular contempt for Red Army POWs and those 'missing without a trace'; a cruel legacy, he charged, of Stalin's dictum that 'There are no prisoners – only traitors'. Such prejudices could have been remedied, Kondrat'yev suggested, by the publication of memoirs that depicted the horrific fate of those who 'fell prisoner', not 'gave themselves over' to imprisonment [the Stalinist expression implying capture was betrayal];[16] but memoirs of defeat, encirclement and capture could not be published in the Soviet era. For Kondrat'yev, refusal to publish such memoirs was to deny future generations a vast number of invaluable 'eyewitness testimonies that recounted "their" war; the war they lived and experienced; and what it was like to be in their shoes'.[17]

The perestroika roundtable of historians and writers called for the 'rehabilitation' of the 'memoir genre', by publishing them 'uncut and uncensored' [*bez kupyur i kon"yunkturnoi pravki*].[18] It would take the demise of the Soviet Union to achieve this. The result has been a series of refreshingly unvarnished memoirs by rank-and-file soldiers – men and, increasingly, women. The view from the trenches is invariably more confronting than that of their military overlords. Blood, filth, fear, ineptitude, revenge, cruelty and sexual harassment are often depicted in such retrospectives to a degree that was near impossible in the largely sanitised Soviet memoir. This is particularly true in relation to POW and women's memoirs.

'MASSACRE OF THE INNOCENTS'

As often as not, especially in the Soviet period, veterans' associations have sponsored the publication of memoir collections: vignettes of wartime experience. But in the post-Soviet period, individual memoirs have appeared, encouraged by invitations from private publishers. Almost all such memoirs, Soviet and post-Soviet alike, speak of a desire to bequeath the heritage of victory in the Great Patriotic War to succeeding generations. Registering a generational shift from 'witness' to 'learned' history,[19] the more recent memoirs also tend to give more personal reasons for writing: age, impending death and the passage of time. Such is the case for a former Red Army Rifle Battalion Commander, Mikhail Shelkov, who at age eighty, prompted by his son and grandsons, in 2003 decided to 'give it a try', knowing that he had forgotten names, events and places, but still recalling a lot, with 'barely a night going by that I don't dream of the war'.[20] A post-Soviet memoir it may be, but Shelkov follows the standard Soviet format: a family history precedes the war, before the 1917 revolution, his grandfather serving with the Tsarist military; in the 1930s, on the receiving end of Stalin's war on the *kulaks*, so-called 'rich farmers'; a violent youth in the Volga city of Rybinsk but also 'a passion' for aviation – spurred on by the Komsomol, the Communist Party youth organisation.[21]

Deliberately avoiding 'idealising the past', unlike most Soviet memoirs, Shelkov does not concentrate on the post-Stalingrad, victorious years of 1943–45. But nor, strangely, does Shelkov's war begin on 22 June 1941. Instead, he starts in August 1941, when due to catastrophic Soviet defeats, 'war thundered all around'. Yet he and others did not receive the expected call-up for aviation training because they were 'of course' uninformed of the destruction of the Soviet air force. Not surprisingly, he felt a 'terrible, fatal uncertainty'. It was soon resolved: he found himself training as an infantryman with a reserve regiment, as the Germans threatened Moscow. Two-year training was condensed into six months. It was also inadequate: rather than battlefield tactics and command, he underwent the gruelling training of the individual infantryman, a 'gap' he 'dearly felt on the front'.[22]

As an eighteen-year-old trainee officer, Shelkov endured brutal discipline for the most minor infractions, yet he and his fellow trainees thought that everything would be 'fine' at the front: they would 'make it hot for the fascists and return as war heroes'. 'Green youths, they were being sent to certain death'; little did they know then that only four out of their fifty-strong Rybinsk cohort would survive: 'A lieutenant at the front survived on average a few weeks; during an offensive, a few hours'. In the telling, Shelkov gives us a rare glimpse into outlawed religious convictions, rather than party-political ones that characterise most Soviet memoirs. He believed that at the time 'God had still not decided his fate'.[23]

Shelkov writes scathingly of Red Army leadership in the first eighteen months of the war, condemnation that would have been unthinkable in the Soviet era. His first instructions as a young lieutenant commanding a decimated platoon defending Rzhev on the Kalinin Front were, he confesses, 'terrible': 'Not one step backwards! [*Ni Shagu nazad!* Stalin's then secret Order No. 227 of 28 July 1942]. If suddenly, God help us, panic broke out, then we had to stand in front of the panicers and mercilessly shoot the main ones'. And he shares his near despair at the needless mass deaths of thousands of Soviet infantry due to the 'ignorance of the military leadership', who threw them into battle in successive waves; First World War tactics rendered obsolescent by automatic weapons. With insufficient artillery to suppress enemy machine-gun 'nests', the infantry were mown down, the officers first, leaving their troops in disarray and panic. Moreover,

> ... We had been led to believe that we would only fight on enemy soil; as the song went, 'We will annihilate the enemy, with little blood but a mighty blow'. Yet here we were in the second year of the war, the Germans in the very heart of Russia and incomprehensible disaster unfolding on the southern fronts, while before us lie thousands of warriors, the flower of our people, slaughtered ignominiously.[24]

Rather than the unalloyed optimism that pervades Soviet era memoirs, Shelkov frequently acknowledges that the troops were in despair. In late October 1942, with the onset of winter, the soldiers huddled in wet, muddy trenches. Stalin's notorious Order No. 227 was in full swing: 'death stalked their heels'. 'Hidden desertion' was occurring, soldiers wounding themselves – for which the penalty was execution or the punishment battalion [*Shtrafbat*]. The Germans, he notes, had no equivalent order; they could retreat as tactically required – and they were 'far more concerned' about their troops. 'But for those who were "there"', Order No. 227 'didn't hasten victory; it simply cost thousands of lives'.[25] This is a significant departure from the tendency of most other memoirs to praise Stalin's 'Not one step backwards!' order as harsh but necessary.

At the end of November 1942, nineteen-year-old Shelkov found himself a senior lieutenant commanding a company of soldiers, many of whom were old enough to be his father. The first six months of his deployment outside Rzhev, the Red Army simply marked time, shedding blood in futile attempts to penetrate enemy defences. Shelkov was delighted when in October 1942 political commissars were subordinated to military commanders, followed in January 1943 by the decision to put commanders immediately behind their troops, thereby reducing the toll, and ensuing chaos, among the rank and file. This was a time when the Soviet air force became more active, automatic weapons replaced the rifle and the famous T-34 tank increasingly made its presence felt. With the Sixth Army surrounded at Stalingrad, German forces suddenly abandoned Rzhev, with the Red Army in 'hot pursuit'.[26]

ATONING IN BLOOD

Shelkov gives a rare insight into a Red Army '*Shtrafrot*' [punishment company]: soldiers who, if they were lucky, could 'atone in blood' for breaches of military discipline. But thrown into battle under threat of immediate execution for the slightest insubordination, *Shtrafrot* soldiers were more likely to be 'completely wiped out in an instant'.[27] He also provides a rare instance of Soviet crimes against German POWs: the summary execution of 'defenceless' POWs, shot in the back of the head by a Red Army political officer. He himself admitted having a German prisoner executed when his unit was encircled, a common practice on both sides when there was nowhere to detain prisoners.[28]

Like so many other male war memoirs, relations with a woman (or women) on the home front runs like a red thread through the narrative, in Shelkov's case then twenty-year-old 'Valechka', his future wife: 'From the moment I was called up, the main source of positive emotions for me were letters from my Valechka ... I couldn't live without her'. Shelkov certainly fought for and was prepared to die for the Motherland, but it is evident that love of Valechka, as much as love of the Motherland, sustained him, especially after being redeployed following a serious stomach wound: 'I WILL RETURN', he declared.[29]

Returning to the front, a veteran lieutenant at age twenty, marked the beginning of the 'most significant, dramatic phase of my life': operation 'Bagration' to liberate Belarus and Lithuania, in June 1944. Shelkov testifies to the enthusiasm with which Red Army forces were welcomed, 'like family', in Belarus. Sixty years on he still recalled 'with excitement' that 'joyful' welcome. German resistance seemingly melted away as the Red Army advanced, but stiffened as they approached the Lithuanian border. But they were aghast to find that Lithuanian peasants, far from welcoming them as 'liberators', literally turned their backs on them. As Shelkov later discovered, they did not expect anything good from the 'cursed' Soviets.[30]

Conflict flared again. The Red Army's recapture of Vilnius saw 'blood flow like a river' in savage 'close combat' with the surrounded German forces. In the course of the taking of Vilnius, Shelkov himself was nearly executed by his 'ignorant', 'monster' regimental commander as a 'scapegoat' for a failed operation that 'doomed' an entire battalion to destruction under enemy tank tracks. Shelkov was threatened with a military tribunal for ordering a tactical retreat to save his own battalion. At stake in this conflict with his superior was the meaning of Stalin's 'Not one step backwards!' decree. Most memoirs depict Stalin's order as a harsh but necessary measure. But Shelkov was and is bold enough challenge this myth. The 'majority' of commanders mindlessly followed this order 'to the letter', thereby 'pitilessly dooming their troops to destruction ... We did not simply defeat the Germans, we inundated them with our blood, and they drowned in it!' Shelkov, however, counts himself among the minority who understood that in this 'devil's game of war' a tactical 'step backwards' was sometimes necessary. Shelkov was prepared for the worst; fortunately for him he was reassigned to the staff of a rifle regiment.³¹

After the bloody battles of Lithuania they reached East Prussia, 'the cradle of German militarism'. Shelkov was stupefied by the extraordinary turnaround in Soviet military fortunes. Two years earlier, 'sitting in a trench outside a burning Rzhev confronted by a field strewn with the bodies of our soldiers, it had been difficult to imagine ... I would eventually be scrutinising the wolf's lair through binoculars. My heart beat faster as my imagination soared'. So did the warfare; the blood of Russian soldiers 'flowed like a river', as the Germans fought fiercely to defend East Prussia, one 'vast, formidable fortress', that would cost thousands of lives to subdue. Germany was obviously 'played out', but so too was Shelkov. Continual, extraordinary losses of young lives took their toll; he admitted suffering from 'deep depression and complete indifference to his own fate'. The death toll was so high among the Soviet infantry that 'every day one survived was a gift from God'. But, Shelkov assures his Russian reader, and perhaps himself, 'This was not cowardice, it was simply a thirst for life in the face of inevitable death'.³²

'TRAITORS'

So deeply has the Soviet heroic-patriotic narrative been entrenched that it has precluded almost any other rendering of experiences forged in the furnace of the Eastern Front. In particular, it has excluded recollections from those who seemingly did not measure up to heroic self-sacrifice and martyrdom that constituted the leitmotiv of the war, above all, former Red Army prisoners of war. Decades after Stalin's infamous Order No. 270 of 16 August 1941, not published until 1988 during Gorbachev's *glasnost'* [openness], equated Soviet soldiers who 'gave themselves over' to the enemy with traitors, POWs bore the seemingly 'indelible stain' of suspicion that they had been cowards, capitulators or collaborators who had betrayed the 'sacred cause' of the anti-fascist war in defence of the Motherland [*Rodina-mat'*].³³ Even under *glasnost'*, former POWs continued to be regarded with such contempt it was almost impossible for them to publish their memoirs; they were dismissed as 'not real soldiers', as the chairman of the All-Union Council of Veterans put it as late as 1988.³⁴

One of the first memoirs to appear after the demise of the Soviet Union that dealt with the issue of POWs in any depth was aptly titled *A Hidden Biography*. It was published in 1996 by a former fighter pilot, Boris

Veselovsky who had endured eight years in the GULAG.[35] Published by Voenizdat, formerly the Soviet Ministry of Defence publishing house, its format is distinctly Soviet, even if its subject matter is not: childhood to war, concentration camp and escape, GULAG and liberation. Veselovsky's motivation to record his recollections is also Soviet and patriotic; it was penned on the 'insistence' of his son, so that the 'young generation' should know about 'everything' he experienced.[36] In distinctly Soviet style, this is not an introspective text, a lament for lost comrades in arms, or conscious coping with trauma. It is a didactic text, in the sense of bequeathing a slice of hidden, personal history in a vast historical drama to future generations.

Shot down over Leningrad in January 1943 and captured, Veselovsky was imprisoned in a concentration camp in Poland. While denying he was a communist (he destroyed his party card – sacrilege from the Soviet perspective, although he does not remark on that), he categorically declares he refused to join the collaborationist 'Russian Free Army' (ROA) led by former Red Army General Vlasov: 'I would not be a traitor'. Veselovsky managed to escape and spent eighteen months with partisan detachments in Poland and Belarus before eventually rejoining his air regiment on the North-West Front, where he took to the skies again with the 15th Air Army in July 1944. But six months later, due to an 'absurd twist of fate', he was condemned by a military tribunal to seven years in a GULAG 'correctional-labour camp' for 'mortally wounding' a sergeant in the course of an affray, defending the honour of army women from a group of drunken soldiers. Given the 'sacred' tenor of the Patriotic War mythology ('Our cause is just', declared Molotov in 1941), revelations of drunkenness, disorder and killing within the Red Army by one of its own were heresy. Even more heretical were Veselovsky's claims about his fate and that of Red Army POWs: interrogated by military counter-intelligence SMERSH (an acronym for 'Death to Spies'), he was subject to summary justice merely to set an example at a time when ill discipline was growing in the 15th Air Army. Stripped of his rank and awards, he was doomed to 'atone' for his crime 'before the Motherland', and punished just like captured enemy saboteurs.

Veselovsky found himself exiled in the far northern Komi Republic, with common criminals and former Red Army soldiers, 'simply' there because they had been in German captivity. Among them, a bomber pilot shot down and captured over Warsaw in 1943 who escaped into Soviet captivity, condemned to ten years in the GULAG as a 'traitor to the Motherland'; his 'burnt face and body insufficient evidence' of innocence. It was not only Red Army POWs who were treated as traitors. Former members of the Italian resistance who had fled 'fascist penal servitude' were imprisoned alongside 'real traitors: former police, executors and Vlasovites: all equally subject to forced labour, hunger and lawlessness in the camp', where 'death, murder ... and terror' could go unpunished. A failed escape attempt saw Veselovsky further condemned for 'counter-revolutionary sabotage'. Eventually, on 13 December 1953, the year Stalin died, Veselovsky was released: 'Freedom!', after eight years, he exclaims. But his passport prohibited him from residing in major cities such as Moscow and 'closed industrial zones', or working in certain industries. He bore the 'stain' of treason. Symptomatic of the views that prevailed within the military, his attempts to gain support for a review of his case from the Secretary of the Veterans' Association, Aleksey Mares'ov, were coldly rebuffed: 'The tribunal has already dealt with this, which means everything is in order. There is nothing I can do'. But, in truly Soviet heroic style, Veselovsky tells the reader he fought to overturn the tribunal's harsh judgement. He finally succeeded after thirteen years of 'torment', in February 1958 during the post-Stalinist 'thaw'. He rejoiced in regaining 'full' Soviet citizenship and, in 1964, readmission to the Communist Party – the ultimate happy ending. 'That's just the way it was' [*Chto bylo, to bylo*], Veselovsky concludes, without a trace of bitterness; a matter of fact acceptance of Soviet social norms in a post-Soviet Russia, a legacy of Veselovsky's upbringing as one of the 1930s 'Stalin generation'.

'"SYNDROME" OF DISTRUST'

Not all ex-POWs are as forgiving as Veselovsky; certainly not of Stalin and his regime. Eighty-eight-year-old former cavalry regiment signaller Dmitry Lomonosov, whose parents' commitment to the 1917 October Revolution had eventually cost them their lives as 'enemies of the people' during Stalin's terror, is deeply cynical about why the Red Army fought so tenaciously and bitter about the price that ordinary soldiers paid for the victory, especially POWs. Nobody fought 'for Stalin', or out of enthusiastic, 'patriotic impulses'; victory was achieved 'despite Stalin's extremely negative role'. For Lomonosov, 'innate' 'duty and obligation', and 'enormous physical staying power', reinforced by 'blocking detachments, military tribunals and punishment battalions', motivated the ordinary soldier in the face of certain death.[37] Coercion and punishment were the drivers of victory.

Lomonosov, wounded and captured in Belarus by the Germans on 14 January 1944, blames Stalin, for whom there were 'no prisoners, only traitors', for the still widespread belief of his compatriots that POWs had 'betrayed' their military oath. Of the 5.7 million POWs, 3.3 million had died in German concentration camps, more than a third of the 8.8 million Soviet dead, yet their 'cruel', 'tragic' fate, he reminds the reader, remains unknown. There were virtually no books, films or memorials dedicated to their treatment as 'sub-humans' by the Nazis or 'traitors' by the NKVD [People's Commissariat of Internal Affairs]. POWs who returned to the Soviet fold if they were not 'repressed', i.e. consigned by the NKVD to the GULAG, faced decades of 'persecution and humiliation'. Up until 1956, ex-POWS such as Lomonosov were not recognised as combatants. And up until the demise of the Soviet Union they had restricted access to jobs, study and travel; not until 1995 were their rights as citizens fully restored. Even now, the 88-year-old ex-POW confronts the '"syndrome" of distrust' that lingers in 'social consciousness'; combatting it and salvaging the reputation of his fellow ex-prisoners largely motivates his memoir.[38]

COURTING COLLABORATION

Under the provocative title, *In German Captivity: Notes of a Survivor*, ninety-year-old Yury Vladimirov details his capture as an eighteen-year-old anti-tank gunner in the 'cauldron' [*kotel*] of encirclement in the battle for Kharkov in May 1942, three years of inhuman incarceration, and then NKVD 'filtration' that saw him assigned to forced labour in the coal mines of the Ukrainian Donbass region on the grounds that 'millions ... laid down their lives and were maimed on the front but thanks to captivity ... we remained alive. Therefore we were obliged through ... many years of labour in the mine to repay, if only partially, the fallen, the crippled and all of Soviet society who had enabled us to survive. Only then could we return home to the motherland with a clear conscience'.[39]

Deported from Dnepropetrovsk (Ukraine) and eventually ending up in Maulberg (Germany), Vladimirov's survival – starving, chronically ill, night-blind – seems nothing short of a miracle, given the extraordinary death rate of 57.7 per cent of the 5.7 million Red Army POWs. For Vladimirov this was a war crime for which he holds Soviet authorities partly responsible; their refusal to sign the Geneva Convention on Prisoners of War, in their belief that POWs were 'traitors', had 'legalis[ed]' mass 'starvation'.

Vladimirov sails perilously close to the wind of collaboration when he explains his survival by his facility with German, which made him a useful go-between for both gaolers and gaoled; ultimately he was assigned to less arduous farm work in Germany. Along the way he reveals less than glorious details of captured comrades: collaborationist '*Hillswillige*' volunteers and members of the ROA; murder and cannibalism by starving POWs; Soviet women workers (*Ostarbeiterinnen*) who had 'volunteered' to go to Germany for 'better wages and clothes'; the murder of barracks 'informers'; and applications by POWs to join the *Wehrmacht*. Extraordinarily, Vladimirov himself admits that enticed by convincing anti-Stalinist propaganda he too almost signed up with the ROA; but others did, he declares, out of conviction or desperation.[40]

Notwithstanding Stalin's view that POWs were traitors, a view that fuelled popular prejudice against them, Vladimirov argues that he was in no position to flee back to the Soviet side, to sabotage the German war effort or to take revenge on his captors: 'this would have been an evil, inhuman act'. And he laments that 'many' POWs gave little thought to patriotism or their Red Army comrades giving their lives for POW freedom. Despite the enormous pressure to collaborate, Vladimirov recalls the POWs' continued identification with their Motherland [*Rodina*], especially in the wake of victory at Stalingrad: they resolved to combat ROA recruitment and propaganda. He also records the post-Stalingrad influx of detainees, as European resistance movements were galvanised by the catastrophic German defeat, and the changed, post-Stalingrad mood among captors and prisoners alike. For the latter, elation displaced despair.[41]

Vladimirov's detailed account of his incarceration and internment entails keen, nuanced observations of daily life, avoiding stereotypes about his German overlords, not all of whom were Nazi monsters, he suggests, coupled with sustained reflections on the political and military situation. This political dimension of Vladimirov's memoir puts it firmly in the Soviet mould. But in an audacious aside, in which he suggests that 'some believed General Vlasov was motivated to establish the ROA in order to deceive Hitler and his circle and thereby save millions of Soviet prisoners of war from starving to death',[42] Vladimirov betrays considerable sympathy for the reviled ROA. In doing so, Vladimirov is completely at odds with the Soviet and Russian patriotic narrative, courting the charge of 'traitor'. Such a memoir would never have been published in the Soviet era.

WAR'S 'WOMANLY FACE'

It is not only Russian male soldiers who feel impelled to recall the Patriotic War. Given that some one million women served in the Red Army, Russia is one of the few states where women's war memoirs have had a significant and increasing presence, challenging the masculinist mould of fighting brotherhood that has dominated the genre everywhere since its emergence.[43] In the Soviet era, collective memoirs were often the norm, 'testimonial narratives' in which individual identity was subordinated to collective identity and commitment to Soviet ideals.[44] But in post-Soviet Russia, increasingly, uncensored, individual memoirs have appeared. Unlike men's memoirs, most women's memoirs show little or no interest in military feats of arms, tactics or weaponry. There are exceptions, however, such as the 2006 memoirs of Yulya Zhukova, *Young Woman with a Sniper's Rifle*, which detail her bloody path in 1943-44 as an eighteen-year-old from the Urals factory front to the horrors of East Prussia.[45] But in the main, as military personnel, women's memoirs recall experiences that seem specifically female, particularly the human and social dimension of war. Red Army women credited themselves with raising the 'cultural level' of military men, civilising them, so to speak. In the post-Soviet era, women have written with increased openness of the distinctive roles and experiences of women at war that, while largely embracing its heroic, patriotic gloss, nevertheless have begun to depict the demeaning sexism of their male comrades at war. And some have depicted the cruel accusation of treason that was also directed at repatriated Red Army women POWs.

Even in the post-Stalin Soviet period, the ruthless treatment to which women POWs could be subject on their return home occasionally surfaced in published memoirs. Such was the paranoid Russian chauvinism that engulfed the Soviet Union in the immediate post-war years that even the most extraordinary heroism was no safeguard against suspicion. Red Army pilot Anna Timofeyeva-Yegorova, one of the few women to fly the challenging Il-2 *shturmovik* ground-attack aircraft, the so-called 'flying tank', was also one of the few women aviators to be captured. Shot down on 20 August 1944 over Poland on her 277th mission, she was imprisoned for five months in a German concentration camp until her release by a Red Army tank unit on 31 January 1945. She was lucky to survive: severely injured – 'broken arms, a broken leg, back and head injuries, and burns' – this 'flying witch', as the enemy dubbed her, received virtually no treatment while imprisoned. Her ordeal, however, was not sufficient to convince SMERSH, who subjected her to ten days' *filtratsiya* [interrogation], then invited her to join them – which she refused to do. Demobilised as an invalid, eventually, in May 1965, she was awarded a Hero of the Soviet Union gold star. In fact, Timofeyeva-Yegorova had won the Soviet Union's highest military award in 1944 on the assumption that she had been killed, but it was then withdrawn when it was discovered she had been a POW.[46]

Surprisingly, Timofeyeva-Yegorova's tale of cruel betrayal was first published towards the end of the Brezhnev years, when the cult of the Patriotic War was at its zenith. But her revelations then are mute compared to those published in an expanded edition of her memoirs published in 1999. Despite Timofeyeva-Yegorova's reluctance to 'indulge memory' because 'memory is one thing and life another', her post-Soviet memoirs detail her prolonged, pitiless interrogation by the counter-intelligence agency SMERSH as a 'lying', 'fascist bitch' and her struggle for several years thereafter to clear her name and reinstate her Communist Party membership.[47]

AN 'INDELIBLE STAIN'

Very few former POWs were accorded hero status. Sofya Anvayer, a Jewish Red Army nurse who had been held prisoner for more than three years, far from being hailed as a heroine on her return, like so many other Soviet POWs was stigmatised as a traitor. She suffered the opprobrium of having been a prisoner of war for the rest of her life. *Bleeds My Memory*, her poignant, posthumous memoir, was finally published in 2005 on the 60th anniversary of the victory.[48]

Anvayer's tale is harrowing. As a 21-year-old Moscow medical student, she volunteered for the Red Army within twenty-four hours of the outbreak of war. Rebuffed as a soldier, she joined a field hospital, only to be captured in late October 1941 in the 'hell' of the Vyazma 'cauldron'. Condemned to more than three horrendous years as a POW in occupied Poland, she escaped the 'annihilation' of Jews by adopting a gentile name. Saved from the crematorium, she only survived the Nazi 'death marches', the forced evacuation in winter 1945 of concentration camp inmates towards Germany, by luck. Reunited with the advancing Red Army, she volunteered to 'fight the fascists', to no avail. In the spring of 1945 she was turned over to SMERSH and mercilessly subjected to '*spetsproverka*' [special checks] to verify that she was not a traitor.[49] Accused of sexual collaboration, she attempted to take her own life. Although finally released in March 1946, after a year's detention by her 'own', she bore the 'stain' of suspicion that as a former POW she was a traitor, an ignominy she was forced to endure for the rest of her life.

It is a measure of the degree to which Stalin clamped down on war remembering, heroic or otherwise, that only in the wake of Khrushchev's 'thaw' could Anvayer first publish her 'unforgettable' experiences as a POW in a German labour camp, in the journal *Znamya*, in September 1956.[50] Just three months earlier, on 29 June 1956, the Communist Party Central Committee had adopted a secret resolution for 'the elimination of the consequences of gross violations of legality in relation to former prisoners of war and the families'; it scarcely changed the status of either former POWs or their families.[51] It would be another ten years, 1966, before Anvayer could write of her horrific concentration camp experiences.[52] But of her subsequent treatment at the hands of her 'own', she could write only long after the demise of the Soviet Union: her 'bitterness' at the injustice; her fight for the right to live at home in Moscow and for a passport, only to discover in 1953 that its serial number indicated that the bearer was 'unreliable'; and the suspicion that she remained under due to her 'indelible stain'.[53]

Anvayer's vivid depiction of her '*filtratsiya*' at the hands of SMERSH reveals the depth of suspicion that prevailed among Soviet military intelligence towards former POWs, especially a Jewish woman, undoubtedly fanned by Stalinist fears of 'neo-Decembrist' and 'western' infections carried by returning soldiers.[54] In Anvayer's words, she was interrogated by an 'unprepossessing' individual, who evidently did 'not want to believe anything' she said: 'A Jewess? Jews don't come back alive from there'. She was accused of inventing 'fairy tales' about pretending she was Georgian, the SMERSH officer demanding to know 'Where and when you surrendered? [*sdalas' v plen*]. When she protested that she had 'not surrendered' but had been captured in the Vyazma cauldron, 'encircled by five armies', had 'attempted to break through to the front', and that she had been captured 'half-alive' in a forest where she had been attempting to help a 'badly wounded comrade', the response was brutally curt: 'Don't make things up ... Only cowards were taken prisoner, in the worst circumstances people shot themselves'. All attempts on Anvayer's part to speak of 'resistance' were rebuffed: 'Lyricism. Fantasies. You need to say what really happened'. 'Whom did you betray to the Gestapo?' 'You will regret this', she was warned, and she did: thrown into solitary confinement she threatened a 'hunger strike', which was callously dismissed as 'your decision'. Imprisoned for a third time, Anvayer was assigned to medical duties alongside German POW medical staff, forced to cope with outbreaks of lice, typhus and diphtheria which an incompetent, drunken Red Army major would not deal with.[55]

Anvayer seems to have shown just a little too much sympathy for the German POW medical staff with whom she was working. Defending a German POW surgeon from a vindictive woman junior lieutenant from the Red Army medical service, a 'vulgar hussy', Anvayer incurred her wrath: 'Ignoramus! German whore! Get to Siberia. You will soon be sent to the camps! You will find out what it means to betray the motherland!'[56]

Anvayer's experiences at the hands of SMERSH and their lifelong aftermath tell us a great deal about the extraordinary ruthlessness of the Stalinist state at war, Stalin's paranoia about 'neo-Decembrist' sentiments among returning soldiers infecting the Soviet polity, and the unforgiving patriotism, bordering on chauvinism, with which the war was waged that would linger long after Stalin was gone. Perhaps most remarkable about

Anvayer's tragic tale is that despite her ordeals, the wartime story she tells is in most respects the same heroic-patriotic saga as those veterans whose stories accorded with the official, sanitised history of the Great Patriotic War. There is no repudiation of her original commitment, despite the seeming betrayal by her 'own' Soviet authorities. Anvayer's public proclamation of her loyalty, despite the humiliation she bore as a former prisoner of war, may be seen as her attempt to find acceptance in Soviet society. But it should also be seen as a testimony to the extraordinary depth of conviction, the *mentalité* that motivated the 'Stalin' generation of Soviet women to volunteer to fight fascism on the front. It is also testimony to one of the sources of the enduring power of the patriotic myth of the Great Patriotic War in Soviet and post-Soviet societies, beyond the posturing of monumental state propaganda: it struck a real resonance with the life and death experiences of millions of Soviet citizens – civilians, veterans and POWs. Above all, it is testimony to the unassailable sacralisation of the Patriotic War myth that Anvayer's blasphemous tale could only be published in post-Soviet Russia, and then only posthumously.[57]

TABOO THEMES

The POW taboo is not the only one that has been broken by women veterans. Sexual relations and harassment have also been confronted in contemporary women's memoirs; among the most controversial, the phenomenon of the so-called 'mobile field wife' or *PPZhe* [*Polevaya pokhodnaya zhena*], based on rumours that *frontovichki* [female frontline soldiers] were no more than officers' mistresses.[58] Primarily, the *PPZhe* slur was a home front 'moral panic' about very young women living alongside hundreds of men. It was a slur that precluded the possibility of women entering into a relationship with an officer for 'love' or otherwise, that might have offered her some comforts and companionship, and shielded her somewhat from predatory, young male soldiers, in an army without brothels, with whom she might find herself alone in a *zemlyanka* [earthen dugout].[59]

Predatory relations between officers and young women is another taboo to have surfaced in post-Soviet women's memoirs, even among the most loyal. Occasionally, Soviet memoirs had hinted at personal passions that embroiled young women and men at the front: a stolen kiss or even an 'eternal triangle'. But in spring 1942, with the mass recruitment of women into the military, the Red Army's Main Political Directorate [GPU] had expressed anxiety about drunken, 'amoral relations' between commanders and commissars and women, nurses in particular.[60]

Six decades on, military nurse Irina Bogacheva, in her 2005 memoir *The Roads We Choose*, wrote of 'love' between young men and women soldiers as a natural, 'human' phenomenon, especially in wartime when all feared dying 'without having loved'. Sometimes, such liaisons culminated in marriage. She acknowledged, however, that married male soldiers on the front were more likely to abandon their peacetime inhibitions about sexual relations with other young women.[61] But sniper Zhukova went rather further. She explicitly recalled being assigned to an artillery regiment, where she found herself alone, without the support of other women, and prey to a division captain notorious for his love of alcohol and women. On her very first night she was summoned by the captain, threatened with a tribunal if she disobeyed. Even at that time she had 'already heard all sorts of stories of the amorous pretensions of certain officers, of deceived young women and of those contemptuously referred to as *PPZhe*'. Eventually summoned under armed guard, due to the drunkenness of the commander she escaped a situation she could not even bring herself to write about. Thereafter she survived under the protection of three 'true knights' in the regiment.[62]

Notwithstanding the fact that the experiences and fate of Soviet women soldiers and veterans are clearly gendered issues, patriotism has trumped any feminist consciousness as understood in the West. Despite some voicing of these taboo topics, silences remain, born of censorship or self-censorship out of respect for the patriotic 'sacred cause'. In particular, little or nothing has been written about the post-war life of women veterans: the official pressure to return to family and working life; the stigma of the *PPZhe*; or the fate of women invalids, physically or psychologically crippled, or those not recognised as heroes. Their story remains locked up in archives to secure the unsullied, celebratory mythology of the Great Patriotic War.

Witness, for example, the unpublished, crude, harrowing retrospective of despair, written a half-century on in a faltering hand by a young woman paramedic. Yefrosiya Savoskina managed to survive the catastrophic destruction of her ill-fated, ill-armed, volunteer civilian militia [*opolchenie*] division outside Moscow during the *Wehrmacht* onslaught in July–September 1941. But many of her young girlfriends did not. It is really a story of unresolved trauma that Savoskina bore all her life: horrific death and suffering, accusations of betrayal, and guilt about survival. 'War [*voina*]. What a horrific word it is', she begins her recollection, 'I can't believe we young women survived all that'. This memoir is a litany of horrors: maiming, haemorrhaging, infected wounds, suicide, desperate hunger, summary execution, atrocities and the appalling deaths of close friends. In Savoskina's never-ending nightmare, there is not even the redeeming notion of sacrifice for the Motherland.[63]

HUMANISING WAR

Surveys of Russian public opinion confirm that six decades on, the Great Patriotic War occupies the defining place in mass 'historical consciousness'. Despite the demise of the Soviet Union, victory in that war has become the touchstone of Russian national pride, despite attempts in the 1990s to undermine it. In the twenty-first century, the increasingly authoritarian Putin administration has worked overtime to ensure the inviolability of the mystique of the Patriotic War. The 60th jubilee of 'The Victory' in 2005 was central to President Putin's drive to reinvigorate Russian patriotism; he hailed Victory Day as the most 'sacred', 'inclusive' and 'festive' day for Russia. Under Putin, militarist patriotism has become the decisive unifying element in state ideology and popular consciousness, most recently manifest with the establishment of the Russian Military History Society, the imperial predecessor of which was disbanded in 1917.[64] Amidst this resurgent patriotism, there is little popular tolerance of revisionist challenges to the mythology of the war.[65] Despite the fact that most of the Russian military memoirs examined here have encroached on the heroic, 'sacrificial teleology' of the Patriotic War,[66] particularly those of former POWs, none, even those recollections that remain unpublished, have blasphemed against its core belief that this was a 'sacred war' against a satanic enemy. On the contrary, almost all the memoirists have reaffirmed the righteousness of the war and their role in it by seemingly more truthful depictions of their experiences, thereby reaffirming their place in a more humanised, and therefore more credible, Great Patriotic War grand narrative.

NOTES

1. 'It seems that the circumstances of war intensify the distortions and increase the difficulties of putting events into words.' Samuel Hynes, *The Soldiers' Tale: Bearing Witness to Modern War* (New York, 1998), 15–16, 23–25.
2. Lorina Repina, 'Historical Memory and Contemporary Historical Scholarship', *Russian Studies in History* 49(1) (2010), 15.
3. N.E. Rozhkova, 'Voennye memuary kak istoriya i kak literatura', *Novye rossisskiye gumanitarnye issledovaniya*, 6 July 2007, 3, 9 (emphasis in the original), available at: http://www.nrgumis.ru/articles/article (accessed 15 April 2012).
4. Nina Tumarkin, *The Living and the Dead: The Rise and Fall of the Cult of World War II in Russia* (New York, 1994), 132–36.
5. Mark Edele, *Soviet Veterans of World War II: A Popular Movement in an Authoritarian Society, 1941–1991* (Oxford and New York, 2008).

6. Joachim Hösler, 'Aufarbeitung der Vergangenheit? Der Große Vaterländische Krieg in der Historiographie der UdSSR und in Rußland' [Reworking the Past? The Great Fatherland War in the Historiography of the USSR and Russia], *Osteuropa* 55(4–5) (2005), 115–25.
7. Hiroaki Kuromiya, 'Soviet Memoirs as a Historical Source', in Sheila Fitzpatrick and Lynne Viola (eds), *A Researcher's Guide to Sources on Soviet Social History in the 1930s* (New York and London, 1992), 235; Peter Jahn, 'Opora pamyati – vremya pamyati' [The Basis of Memory is the Time of Memory], in Peter Jahn (ed.), *Triumph und Trauma: Sowetische und Post Sowetische Erinnerung an der Krieg 1941–45* (Berlin-Karlshorst, 2005), 17–19.
8. See Roger D. Markwick, 'The Great Patriotic War in Soviet and Post-Soviet Collective Memory', in Dan Stone (ed.), *The Oxford Handbook of Postwar European History* (Oxford, 2012), 692–713.
9. Testimony to this are the Russian websites dedicated to memoirs and memory about the Great Patriotic War, notably *Voennaya Literatura* (http://militera.lib.ru/memo/index.html) and *Ya Pomnyu. I Remember* (http://iremember.ru/).
10. As Barbara Walker has so eloquently said of Russian-Soviet memoir tradition: 'The value of these documents lies at certain key moments less in their accurate reflection of what actually happened in the past, and more in how they reflect the ways that their authors, as participants in Russian culture, view the world: how they think of their past, and how they connect it to their present; how they believe that society should work, and what they see as appropriate or ideal social, economic, and political behavior. These memoirs offer invaluable insights into some of the twists and turns of Soviet Russian culture, as well as into the internal cultural logic of Russian discourse about Soviet history'. Walker, 'On Reading Soviet Memoirs: A History of the "Contemporaries" Genre as an Institution of Russian Intelligentsia Culture from the 1790s to the 1970s', *Russian Review* 59(3) (2000), 329.
11. Tumarkin, *The Living and the Dead*, 188, 190, 193.
12. R.W. Davies, *Soviet History in the Gorbachev Revolution* (Houndmills, 1989), 100–11.
13. 'Velikaya otechestvennaya voina: fakt i dokument v istoricheskikh issledovaniyakh i khudozhestvennoi literature. Beseda istorikov i pisatelei za "kruglym stolom"', *Istoriya SSSR*, 1988 (4), 3–44.
14. 'Velikaya otechestvennaya voina: fakt i dokument', 33. Two volumes of her memoirs were published at the height of perestroika: *Berlin, mai 1945* [Berlin, May 1945] (1985) and *Blizhnye podstupy* [Immediate Approaches] (1986), both available at: http://militera.lib.ru/memo/1/abc/r.html (accessed 8 April 2013).
15. Konstantin Simonov, 'O vospominaniakh. Zametki pisatel'ya', *Krasnaya Zvezda*, 17 April 1960; 'Pered glazami', *Krasnaya Zvezda*, 24 April 1960. Apparently Kondrat'yev was unaware that in 1980 the literary journal *Ogonyek* had appealed to war veterans and their families to submit war memorabilia, including recollections, letters and photos. These are now held in the Moscow archive of the former Communist Party youth organisation, the Komsomol.
16. Edele, *Soviet Veterans of World War II*, 115–16.

17. 'Velikaya otechestvennaya voina: fakt i dokument', 34–35. In September 1993, when he was seriously ill, then 73-year-old Kondrat'yev committed suicide; http://tvervov.tverlib.ru/person/tv-015-kondratiev.htm (accessed 19 May 2012).
18. 'Velikaya otechestvennaya voina: fakt i dokument', 13.
19. Ekaterina Makhotina, 'Refracted Memories. The Great Patriotic War in Russia Today', in Claudia Freytag et al. (eds), *Juni 1941 Der Tiefe Schnitt / June 1941 The Deepest Cut* (Berlin-Karlshorst, 2011), 39.
20. Mikhail Shelkov, *Zapiski komandira strelkovovo batal'yona. Ot Rzheva do Vostochnoi Prussii. 1942–1945* [Notes of a Rifle Battalion Commander. From Rezhev to East Prussia, 1942–1945] (Moscow, 2010), 3.
21. Shelkov, *Zapiski komandira*, 12.
22. Shelkov, *Zapiski komandira*, 11, 15, 17.
23. Shelkov, *Zapiski komandira*, 21–22, 27–29.
24. Shelkov, *Zapiski komandira*, 33, 35–36, 41.
25. Shelkov, *Zapiski komandira*, 45–46, 58, 94.
26. Shelkov, *Zapiski komandira*, 47, 50–53.
27. Shelkov was by no means the first to publicise Red Army penal units. In 2004 *Shtrafbat* [Penalty Battalion], an eleven-part television series directed by Nikolai Dostal, was received with acclaim, despite resurgent Great Patriotic War pride in Putin's Russia.
28. Shelkov, *Zapiski komandira*, 53, 58–59, 152.
29. Shelkov, *Zapiski komandira*, 77, 79.
30. Shelkov, *Zapiski komandira*, 97, 103, 118, 124, 133, 144.
31. Shelkov, *Zapiski komandira*, 126–27, 134, 146, 150–53.
32. Shelkov, *Zapiski komandira*, 192, 200, 209, 233, 244.
33. Lev Kokin, 'O Sof'ye Anvayer i ee memuarakh. Posleslovie redaktora', in Sof'ye Anvayer, *Krovotochit moya pamyat': iz zapisok studentki-medichki* [Bleeds My Memory: Notes of a Female Medical Student] (Moscow, 2005), 206; V. Naumov, 'Sud'ba voennoplennykh i deportirovannykh grazhdan SSSR. Materialy komissii po reabilitatsii zhertv politicheskikh repressi,' [The Fate of Prisoners of War and Deported Citizens of the USSR. Information from the Commission for the Rehabilitation of the Victims of Political Repression] *Novaya i noveishaya istoriya* 2 (1996), 91–112.
34. Leon Aron, *Roads to the Temple. Truth, Memory, Ideas, and Ideals in the Making of the Russian Revolution, 1987–1991* (New Haven and London, 2012), 167–70. For Order No. 270, see Frank Ellis, *The Damned and the Dead. The Eastern Front the Eyes of Soviet and Russian Novelists* (Lawrence, KS, 2011), Appendix A, 285–88.
35. Boris Vladmirovich Veselovsky, *Skrytaya biografiya* [Secret Biography] (Moscow, 1996), available at: http://militera.lib.ru/memo/russian/veselovsky_bv/index.html (accessed 9 April 2013). The online text is not paginated, so sections only are referred to.
36. Veselovsky, *Skrytaya biografiya*, 'Tetrad' chetvertaya: 3. Vozvrashchenie aviatsiyu'.

37. Dmitry Lomonosov, *Zapiski ryadovo radista. Front. Plen. Vozvrashchenie 1941–1946* [Notes of a Rank and File Radio Operator. Frontline. Imprisonment. Return. 1941–1946] (Moscow, 2012), 341–43.
38. Lomonosov, *Zapiski ryadovo radista*, 214–17.
39. Yury Vladimirov, *V Nemetskom plenu. Zapiski vyzhivshevo 1942–1945* [In German Captivity. Notes of a Survivor 1942–1945] (Moscow, 2010), 7–8, 364, 370, 389.
40. Vladimirov, *V Nemetskom plenu*, 45–46, 71, 73, 83, 89, 94, 97, 107–8, 118–19, 131, 145.
41. Vladimirov, *V Nemetskom plenu*, 131, 133, 137, 179–80, 198, 211.
42. Vladimirov, *V Nemetskom plenu*, 145.
43. Roger D. Markwick, '"A Sacred Duty": Red Army Women Veterans Remembering the Great Fatherland War, 1941–1945', *Australian Journal of Politics and History* 54(3) (2008), 403–20.
44. Marianne Liljeström, 'The Remarkable Revolutionary Woman: Rituality and Performativity in Soviet Women's Autobiographical Texts from the 1970s', in Marianne Liljeström, Arja Rosenholm and Irina Savkina (eds), *Models of Self: Russian Women's Autobiographical Texts* (Helsinki, 2000), 81–82.
45. Yulya Zhukova, *Devushka so snaiperskoi vintovkoi: Vospominanii vypusknitsy tsentral"noi zhenskoi shkoly snaiperskoi podgotovki 1944–1945* [Young Woman with a Sniper's Rifle: Memoirs of a Graduate of the Central Women's Sniper Training School 1944–1945]. (Moscow, 2006). See Roger D. Markwick and Euridice Charon Cardona, *Soviet Women on the Frontline in the Second World War* (Basingstoke, 2012), 213–28.
46. A.A. Timofeyeva-Yegorova, *Derzhis, Sestrenka!* [Stand Firm, Little Sister!] (Moscow, 1983), 154–69, 174. This particular memoir had a print run of 100,000. Contrast this with the average 3,000 to 4,000 copies of current memoirs.
47. A.A. Timofeyeva-Yegorova, *'Ya beryoza, kak shlyshite menya?'* ['Birch Tree Here. Do You Hear Me?'] (Moscow, 1999), available at: http://militera.lib.ru/memo/russian/egorova/index.html, published in English as Anna Timofeyeva-Yegorova, *Red Sky, Black Death. A Soviet Women Pilot's Memoir of the Eastern Front*, trans. by Margarita Ponomareva and Kim Green (Bloomington, 2009), 195–96, 206–7.
48. Anvayer, *Krovotochit moya pamyat'*.
49. Anvayer, *Krovotochit moya pamyat'*, 20, 197–98.
50. Sof'ya Anvayer, 'Nezabyvaemoe', *Znamya* 9 (September 1956), 114–36.
51. Postanovlenie TsK KPSS (29 June 1956) No. 898-490s, 'Ob ustranenii posledstvii grubykh narushenii zakonnosti v otnoshenii byvshikh voennoplennykh i chlenov ikh semei', *Voenno-istorichesky zhurnal* 8 (1991), 32–34; Naumov, 'Sud'ba voennoplennykh', 109.
52. S.I. Anvayer, 'Kontslager' Shtutgof' [Shtutgof Concentration Camp], in *Lyudi pobedivshie smert'* [People Who Defeated Death] (Leningrad, 1968), 278–313. Anvayer claims (184) that the catalyst for writing of her POW experience was a publication by Yury Pilyar, 'Vse eto bylo' [All This was True], *Novy mir*, Nos. 11 and 12, 1955, 'the first swallow' of literature about 'a fascist concentration camp and resistance'.

53. Markwick and Charon Cardona, *Soviet Women on the Frontline*, 244.
54. Elena Zubkova, *Russia after the War. Hopes, Illusions, and Disappointments, 1945–1957*, trans. and ed. by Hugh Ragsdale (New York and London, 1998), 25–27, 105; Kees Boterbloem, 'Soviet GIs or Decembrists? The Reintegration into Postwar Soviet Society of Russian Soldiers, POWs, Partisans, and Civilians who Lived under German Occupation', *War & Society* 25(1) (May 2006), 77–87.
55. Anvayer, *Krovotochit moya pamyat'*, 134–36, 146–47.
56. Anvayer, *Krovotochit moya pamyat'*, 148.
57. To the author's knowledge there have been no Russian reviews of *Krovotochit moya pamyat'*. Anvayer's memoir is strikingly absent from the website *Voennaya Literatura* (see above, note 9).
58. Barbara Alpern Engel, 'The Womanly Face of War. Soviet Women Remember World War II', in Nicole Ann Dombrovski (ed.), *Women and War in the Twentieth Century. Enlisted with or without Consent* (New York and London, 1999), 138–59.
59. Markwick and Charon Cardona, *Soviet Women on the Frontline*, 80, 228.
60. Markwick and Charon Cardona, *Soviet Women on the Frontline*, 80.
61. I.Ye. Bogacheva, *Dorogi, kotorye my vybiraem: Vospominaniya i razmyshleniya voennoi medsestry* [The Roads We Choose: Memoirs and Reflections of a Military Nurse], 2nd ed. (Voronezh, 2005), 54–55.
62. Zhukova, *Devushka so snaiperskoi vintovkoi*, 156–61; Markwick and Charon Cardona, *Soviet Women on the Frontline*, 228.
63. 'Vospominaniya Savoskinoi E.K.', manuscript from the Central Museum of the Great Patriotic War, Moscow (TsMVOV). See Markwick and Charon Cardona, *Soviet Women on the Frontline*, 47–48.
64. Markwick, 'The Great Patriotic War', 711–13; 'Moscow Hosts First Meeting of Russian Military History Society', available at: http://english.ruvr.ru/2013_03_14/Moscow-hosts-first-meeting-of-Russian-Military-History-Society/ (accessed 28 April 2013).
65. Zhan T. Toshchenko, 'Historical Consciousness and Historical Memory: An Analysis of the Current Situation', *Russian Studies in History* 49(1) (Summer 2010), 40–42; Aleksandr S. Seniavskii and Elena S. Seniavskaia, 'The Historical Memory of Twentieth-Century Wars as an Arena of Ideological, Political, and Psychological Confrontation', *Russian Studies in History* 49(1) (Summer 2010), 72–73.
66. Makhotina, 'Refracted Memories', 31.

BIBLIOGRAPHY

Memoirs

Anvayer, S. *Krovotochit moya pamyat': iz zapisok studentki-medichki* [Bleeds My Memory: Notes of a Female Medical Student]. Moscow, ROSSPEN, 2005.

Anvayer, S.I. 'Kontslager' Shtutgof' [Shtutgof Concentration Camp], in *Lyudi pobedivshie smert'* [People Who Defeated Death] (Leningrad, 1968), 278–313.

Bogacheva, I.Ye. *Dorogi, kotorye my vybiraem: Vospominaniya i razmyshleniya voennoi medsestry* [The Roads We Choose: Memoirs and Reflections of a Military Nurse], 2nd ed. Voronezh: VGU, 2005.

Jahn, P. 'Opora pamyati – vremya pamyati' [The Basis of Memory is the Time of Memory], in P. Jahn (ed.), *Triumph und Trauma: Sowetische und Post Sowetische Erinnerung an der Krieg 1941–45* [Triumph and Trauma: Soviet and Post-Soviet Memory of the War, 1941-45](Berlin-Karlshorst: Christoph Links-Verlag, 2005), 8–21.

Lomonosov, D. *Zapiski ryadovo radista. Front. Plen. Vozvrashchenie. 1941–1946* [Notes of a Rank and File Radio Operator. Frontline. Imprisonment. Return. 1941–1946]. Moscow: Tsentropoligraf, 2012.

Shelkov, Mikhail. *Zapiski komandira strelkovovo batal'ona. Ot Rzheva do Vostochnoi Prussii. 1942–1945* [Notes of a Rifle Battalion Commander. From Rezhev to East Prussia, 1942–1945]. Moscow: Tsentropoligraf, 2010.

Timofeyeva-Yegorova, A. *Red Sky, Black Death. A Soviet Women Pilot's Memoir of the Eastern Front*, trans. by M. Ponomareva and K. Green. Bloomington, IN: Slavica, 2009.

Timofeyeva-Yegorova, A.A. *Derzhis, Sestrenka!* [Stand Firm, Little Sister!] (Moscow, 1983).

Vladimirov, Y. *V Nemetskom plenu. Zapiski vyzhivshevo 1942–1945* [In German Captivity. Notes of a Survivor]. Moscow: Tsentropoligraf, 2010.

Zhukova, Y. *Devushka so snaiperskoi vintovkoi: Vospominanii vypusknitsy tsentral"noi zhenskoi shkoly snaiperskoi podgotovki 1944–1945* [Young Woman with a Sniper's Rifle: Memoirs of a Graduate of the Central Women's Sniper Training School 1944–1945]. Moscow: Tsentropoligraf, 2006.

Zubkova, E. *Russia after the War. Hopes, Illusions, and Disappointments, 1945–1957*, trans. and ed. by H. Ragsdale. New York and London: M.E. Sharpe, 1998.

Secondary Sources

Alpern Engel, B. 'The Womanly Face of War. Soviet Women Remember World War II', in N.A. Dombrovski (ed.), *Women and War in the Twentieth Century. Enlisted with or without Consent* (New York and London: Garland Publishing, 1999), 138–59.

Aron, L. *Roads to the Temple. Truth, Memory, Ideas, and Ideals in the Making of the Russian Revolution, 1987–1991*. New Haven and London: Yale University Press, 2012.

Boterbloem, K. 'Soviet GIs or Decembrists? The Reintegration into Postwar Soviet Society of Russian Soldiers, POWs, Partisans, and Civilians who Lived under German Occupation'. *War & Society* 25(1) (May 2006), 77–87.

Davies, R.W. *Soviet History in the Gorbachev Revolution*. Houndmills, Basingstoke: MacMillan Press, 1989.

Edele, M. *Soviet Veterans of World War II: A Popular Movement in an Authoritarian Society, 1941–1991*. Oxford and New York: Oxford University Press, 2008.

Ellis, F. *The Damned and the Dead. The Eastern Front through the eyes of Soviet and Russian Novelists*. Lawrence, KS: University of Kansas Press, 2011.

Hösler, J. 'Aufarbeitung der Vergangenheit? Der Große Vaterländische Krieg in der Historiographie der UdSSR und in Rußland' [Reworking the Past? The Great Fatherland War in the Historiography of the USSR and Russia]. *Osteuropa* 55(4–5) (2005), 115–25.

Hynes, S. *The Soldiers' Tale: Bearing Witness to Modern War*. New York: Penguin Books, 1998.

Kuromiya, H. 'Soviet Memoirs as a Historical Source', in S. Fitzpatrick and L. Viola (eds), *A Researcher's Guide to Sources on Soviet Social History in the 1930s* (New York and London: M.E. Sharpe, 1992), 233–54.

Liljeström, M. 'The Remarkable Revolutionary Woman: Rituality and Performativity in Soviet Women's Autobiographical Texts from the 1970s', in M. Liljeström, A. Rosenholm and I. Savkina (eds), *Models of Self: Russian Women's Autobiographical Texts* (Helsinki: Kikimora Publications, 2000), 81–100.

Makhotina, E. 'Refracted Memories. The Great Patriotic War in Russia Today', in C. Freytag et al. (eds), *Juni 1941 Der Tiefe Schnitt / June 1941 The Deepest Cut* (Berlin-Karlshorst: Ch. Links Verlag, 2011), 28–39.

Markwick, R.D. 'Censorship and Fear: Historical Research in the Soviet Union'. *Groniek. Historisch Tijdschrift* 46(201) (Winter 2014/2015), 371–86.

Markwick, R.D. 'The Great Patriotic War in Soviet and Post-Soviet Collective Memory', in D. Stone (ed.), *The Oxford Handbook of Postwar European History* (Oxford: Oxford University Press, 2012), 692–713.

Markwick, R.D. '"A Sacred Duty": Red Army Women Veterans Remembering the Great Fatherland War, 1941–1945'. *Australian Journal of Politics and History* 54(3) (2008), 403–20.

Markwick, R.D., and E. Charon Cardona. *Soviet Women on the Frontline in the Second World War*. Basingstoke: Palgrave Macmillan, 2012.

Naumov, V. 'Sud'ba voennoplennykh i deportirovannykh grazhdan SSSR. Materialy komissii po reabilitatsii zhertv politicheskikh repressi,' [The Fate of Prisoners of War and Deported Citizens of the USSR. Information from the Commission for the Rehabilitation of the Victims of Political Repression] *Novaya i noveishaya istoriya* 2 (1996), 91–112.

Repina, L.P. 'Historical Memory and Contemporary Historical Scholarship'. *Russian Studies in History* 49(1) (2010), 8–25.

Seniavskii, A.S., and E.S. Seniavskaia. 'The Historical Memory of Twentieth-Century Wars as an Arena of Ideological, Political, and Psychological Confrontation'. *Russian Studies in History* 49(1) (Summer 2010), 53–91.

Toshchenko, Zh. T. 'Historical Consciousness and Historical Memory: An Analysis of the Current Situation'. *Russian Studies in History* 49(1) (Summer 2010), 37–52.

Tumarkin, N. *The Living and the Dead: The Rise and Fall of the Cult of World War II in Russia*. New York: Basic Books, 1994.

Walker, B. 'On Reading Soviet Memoirs: A History of the "Contemporaries" Genre as an Institution of Russian Intelligentsia Culture from the 1790s to the 1970s'. *The Russian Review* 59(3) (2000), 327–52.

Roger D. Markwick is Professor of Modern European History, the University of Newcastle, Australia. He is the lead co-author of *Soviet Women on the Frontline in the Second World War* (Palgrave-McMillan, 2012), which was shortlisted for the 2013 NSW Premier's History Awards. His *Rewriting History in Soviet Russia: The Politics of Revisionist Historiography in the Soviet Union, 1956–1974* (Palgrave-McMillan, 2001) won the Alexander Nove Prize in Russian, Soviet, and Post-Soviet Studies in 2003. He co-authored *Russia's Stillborn Democracy? From Gorbachev to Yeltsin* (Oxford University Press, 2000). Roger Markwick's latest research, supported by an ARC Discovery Project grant, is on Soviet women on the home front during the Second World War.

Chapter 8

Reimagining the Yugoslav Partisan Epic

Vesna Drapac

A Yugoslav state was established twice in the wake of war. The experience, memory and abuse of the memory of war shaped the history of these states. This was as much the case after 1918 as it was after 1945. It was commonly argued that war had channelled the Yugoslav revolutions, nationalist in 1918 and socialist in 1945. The Partisan Epic in many ways eclipsed the memory of the First World War and was the creation story on which the new Yugoslavia was built. It recounted how a small band of guerrilla fighters under the command of Josip Broz Tito (1892–1980) won over the hearts and minds of the majority of Yugoslavs to form a 'people's army' which expelled the foreign fascists and defeated their local collaborators. This epic was documented and idealised in different sources including memoirs. It became an integral component of the official historiography of the war, the main contours of which could be said to have remained in place until Tito's death.

While there were challenges to the idealised version of the Partisans' war during Tito's lifetime, it was after 1980 that revisionism grew exponentially. This was particularly evident in the Serbian academy, as has been demonstrated clearly by several historians.[1] There were a number of components to the revisionist push.[2] It included an attack on the official historiography of the war with a particular focus on the accusation of collaboration against the Serbian-led remnants of the Yugoslav army, commonly referred to as the Chetniks, and their leader, Dragoljub (Draža) Mihailović (1893–1946). Mihailović was tried and found guilty of war crimes and high treason and was executed in 1946. In the new Serbian histories of the Second World War the Chetniks' reputation as true heroes of the resistance was restored.

This chapter is timely because of the now complete official rehabilitation of Mihailović. The process of rehabilitation was facilitated, even propelled, by the partial, ideologised and gendered articulation of the resistance ideal and an inflexible interpretation of collaboration in the official historiography. The collapse of communism led to the collapse of the Partisan Epic in many quarters and then to the implantation of a number of counter-myths. I do not present a systematic or comprehensive study of the vast memoir literature here. Such an undertaking would be well beyond the scope of the chapter. My goal is limited to arguing that the revisionist pendulum has swung too far from the resistance ideal and that the memoir literature can help us understand both why this was possible and how we might restore some sense of equilibrium.

A WAR OF ABSOLUTES

It is important to have a sense of the way in which the war was conceptualised in order to understand the historiographical fragmentation that accompanied revisionism. In their descriptions of resistance in Yugoslavia many historians inside and outside the country evoked the Balkanist paradigm, depicting an exceptionally savage war in which primitive peoples, easily manipulated or driven by dark passions and age-old ethnic hatreds, ran amuck. It was also a war of absolutes. One was for the enemy or against him. Conversion narratives notwithstanding, there were generally no grey areas of thought and behaviour in the resistance narrative in which a supranational Yugoslav resistance triumphed magnificently over foreign oppression and extreme collaboration.

Academic writing on the war generally reinforced this image. The official Yugoslav history of the great, patriotic, all-national, anti-fascist struggle was also instrumentalised and became fixed. It did not and could not acknowledge the coexistence of multiple resistances. It was not a historiography of nuances or of subtleties in behaviour and remained untouched by the impact of social histories of the war and occupation regimes as they evolved in Western European historiography from the late 1960s.

What complicates the case of the historiography of Yugoslav resistance and revisionism is the national question. In some respects this national question is (understandably) obscured in the memoir literature, which celebrates the cross-national appeal of the Partisans and their call to arms on the foundation stone of 'brotherhood and unity'. But there were important differences in the experience and depiction of resistance and collaboration among and within the nationalities. For coherence and clarity, this chapter will focus largely though not entirely on the Serbian example.[3] The dominance of Serbs in the resistance narrative and in debates about resistance and revisionism warrants this focus. One of the premises of the Partisan Epic was that during the war a new (federative) Yugoslavism, born of the revolutionary impulse, eclipsed the system of Serb domination under a royal dictatorship. The highly centralised Yugoslav Kingdom had to be overthrown because it was corrupt, unrepresentative and oppressed non-Serbs. Further, the agents of that government – whether in London or in Serbia – had as their primary goal not the liberation of the country, but the restoration of the old regime. These arguments, among other basic assumptions in the memoir literature and in what became the official historiography, were the first casualties in the near total rejection of the Partisan Epic by revisionists after the death of Tito and prior to the collapse of Yugoslavia. Historians began to speak of the 'myth' of Serbian domination in the first Yugoslavia.[4]

The Partisan Epic was created during the war itself but, simultaneously, an alternative resistance story was promoted by the Yugoslav government-in-exile in London. This alternative narrative focused on Chetniks as resisters of the first hour. The Chetniks were subsequently 'betrayed' by the Allies who were duped into believing that the communists were the more effective resistance force and that the Chetniks were collaborating in order to neutralise their main rivals, the Partisans. This version of events was expanded upon relentlessly by anti-communist Serb émigrés, a group of British and American historians as well as veterans of the war.[5] Tomislav Dulić has shown that diasporic communities and émigrés who became academics played a vital role in forming the 'social memory' of Chetnik resistance.[6] This strand of writing on the war in Yugoslavia was continuous outside the country from the 1940s. It aligned itself with the Serbian nationalist revival of the 1980s, which drew on the memory of both world wars, and informed the revisionist interpretations of the Partisan Epic.[7]

As is the case elsewhere, Yugoslav resistance has undergone a general process of demythologisation whereby the early post-war resistance ideal is now routinely debunked in many quarters. In 1988, John Sweets argued that the new historiography of France as a 'nation of collaborators' led to distortions in the interpretation of French resistance.[8] I would add that it led to still greater distortions in the interpretation of collaboration.[9] Unlike in France, however, the Yugoslav resistance story was also prone to nationalist manipulation and appropriation.[10] This was in part because, as many have argued, the memory of 'ethnic hatreds' that flared up in the war was suppressed in the official historiography. However, ethnicised interpretations of the war were embedded in the Partisan Epic even when they were masked by slogans about the cross-national basis of the anti-fascist struggle and the realisation of 'brotherhood and unity'.

Resistance as depicted in the Partisan Epic was almost exclusively military, political and, in spite of the large numbers of women involved, masculine. In this sense it was not unlike the idealised depiction of resistance in other countries which focused on the outcomes of resistance rather than the processes that made it possible.[11] The simplistic explanation of the success of resistance over collaboration and foreign occupation from within these narrow interpretative parameters (military, political and masculine) is the most important factor contributing to the demise of the resistance ideal in Europe and, in our case, the demystification of the Partisan Epic.

THE MEMOIR LITERATURE AT A GLANCE

In Yugoslav Partisan writings we have a blurring of the lines between personal memoirs, diaries, propaganda, popular culture, official histories and the work of academic historians. A Partisan memoir might be a composite of notes taken during the war, a diary and documents collected retrospectively. It might draw predominantly on memory or on one's wartime writings and speeches. Some of the memoirs are highly detailed, covering multiple volumes or devoting hundreds of pages to a particular area or event. Given the ubiquitousness over the last two decades of approaches to history drawing on memory, and given the centrality of the world wars to the history of both Yugoslavias, it is perhaps surprising that there is no systematic study of these writings.[12] This gap in the literature may in part be explained by the fact that works on memory and history have generally focused on cultural rather than social and political themes.[13] Furthermore, the memoirs are often very long and stylistically unimaginative or formulaic. The writing can be turgid, episodic, repetitive and formal, not to say wooden. There are exceptions, including, for example, *Wartime* (1977) by the famous dissident Milovan Djilas (1911–95) and *Tebi, moja Dolores* (1978) by Saša Božović (1912–95). *Wartime*, first published in English, was hailed as a classic of the genre by Djilas's Anglophone reviewers and Božović's highly personal account of her years as a Partisan doctor, published in Belgrade, enjoyed great success.

My reflections on this literature are informed by the work of historians like Mark Hewitson and Yuval Harari who have stimulated a renewed interest in 'ego documents' relating to the experience of war.[14] Robert Gildea and Omer Bartov, among others, argue that concerns about the reliability of witness testimony and personal narratives have led to an overly cautious approach to their use.[15] Gildea writes that first-hand accounts are important for many reasons, including because they reveal the meaning resisters gave to their actions.[16] New histories of the war in Yugoslavia draw on this kind of material to good effect.[17] Evidently, we should approach the memoirs cautiously and interrogate them as we would any other historical sources. The memoirs are partial and often self-serving. Many were written by powerful men who sought to celebrate their military achievements, to discredit their political enemies and to legitimise their ascendancy after 1945. The selective and very specific local or regional focus of some memoirs makes it difficult to generalise from particular examples. However, the memoirs also present us with a fascinating and instructive body of material and are deserving of much closer attention as sources in themselves. It is precisely their partiality that makes these works so valuable, providing a unique glimpse into the life and mentality of elite Partisans as well as less well-known resisters. As the official story of the war was regulated, the memoirs also illustrate what was deemed important and acceptable in conveying the resistance story and why.

Often memoirists write that their primary goal is simply to 'tell the truth', to present the story as they remember it for posterity. Rodoljub Čolaković (1900–83) was political commissar to the Partisan detachments in Bosnia-Herzegovina and a factional rival of Tito. His multivolume memoir was first published in 1956 and then condensed into one volume and translated into English in 1962. He commented that he was not interested in writing 'history' but in providing the 'raw material' for the histories others would write. He believed that eyewitness accounts 'prompt reflection' and that as he had contributed to key military and political decisions, there would surely be some interest in what he had to say. *Winning Freedom*, as his work was evocatively titled in English,[18] suggests succinctly what we might expect in the story about to unfold. Similarly, Peko Dapčević (1913–99), who became commander of the 1st and 4th armies and participated in the liberation of Belgrade, informs us that, while he is no historian, he has much to teach his readers on the nature and evolution of Partisan warfare.[19]

The most important factor conveyed in this literature is that under the leadership of Tito and the Communist Party a highly effective military force was created. A people's army emerged from a small band of poorly equipped but independent, united and determined believers and heroes. Dapčević focuses on strategy and tactics to explain this successful transition. Over 243 pages he explains why the Partisans were able to defeat a much better armed and larger force. The combination of small-scale manoeuvres and regular offensives surprised and wore down the invaders and their local lackeys. These tactics were underpinned by unity of vision and an indefatigable determination to expel an enemy that was unprepared for the kind of war the Partisans waged.[20]

The memoirs show how the war and revolution became entangled. This convergence legitimised the new state. In any single volume we find repeated, several times, stock phrases about the Partisans' action as the articulation of the people's will. Detailed descriptions of key political moments, including the first and second meetings of the Anti-Fascist Council for the People's Liberation of Yugoslavia (AVNOJ) in Bihać (November 1942) and Jajce (November 1943) and the resolutions resulting from those meetings, are common. We learn that, as they expelled the occupiers and neutralised their local collaborators, the Partisans made a new country and that, above all, the revolutionary transition was legal. Significantly, we also learn that the Partisans made and liberated the new Yugoslavia independently. The Allies did not hand them victory, nor did the Soviets make the Yugoslavs' revolution. This emphasis on the singularity of the Yugoslavs' war was evident in writings prior to the split with the Soviet Union in 1948, but more strident thereafter. Mitra Mitrović (1912–2001) joined the Communist Party in 1933 and was a prominent feminist, a leader in the Anti-Fascist Front of Women and an editor of the chief organ of the Communist Party, *Borba*, which was published underground during the war.[21] Mitrović was not alone when she noted, pointedly, that Stalin had not recognised the Yugoslavs or their battle. In fact, the Soviets were dismissive. Moreover, they were not worthy to lead the Yugoslav revolutionaries. After a meeting with the Soviet Mission, Mitrović was left with a negative impression of the Russians as morally reprehensible men who drank too much and who seemed to expect to be entertained or 'serviced' by local women.[22]

Stories of suffering, sacrifice and extreme hardship abound in firsthand accounts of Partisan warfare. There are long descriptions of columns trudging through snow, making their way across fast flowing rivers and climbing perilously steep mountain passes. The Partisans cobbled together uniforms from whatever they could lay their hands on, even if it meant using parts of the uniforms of dead enemy soldiers. They ate grass when there was nothing else or when the local populations were unwelcoming. The memoirs, with their descriptions of the constant marching back and forth over territory that is taken, lost and retaken, suggest that men and women who were less driven would have given up the battle. The Partisans were able to continue because of their superhuman determination, their courage, their loyalty, the knowledge that they were fighting for a just and urgent cause, and because 'the people', recognising these qualities, were inspired to follow them.

The memoirs thus invariably document how ordinary women and men either supported the Partisans from the outset, or were won over to their cause in greater and greater numbers. Mitrović notes that guards who were persuaded to 'cross over' helped her and others to escape when they were arrested in Belgrade. She acknowledges that sometimes it was hard for peasants to know what to do and who to support, or even who it was that was passing through their village.[23] But over time the majority of people became convinced that the Partisans best served their interests. One of the underlying premises is that individually and collectively Partisans were morally upright humanitarians and that this was one of the reasons for their appeal. The memoirists paint themselves as respectful, dignified and mindful of their reputation. Famously, this was evident in the fact that there were to be no romantic liaisons between the fighting men and women. This unrealistic (and unrealisable) image of noble heroism and moral probity travelled well and was embraced and publicised internationally during the war. There is an emphasis always on the fact that nothing was taken from farms or villages without permission and we learn that if desperately needed supplies were not freely offered by the local population, the Partisans would not ask for them. In due course some of the Partisans broached the question of communists confiscating supplies from unsympathetic peasants, but for others this 'revelation' was contentious to the end. Božović, for example, never diverged from the idealised version of the epic on that score. She notes how the Partisans would not take a plum or an apple that had fallen from a tree, even where the orchards were bursting with summer produce.[24] Božović unfailingly comments on the generosity of people who shared their food spontaneously with the Partisans for the simple reason that they had faith in them. Partisans relied on and gladly accepted this help from (generally unnamed) locals. While, for the most part, there is a notable absence of humility in the men's memoirs, the mere acceptance of such generosity, it becomes evident, could be humbling in itself. Given what we know about the numbers of people involved directly or indirectly with the Partisans, it had to be the case that ever-widening circles of sympathisers sustained the insurgents.

On the occasions we glimpse the Partisans as emotional beings it becomes evident that the memoirs can provide nuanced insights into the mental world of the activists. Descriptions of the care of their wounded provide a good example of this. The fourth enemy offensive, Operation Weiss or the Battle of the River Neretva (February–March 1943), was known also as the Battle for the Wounded. Time after time we read that the Partisans would not leave the wounded behind because their fate, if they were caught by the enemy, would be certain death. Mitrović mentions this when describing how the wounded were transported carefully across the River Piva in spite of the urgency of the situation, the great risk this posed to all and the enormous effort it involved. The wounded did not want to hold up their comrades but it was out of the question that they would be abandoned.[25] When under heavy attack or trapped, the wounded were hidden in caves. Božović's memoir commemorates the work of the medical attachments and the multitude of volunteers who ensured that the wounded would be protected. It also describes the gratitude of the wounded towards those who helped them.

Nothing reveals as much about the emotional lives of the Partisans, men and women, as the descriptions of the death of family members. Božović suffered the loss of her daughter, Dolores, who was born while she was interned and died eighteen months later from exposure.[26] The way Božović dealt with her grief – through the comfort of her friends and by getting on with the job at hand – evidently moved her readers. Her memoir was clearly a kind of dedication to the lost child. Schoolchildren's reactions to the first printing of the book were documented in later editions. Many teachers had organised class projects inspired by Božović's story. Some pupils wrote poems in her honour while men and women inundated Božović with letters of support and sympathy. The book was a publishing phenomenon, possibly in part because it told a simple and accessible Partisan story that was largely unfamiliar or that had been obscured over the decades by cynicism and revelations about the far from positive side of Partisan action in the field. Other deaths – of friends and fellow fighters or, in the case of Božović, the doctors and nurses with whom she worked, as well as her patients – are also recorded poignantly in the memoir literature.[27]

CRACKS IN THE FACADE

The points discussed thus far indicate the wealth of anecdotal and generic material contained within the memoirs and hint at the integrative potential of the Partisan Epic. However, it is also evident that the memoirs constructed the epic in such a way as to make it vulnerable to distortion over time. Historians in the successor states of the former Yugoslavia have reinterpreted, re-evaluated and revised the official Tito-centred historiography of the war – and the embedded Partisan Epic – differently. While some questions have overarching relevance (for example the nature of resistance itself), there are concerns, priorities and debates that are specific to particular regions or republics. My focus on the example of Serbia is pertinent because it reveals how one historiographical tradition has been so effectively displaced by another and why this is problematic. I have identified four themes from the memoirs that illustrate especially well why the official story was easily undermined. The first is creating order out of chaos, necessitating the replacement of an unjust regime with one that was just. The second is the treatment of collaboration. The third is the place of Tito in the narrative. The fourth is the narrow, gendered understanding of what it meant to resist.

Creating Order out of Chaos

The Partisans claimed that they created unity out of disunity and order out of chaos. Their motivation was to replace an unrepresentative regime with one that was representative. Expelling the occupier was not enough; his departure had to be accompanied by the establishment of a new Yugoslavia. Creating unity out of disunity was possible because of good leadership and because of the constancy and single-mindedness of the Partisan warriors, many of whom came to the war with a pedigree of suffering having spent years in the political prisons of the Kingdom of Yugoslavia.[28] Loyalty came from ideological cohesion. The 'conversions', and the mass support that ensued, were evidence of the fact that the Partisans had convinced the wider population of the correctness of their interpretation of events, and of history itself. The unity forged in war precipitated and legitimised the post-war seizure of power or, as many would come to refer to it, the second Yugoslav revolution.

A sense of order is reinforced by the way the memoirists recall the most important components of what is termed 'Partisan culture'. We are told that meetings, properly chaired and during which the views of all were welcome and respected, are central to the basic organisational structures put in place where the Partisans had wrested power from the occupiers or from the collaborators. Theatrical and musical evenings, dancing the *kolo*, singing and poetry readings elevated their gatherings. The new administrative and educational centres showed what was possible in the realm of progressive social policy to those (mostly peasant) Yugoslavs whom the old regime had left on the periphery. Božović's memoir provides consistent support for this position with her representation of the morally upright Partisan. She was writing a little later than Djilas, who, by contrast undermined this cornerstone of the Partisan legend with his 'honest' appraisal of Partisan violence, which he described as endemic to the inhabitants of the land itself.

Djilas was well known for his dissidence and his classic critique of communist totalitarianism, *The New Class* (1957). The book brought him considerable international attention and admiration.[29] We have seen that *Wartime* was also highly praised. Critics noted that it acknowledged Partisan excesses while stopping short of relativising them. This was viewed as one of the greatest strengths of *Wartime*, showing its authenticity and the author's integrity while at the same time revealing that bad things had to be done to win the 'good' Second World War. But, in reality, Djilas reprises all the old truths about the nature of the 'very bad' or 'dirty' Balkan war, suggesting that it was necessary to put a heavy lid on the hotbed of extreme and primal passions the region had spawned over centuries.

Djilas frequently refers to the violence embedded in the landscape and in the very being of 'Yugoslav' people. The violence of the 'Balkan man' was a recurring motif in much of his work and evidence of the salience of the Balkanist discourse embraced by notable writers and thinkers in the region.[30] The example he draws on is, often, his native Montenegro, the 'land without justice'.[31] He described a much admired Montenegrin-born Partisan, Sava Kovačević (1905–43), as a natural born rebel 'beyond consciousness and ideology', a leader and symbol 'apart from the party'. Djilas continued: 'Inside him ... warfare and struggle were inevitable, particularly on the soil which bore him and at the time he lived in'.[32] Djilas noted how 'hatreds flared' in all their 'elemental and destructive dimensions'. This was generalised across all the warring groups: 'we, high up in the party, did not really comprehend [these hatreds] even though we had inflamed them'.[33] It was by harnessing and redirecting this destructive energy that the forces for good would triumph (if only temporarily). He conveys the idea of war as a cleansing agent and a necessary precondition for peace in Yugoslavia. This was seen to be a reasonable position and, because he was no longer in good standing with the regime and therefore apparently had nothing to gain or lose by what he wrote, his was, by default, a 'balanced' account. Regardless of his intentions, it was only a short step from *Wartime* to the extreme revisionism of the following decade. A key element of the demystification of Partisan resistance involved gradual revelations about their violence and punitive campaigns against local opponents. These revelations were central to the rationalisation and justification – and then the denial – of Chetnik collaboration.

Interpreting Collaboration

The treatment of the obvious 'quislings' varies little over time in the memoirs and the official historiography. This is as true of the Croat Ante Pavelić (1889–1959) and the Ustaše he led in the Independent State of Croatia (Nezavisna Država Hrvatska) as it is of the Serb collaborators. The latter included the Yugoslav government-in-exile, their representative on the ground, Mihailović, and Milan Nedić (1877–1946), the prime minister of the so-called Government of National Salvation between 1941 and 1944. Collaborationists represent the desperate expression of the old bourgeois elites who exhibited reactionary and chauvinistic tendencies. But the treatment of the *faux* resisters, the Chetniks, was more challenging given the historic ties of the Allies and the Serbs and the role of the Yugoslavs in London. It was also a question of rivalry between the Partisans and Chetniks for resources and support, which resulted in the ruthless clashes between them and a legacy of bitterness. There could be no 'alliance' between Partisans and Chetniks or a plurality of 'resistances' in this context.

As noted above, a constant refrain was that the government-in-exile stood for Serbian hegemony and Serbian ultra-nationalism. It did not and could not represent true Yugoslavism but spoke for a now defunct antidemocratic monarchical order. According to the Partisans, the London Yugoslavs, the Chetniks and Nedić, effectively, worked as one. All had as their main goal to eradicate or 'crush' the Partisans, their greatest enemy. They were prepared to do this even if it meant using the materiel provided by the Allies for the fight against the Axis forces, against the Partisans. The Chetniks were therefore more insidious than the Ustaše, who were always beholden to the Germans and without whose support they would have been overthrown. Their proximity to the Allied leadership in London assured the Chetniks of power and influence disproportionate to their support among Yugoslavs. Čolaković refers to his fellow Serbs who were collaborating as the 'scum of the land'.[34] Djilas writes that the Chetniks were merely 'an auxiliary army of the invaders'.[35] Set pieces in the memoirs include the 'coming across' of Yugoslav army personnel who grew frustrated with the Chetniks' policy of inaction towards the enemy on the one hand, and their desperate pursuit of the Partisans on the other. As he abandoned the Chetniks for the Partisans, one such 'convert' remarked of his commanding officer that 'it's all *wait* with him' and added that Mihailović was 'a camouflaged fifth columnist'.[36]

The crudely propagandistic assessment of all collaboration remained static from the 1940s and is one of the key tributaries to Serbian revisionism of the 1980s. The failure to consider the range of motivations behind the Chetniks' inaction, including self-interest, pragmatism, ideology, the changing circumstances of the war, and the fear of reprisals – if only to reject their validity – allowed the revisionists eventually to ignore and deny completely the accusation of Chetnik collaboration. Veselin Djuretić's 1985 monograph, for example, *Saveznici i jugoslovenska ratna drama* [The Allies and the Yugoslav War Drama], has been described as having 'provided the most radical reappraisal of the Second World War and the [heretofore] proscribed Chetniks',[37] but he was not alone.[38] Typically, in order to gloss over the Chetniks' wartime transgressions, historians would present known Chetnik collaborators as unrepresentative renegades, 'irregulars' on the periphery and out of the control of the leadership. The revisionists were then able to replace what they termed the 'communists' lies' with their own, and to present a history of Chetniks that overlooks or relativises their collaboration and their national exclusivism. This approach has reinforced the exceptionalist paradigm and stereotypical (ethnicised) interpretations of collaboration. Neither denying collaboration nor categorising it exclusively as extreme helps us to understand or explain it.

Fallen Hero

The toppling of the greatest hero of the Partisan Epic, Tito, from his pedestal was the most definitive act of revisionism. In most of the memoirs Tito is a distant and respected figure but the Partisans still tend to exhibit a strong personal attachment to him. Mitrović writes that he was the main target of the collaborators and the occupiers and that the Germans were much more aggressive in their aerial attacks when they thought Tito was present. Tito's concern for the rank and file is communicated in a multitude of anecdotes. Mitrović notes that when they heard that Tito would not cross the River Neretva until the last of the wounded had reached the other side, local peasants burst into tears so fearful were they for his safety.[39]

As Djilas became less ideologically dogmatic and then overtly critical of communism, he was more disparaging towards his former master, Tito. (Other Partisans expressed similar sentiments soon after.)[40] Academic reviewers were particularly interested in the way Djilas described Tito. As mentioned above, it seemed at the time as if Djilas's was a balanced approach: he had simply and unceremoniously demystified Tito by showing his flaws. It was generally agreed that if Djilas had 'dissected the Partisan myth', it was in an even-handed way.[41] This was seen to be all the more laudable given that Djilas had spent years in prison for his ideological transgressions and criticisms of the Party. In fact, Djilas is derisive and condescending towards Tito, whom he regards as his intellectual inferior. Djilas wrote that '[t]he talent of revolutionary leaders is measured by their organizational inventiveness and political acumen'.[42] As we proceed through *Wartime*, it becomes obvious that he was referring to his own talent as a leader, not Tito's. Far from creative, Tito had, according to Djilas, a 'way of quietly absorbing the ideas of others only to put them forward later as his own, when they had passed through the sieve of his pragmatism'.[43] Evidently Djilas's ideas were among those Tito 'absorbed'. While energetic and persevering, Tito was also derivative, dogmatic and soft. Already in the war he expected and accepted privileges. A cow was in tow to provide him with fresh milk and his female companion was also in close proximity. Djilas in his 'innocence' had not realised that during the war Tito's secretary was really his mistress and suggests that he was put out by the fact that that the rules on moral probity did not seem to apply to Tito himself.

It was not long after his death that Tito, the charismatic leader of the resistance, came to be seen as one of the century's greatest hoaxers and tyrants. Henceforth there were few obstacles to the dismantling of the Partisan Epic. It is not a question of reclaiming the lost honour of Partisan heroes. The problem is, rather, the heroicisation of resistance itself. The dichotomous approach which depends on the identification of absolute heroes and victims on the one hand, and absolute villains on the other, persists under a different guise. The obsessive need to exonerate or to condemn those who lived the war has had a negative impact on the history and memory of resistance and collaboration everywhere. Serbian historiography is no different on that score.

Gender Blindness

One of the most obvious gaps in the official historiography, and one which smoothed the path of revisionism, is the near complete failure to incorporate gender into the master narrative of the Partisan Epic. Both resistance and collaboration were understood from within a narrowly political, military or ethnicised interpretative framework. Women's writing and reminiscences reveal that there was not a single model of resistance and invite further speculation on what it meant to resist in Yugoslavia, a definitional question that has been (and continues to be) neglected. The taxonomies of resistance and collaboration, which perhaps have been over-theorised in central and western European historiography, are barely acknowledged in histories of the Yugoslavs' war. The result is a simplistic understanding of wartime behaviour generally, and of resistance and collaboration in particular.

There have been a number of important and detailed studies of women Partisans.[44] During the war, the 'fighting women of Yugoslavia' were praised in the Allied press. Some early reports incorrectly identified these 'fighting women' with Chetnik resistance, though this misapprehension was rectified in due course. According to the Allies, women's activism indicated the widespread popularity of the Partisan resistance movement as well as the bravery of the female combatants. So the problem is not that we are unaware of the role of women in the resistance, but that our approach to this question is determined by relatively narrow criteria and women are normally treated in a parallel historiography. A range of issues that do not necessarily shed light on resistance (or collaboration) thus become entangled. For example, in some studies the key questions are whether or not women were treated equally in the Partisan movement (which, of course, they were not) or whether, collectively, they emerged from the war 'emancipated' or 'liberated' in a social sense due to their resistance experiences (which, again, they did not). The focus on women as secondary in the organised resistance blinds us to the broader understanding of resistance and collaboration a general study of women's lives can afford. The idea of gender blindness therefore relates to the way in which resistance has been conceptualised and the overriding focus on organised resistance and resistance structures where the dominance of men was to be expected.[45]

The memoirs of outsiders indicate their fascination with the participation of women in the resistance. Major William Jones, a Special Operations Executive (SOE) operative who spent a year with the Partisans in Slovenia and Croatia from May 1943 wrote *Twelve Months with Tito's Partisans* before the war had ended and it was published in 1946. Jones mentions women, often, throughout the book. But he goes further, devoting an entire chapter to women in the National Liberation Movement. He opens this chapter with the following words: 'Full recognition must be given to the women of Jugoslavia, for their part in the struggle for freedom was equally as great as that of their men. They were an indispensable part of the Freedom Movement, and without them, the men readily admitted, this movement could not have existed'.[46] Jones anticipated by over three decades the new history of resistance, or as the French would say, 'resistances', which sought to bring women in from the fringes to the centre of the resistance narrative. Basil Davidson, one time head of the Yugoslav section of the SOE, was parachuted into Bosnia in 1943. His memoir also devotes considerable space to women. Recognisable female stereotypes are fleshed out with descriptions recounting what he knew of their background and their public and private lives.[47]

The Partisan men mention women in their memoirs too. There are routine references to women's bravery and commitment. Many also glibly remark that women were often more heroic than men, and there the story generally ends. For the most part these women remain faceless. The women's writing, however, indicates something different, including the fact that resistance took many forms. Writing in 1953, Mitrović was close to her male counterparts in the topics covered and in her matter of fact style. While praised, her work was nonetheless described as, characteristically, the work of a woman, emotive and unscientific.[48] Mitrović is more overtly political than Božović and focuses on the more traditional themes of the Partisan story, including the violence and cruelty of the occupiers and the collaborators. But both women emphasize the wider social processes sustaining the Partisans. Mitrović notes that women from Montenegro were proud to be fighting alongside men and writes about the case of a brother and sister who wanted to fight together and eventually got permission to do so.[49] She makes the point that, while women were eager to join the Partisans, there were no women fighting on the side of the occupiers. Tito's December 1942 address to women resisters is a noteworthy event for her and others, as are various communal manifestations.[50] Mitrović further points out that young women in Serbian villages in Lika welcomed her both because she had served with the proletarian units and because she was Serbian.[51] Unsurprisingly, given that she was writing at the high point of the new Yugoslavism and the triumph of 'brotherhood and unity', she observes also that Croatian, Serbian and Montenegrin women willingly assisted the Partisans in spite of the 'traitors' within their respective national groups.[52]

Božović's memoir builds on some of Mitrović's themes but her reflections are still more woman-centred. She draws attention to the necessary preconditions for the emergence of resistance, including the social milieu which nurtured and sustained it. Without due recognition of these preconditions resistance is distanced from its societal roots and resisters' acts are reduced to military heroics informed by communist slogans. Božović focuses on the daily routines and difficulties of her life as a doctor. The personal relationships forged with others (notably the nurses) were central to her work and her choice to resist. She is modest about her achievements. She unfailingly places herself within a collective of supporters and friends, reminding the reader that in such a war one could not function alone and that all victories, large and small, belonged to the group. Božović remained wedded to the idea of what she calls the 'humanism' that defined the Partisan movement. According to her, it was the commendable behaviour of the Partisans, their leadership by example, which enabled them to win more and more supporters. Interestingly, too, her Orthodox religious identity sat easily with her developing communist identity. Her reminiscences were in marked contrast to those of most of the male Partisans and at odds with the increasingly exclusive nationalism of the Serbian academy and its interpretation of the Second World War.

In the foreword to the fifth edition of Božović's memoir, published in 1981, a year after Tito's death, we read that her story is especially apposite. The 'ominous clouds' on the horizon were worrying and her book reminded readers, the younger generation in particular, that only with great sacrifices had the Partisans been able to rebuild the country after its inglorious defeat in 1941, a defeat that had been precipitated by the corruption of the old monarchical regime.[53] But there was a deep satisfaction among those who had taken part in the resistance struggle because they were united around a common and noble cause. Božović, like Djilas, evoked the grandeur of the struggle against fascism but she did not subvert it, consciously or unconsciously. In part this is because her intention was different from Djilas's and because the memories she drew on did not lend themselves to such subversion. She describes the daily challenges of a woman Partisan doctor, rather than tactics and strategy, political rivalries or the international context. Moreover, while she does write about the Partisans' experience of epic battles, it is from the perspective of their frailty and, often, from the perspective of the great resilience of the wounded and the devotion of their carers. Božović's memoir predates the revisionism that came after Tito's death, but the references in the foreword to the uncertainty of the times and the need to focus on the sacrifices of the heroic and the humble that had led to the birth of the new Yugoslavia, suggest that the fragmentation of the epic was well underway.

CONCLUSION

As Yugoslavia was collapsing in the 1990s more memoirists came out of the woodwork, including, interestingly, academics like Dimitrije Djordjevic. He had enjoyed a career in the United States and was a past president of the Association of Slavic History. In the 1990s he was counselling Serbs to restore their national integrity, by force if necessary. He wrote that his own memories had 'slumbered for half a century' because he had devoted himself 'to teaching and to historical research into the past of the Balkans'. Then he added:

> Memories resurged as my life is closing, as an answer to the request of a friend, a pro-Western follower of Mihailovich, shot by the Nazis at Banjica in 1942: 'Don't let them forget us!' In half a century of communist party rule in Yugoslavia the past was covered over and buried under one-sided and false claims. One forgets today the role which the anti-communist, pro-Western, pro-American and Serbian inspired Mihailovich movement played during World War II and the way it was sacrificed to the needs of international inter-allied politics. [...] The generation to which I belonged led the charge against overwhelming odds and was vanquished.[54]

It is important for us to recognise, as Dulić avers, that men like Djordjevic had a role in the shaping of Yugoslav historiography in a way that was ideologically and nationally charged. They were not unique in this sense, but their sympathies were concealed by their vaunted 'objectivity'. A similar trajectory may be found in the example of Stevan K. Pavlowitch whose influence was greater and whose raison d'être as a historian over several decades seems to have been to rehabilitate the London Yugoslavs and the Chetniks and to discredit works remotely positive in their appraisal of the Partisans.[55] Vladislav Marjanović traces the impact of such historians, suggesting that their theses about Yugoslav history gave the revisionists their launching pad and invested their work with credibility.[56]

The communists evoked a heroic paradigm of resistance that did not account fully for the preconditions necessary for successful resistance or explain the range of activities and behaviours that had sustained it. This was common to all epic histories of European resistance. Djilas reflected on why wars are necessary. He wrote that war is an agent facilitating or 'spawn[ing] hope and creativity' and to refuse to acknowledge this would amount to renouncing 'one's own inner nature'. Far from a necessary evil, war brought out the best in men and was the making of the Party. While obscuring or ignoring the role of women in the movement (and hence the war's many faces and the range of motivations of its combatants and non-combatants), Djilas especially praised Serbs, 'true warriors[,] a people who regard the army as their own, and war as something natural'.[57] The Partisan Epic was thus reduced to a series of nationalist struggles and alternative insights afforded by various sources, including the memoir literature, written off as mere propaganda.

The fact that official Yugoslav historiography could not accommodate deviations from the accepted interpretations of the war accounts in large part for the intensity and success of revisionism. As women were not integrated into this historiography and as it was gender blind, the complexity and nuanced nature of the resistance specifically, and the liberation movement as a whole, could never be conveyed properly. The fixed image of the female combatant as an honorary (or lesser) man reinforced the stereotypes of resistance. The dominant paradigm overemphasised heroic, masculine, individual refusal over the collective action of men and women, and overemphasised (the seemingly exceptionalist) nationalist confrontation over the cohesion that was necessary to expel the occupying forces and liberate the country. More serious reflection on the layered significance of women's involvement in the Partisan Epic might have provided an important contribution to European resistance historiography. But the ideologues were more concerned with making history serve political ends. The historiographical void they created was filled by their political enemies whose misrepresentation of the Partisan Epic has rendered the resistance narrative unrecognisable. The memoirs help us understand why this was the case. However, they can also provide the basis for a renewed study of the Partisans and the personal, social, political and cultural contexts in which they waged their war.

NOTES

1. For a comprehensive study, see J. Dragović-Soso, '*Saviours of the Nation*': *Serbia's Intellectual Opposition and the Revival of Nationalism* (London, 2002). See also D. Stojanović, 'Revisions of Second World War History in Contemporary Serbia', in S. Ramet and O. Listhaug (eds), *Serbia and the Serbs in World War Two* (Basingstoke, 2011), 247–64.
2. See V. Marjanović, 'L'historiographie contemporaine serbe des années 80: de la démystification idéologique à la mystification nationaliste', and 'L'histoire politisée. L'historiographie serbe depuis 1989', in A. Marès (ed.), *Histoire et pouvoir en Europe médiane* (Paris and Montreal, 1996), 139–70 and 283–308. See also S. Cvijic, 'Swinging the Pendulum: World War II History, Politics, National Identity and Difficulties of Reconciliation in Croatia and Serbia', *Nationalities Papers* 36(4) (2008), 713–40; and S. Cirković, 'Historiography in Isolation: Serbian Historiography Today', *Helsinki Monitor* 35 (1994), 35–40.
3. While this chapter draws on a range of memoirs, it refers predominantly to the following sample: S. Božović, *Tebi, moja Dolores*, 5th ed. (Belgrade, 1981 [1978]); R. Čolaković, *Winning Freedom*, trans. by A. Brown (London, 1962); P. Dapčević, *Kako smo vodili rat* (Belgrade, 1975 [1956]); B. Davidson, *Partisan Picture* (Bedford, 1946); M. Djilas, *Wartime: With Tito and the Partisans*, trans. by M. Petrovich (London, 1980 [1977]); W. Jones, *Twelve Months with Tito's Partisans* (Bedford, 1946); E. Kardelj, *Put nove Jugoslavije: članci i govori iz narodno-oslobodilačke borbe, 1941–1945* (Belgrade and Zagreb, 1946); E. Kardelj, *Reminiscences: The Struggle for Recognition and Independence: The New Yugoslavia, 1944–1957*, trans. by D. Norris, S. Peić and J. Wrench (London, 1982 [1980]); M. Mitrović, *Ratno putovanje* (Belgrade, 1962 [1953]); I. Ribar, *Uspomene iz narodno oslobodilačke borbe* (Belgrade, 1961); and V. Velebit, *Sećanja* (Zagreb, 1983).
4. See, for example, A. Dragnich, 'The Anatomy of a Myth: Serbian Hegemony', *Slavic Review* 50(3) (1991), 659–62.
5. A small selection includes M. Lees, *The Rape of Serbia: The British Role in Tito's Grab for Power 1943–1944* (New York, 1990); D. Martin, *Ally Betrayed: The Uncensored Story of Tito and Mihailovich*, foreword by R. West (New York, 1946); R. Mitchell, *Ruth Mitchell, Chetnik, Tells the Facts about the Fighting Serbs: Mihailovich and 'Yugoslavia'* (Arlington, VA, 1943); R. Mitchell, *The Serbs Choose*

War (New York, 1943); and J. Rootham, *Miss Fire: The Chronicle of a British Mission to Mihailovich, 1943–1944* (London, 1946).
6. T. Dulić, 'Sentenced "for Ideological and Political Reasons"? The Rehabilitation of Dragoljub "Draža" Mihailović in Serbia', *Sociologija* 54(4) (2012), 625–48.
7. Space does not allow for a discussion of the importance of the layering of the memories of both world wars in the memoir literature and revisionist discourse. I have broached this theme in V. Drapac, *Constructing Yugoslavia: A Transnational History* (Basingstoke, 2010).
8. J. Sweets, 'Hold that Pendulum! Redefining Fascism, Collaborationism and Resistance in France', *French Historical Studies* 15(4) (1988), 731–58.
9. See V. Drapac and G. Pritchard, 'Beyond Resistance and Collaboration: Towards a Social History of Politics in Hitler's Empire', *Journal of Social History* 48(4) (2015), 865–91.
10. See M. Hoare, 'Whose is the Partisan Movement? Serbs, Croats and the Legacy of a Shared Resistance', *Journal of Slavic Military Studies* 15(4) (2002), 24–41.
11. For a good summary of the changing perceptions and evolving historiography of resistance in France, see J. Jackson 'Introduction: Historians and the Occupation', in *France: The Dark Years, 1940–1944* (Oxford, 2003 [2001]), 1–20.
12. Memoirs and personal testimony, however, hold an important place in a number of key works on the subject. J. Batinić and M. Hoare, for example, draw on personal narratives and eyewitness accounts. Hoare also conducted interviews with Partisans. See J. Batinić, *Women and Yugoslav Partisans: A History of World War II Resistance* (New York, 2015); M. Hoare, *Genocide and Resistance in Hitler's Bosnia: The Partisans and the Chetniks, 1941–1943* (Oxford, 2006). M. Hoare, *The Bosnian Muslims in the Second World War: A History* (London, 2013);
13. J.-W. Müller argues this in *Memory and Power in Post-War Europe. Studies in the Presence of the Past* (Cambridge, 2002). For a study of recent political memoirs, see C. Whitehead, 'Political Memoirs, Myth, Policy, and the Wars of Yugoslav Succession', *Past Imperfect* 15 (2009), 154–92. For interesting discussions of social and cultural commemorative practices associated with the Partisan heritage, see H. Karge, 'Mediated Remembrance: Local Practices of Remembering the Second World War in Tito's Yugoslavia', *European Review of History – Revue européenne d'histoire* 16(1) (2009), 49–62; H. Karge, 'Practices and Politics of Second World War Remembrance: (Trans-)National Perspectives from Eastern and South-Eastern Europe', in M. Pakier and B. Stråth (eds), *A European Memory? Contested Histories and Politics of Remembrance* (New York and Oxford, 2010), 137–46; R. Mills, 'Commemorating a Disputed Past: Football Club and Supporters' Group War Memorials in the Former Yugoslavia', *History* 97(328) (2012), 540–77; and W. Hoepken, 'War, Memory, and Education in a Fragmented Society: The Case of Yugoslavia', *East European Politics and Societies* 13(1) (1999), 190–227.
14. Y. Harari, 'Martial Illusions: War and Disillusionment in Twentieth-Century and Renaissance Military Memoirs', *Journal of Military History* 69(1) (2005),

43–72; Y. Harari, 'Military Memoirs: A Historical Overview of the Genre from the Middle Ages to the Late Modern Era', *War in History* 14(3) (2007), 289–309; and M. Hewitson, '"I Witnesses": Soldiers, Selfhood and Testimony in Modern Wars', *German History* 28(3) (2010), 310–25.
15. O. Bartov, 'Eastern Europe as the Site of Genocide', *Journal of Modern History* 80 (3) (2008), 557–93; R. Gildea, *Fighters in the Shadows: A New History of the French Resistance* (London, 2015), 15.
16. Gildea, *Fighters in the Shadows*, 15.
17. See note 12 above.
18. The original title was *Zapisi iz oslobodilačkog rata* [Notes from the Liberation War]. The work comprised several volumes, the first of which was published in 1947.
19. Dapčević, *Kako smo vodili rat*.
20. See, especially, Dapčević, *Kako smo vodili rat*, 164–82.
21. Mitrović was married to Milovan Djilas from whom she became estranged during the war. They separated in the late 1940s and divorced in 1952.
22. Mitrović, *Ratno putovanje*, 94, 206.
23. Mitrović, *Ratno putovanje*, 87ff.
24. See, for example, Božović, *Tebi, moja Dolores*, 65, 175–76.
25. Mitrović, *Ratno putovanje*, 164ff.
26. Božović, *Tebi, moja Dolores*, 103ff. Dolores died in March 1943.
27. The Croat Ivan Ribar's description in *Uspomene* of the loss of both his sons is similarly affecting.
28. The Communist Party was outlawed in the Kingdom in 1921 but its adherents continued to be active underground. For a good introduction to interwar Yugoslav politics, see S. Ramet, *Three Yugoslavias: State-Building and Legitimation, 1918–2005* (Bloomington, Indianapolis and Washington, DC, 2006) chs 2 and 3.
29. Djilas's work was published outside the country in English and generally well received. *The New Class* first appeared in the United States in 1957 and established Djilas's credentials as a fearless and articulate dissident.
30. See the now classic text by M. Todorova, *Imagining the Balkans* (Oxford and New York, 1997) for an analysis of this discourse. See also M. Todorova, 'The Trap of Backwardness: Modernity, Temporality and the Study of East European Nationalism', *Slavic Review* 64(1) (2005), 140–64; and P. Garde, *Le discours balkanique. Des mots et des hommes* (Paris, 2004).
31. His first autobiographical book, entitled *Land without Justice*, was published in 1958.
32. Djilas, *Wartime*, 152–53.
33. Djilas, *Wartime*, 88.
34. Čolaković, *Winning Freedom*, 39.
35. Djilas, *Wartime*, 160.
36. Čolaković, *Winning Freedom*, 33. Emphasis in the original.
37. Dragović-Soso, '*Saviours of the Nation*', 101.

38. See S. Lazić, 'The Re-evaluation of Milan Nedić and Draža Mihailović in Serbia', in Ramet and Listhaug, *Serbia and the Serbs in World War Two*, 265–82. See also Cvijić, 'Swinging the Pendulum'.
39. Mitrović, *Ratno putovanje*, 228.
40. Most famously, regime 'historian' Vladimir Dedijer strategically published his revised (critical) study of Tito after the latter's death. See V. Dedijer *Novi prilozi za biografiju Josipa Broza Tita*, 2 vols (Rijeka, 1981).
41. W. Roberts, 'Wartime in Yugoslavia' (review of *Wartime*), *Slavic Review*, 37(3) (1978), 491–94.
42. Djilas, *Wartime*, 59.
43. Djilas, *Wartime*, 142–43.
44. A recent example in English is Batinić's *Women and Yugoslav Partisans*. See also B. Jancar-Webster, *Women and Revolution in Yugoslavia, 1941–1945* (Denver, 1990).
45. I have elaborated on this point in V. Drapac, 'Women, Resistance and the Politics of Daily Life in Hitler's Europe: The Case of Yugoslavia in a Comparative Perspective', *Aspasia* 3 (2009), 55–78.
46. Jones, *Twelve Months with Tito's Partisans*, 77.
47. Davidson, *Partisan Picture*, passim.
48. B. Mihajlović, 'Predgovor' [Preface] in Mitrović, *Ratno putovanje*, 7–17.
49. Mitrović, *Ratno putovanje*, 113.
50. Mitrović, *Ratno putovanje*, 138, 140, 154. It is interesting to compare this experience with that of Soviet women. See, for example, B. Engel, 'The Womanly Face of War: Soviet Women Remember World War II', in N. Dombrowski (ed.), *Women and War in the Twentieth Century: Enlisted With or Without Consent* (New York, 1999), 138–59; A. Krylova, *Soviet Women in Combat: A History of Violence on the Eastern Front* (Cambridge and New York, 2010); and Roger Markwick, '"A Sacred Duty": Red Army Women Veterans Remembering the Great Fatherland War, 1941–1945', *Australian Journal of Politics and History* 54(3) (2008), 403–20.
51. Mitrović, *Ratno putovanje*, 188.
52. Mitrović, *Ratno putovanje*, 226.
53. See B. Ćopić and M. Alečković in Božović, *Tebi, moja Dolores*, IX–XVI.
54. D. Djordjevic, *Scars and Memory: Four Lives in One Lifetime* (Boulder, CO, 1997), Preface, n.p.
55. There are many examples of his work in which this tendency is evident. A good indication of his particular vigilance is his review of F.W.D. Deakin's *The Embattled Mountain* (1971) in *European Studies Review*, 3 (1) (1973), 88–95.
56. Marjanović, 'L'historiographie contemporaine serbe des années 80' and 'L'histoire politisée'. See also Dulić, 'Sentenced "for Ideological and Political Reasons"?'.
57. Djilas, *Wartime*, 22, 115.

BIBLIOGRAPHY

Memoirs and Primary Sources

Božović, S. *Tebi, moja Dolores*. 5th ed. Belgrade: NIRO 'Četvrti Jul', 1981 [1978].
Čolaković, R. *Winning Freedom*. Trans. by A. Brown. London: Lincolns-Prager, 1962.
Dapčević, P. *Kako smo vodili rat*. Belgrade: NIGP 'Privredni Pregled', 1975 [1956].
Davidson, B. *Partisan Picture*. Bedford: Bedford Books, 1946.
Djilas, M. *The New Class: An Analysis of the Communist System*. New York: Praeger, 1957.
Djilas, M. *Land Without Justice*. London: Methuen, 1958.
Djilas, M. *Wartime: With Tito and the Partisans*. Trans. by M. Petrovich. London: Secker and Warburg, 1980 [1977].
Djordjevic, D. *Scars and Memory: Four Lives in One Lifetime*. Boulder, CO: East European Monographs, Distributed by Columbia University Press, New York, 1997.
Jones, W. *Twelve Months with Tito's Partisans*. Bedford: Bedford Books, 1946.
Kardelj, E. *Put nove Jugoslavije: članci i govori iz Narodno-Oslobodilačke Borbe 1941–1945*. Belgrade and Zagreb: Kultura, 1946.
Kardelj, E. *Reminiscences: The Struggle for Recognition and Independence: The New Yugoslavia, 1944–1957*. Trans. by D. Norris, S. Peić and J. Wrench. London: Blond and Briggs and Summerfield Press, 1982 [1980].
Martin, D. *Ally Betrayed: The Uncensored Story of Tito and Mihailovich*, foreword by R. West. New York: Prentice-Hall, 1946.
Mitchell, R. *'Ruth Mitchell, Chetnik, Tells the Facts about the Fighting Serbs: Mihailovich and 'Yugoslavia'*. Arlington, VA: Serbian National Defense Council, 1943.
Mitchell, R. *The Serbs Choose War*. New York: Doubleday Doran, 1943.
Mitrović, M. *Ratno putovanje*. Prosveta: Belgrade, 1962 [1953].
Ribar, I. *Uspomene iz narodno oslobodilačke borbe*. Belgrade: Vojnoizdavački Zavod JNA, 'Vojno Delo', 1961.
Rootham, J. *Miss Fire: The Chronicle of a British Mission to Mihailovich, 1943–1944*. London: Chatto and Windus, 1946.
Velebit, V. *Sećanja*. Zagreb: Globus, 1983.

Secondary Sources

Bartov, O. 'Eastern Europe as the Site of Genocide'. *Journal of Modern History* 80(3) (2008), 557–93.
Batinić, J. *Women and Yugoslav Partisans: A History of World War II Resistance*. New York: Cambridge University Press, 2015.
Cirković, S. 'Historiography in Isolation: Serbian Historiography Today'. *Helsinki Monitor* 35 (1994), 35–40.
Cvijic, S. 'Swinging the Pendulum: World War II History, Politics, National Identity and Difficulties of Reconciliation in Croatia and Serbia'. *Nationalities Papers* 36(4) (2008), 713–40.

Dedijer, V. *Novi prilozi za biografiju Josipa Broza Tita*. 2 vols. Rijeka: Liburnija, 1981.
Djuretić, V. *Saveznici i jugoslovenska ratna drama*. 2 vols. Belgrade: Politika, 1985.
Dragnich, A. 'The Anatomy of a Myth: Serbian Hegemony', *Slavic Review* 50(3) (1991), 659–62.
Dragović-Soso, J. *'Saviours of the Nation': Serbia's Intellectual Opposition and the Revival of Nationalism*. London: Hurst and Co., 2002.
Drapac, V. 'Women Resistance and the Politics of Daily Life in Hitler's Europe: The Case of Yugoslavia in a Comparative Perspective'. *Aspasia* 3 (2009), 55–78.
Drapac, V. *Constructing Yugoslavia: A Transnational History*. Basingstoke: Palgrave Macmillan, 2010.
Drapac, V., and Pritchard, G. 'Beyond Resistance and Collaboration: Towards a Social History of Politics in Hitler's Empire', *Journal of Social History* 48(4) (2015), 865–91.
Dulić, T. 'Sentenced "for Ideological and Political Reasons"? The Rehabilitation of Dragoljub "Draža" Mihailović in Serbia'. *Sociologija* 54(4) (2012), 625–48.
Engel, B. 'The Womanly Face of War: Soviet Women Remember World War II', in N. Dombrowski (ed.), *Women and War in the Twentieth Century: Enlisted With or Without Consent* (New York: Garland Publishing Inc., 1999), 138–59.
Garde, P. *Le discours balkanique. Des mots et des hommes*. Paris: Fayard, 2004.
Gildea, R. *Fighters in the Shadows: A New History of the French Resistance*. London: Faber and Faber, 2015.
Harari, Y. 'Martial Illusions: War and Disillusionment in Twentieth-Century and Renaissance Military Memoirs'. *Journal of Military History* 69(1) (2005), 43–72.
Harari, Y. 'Military Memoirs: A Historical Overview of the Genre from the Middle Ages to the Late Modern Era'. *War in History* 14(3) (2007), 289–309.
Hewitson, M. '"I Witnesses": Soldiers, Selfhood and Testimony in Modern Wars'. *German History* 28(3) (2010), 310–25.
Hoare, M. 'Whose is the Partisan Movement? Serbs, Croats and the Legacy of a Shared Resistance'. *Journal of Slavic Military Studies* 15(4) (2002), 24–41.
Hoare, M. *Genocide and Resistance in Hitler's Bosnia: The Partisans and the Chetniks, 1941–1943*. Oxford: Oxford University Press, 2006.
Hoare, M. *The Bosnian Muslims in the Second World War: A History*. London: Hurst & Company, 2013.
Hoepken, W. 'War, Memory, and Education in a Fragmented Society: The Case of Yugoslavia'. *East European Politics and Societies* 13(1) (1999), 190–227.
Jackson, J. *France: The Dark Years, 1940–1944*. Oxford: Oxford University Press, 2003 [2001].
Jancar-Webster, B. *Women and Revolution in Yugoslavia, 1941–1945*. Denver: Arden Press, 1990.
Jancar-Webster, B. 'Women in the Yugoslav National Liberation Movement', in S. Ramet (ed.), *Gender Politics in the Western Balkans: Women and Society in Yugoslavia and the Yugoslav Successor States* (University Park, PA: The Pennsylvania State University Press, 1999), 67–87.

Karge, H. 'Mediated Remembrance: Local Practices of Remembering the Second World War in Tito's Yugoslavia'. *European Review of History – Revue européenne d'histoire* 16(1) (2009), 49–62.

Karge, H. 'Practices and Politics of Second World War Remembrance: (Trans-) National Perspectives from Eastern and South-Eastern Europe', in M. Pakier and B. Stråth (eds), *A European Memory? Contested Histories and Politics of Remembrance* (New York and Oxford: Berghahn, 2010), 137–46.

Krylova, A. *Soviet Women in Combat: A History of Violence on the Eastern Front.* Cambridge and New York: Cambridge University Press, 2010.

Lazić, S. 'The Re-evaluation of Milan Nedić and Draža Mihailović in Serbia', in S. Ramet and O. Listhaug (eds), *Serbia and the Serbs in World War Two* (Basingstoke: Palgrave Macmillan, 2011), 265–82.

Lees, M. *The Rape of Serbia: The British Role in Tito's Grab for Power, 1943–1944.* New York: Harcourt Brace Jovanovich, 1990.

Marjanović, V. 'L'historiographie contemporaine serbe des années 80: de la démystification idéologique à la mystification nationaliste' and 'L'histoire politisée. L'historiographie serbe depuis 1989', in A. Marès (ed.), *Histoire et pouvoir en Europe médiane* (Paris and Montreal: L'Harmattan, 1996), 139–70 and 283–308.

Markwick, R. '"A Sacred Duty": Red Army Women Veterans Remembering the Great Fatherland War, 1941–1945'. *Australian Journal of Politics and History* 54(3) (2008), 403–20.

Mills, R. 'Commemorating a Disputed Past: Football Club and Supporters' Group War Memorials in the Former Yugoslavia'. *History* 97(328) (2012), 540–77.

Müller, J.-W. (ed.) *Memory and Power in Post-War Europe. Studies in the Presence of the Past.* Cambridge: Cambridge University Press, 2002.

Ramet, S. *Three Yugoslavias: State-Building and Legitimation, 1918–2005.* Bloomington and Indianapolis: Indiana University Press and Washington, DC: Woodrow Wilson Center Press, 2006.

Ramet, S., and O. Listhaug (eds). *Serbia and the Serbs in World War Two.* Basingstoke: Palgrave Macmillan, 2011.

Roberts, W. 'Wartime in Yugoslavia' (review of *Wartime*), *Slavic Review*, 37(3) (1978), 491–94.

Shepherd, B., and J. Pattinson (eds). *War in a Twilight World: Partisan and Anti-Partisan Warfare in Eastern Europe, 1939–45.* Basingstoke: Palgrave Macmillan, 2010.

Stojanović, D. 'Revisions of Second World War History in Contemporary Serbia', in S. Ramet and O. Listhaug (eds), *Serbia and the Serbs in World War Two.* Basingstoke: Palgrave Macmillan, 2011, 247–64.

Sweets, J. 'Hold that Pendulum! Redefining Fascism, Collaborationism and Resistance in France'. *French Historical Studies* 15(4) (1988), 731–58.

Todorova, M. *Imagining the Balkans.* Oxford and New York: Oxford University Press, 1997.

Todorova, M. 'The Trap of Backwardness: Modernity, Temporality and the Study of East European Nationalism'. *Slavic Review* 64(1) (2005), 140–64.

Whitehead, C. 'Political Memoirs, Myth, Policy, and the Wars of Yugoslav Succession'. *Past Imperfect* 15 (2009), 154–92.

Vesna Drapac is a member of the History Department at the University of Adelaide. She is interested in social, religious and cultural responses to international crisis in the twentieth century and her publications include *War and Religion: Catholics in the Churches of Occupied Paris* (Washington, DC, 1998) and, *Constructing Yugoslavia: A Transnational History* (Basingstoke, 2010).

Chapter 9

The War That Was Not
1948 Israeli War Memoirs

Ilan Pappe

INTRODUCTION

'The 1948 War' is a title recently given to the events that shook the land of Palestine between November 1947 and June 1949. It is a neutral term that replaced in the Western media and academia previous titles all of which, in one way or another, reflected the Israeli historical narrative. 'Genesis 1948', as Dan Kurzman's book would have it, or the more common term 'The War of Independence' were typical examples of this direction.[1] Palestinian historiography, on the other hand – popular as well as academic – attempted to challenge these descriptions by referring to the events of that year as the Palestinian *Nakbah* (catastrophe in Arabic). This reference informs Palestinian collective memory and interpretations of the 1948–49 events up to the present day.

What the two narratives had in common was the reference to the events in those years as a war that allowed a more recent and professional historiography to produce the 'neutral' term, the 1948 war. This title was heard often after the emergence of the Israeli 'new history' – a group of professional historians in Israel who used local and foreign archives and who validated in their works principal episodes in the Palestinian narrative. Several leading textbooks and curricula in the West reflect this new development.[2]

However, the most up-to-date views on the war challenge even this seemingly 'neutral' title. What transpires now is a dichotomous historiographical picture of two fronts of violence. The first front consists of a conventional military confrontation that raged between the newly formed Jewish state and the Arab units entering Palestine on the day the British mandate ended, on 15 May 1948. The other, second front was not really a 'war'; it was an ethnic cleansing operation. It was, in the main, an intensive military activity by Israeli troops within the civil, rural and urban Palestinian space, in which very little resistance, if any at all, occurred.[3]

The very different nature of the two 'wars' also produced different kinds of war memories and memoirs. Those who fought in the conventional war, as in so many other historical case studies, show similarities from both sides of the divide. We have very few individual soldiers' memoirs from the Arab side, while those on the Jewish-Israeli side are quite abundant. (Just recently the Israeli archives released from the files of the military censor a considerable correspondence between the front and home. There may be such a treasure in various Arab countries, but it has not as yet been made accessible).[4]

This chapter is concerned mainly with one particular genre and type of 1948 war memories and memoirs: those of the Palestinian survivors of the 1948 ethnic cleansing. Nonetheless, they still provide only part of the historical picture and thus should be juxtaposed, for the purpose of this chapter, against two other more marginal memoirs: those of Israeli soldiers and officers and a very select number of top Arab officers.[5] The top officers on both sides help the historian reconstruct the story of the war and the year as a whole from above while the memories of the troops and the Palestinians give an insight into the micro-history of the Palestinian catastrophe of each and every location on the map.

I have decided to single out the Palestinian war memoirs in order to make two points still not accepted everywhere or even adequately acknowledged. The first is that there is a distinct difference between the war memories of Israelis and Palestinians from that war. The Jewish literature consists of classical battlefront memories, with little in the form of home front recollections. On the other hand, there are hardly any Palestinian battlefront memoirs, memories or recollections. There were hardly any Palestinian fighting men. For the Israelis, the war was a conventional confrontation with regular armies; for the Palestinians, it was a military assault on their villages, towns and homes. The second point of difference is that for the Israeli Jews the 1948 episode is closed. Time and historical distance have allowed a more sober and less idealised view of the war. For the Palestinians, 1948 is an inconclusive chapter; the Nakbah is still celebrated each year.

As Ahmad Sa'di and Lila Abu Lughod explain in their seminal work, the Palestinian memories of 1948 are a relevant and ever present constituent in the way their reality and collective identity is formulated.[6] For them, as these authors argue, the iniquities of the present are experienced as a continuous replay of the injustice of the past. The contemporary Palestinian experience and moral claims for justice and redress are based on these memory reservoirs. Moreover, Palestinian political life after 1948 was organised around the Nakbah and the way it was remembered. These oral histories and memories inspire and inform most of the Palestinian literature, arts, cinema and plays as well the national consensus despite the fragmentation and political diversification of Palestinian politics since 1948. Dina Matar has shown how these memories, which she defines as 'composite biography' – her work covers a wider chronological span from 1936 to 1993 – unify the disparate worlds of Palestinians living in Israel, the West Bank, Lebanon and Syria.[7]

THE VIEW FROM ABOVE

Most of the professional historiography of the 1948 war, whether it represented or challenged the Zionist narrative, as did the 'new historians' in Israel, and to a lesser extent Palestinian historians, tended to belittle the importance of evidence that transcended the written, military or political document. The Oxford-based historian Avi Shlaim was an exception. His politics-from-above narrative relied heavily on in-depth interviews with the politicians and generals of the hour.[8]

The absence of proper archives in the Arab countries, including Palestinian documentation, has turned the handful of published military and political memoirs of the 1948 war into a source that can provide some balance to the heavy reliance on the well-organised and accessible Israel and Zionist archives. As the 1948 campaign was, to put it mildly, hardly a glorious military success for the Arabs, there are more politicians than generals who wrote memoirs. The politicians and diplomats who bothered to reminisce did so mainly in order to salvage their personal role within a more general Arab fiasco. Surprisingly, Palestinian politicians have been quite prolific in writing about this period; they were such secondary actors on the ground that they could describe the catastrophe without assuming any of the blame (for example, in not preparing their people in time for the imminent catastrophe). These included the memoirs of the leader of the Palestinian community, Haj Amin al-Husayani, his secretary and heir Ahmad al-Shuqairi, later the first chair of the Palestinian Liberation Organization, and many others.[9]

Despite the abundance of Arab political memoirs, the number pales in comparison to the verbose Israeli memorial industry of the 1948 war. Since it is regarded as the golden moment of the birth of the state of Israel, participation in the war almost automatically grants one a place in the national pantheon. It explains the wish to idealise and exaggerate one's own role in that 'sacred' event. Some people did indeed play a leading role, such as the first Prime Minister of Israel, David Ben-Gurion, whose war diary became a three-volume book that attempted to engrave in the local and international collective memory the Zionist version of events.[10] When his entries were read later on by the more critical 'new historians' in Israel, they exposed, contrary to the wishes of the man himself, unpleasant truths about Israel's overall conduct in the war in general, and towards the local indigenous population of Palestine in particular. One famous case, exposed by the historian Nur Masalha, was a letter from Ben-Gurion to his son in 1937 found in his personal archives, in which he explicitly called for the expulsion of the Palestinians. Ben-Gurion himself republished the letter many years later expunging the quote, but the original remained in the archives.[11]

It was, however, mainly the generals and officers of those years who had two distinct forms of depositing their individual memories into the collective memory bank of the nation. One of those forms was writing autobiographical accounts, more often than not a few years after the war, so that other wars could be included; the other form was writing segments in the Brigade books of 1948 – there were a dozen of them – very soon after the war. In those Brigade books these officers contributed by writing the editorial passages between the collation of individual stories and memoirs. Rafi Nets-Zehngut wrote a comprehensive work on Israeli veteran war memories and counted about seventy such published memoirs.[12] These autobiographical recollections have also turned out to be a very useful companion to the material stored in the military and political archives. Top officers on the Israeli side were also interested in local occurrences and their memories help to expand the historiographical picture that until recently was based solely on the written documents unearthed in the Israeli archives. These two set of memories, of the soldiers on the ground and the civilians in the midst of the military action, are significant not only for completing the historiographical picture of this crucial landmark in the history of Palestine and indeed of the Middle East as a whole, but also because they tie into the long-running debates about the place of oral evidence and personal memoirs in the reconstruction of the past.

CHALLENGES TO THE HEGEMONIC NARRATIVE

Individual memories can either serve as a tool in the hands of the collective, structured and manipulated from above, or become a means of subverting collective memory.[13] The former Yugoslavia is one region where the most impressive work on these interrelations has been recently conducted. In post-Second World War Yugoslavia, historical narratives were shaped and framed from above, and were accepted for a while by individuals because there were no outlets for personal reminiscences that might have countered the official narratives.[14] The temporal and physical distance from the event, not to mention state structures, made it difficult for the individual to disprove or oppose official communist memory. However, as we have already noted, the role of memory between the individual and the collective is a two-way process. Personal memories are the main resources from which collective memory draws, suggesting that mythologised historical narratives can be opposed by active participation of individual memories (both through experience and by word of mouth) within society.[15] Although individuals may not be able to disprove a particular collective memory, they can oppose the influence a dominant narrative has on collective memory and on a community's identity by offering alternative, competing personal memories.

In some cases, the Israeli generals who participated in the 1948 war underwent such a transformation and became more subversive towards the collective memory. As such, they turned into a more intriguing source for completing the picture and in ways that tally well with Palestinian oral history of the events, which I have chosen to describe elsewhere as 'ethnic cleansing'.[16] When they were originally written in the 1950s, there was a certain amount of self-censorship brought about by an awareness that the proud actions they were commended for by Israeli society could be considered war crimes, or that boasting about blowing up villages or orders to kill villagers en masse would no longer be viewed as heroic in the world of the 1990s, a world shocked by the cruelty of ethnic conflict in Eastern Europe and Africa. As a consequence, some of the Israeli generals who participated in the 1948 war moved from representing the hegemonic narrative to challenging it. When this happens the dichotomous and simplified picture the collective memory conveys of the other in any historical event can become blurred.

A prime example of this is General Moshe Carmel, commander of the Northern Front, whose orders to expel Palestinians were exposed by the new historians and were later incorporated into newspaper articles on his role. He went from a position of total denial of any wrongdoing to inserting more than a modicum of doubt and regret into his own recollections.[17] The same applies to General Shmuel Mula Cohen, commander of the Iftach Brigade in 1948. Within a period of twenty years he provided two different versions of the same events, the latter less complimentary to official Israeli memory, to put it mildly.[18] Finally, one can mention General Nahum Golan, commander of the Golani Brigade in 1948 who underwent a similar process. All three generals cited here eventually gave a more honest, and much less sympathetic picture of what they and their brigades did in the 1948 war.[19]

Once we cast these two sets of war memories, by the Jewish troops and the Palestinian survivors, into one narrative – what one may call a joint narrative of the victims and the victimisers – we can significantly contribute to a more complete historiographical picture of the 1948 war. Put another way, the fusion of these two sources with military declassified material present in the Israeli, British and United Nations archives provides the micro-history, and a history from below, of the 1948 war so crucial for understanding the Palestinian narrative of the Nakbah.

Sources, however, have different qualities and different potential. While one cannot doubt the importance of personal Israeli Jewish soldiers' memoirs, especially in their more critical form, in challenging the dominant Zionist narrative, it is the reservoir of Palestinian personal recollections that has the most powerful potential to transform and in many ways repudiate the Zionist narrative of the 1948 war. Nonetheless, a dialectical relationship with all historical sources on the Jewish side can expand the historical picture to its maximum.

THE VICTIMS' VIEW

For Palestinians, and anyone who refused to buy into the Zionist narrative, the validity of oral testimony and memoirs as a legitimate historical source was never doubted. About thirty years ago, the Palestinian victims of the Nakbah started reassembling the historical picture that the official Israeli narrative of 1948 had done everything to conceal and distort. The tale Israeli historiography had concocted spoke of a massive 'voluntary transfer' of hundreds of thousands of Palestinians who had decided temporarily to leave their homes and villages so as to make way for the invading Arab armies bent on destroying the fledgling Jewish state. By collecting authentic memories and documents about what happened to their people, Palestinian historians in the 1970s, Walid Khalidi foremost among them, were able to retrieve a significant part of the picture Israel had tried to erase.[20] But they were quickly overshadowed by publications such as Dan Kurzman's *Genesis 1948*, which appeared in 1970 and again in 1992 (the later edition with an introduction from the then Israeli Prime Minister, Yitzhak Rabin).[21] There were also some who came out in support of the Palestinian endeavour, like Michael Palumbo whose *The Palestinian Catastrophe*, published in 1987, validated the Palestinian version of 1948 events with the help of UN documents and interviews with Palestinian refugees and exiles, whose memories of what they had gone through during the Nakbah still proved to be hauntingly vivid.[22]

A breakthrough in the battle over memory in Palestine could have occurred with the appearance on the scene in the 1980s of the so-called 'new history' in Israel. This was an attempt by a small group of Israeli historians to revise the Zionist narrative of the 1948 war.[23] This writer was one of them. But we, the new historians, never contributed significantly to the struggle against the Nakbah denial as we sidestepped the question of Israeli moral responsibility for what in my eyes now looks like the ethnic cleansing of Palestine. Nevertheless, using primarily Israeli military archives, the revisionist Israeli historians did succeed in showing how false and absurd was the Israeli claim that the Palestinians had left 'of their own accord'. They were able to confirm many cases of massive expulsions from villages and towns and revealed that the Jewish forces had committed a considerable number of atrocities, including massacres.

One of the best-known figures writing on this subject was the Israeli historian Benny Morris. Since he exclusively relied on documents from the Israeli military archives, Morris ended up with a very partial picture of what happened on the ground. Still, this was enough for some of his Israeli readers to realise that the 'voluntary flight' of the Palestinians had been a myth and that the Israeli self-image of having waged a 'moral' war in 1948 against a 'primitive' and hostile Arab world was considerably flawed and possibility already bankrupt.[24] The picture was partial because Morris took the Israeli military reports he found in the archive at face value or even as an absolute truth. Thus, he ignored such atrocities as the poisoning of the water supply into Acre with typhoid, numerous cases of rape and dozens of massacres perpetrated by the Jews. He also repeatedly insisted – wrongly – that before 15 May 1948 there had been no forced evictions. Palestinian memoirs and oral history show clearly how months before the entry of Arab forces into Palestine, and while the British were still responsible for law and order in the country – namely before 15 May – the Jewish forces had already succeeded in forcibly expelling almost a quarter of a million Palestinians.[25] Had Morris and others used Arab sources, or turned to oral history, they might have been able to get a better grasp of the systematic planning behind the expulsion of the Palestinians in 1948 and provide a more truthful description of the enormity of the crimes the Israeli soldiers committed.

There was then, and there is now still, a need, both historical and political, to go beyond descriptions such as the one we find in Morris, not only in order to complete the picture (in fact, to provide the second half of it), but also – and far more importantly – because there is no other way to fully understand the roots of the contemporary Israeli-Palestinian conflict. But above all, of course, there is a moral imperative to continue the struggle against the denial of the crime. The endeavour to go further has already been attempted. The most important work, to be expected given his previous significant contributions to the struggle against the denial, was Walid Khalidi's essential book *All That Remains*,[26] which is based among other sources on a variety of memoirs and recollections. This is an almanac of the destroyed villages, and is still an essential guide for anyone wishing to comprehend the enormity of the catastrophe. But it not only provided the Palestinian 'side of the story'; it gave us the thick description of the microhistory of that war, the individual human story that makes every unique case study of inhumanity into a global phenomenon.

The descriptions in archives are very slim and positivist historians usually do not dare to add layers to the bare narrative according to their imagination. The individual stories can only be filled with the help of oral history. Oral history is extensively used in the Israeli historiography of the Holocaust but is totally de-legitimised if attempted by Palestinian historians reconstructing the Nakbah. Oral history is a crucial methodology for pursuing further the research on the 1948 war. It is indeed, as in the case of other subaltern groups, a vital tool for salvaging the voices of the Palestinian victims of the 1948 war.

In recent years oral history has been acknowledged in the global academic community as a respected sub-discipline. There are more than a thousand programmes of oral history in American universities alone. In a parallel development, the written document's status has declined and it is no longer considered any more authentic or reliable than oral testimony. How much this reassessment is valid with regard to Israel and Palestine can be seen from a closer look at the *Israel Defense Forces* and Defense Establishment *Archives* (IDFA) and the relevant 1948 documents. Most of these documents consist of correspondence between soldiers, the purpose of which is not only to report from the front, but quite often to glorify their part in the campaign and conceal fiascos and misdeeds. Positivist historians who rely exclusively on written documents quite often resort to guesswork and imagination, without admitting it, when reconstructing the past from the documents (a truism already articulated in 1934 by Robin George Collingwood, who asserted that all historians have to use their imagination when emplotting the story of the past).[27]

Oral history is not a substitute for archival sources, but it can provide crucial material to fill gaps and to confirm written evidence that quite often supplies us only with the 'bare bones' of events. Thus, when the official Israeli military book on the 1948 war, the *Hagana Book*, refers very briefly to an occupation of a Palestinian village by Jewish forces or the 'purifying' of another in the 1948 war, the event appears in a detailed and graphic form in the Palestinian collective memory: quite often a tale of expulsion and sometimes massacre.[28]

Indeed, some of the more infamous massacres committed in 1948, such as the massacre in the village of Tantura, could not have been discovered or even debated if at least part of the Palestinian and Jewish testimonies about it were not trusted as valid sources.[29] Illicit and indirect references to an event in the military documents become clearer when juxtaposed with oral testimonies or war memoirs, as the case of the massacre in Dawaima proves. Even a positivist historian who totally rejects the validity of oral testimony or memory, and in particular that coming from the Palestinian side, had to rely on oral testimonies and war memoirs to complete the historiographical picture.[30]

Alessandro Portelli, who has dealt extensively with oral history, insists that it tells us less about events in history and much more about their significance.[31] Portelli has also looked at the murder trial of Aldo Moro in Italy in 1987. His main conclusion was that written documents are themselves quite often a processing of oral testimonies and hence do not deserve preferential treatment. Oral history is indeed as authentic as the documented one. Both materials are broken pieces of clay pottery from the past, which are themselves interpretations of a reality that historians, like archaeologists, claim they can reconstruct. The reassemblage quite often is done according to a contemporary agenda and not necessarily an accurate reflection of the past. Fifty years from today, these clay pieces might be the basis for telling the story of the last two *Intifadas*, both Israeli wars in Lebanon, the assault on Gaza and the attack on the passenger ship, the *Mavi Marmara*. Their history would be written on the basis of IDFA archives, media reports and memories of Palestinian victims. There will be few narratives, all substantiated by evidence and all conforming to the academic game, whatever it might be in the middle of this century.

While 1948 memories of Palestinians help to fill the gaps left by the mainly Israeli military archives on the micro-historical evidence about the war, they also provide other angles on the events of that year that written documents fail to do. One of them is mapping the road of exodus. These memories allowed Salman Abu Sitta, a refugee from 1948, who spent years cataloguing the course and consequences of the Nakbah, to map the routes of exile as well as the structure of the villages.[32] In several houses inside and outside of Palestine, a visual memorised map was translated into a wall painting of the lost and destroyed village. The power of these memories will fade if these witnesses are not properly recorded, as many of them are aging and many have not been interviewed. Their memories, live or recorded, will play a very important role in the history of the conflict.

FUTURE RESEARCH

There is still more research to be done on the 1948 war based on war memories. Significant progress has been made by the authors who contributed to the volume mentioned earlier, edited by Sa'di and Abu Lughod.[33] They have begun connecting a matrix of factors and examined their impact on the quality and usefulness of Palestinian memories. The 1948 Palestine memories were, so it transpires, different depending on class, gender, generation and geographical location.[34] A number of postgraduate students have recently focused on women's memoirs from 1948. The war was a double catastrophe for women for whom the house, the home, was their entire world.[35] This is a dimension quite often not associated with war memoirs, but as I have tried to argue in this chapter, it depends on how we define the 'war' in the case of 1948.

Another possible angle is using a more integrative approach to the oral histories of both sides. The Israeli anthropologist Efrat Ben-Zeev has already attempted this. She looks at the way personal narratives clashed with the national ones and does so concurrently for three groups involved in 1948: the Palestinian villagers; the Jewish soldiers; and the British policemen.[36] This could open the way for an even more ambitious project – the construction of a joint archive for the testimonies of both the victimisers and victims of the 1948 war. Such a project is now in the making.[37]

One should not place too much hope on the role of these memories in the political realm but it may even have an impact in this respect as well. Recently several Israeli scholars have stated their opinion that deconstructing the collective memory and juxtaposing it with the private one can promote peace.[38] This may be overly optimistic but what it definitely does is contain and curb the self-idealisation so often promoted through the collective memory. The memories of the victims do not allow that idealisation to go very far, nor do honest recollections of the victimisers. And when both, as happened in Israel in the 1990s, are supported by the work of professional historians, then indeed the war memoirs open the way for a more sober look at the past for the sake of the future.

NOTES

1. Dan Kurzman, *Genesis 1948: The First Arab-Israeli War* (New York, 1992).
2. Ilan Pappe, 'Post-Zionist Discourse in Israel, 1991–2001', *Holy Land Studies* 1(1) (2002), 3–20.
3. Ilan Pappe, *The Ethnic Cleansing of Palestine* (Oxford, 2006).
4. The archive became open in the summer of 2008 and is hosted in the Israel Defense Forces (IDF) archives.
5. Sources include the following: the personal aide to the secretary general of the Arab League at the time wrote the book, Wahid al-Daly, *The Secrets of the Arab League and Abd al-Rahman Azzam* (Cairo, 1978) (Arabic); Adil Arslan, who was the Syrian Foreign Minister at the time, wrote his memoirs edited by Yusuf Ibish in Yusuf Ibish (ed.), *The Memoirs of the Amir Adil Arslan* (Beirut, 1983); Jordanian General Abdullah al-Tal's memoirs, *The Palestine Disaster* (Cairo, 1959) (Arabic); and Iraqi General Taha al-Hashimi's *War Memoirs*, 2 vols (Beirut, 1978) (Arabic). The Leading Israeli source was the diaries of David Ben-Gurion: Gershon Rivlin and Elhanan Oren (eds), *The War of Independence: Ben-Gurion's War Diary*, 3 vols (Tel-Aviv, 1982) (Hebrew). His nemesis, Menachem Begin, also published his *The Story of the Irgun* (New York, 1951). The Israeli diplomats wrote too. See the first ambassador to the United States, Eliahu Eilat, *The Struggle for Statehood*, 2 vols (Tel-Aviv, 1982) (Hebrew); Eliahu Sasson, *On the Road to Peace* (Tel-Aviv, 1978) (Hebrew); and Moshe Sharett, *On the Brink of Statehood* (Tel-Aviv, 1958) (Hebrew). The generals' memoirs appear among other sources in Yehuda Sluzki, *The Hagana Book* (Tel-Aviv, 1978) (Hebrew). The commander of the Hagana intelligence unit in the Jerusalem area published his memoirs: Itzhak Levi, *Jerusalem in the War of Independence* (Jerusalem, 1986) (Hebrew); and Uri Ben Ari, *Follow Me* (Tel-Aviv, 1994) (Hebrew). All the brigades of the Hagana published almanacs: Binyamin Etizoni (ed.), *The Golani Brigade in the War* (Tel-Aviv, no date) (Hebrew); Eashel Zadok (ed.), *The Carmeli Brigade in the War of Independence* (Tel-Aviv, 1973) (Hebrew); Zvi Sinai and Gershon Rivlin (eds), *The Alexandroni Brigade in the War of Independence* (Tel-Aviv, 1964) (Hebrew); and Israel Even Nur (ed.), *The Yiftach-Palmach Story* (Bat Yam, no date) (Hebrew). More junior but very telling memories are those of female soldiers, such as Netiva Ben Yehuda, *Between the Knots* (Jerusalem, 1985) (Hebrew); and Geula Cohen, *Woman of Violence: Memories of a Young Terrorist, 1945–1948* (New York, 1966).
6. Ahmad Sa'di and Lila Abu Lughod, *Nakba: Palestine, 1948, and the Claims of Memory* (New York, 2007).

7. Dina Matar, *What It Means to Be Palestinian: Stories of Palestinian Peoplehood* (London and New York, 2010).
8. Avi Shlaim, *Collusion across the Jordan: King Abdullah, the Zionist Movement, and the Partition of Palestine* (New York, 1988).
9. Several members of the Palestinian elite and known figures in the local society published their memoirs. The leader of the community, Haj Amin al-Husayni, published several books. The most relevant to our case study is his *The Truth about Palestine* (Cairo, 1956) (Arabic). His secretary Ahmad al-Shuqairi's book also deals with the same period, *Forty Years in the Arab and International History* (Beirut, 1960) (Arabic). Other books include Arif al-Arif, *The Catastrophe*, 3 vols (Beirut, 1988) (Arabic); Muhammad Izzat Darwaza, *About the Modern Arab Movement*, 2 vols (Sidon, 1959) (Arabic); Muhammad Nimr Al-Hawari, *The Road to Catastrophe* (Cairo, 1969) (Arabic).
10. Sa'di and Abu Lughod, *Nakba*.
11. See the discussion in *The Journal of Palestine Studies*, 164(4) (2012), 1–3 on this quote and similar ones.
12. Rafi Nets-Zehngut, 'Internal and External Collective Memories of Conflicts: Israel and the 1948 Palestinian Exodus', *International Journal of Conflict and Violence* 6(1) (2012), 126–40.
13. James Booth, 'The Unforgotten: Memories of Justice', *American Political Science Review* 95(4) (2001), 777–91; Stephanie Lawsin and Seiko Tannaka, 'War Memories and Japan's "Normalization" as an International Actor: A Critical Analysis', *European Journal of International Relations* 17(3) (2011), 405–28.
14. See Vesna Drapac in this collection.
15. Michael G. Kenny, 'A Place for Memory: The Interface between Individual and Collective History', *Comparative Studies in Society and History* 41(3) (1999), 420–37.
16. Pappe, *The Ethnic Cleansing*.
17. The early version: Moshe Carmel, *The North Front Battles* (Tel-Aviv, 1949) (Hebrew); the later version: 'Responding Comments', in Omri Refael and Magen Amnon (eds), *Conquering the Arab and Mixed Cities in the War of Independence* (Ramat Efal, 1989) (Hebrew), 31–32.
18. This comparison is ably done by Rafi Nets-Zehngut, 'Internal and External Collective Memories of Conflicts'.
19. Nets-Zehngut, 'Internal and External Collective Memories of Conflicts'.
20. Nets-Zehngut, 'Internal and External Collective Memories of Conflicts'.
21. Dan Kurzman, *Genesis 1948: The First Arab-Israeli War* (London, 1970,1992).
22. Michael Palumbo, *The Palestinian Catastrophe: The 1948 Expulsion of the Palestinians from Their Homeland* (New York, 1987).
23. See Pappe, 'Post-Zionist Discourse in Israel'.
24. Benny Morris, *The Birth of the Palestinian Refugee Problem* (Cambridge, 2004).
25. Pappe, *The Ethnic Cleansing*.
26. Walid Khalidi (ed.), *All That Remains: The Palestinian Villages Occupied and Depopulated by Israel in 1948* (Washington, DC, 1992).

27. R.G. Collingwood, *The Idea of History* (Oxford, 1994).
28. Pappe, *The Ethnic Cleansing*.
29. Ilan Papppe, 'The Tantura Case in Israel: The Katz Research and Trial', *Journal of Palestine Studies* 30(3) (2001), 19–39.
30. See Pappe, *The Ethnic Cleansing*, 195–98 and Morris, *The Birth*, 222–23.
31. Alessandro Portelli, *The Order Has Been Carried Out: History, Memory, and Meaning of a Nazi Massacre in Rome* (London and New York, 2007).
32. Salman Abu Sitta, *Atlas of Palestine 1948* (London, 2005).
33. Sa'di and Abu Lughod, *Nakba*.
34. Sa'di and Abu Lughod, *Nakba*.
35. Fatma Kassem, *Palestinian Women: Narrative Histories and Gendered Memories* (London, 2011).
36. Efrat Ben Ze'ev, *Remembering Palestine in 1948: Beyond National Narratives* (Cambridge, 2011).
37. The Common Narrative, an Arts and Humanities Research Council (AHRC) project led by Ilan Pappe and Eyal Sivan (soon to become a website).
38. These sources are quoted in full in Nets-Zehngut, 'Internal and External Collective Memories of Conflicts'.

BIBLIOGRAPHY

Memoirs

Arslan, Adil. *The Memoirs of the Amir Adil Arselan* (edited by Yusuf Ibish). Beirut: no publisher, 1983 (Arabic).
Al-Arif, Arif. *The Catastrophe*. 3 vols. Beirut: no publisher, 1988 (Arabic).
Al-Daly, Wahid. *The Secrets of the Arab League and Abd al-Rahman Azzam*. Cairo: no publisher, 1978 (Arabic).
Al-Hashimi, Taha. *War Memoirs*. 2 vols. Beirut: no publisher, 1978 (Arabic).
Al-Hawari, Muhammad Nimr. *The Road to Catastrophe*. Cairo: no publisher, 1969 (Arabic).
Al-Husayni, Haj Amin. *The Truth about Palestine*. Cairo: no publisher, 1956 (Arabic).
Al-Shuqairi, Ahmad. *Forty Years in the Arab and International History*. Beirut: no publisher, 1960 (Arabic).
Al-Tal, Abdullah. *The Palestine Disaster*. Cairo: no publisher, 1959 (Arabic).
Begin, Menachem. *The Story of the Irgun*. New York: Henry Schuman, 1951.
Ben Ari, Uri. *Follow Me*. Tel-Aviv: Maariv, 1994 (Hebrew).
Ben Yehuda, Netiva. *Between the Knots*. Jerusalem: Domino, 1985 (Hebrew).
Carmel, Moshe. *The North Front Battles*. Tel-Aviv: Ministry of Defence Publication, 1949 (Hebrew).
Carmel, Moshe. 'Responding Comments', in Omri Refael and Magen Amnon (eds), *Conquering the Arab and Mixed Cities in the War of Independence* (Ramat Efal: Hagana Publications, 1989), pp. 149–62 (Hebrew).

Cohen, Geula. *Woman of Violence: Memories of a Young Terrorist, 1945–1948*. New York: Holt, Rinehart and Winston, 1966.
Eilat, Eliahu. *The Struggle for Statehood*. 2 vols. Tel-Aviv: Shoken, 1982 (Hebrew).
Etizoni, Binyamin (ed.). *The Golani Brigade in the War*. Tel-Aviv: Ministry of Defence Publications, no date (Hebrew).
Even Nur, Israel (ed.). *The Yiftach-Palmach Story*. Bat Yam: Palmach Publications, no date (Hebrew).
Izzat Darwaza, Muhammad. *About the Modern Arab Movement*. 2 vols. Sidon: al-Maktaba al-Asriyya, 1959 (Arabic).
Levi, Itzhak. *Jerusalem in the War of Independence*. Jerusalem: Ministry of Defence Publication, 1986 (Hebrew).
Rivlin, Gershon, and Elhanan Oren (eds). *The War of Independence: Ben-Gurion's War Diary*, 3 vols. Tel-Aviv: Ministry of Defence Publications, 1982 (Hebrew).
Sasson, Eliahu. *On the Road to Peace*. Tel-Aviv: Am Oved, 1978 (Hebrew).
Sharett, Moshe. *On the Brink of Statehood*. Tel-Aviv: Am Oved, 1958 (Hebrew).
Sinai, Zvi, and Gershon Rivlin (eds). *The Alexandroni Brigade in the War of Independence*. Tel-Aviv: Ministry of Defence Publications, 1964 (Hebrew).
Sluzki, Yehuda. *The Hagana Book*. Tel-Aviv: IDF Publications, 1978 (Hebrew).
Zadok, Eashel (ed.). *The Carmeli Brigade in the War of Independence*. Tel-Aviv: Ministry of Defence Publications, 1973 (Hebrew).

Secondary Sources

Abu Sitta, Salman. *Atlas of Palestine 1948*. London: Palestine Land Society, 2005.
Ben Ze'ev, Efrat. *Remembering Palestine in 1948: Beyond National Narratives*. Cambridge: Cambridge University Press, 2011.
Booth, James. 'The Unforgotten: Memories of Justice'. *American Political Science Review* 95(4) (2001), 777–91.
Collingwood, R.G. *The Idea of History*. Oxford: Oxford University Press, 1994.
Kassem, Fatma. *Palestinian Women: Narrative Histories and Gendered Memories*. London: Zed Books, 2011.
Kenny, Michael G. 'A Place for Memory: The Interface between Individual and Collective History'. *Comparative Studies in Society and History* 41(3) (1999), 420–37.
Khalidi, Walid (ed.). *All That Remains: The Palestinian Villages Occupied and Depopulated by Israel in 1948*. Washington, DC: Institute for Palestine Studies, 1992.
Kurzman, Dan. *Genesis 1948: The First Arab-Israeli War*. New York: Da Capo Press, 1992.
Lawsin, Stephanie, and Seiko Tannaka. 'War Memories and Japan's "Normalization" as an International Actor: A Critical Analysis'. *European Journal of International Relations* 17(3) (2011), 405–28.
Matar, Dina. *What It Means to Be Palestinian: Stories of Palestinian Peoplehood*. London and New York: I.B. Tauris, 2010.

Morris, Benny. *The Birth of the Palestinian Refugee Problem*. Cambridge: Cambridge University Press, 2004.
Nets-Zehngut, Rafi. 'Internal and External Collective Memories of Conflicts: Israel and the 1948 Palestinian Exodus'. *International Journal of Conflict and Violence* 6(1) (2012), 126–40.
Palumbo, Michael. *The Palestinian Catastrophe: The 1948 Expulsion of the Palestinians from Their Homeland*. New York: Quartet Books, 1989.
Pappe, Ilan. *The Ethnic Cleansing of Palestine*. Oxford: Oneworld Publications, 2006.
Pappe, Ilan. 'Post-Zionist Discourse in Israel, 1991–2001'. *Holy Land Studies* 1(1) (2002), 3–20.
Pappe, Ilan. 'The Tantura Case in Israel: The Katz Research and Trial'. *Journal of Palestine Studies* 30(3) (2001), 19–39.
Portelli, Alessandro. *The Order Has Been Carried Out: History, Memory, and Meaning of a Nazi Massacre in Rome*. London and New York: Palgrave Macmillan, 2007.
Sa'di, Ahmad, and Lila Abu Lughod. *Nakba: Palestine, 1948, and the Claims of Memory*. New York: Columbia University Press, 2007.
Shlaim, Avi. *Collusion across the Jordan: King Abdullah, the Zionist Movement, and the Partition of Palestine*. New York: Columbia University Press, 1988.

Ilan Pappe is Professor of History, Director of the European Centre for Palestine Studies and Co-Director for the Exeter Centre for Ethno-Political Studies at the University of Exeter. He is a prolific author on questions of Israel, Palestine and the Middle East. He is the author of, among other books, *The Forgotten Palestinians: A History of the Palestinian Minority in Israel* (New Hampshire, 2011); *The Husyanis: The Rise and Fall of a Palestinian Aristocracy* (Berkeley, 2010); and *The Modern History Palestine, One Land, Two Peoples* (Cambridge, 2003).

Chapter 10

Remembering the 'Endless' Partition
From Memoirs about the 1947 Conflict to the Post-Memoir

Tarun K. Saint

In this chapter I propose to critically analyse a selection of important memoirs written in the wake of the partition of the subcontinent. The partition of India in 1947, following the British Labour government's decision to transfer power, led to widespread and unprecedented collective violence, reaching its peak in Punjab from August 1947 to January 1948, with loss of life comparable to that of major wars.[1] Even so, the differences between conventional wars and the partition need to be underlined as well. Unlike situations of conflict between alliances of nations and/or states during wars such as the Great War or the Second World War, the violence during the period 1947–48 was closer to a civil war, as communities (especially across north India) engaged in forms of reciprocal violence and what Paul Brass calls 'retributive genocide'.[2] However, unlike most full-on civil wars, the partition was marked by targeted violence primarily directed at minorities, whether the Muslim community in India, or Sikhs or Hindus in Pakistan, who had earlier been deemed hostages to the welfare of the minority in the 'other' country.[3] Indeed, attacks were often initiated by refugees who had reached the other side of the newly drawn border. As Faisal Devji argues, this led to a kind of mutual devastation, never seen before in the subcontinent.[4] Such large-scale killing, ironically enough, accompanied the process of attainment of freedom from colonial rule by the British, in the wake of a mostly nonviolent campaign led by Mohandas Karamchand Gandhi, among others. This blood-letting in 'civil' society preceded the later wars between the newly born nation-states, India and Pakistan – the first war was fought in Kashmir in 1948, followed by later wars in 1965, 1971 (which resulted in the creation of Bangladesh) and the Kargil debacle in 1999. During the partition, the death toll exceeded one million, while at least 75,000 women were abducted and between ten and fifteen million people displaced on both sides of the subcontinent. Indeed, partition-related violence approached near-genocidal levels of intensity in some areas of north-west India.[5]

This rupture in historical time was reckoned with by historians, novelists, artists and writers of memoirs in different ways, often after a gap in time, as a result of the attempt to make sense of the after-effects of the partition in personal and social life. If, as Paul Fussell argues, the Great War bequeathed the memory of seemingly never-ending attrition, the endless war,[6] the partition, has left behind the idea of a partition that has not ended, indeed what may seem like an endless partition, one that has yet to come to a close.[7] Just as the Great War transformed the collective consciousness and had an impact on successive generations (responded to often by writers in terms of a terrible irony, as Fussell shows),[8] the historical trauma of the partition has had ripple effects on at least three generations.

I will focus in the discussion to come on some important memoirs dealing with the partition, as well its afterlife, culminating in a new form that one might term the post-memoir. While a number of life-writings in different Indian languages such as Urdu, Hindi, Punjabi and Bengali, as well as Sindhi (besides English) came to be written soon after 1947, the subject was not easy to broach in printed form due to societal taboos and a resulting silence in the public domain. At least one major memoir in Urdu (*In Freedom's Shade* by Anis Kidwai), while composed soon after partition, faced many hindrances before being eventually published in 1974.[9] It was perhaps the publication of Alok Bhalla's anthology of short stories in 1994 that resulted in a consolidated effort being made to collate and translate such memoirs (indeed, Bhalla's own introduction brought in a strongly autobiographical note while enunciating the reasons for undertaking the task of unearthing and translating partition fiction).[10] In the 1990s, anthologies such as Mushirul Hasan's *India Partitioned* (2 vols.) appeared; the second volume opened with an extract from Mumtaz Shah Nawaz's autobiographical novel *The Heart Divided*, along with selections from memoirs by and interviews with writers and activists such as Kamla Patel, Josh Malihabadi, Aruna Asaf Ali and Lakshmi Sahgal, among others.[11] Later, in Ahmad Salim's *Lahore 1947*, we find an extract from 'The Sixth River', a satirical fictive memoir by Fikr Taunsvi, as well as first-person accounts by artist Satish

Gujral, novelist Khushwant Singh and poet Amrita Pritam, among others.[12] Subsequently, Ritu Menon's *No Woman's Land* brought together life-writings negotiating the traumatic experience of the partition by women from across South Asia, featuring pieces by diasporic writers such as Sara Suleri, as well as well-known voices such as Ismat Chughtai, Kidwai, and Patel.[13] More recently, Rita Kothari's *Unbordered Memories* juxtaposed memoirs with fictional accounts by Sindhi writers from both sides of the border.[14]

Given the fact that the Second World War had ended two years before the partition, it is not surprising that one of the earliest memoirs about the event by a well-known historian makes explicit reference to war experiences across the globe during the first part of the twentieth century (which I will address later). B.R. Nanda, in *Witness to Partition: A Memoir*, written in December 1947 but published pseudonymously under the title *Punjab Uprooted* with a postscript in February 1948 (after Gandhi's assassination in January 1948), draws on personal recollections of the catastrophe in the Punjab, on both sides of the border.[15] The volume was reprinted with a new introduction by this well-established Indian historian in 2003, in the wake of resurgence of interest in partition memories. In the original preface, the author allows a subjective dimension to enter at the outset, before attempting to assume an objective stance, casting himself as historian of the moment. Nanda describes his own position as being analogous to that of an onlooker watching two trains on the same track head towards each other. He speaks of often brooding like such an onlooker during the year of communal frenzy leading up to the disaster, as a witness to a tragedy that he cannot prevent, but can foresee. After the collision, people became so preoccupied with comparing the details of the wreckage and tabulating the number of the dead that they did not tend to the wounded, or reflect on the blunder of the stationmaster who started the train. For Nanda, the disaster in the Punjab is like such a train accident; its story will be compiled from various sources, while a few historians will examine the underlying causes of the accident and the mental state of the stationmaster.[16] This leads Nanda to declare his interest in the causes of the communal frenzy at the time, rather than its manifestations. For Nanda, Mohammed Ali Jinnah was like a magician who convinced a crowd of his bona fides, then opened (using a mixed metaphor) Pandora's box, out of which emerged a cobra that he could not control, and which stung him.[17] He locates himself as an Indian historian-in-the-making, unambiguously articulating a nationalist standpoint while analysing the causal factors in question. While the account that follows is framed by such an Indian nationalist point of view, and a tendency to indulge in the rhetoric of blame, Nanda's first-hand observations do at times offer insights that rise above the purely ideological.

Chapter One begins with an evocation of life in Lahore in 1946, where there seemed to be no hint of the disaster to follow.[18] While much of the rest of India was in turmoil after the Great Calcutta Killing (after Jinnah declared Direct Action Day on 16 August 1946), the Punjab seemed to be enjoying a moment of peace. While the Unionists (a party comprised largely of zamindars/landowners of different religious backgrounds) and the coalition they led were in power, it seemed that the communal balance in the Punjab could be retained.[19] This conception of communal balance is crucial to Nanda's argument, for according to him it is the provocative rhetoric of the Muslim League that tilts the situation towards the point of no return, especially after the banning by this provincial coalition government of private armies such as the Muslim League's National Guard and the Rashtriya Swayam Sevak Sangh (RSSS, or RSS as it is now known) in early 1947.[20] However, Nanda reserves his ire for the votaries of the Muslim League, rather than also look in detail at the actions of the RSS and its associate organisations such as the Hindu Mahasabha. Here the imbalance in the analysis of causes becomes evident. In Hajari's more recent account, such far-right Hindu organisations had increased recruitment and taken a militant turn, especially after the Noakhali killings in 1946, training cadres in the use of arms and bomb-making.[21] Similarly, by the end of 1946, the Muslim League's National Guards' strength had grown from 1,500 to 60,000, with the emphasis on arming these 'volunteers'.[22]

Nanda squarely blames British premier Clement Attlee for the Punjab disturbances of March 1946, after the naming of a date for transfer of power.[23] The possibility of power being transferred in some areas to the provincial government (according to the declaration made by Attlee), in his view, led Muslim League leaders to believe that Pakistan had become a concrete possibility. In his discussion of the reasons for the March riots, he ostensibly tries not to ascribe a monopoly of guilt to one party or the other,[24] but in practice he insistently focuses on the well-known political strategies of mobilisation of the Muslim League and Jinnah. An element of bias seems evident as Nanda asserts that the rioting was worse in Muslim-dominated areas such as Rawalpindi and Multan, in comparison with East Punjab, though he does admit to varied local factors coming into play in West Punjab. The 'March anarchy' in Rawalpindi and Multan in his description was quelled by efficient military action, despite Jinnah's reluctance to visit these areas.[25] For Nanda, this 'competitive degradation of communal frenzy' led to the erosion of individual morality and social conscience.[26] While the Muslim League leaders failed to grasp this, as a result Congress leaders became reconciled to the prospect of the partition.[27] The role played by right-wing Hindu nationalists (who had made inroads into the Congress as well)[28] in consolidating the polarised positions of the time is largely ignored by Nanda. As Devji has shown, when the president of the Muslim League compared the Muslims to the Sudeten Germans, as a minority group acting as a beachhead for a larger number of co-religionists in other lands, the president of the Hindu Mahasabha argued that a more apt parallel would be with the German Jews, with whose fate he threatened India's Muslims.[29]

In Nanda's account, there was a period of quiet from the end of March 1947 to the middle of August 1947–actually it was the silence of the grave that prevailed. However, the underlying tension was manifested in the gathering of recruits by communal armies. He differentiates this moment from earlier civil wars such as the conflicts between Cavaliers and Roundheads in seventeenth-century England and Republicans and Falangists in twentieth-century Spain by highlighting the role played by religious identity here, as one could be attacked for simply being born into a particular faith.[30] While acknowledging the difficulty of identifying those responsible for starting the worst of the violence in August, he details the setting up of the Boundary Commission headed by Cyril Radcliffe and the formulation of the partition plan, with the date advanced to 15 August.[31] Ultimately, however, it is the economic motivation of Muslims attracted by the possibilities of self-advancement in Pakistan (unleashed by Jinnah) that is underlined by Nanda as a crucial factor. He strives to prove his contention about vested interests being stronger in West Punjab by emphasising the greater holdings of Sikhs and Hindus in West Punjab, compared to Muslim holdings in the East.[32] The reductivism of this argument seems apparent, as greed and the drive to material self-aggrandisement on the part of Muslims seem to override all other human motivations. Furthermore, this rather crude explanation fails to come to terms with the near-genocidal intensity of reciprocal violence in the Punjab, which led to West Punjab being cleared of Hindus and Sikhs, and East Punjab being depopulated of Muslims (except in Malerkotla).

In the seventh chapter Nanda dismisses Jinnah's conspiracy theories as regards a plot by India to enfeeble Pakistan.[33] The predatory attacks on Muslims in East Punjab are eventually mentioned with the caveat that this was part of a 'chain reaction of an atomic explosion' that had been set off.[34] This rather clichéd and hyperbolic image seems to normalise the brutality that ensued, especially the attacks on women and children. The echo of the explosions at Hiroshima and Nagasaki is apt only insofar as large numbers of non-combatants were targeted in the mass slaughter that occurred on both sides of the Punjab. The rather passive role played by Jinnah (on account of his health) is contrasted by Nanda with the courageous interventions of Jawaharlal Nehru and Gandhi, especially with respect to the calming of Calcutta by Gandhi's fasting.³⁵ He pinpoints the role of the Muslim League's National Guard (formed in 1946) in fomenting violence, and the failure of the Pakistani leadership and state to contain this, while attempting to establish a contrast with the more disciplined Congress Seva Dal.³⁶ The more accurate comparison might be with the RSS and the Akal Sainas (a militant wing of the Sikh Akali party), civil militias that expanded their ranks also as a result of the demobilisation of soldiers en masse after the Second World War. Such militias were well equipped with arms (not surrendered at the time of demobilisation from the army) that were used extensively in mass killing, as Kamtekar has shown.³⁷ Nanda draws a parallel with SS troops of the Nazi party, who initially followed a given leader, but possibly themselves became the master later; this is of a piece with the rhetoric of the times.³⁸ As Devji shows, allegations of harbouring fascist tendencies were being hurled by both the Muslim League and the Congress at the time. Jinnah, for example, accused Gandhi of behaving like a *fuehrer*, exercising an extra-constitutional influence on the Congress.³⁹

Nanda is critical of the notion of a 'surgical solution' to the minority problem, as had been envisaged by Jinnah since 1940. He waxes metaphoric while alluding to the 'quackery' underlying the political surgery that was deployed to achieve this goal. The exchange of populations idea had been tried elsewhere (he refers to south-eastern Europe after the First World War) but had not succeeded in resolving the minority problem.⁴⁰ Nanda's account shifts to a more emotional register while recounting the exodus of the refugees (though he falls prey to predictable rhetoric at times –'the flight of the minorities... enacted a tragedy beyond the power of words to describe').⁴¹ He acknowledges the opportunism afoot as many sought to take advantage of the desperation of fleeing refugees, travelling by train or in convoys on foot. There were also acts of kindness and expressions of solidarity across the threshold of religious difference. The difficulty of rehabilitating these people is underlined, both in terms of physical and mental needs. Several literary references appear; Nanda quotes Marcel Proust on suffering: 'We are healed by suffering only by experiencing it to the full'.⁴² Here the need to face up to traumatic memories is underlined, which might otherwise fester. However, he also believes that the people of Punjab have not reached the stage of Fyodor Dostoyevsky's intense grappling with and acceptance of suffering – the will and capacity to learn from adversity seemed missing.⁴³ Such self-critical remarks lead up to the concluding section of the narrative, in which Nanda offers recommendations for how to deal with the situation at the administrative and social levels. Here Nanda expands the scope of his concerns beyond the immediacy of the partition, advocating a new outlook and a plan for the future of India.⁴⁴

Nanda's postscript (written as the volume was going to press) comes to terms with Gandhi's legacy in the wake of his assassination. His moving tribute includes the observation that the refugees from West Punjab who were most baffled by Gandhi's appeals for patience, restraint and forgiveness were hit hardest by his death; an ironic reversal that has had cascading effects over the following decades.[45] The general drift of Nanda's memoir converges with mainstream Indian nationalist historiography (this is also the case with his introduction, written in 2003; indeed, recent advances in subaltern and feminist historiography with respect to the partition are largely ignored here). Nevertheless, it is such pointed self-critical remarks that elevate the discussion above the polemical and mundane, allowing for a reflection on the event that probes deeper than causal factors. It is at such moments that this memoir begins to approximate to testimony, devising a mode of bearing witness to partition.

It was perhaps inevitable that major leaders of the nationalist movement should reflect on the debacle of the partition soon after the event. Former Congress president Maulana Azad's *India Wins Freedom* was published in shortened form in 1959 as a result of his hesitation over whether prospective readers were ready for his sharply critical views of the role of the Congress leadership.[46] The complete edition was eventually published much later, in 2003, generating some controversy, especially as regards Nehru's and Patel's role in the processes leading up to the partition. Azad's comprehensive rejection of the hostage population theory and any acceptance of the partition on the basis of minorities in each country being held hostage to the security of minorities in the other are significant; the notion of retaliation as a method of ensuring the rights of minorities seemed barbarous to him.[47]

However, to get a sense of the traumatic effects of the changes wrought by the partition, we need to turn to other sources. We may take up for contrast a short 'fictive' memoir, written in a satirical vein, by the Urdu writer Sa'adat Hasan Manto. In 'Savere Jo Kal Meri Ankh Khuli' (trans. 'A Stroll through the New Pakistan') Manto evokes the profound disorientation wrought by the event.[48] Manto migrated from Bombay to Lahore after the partition, the results of which shocked him to the core. Indeed, even such a prolific writer as Manto was unable to write for months after moving from Bombay, where he was a successful script-writer for Hindi films, also establishing a growing reputation as a writer of unconventional, formally innovative Urdu short stories. His initial response was in the form of short vignettes ('Siyah Hashye', trans. 'Black Margins'), which vividly captured the splintered reality of the times, at times incorporating elements of black humour.[49] This tone is carried over into this fragmentary 'fictive' memoir about the moment of arrival of the newly born nation-state, Pakistan. 'It was a strange season and a strange morning'⁵⁰; Manto's first-person account begins this way as his narrator-persona takes a stroll through the streets of Lahore, now in Pakistan. The narrator remarks that he had certainly seen these streets and neighbourhoods before, but it was as if the previous day (after the birth of Pakistan) he had seen them for the first time. Everywhere he looks the slogan 'Pakistan Zindabad' ('Long live Pakistan') is to be seen, appended to shops, homes and even hospitals. The zeal for renaming seems to connote a certain territorial triumphalism, which the narrative debunks. On one building he sees the sign 'Pakistan Zindabad–this property belongs to a Parsi', which he takes to mean that it should not be mistakenly allotted (to a refugee family) thinking it to be a Hindu's.⁵¹ Manto's irony is at the expense of such strategies resorted to by some belonging to 'neutral' minorities like the Parsis to safeguard their homes at this time of reallocation of evacuee properties.

The narrator next visits a *halvai* (maker of sweets) and notices that the fan is turned away from the customers and the owner. He asks the owner about this; he glares at the narrator and asks him to look again. The narrator then notices that the fan is actually pointed towards a poster of their great leader Jinnah. He exclaims 'Pakistan Zindabad' and leaves without drinking his *lassi* (buttermilk).⁵² The irrationality and absurdity of hypernationalism (including such bizarre forms of hero worship) is brought to the fore here. After describing a number of similar absurdities, the narrator comes to a well-known chowk, where he notices that a familiar statue is missing. He asks what happened to it, and is told that the statue has been transferred to a museum. He then prays to God, '...please don't let me be around when they put people in a museum just because they are different'.⁵³ The divisive calculus underpinning the partition is here effectively critiqued as Manto ironises the notion of absolutising difference.

He eventually reaches his destination, a popular park called Lawrence Bagh. As he leaves the place he is informed that it has been renamed Bagh-e-Jinnah. The narrator replies, 'Pakistan Zindabad!', upon which his informant laughs loudly and enters the park. The narrator's concluding remark is that he felt he was coming out of hell.⁵⁴ For it is the perception of the gap between nationalist jingoism and sloganeering and the grotesque reality of what accompanied the partition that generates the ironic consciousness underpinning this 'fictive' memoir. The hubris of nation-building manifested in the accelerated pace of renaming places is effectively satirised by Manto. Furthermore, there is a sense that the process of partitioning of consciousness had acquired a sinister momentum, as if a new kind of instrumental rationality underpinned such acts of redefining space and geography, bereft of real feeling (whether of patriotism or adulation for the leader in question).

In his short memoir about his time in Bombay during the partition, Manto vividly captures the far-reaching transformations afoot.[55] While in earlier instances of communal violence the killings were evenly distributed among the communities, violence had now acquired a new character. As an instance of this he describes coming across the corpse of an ice-seller, a Hindu, near Claire Road. His cart was next to him, and the ice was melting; as it did, the drops mingled with the blood that had coagulated around him. 'It looked like jelly', observes Manto.[56] This incident led to the penning of one of the most striking vignettes in 'Siyah Hashye', titled 'Jelly'.[57] The searing image, however seemingly incongruous, drives home the at times surreal dimensions of the experience of partition. Indeed, Manto again underlines the grotesquerie of the times. As he says, 'There was chaos, mayhem, panic everywhere and from the womb of this anarchy were born two nations. Independent India and independent Pakistan'.[58] Manto is equally unsparing when it comes to illusions harboured by flag-bearers of various stripes. Even as the tricolour of the Indian flag went up in many places, in Bhendi bazaar (the Muslim minority area), posters of Jinnah were up, along with green flags. No one seemed to have a clue about the whereabouts of Pakistan, or the meaning of Independence and its implications for their lives, even as they exulted at the achievement of freedom.[59]

Matters were little different in the newly founded Islamic Republic, as Manto finds. On the previous Independence Day he discovered a man cutting down a tree in front of his house. On chiding the man, he received the answer, 'This is Pakistan. It belongs to us'.[60] Manto's unravelling of the hypocrisy and self-serving nature of much nationalist humbug is candid, and based on personal memories eventually transmuted into fiction. The cartographic anxiety that spread across north India like wildfire, dislocating perceptions of selfhood, ideas of home and of belonging, is most brilliantly evoked in his masterpiece, the short story 'Toba Tek Singh'.[61] Manto bears witness to the damage done to identity at the deepest level by the pressures of demagoguery and often hollow nationalist bluster in this short story, as well as in his 'fictive' memoirs about the partition.

More recently, innovative work by Urvashi Butalia,[62] Ritu Menon and Kamla Bhasin[63] and Veena Das,[64] as well as Gyanendra Pandey,[65] has enabled a shift in focus from national/political history to social and cultural history, with an emphasis on reconstructing the archives using new sources and tools, including the resources of oral history. Indeed, it may be argued that it was personal accounts as well as memoirs by activists such as Anis Kidwai's *In Freedom's Shade* and Kamla Patel's *Torn from the Roots* that helped create space for the feminist and subaltern turn in partition historiography.[66] Both these memoirs by prominent social workers (who worked to rehabilitate refugee women in particular) take up the issue of the recovery of abducted women by the two nation-states, in the wake of large-scale sexual violence.[67] These memoirs continue to provide models for those reckoning with the impact of gendered forms of violence on the mind and in society, whether social scientists, activists or imaginative writers. Ayesha Kidwai, the translator of Kidwai's memoir, began reading her grandmother's memoir after the Gujarat pogrom of 2002,[68] which led her to translate this memoir for a contemporary audience, while thinking afresh about the ways in which partition-era forms of violence tend to reappear.

In Freedom's Shade, written in Urdu in 1949 but published in 1974 (translated into English in 2011), is a striking memoir in many respects.[69] Kidwai's memories of years spent working towards the rehabilitation of refugees (at camps set up at Lal Qila and Humayun's Tomb for those migrating to Pakistan as well as at many camps for those arriving from West Punjab) are interspersed with literary allusions and personal anecdotes of meetings with leaders as well as common folk. In a chilling instance, the targeting of Muslims in Ajmer, Rajasthan, in December 1947 based on maps provided by officers in the food supply and rationing departments is described by Kidwai, a form of bureaucratised violence that has since been seen repeatedly in independent India.[70] The hushed residences of the few Muslims who remained, marked by emptiness and unease, testified to the trauma of the massacres that took place in early 1948, even a year afterwards when Kidwai visited Ajmer in January 1949.[71]

Kidwai is able to sensitively capture minority anxieties at the time as she gives us an account of the mood after Gandhi's assassination, when the rumour was spread that his killer was Muslim. She acknowledges the importance of Nehru's and Patel's announcements that the killer (Nathuram Godse) was a Hindu.[72] Otherwise, she notes, there might have been large-scale reprisal attacks on minority groups, whether Muslim or Sikh.[73] Kidwai recounts an uncanny episode from the time of the Calcutta killings in 1946. A year later she met a Muslim lady who had escaped from Calcutta to Dehradun. The lady told her about the distribution of knives to Pathans lined up in the rear lane. When asked the reason, she replied, 'To kill Hindus, of course. The Pathans pounded them to a pulp, didn't they? They were very useful'.[74] The lady went on to talk about the perceived need at the time to revive a Pathan who had committed seven or eight murders after dunking him in water and placing him on ice, for otherwise he might take his own life. This practice was widespread on both sides, it seems; this indicated a high degree of instrumentalisation and orchestration of violence.[75]

In Kidwai's account, the visceral aspects of partition-era violence (as well as its costs on both mind and body) come to the fore, reminiscent at times of Manto's short stories.

In more recently published memoirs we find a rather different take on the events of 1947, often inflected by concerns of the present. Indeed, writings from recent years often recast the mode of the partition memoir from the standpoint of the second and third generation after the event. A greater degree of self-reflexivity about the act of recollection can be seen in these writings, which take on board the baggage of the past from a postmemorial standpoint. Indeed, we might describe some of these works as post-memoirs, given their concern with the intergenerational transmission of traumatic memories.[76] Here I follow Marianne Hirsch's notion of postmemory, of course, to suggest that recent partition memoirs are actually informed by the memories of survivors, and often respond to the sometimes unspoken trauma of the previous generation.[77]

In the concluding part of this chapter I will take up for discussion some memoirs in which elements of such postmemorial consciousness appear. These writings engage with partition's afterlife in different ways, contingent upon varied backgrounds and contexts. I will touch upon some moments in these narratives to illustrate my argument. We get an incipient sense of this in well-known Pakistani journalist and commentator Raza Rumi's *Delhi by Heart: Impressions of a Pakistani Traveller*,[78] actually an extended reflection on his stay in the capital of India. Rumi describes at the outset a conversation with Apa, an elderly agony aunt in Lahore, before setting out for India, and her memory of the burning of the Hindu-dominated Shahalmi area of Lahore in 1947, which she fled along with all her neighbours.[79] The jolt she felt after seeing the burnt houses and empty homes is still palpable, in addition to the personal loss of her dowry ('gobbled up by Partition').[80] Relayed across time, this traumatic memory acquires personal as well as public dimensions, as she shares her story with Rumi. This incident is the prelude for the author's rediscovery of many historical connections between Delhi and Lahore. In New Delhi Rumi has the chance to meet Indian novelist Khushwant Singh and is addressed by the author of *Train to Pakistan* as the boy from his 'hometown'. Rumi underlines the sense of nostalgia, along with unshed tears, that he perceives underlying Singh's narratives about Lahore and the Punjabi identity, in the process causing Singh's sense of historical trauma to intersect with his own (second-generation) experience.[81] He mentions the 'draining' of 300,000 Muslims from Delhi as 500,000 non-Muslims rushed in after the creation of Pakistan. In Rumi's terms, 'that August brought the dark world of Hades into the daylight' – the agony of the times was universal, not specific to any community.[82] This line seems to deliberately echo Manto's description of emerging from hell; again, it is as if a memory of a memory appears. Rumi's humanitarian rereading of the partition's impact is especially significant, given the domination of one-sided narratives about 1947 in Pakistan (where the statist version is taught as part of the Pakistan ideology).

Kavita Panjabi's memoir *Old Maps and New: Legacies of the Partition – A Pakistan Diary* (2005), as well as her personal essay/memoir 'A Unique Grace' (2015),[83] exemplifies the self-consciousness about memory and trauma that I referred to earlier. I will focus here on her more recent piece. Panjabi has been associated with groups working towards peace between India and Pakistan, as well as the women's movement. As the Indian daughter of Sindhi parents who did not often speak about the experience of displacement to Calcutta during partition, she is able to weave together stories of the first generation (based on recovered memory) and her own experiences in both narratives in unusual ways.[84] Panjabi also generates some compelling insights as regards nostalgia and loss, and the problem of mutual culpability, also as a result of actively participating in the peace process. For instance, before visiting Karachi for a peace conference Panjabi has to initially negotiate her father's anxiety about finding 'nothing there' (as a result of the trauma of being forced to leave Karachi in 1947). Panjabi wonders as a result whether one can think of a homeland without a sense of territorial possession. She then mentions the slow abatement of the partition trauma in her family, after which stories about her father's childhood in Sindh began to be shared.[85]

Next, Panjabi affirms the continuing resistance to the will and acts of politicians who reshaped millions of lives. She is critical of notions of loss exclusively focused on a notion of redemption, especially when such loss is irredeemable. Rather, Panjabi highlights the shared history of trauma and dispossession, as well as of mutual culpability that was characteristic of the partition. While Panjabi's evocation of the necessity of unsettling the finality of the partition is based on personal experiences of interactions with ordinary folk in Pakistan, she concludes with an assertion of the importance of sustaining a grace of spirit that may allow a claim to belonging without possession.[86] Such counterstatements may in time contribute to the possibility of emergence from the long shadow cast by the partition on the subcontinent and eventual liberation from the grip of traumatic memory.

The notion of mutual culpability for the violence during the partition articulated by Panjabi may seem somewhat abstract (in the absence of societal recognition for the need for Truth and Reconciliation-style endeavours), and does not address the specificity of perpetrator responsibility on both sides (trials of perpetrators were held only in rare instances). Nonetheless, it is indeed the case that the difference between the historical trauma of

1947 and other experiences of civil conflict (leading to a greater degree of difficulty with respect to achieving resolution) is the large-scale failure to consciously acknowledge any responsibility (let alone mutual culpability) by most survivors, except perhaps as represented in some fictional accounts.[87] Indeed, the desire for ethical reconstruction can only be met by working through ambivalent memories of complicity, abetment and even direct involvement in pre-emptive reprisal killings against the innocent, as well as recollections of instances of solidarity and resistance; acceptance of mutual culpability may be the first step in this collective process.

Important memoirs about the partition and its afterlife, as we have seen, indicate a shift in focus from recounting the story in terms of heroes and villains or the memory of personal loss to a deeper reflection on the reasons for erasure of memory and the difficulties faced while negotiating censorship and selective amnesia. In these distinctive narratives the transition from the desire to affix blame to a more nuanced negotiation with the moment of extreme violence and its after-effects becomes evident. While the occasional tension between Nanda's attempt at first-hand historical analysis and personal observations is interesting to note, Manto's 'fictive' memoirs allow for a more critical interrogation of nationalist euphoria and ill-thought out variants of utopianism prevalent at the time. The accounts by Azad and Kidwai cast light on the extent of deterioration in personal relations among the leaders even as new forms of violence appeared at the ground level. The publication histories of these volumes exemplify the difficulty of articulating dissenting views and public recounting of 'sensitive' memories. Rumi and Panjabi have since brought to bear a personalised postmemorial awareness in their partition-related recollections. This is also evident in 'A Good Education', a graphic narrative by Vishwajyoti Ghosh and Amiya Sen that self-reflexively includes a personalised dialogue between the author (a graphic artist) and the memoir *Aranyalipi* or *The Forest Chronicles*, composed by his grandmother Amiya Sen, who was a social worker working with refuges from East Bengal relocated to the Dandakaranya forest in central India.[88] Such writings exemplify the possibility of generic reinvention; recent memoirs about partition seem to have re-emerged as post-memoirs, even as we seek to come to terms with the still unfolding afterlife of the 'endless' partition.

NOTES

1. Indeed, for at least one major historian, the Second World War and the partition were inextricably intertwined. In Eric Hobsbawm's terms it was 'the

(Second World) war that broke India in two' (Eric Hobsbawm, *The Age of Extremes: A History of the World 1914-1991* [New York, 1994], 219). Hobsbawm refers to the victory in the Second World War as the British Raj's last triumph, but also its last exhausted gasp. According to him, the fear of the Congress sabotaging the war effort led to the systematic exploitation of Hindu–Muslim divisions by the Raj, destroying itself and also its only source of moral legitimation – a united subcontinent (Hobsbawm, *The Age of Extremes*, 219-20).

2. See Paul Brass, 'The Partition of India and Retributive Genocide in the Punjab, 1946-47: Means, Methods and Purposes', in Brass (ed.), *Forms of Collective Violence: Riots, Pogroms and Genocide in Modern India* (New Delhi, 2005; reprint 2006), esp. 11-12, for an account of 'retributive genocide' in Punjab, during which carefully planned attacks were launched to ensure population transfers.

3. The attacks were hardly on the pattern of spontaneous violence between peasants of different religious communities; rather, the massacres (especially on trains) were well orchestrated (as in the case of those carried out by armed Sikh jathas assisted by the maharajahs of Faridkot and Patiala, as Nisid Hajari shows in *Midnight's Furies: The Deadly Legacy of India's Partition* [Gurgaon, 2015], 138-39). Also see Hajari for an account of Jinnah's explicit reference to Sikhsleft behind in Pakistan as hostages who would ensure that Muslims in India would not be illtreated, after the worst violence began in August 1947 (Hajari, *Midnight's Furies*, 121).

4. Faisal Devji, *The Impossible Indian: Gandhi and the Temptation of Violence* (Cambridge, MA, 2012), 169-71.

5. Brass, 'Partition of India', 11-64.

6. Paul Fussell, *The Great War and Modern Memory* (New York, 1977; reprint 2013), 80-81.

7. On the idea of a 'long partition', experienced as such especially by divided Muslim families, see Vazira Fazila-Yacoobali Zamindar, *The Long Partition and the Making of South Asia: Refugees, Boundaries, Histories* (New York, 2007), 1-18.

8. Fussell, *Great War*, 3.

9. Anis Kidwai, *In Freedom's Shade*, trans. by Ayesha Kidwai (New Delhi, 2011). Trans. of *Azadiki Chhaon Mein*, 1974.

10. See Alok Bhalla (ed.), Introduction to *Stories about the Partition of India*, 3 vols. (New Delhi, 1994), i. esp. x–xii.

11. Mushirul Hasan (ed.), *India Partitioned*, 2 vols. (New Delhi, 1997). Also see Mumtaz Shah Nawaz, *The Heart Divided* (Lahore, 1990; first published 1957).

12. Ahmad Salim (ed.), *Lahore 1947* (New Delhi, 2001). Also see Fikr Taunsvi, 'The Sixth River: A Diary of 1947', in Salim, *Lahore 1947* (trans. of extract from *Chatta Darya*, 1948).

13. Ritu Menon (ed.), *No Woman's Land: Women from Pakistan, India and Bangladesh Write on the Partition of India* (New Delhi, 2004).

14. Rita Kothari (ed.), *Unbordered Memories: Sindhi Stories of Partition* (New Delhi, 2009).

15. B.R. Nanda, *Witness to Partition: A Memoir* (New Delhi, 2003; reprint 2006).
16. Nanda, Preface in Nanda, *Witness to Partition*, ix–x.
17. Nanda, *Witness to Partition*, x–xi.
18. Nanda, *Witness to Partition*, 33.
19. Nanda, *Witness to Partition*, 35.
20. Nanda, *Witness to Partition*, 39. This order was issued on 24 January 1947, as a result of such militias growing at a terrifying pace, as Hajari shows (Hajari, *Midnight's Furies*, 71).
21. Hajari, *Midnight's Furies*, 59.
22. Hajari, *Midnight's Furies*, 64.
23. Nanda, *Witness to Partition*, 40.
24. Nanda, *Witness to Partition*, 46.
25. Nanda, *Witness to Partition*, 47–50.
26. Nanda, *Witness to Partition*, 50.
27. Nanda, *Witness to Partition*, 50–51.
28. Hajari draws attention to Congress Home Minister Sardar Patel's greater sympathy for the RSS and Hindu Mahasabha in his recent study (Hajari, *Midnight's Furies*, 66).
29. Devji, *Impossible Indian*, 121.
30. Nanda, *Witness to Partition*, 52–56.
31. Nanda, *Witness to Partition*, 60–64.
32. Nanda, *Witness to Partition*, 68–72.
33. Nanda, *Witness to Partition*, 73–75.
34. Nanda, *Witness to Partition*, 75–76.
35. Nanda, *Witness to Partition*, 80.
36. Nanda, *Witness to Partition*, 82–84.
37. See Indivar Kamtekar, 'The Military Ingredient of Communal Violence in the Punjab, 1947', in *Proceedings of the Indian History Congress, 56th session, 1995* (Calcutta, 1996), 568–72.
38. Nanda, *Witness to Partition*, 84. In the wake of the unrest in Delhi, Nehru called the RSS and Akali cells 'fascists', no different from Jinnah's thugs or Hitler's (Hajari, *Midnight's Furies*, 170).
39. Devji, *Impossible Indian*, 124–25.
40. Nanda, *Witness to Partition*, 87–88.
41. Nanda, *Witness to Partition*, 90.
42. Cited in Nanda, *Witness to Partition*, 98.
43. Cited in Nanda, *Witness to Partition*, 99–100.
44. Nanda, *Witness to Partition*, 103–50. In particular, Nanda follows the recommendations of Tarlok Singh's *Poverty and Social Change* (cited in Nanda, *Witness to Partition*, 138).
45. Nanda, *Witness to Partition*, 162–68.
46. Maulana Abul Kalam Azad, *India Wins Freedom* (New Delhi, 2003; first published 1959; complete version 1988).

47. Azad, *India Wins Freedom*, 216. Socialist leader Ram Manohar Lohia's *Guilty Men of India's Partition* (New Delhi, 1961; reprint 2009), which began as a rejoinder to Azad's volume (Lohia, *Guilty Men*, 1), is even more scathing in its denunciation of the Congress leadership. For a Pakistani perspective, see Jahan Ara Shahnawaz's *Father and Daughter: A Political Autobiography* (Karachi, 2002). She was the wife of Mohammad Shafi, an influential Muslim League leader, and became active after his death. Her daughter Mumtaz Shah Nawaz began her political career as a Congress supporter, but eventually changed her political affiliation and worked for the Muslim League. The dilemmas faced by her daughter (later recounted in fictional form by Mumtaz in her novel *The Heart Divided*) are presented with empathy and insight. Begum Shaista Suhrawardy Ikramullah's *From Purdah to Parliament* (revised and expanded ed. Karachi, 1998; first published 1963) is noteworthy for her personal and candid description of experiences while campaigning for the Muslim League in East Bengal, as well as later as elected Member of Parliament in Pakistan.
48. Sa'adat Hasan Manto, 'A Stroll through the New Pakistan', trans. by Aakar Patel, in *Why I Write: Essays by Sa'adat Hasan Manto* (New Delhi, 2014), 83–90.
49. Sa'adat Hasan Manto, 'Black Margins', trans. by M. Asaduddin of 'Siyah Hashye', in Muhammad Umar Memon (ed.), *Black Margins: Stories* (New Delhi, 2001; reprint 2003), 177–87.
50. Manto, 'Stroll', 82.
51. Manto, 'Stroll', 83–84.
52. Manto, 'Stroll', 84–85.
53. Manto, 'Stroll', 88.
54. Manto, 'Stroll', 89.
55. Sa'adat Hasan Manto, 'Bombay During Partition', trans. by Aakar Patel, in *Why I Write: Essays by Sa'adat Hasan Manto* (New Delhi, 2014), 77–82.
56. Manto, 'Bombay', 78.
57. Sa'adat Hasan Manto, 'Jelly', in Memon, *Black Margins*, 187.
58. Manto, 'Bombay', 78.
59. Manto, 'Bombay', 79–80.
60. Manto, 'Bombay', 80.
61. Sa'adat Hasan Manto, 'Toba Tek Singh', trans. by M. Asaduddin, in Memon (ed.), *Black Margins*, 212–20.
62. Urvashi Butalia, *The Other Side of Silence: Voices from the Partition of India* (New Delhi, 1998).
63. Ritu Menon and Kamla Bhasin, *Borders and Boundaries: Women in India's Partition* (New Delhi, 1998).
64. Veena Das, *Critical Events: An Anthropological Perspective on Contemporary India* (New Delhi, 1996). See also Das, *Life and Words: Violence and the Descent into the Ordinary* (New Delhi, 2007).
65. Gyanendra Pandey, *Memory, History and the Question of Violence: Reflections on the Reconstruction of Partition* (Calcutta, 1999). Also see Pandey, *Remembering Partition* (Cambridge, 2001).

66. See Kidwai, *In Freedom's Shade* and Kamla Patel, *Torn from the Roots: A Partition Memoir*, trans. by Uma Randeria (New Delhi, 2006). Trans. of *Mool Sotan Ukhdelan*, 1977.
67. I have discussed this aspect of these memoirs in greater detail in a related essay; see Tarun K. Saint, 'Exorcizing the Ghosts of Times Past: Partition Memoirs as Testimony', in Amritjit Singh, Nalini Iyer and Rahul K. Gairola (eds), *Revisiting Partition: New Essays in Memory, Culture and Politics* (Lanham, MD: Lexington Press, 2016), esp. 75–80.
68. Ayesha Kidwai, introduction to *In Freedom's Shade*, by Anis Kidwai (New Delhi, 2011), vii. Trans. of *Azadi ki Chhaon Mein*, 1974.
69. Kidwai, *In Freedom's Shade*.
70. Kidwai, *In Freedom's Shade*, 99–100.
71. Kidwai, *In Freedom's Shade*, 99.
72. For an interesting psychobiography of Madanlal Pahwa, one of the men who attempted to kill Gandhi, see Ashis Nandy, 'Coming Home: Religion, Mass Violence, and the Exiled and Secret Selves of a Citizen Killer', in Ashis Nandy, *Regimes of Narcissism, Regimes of Despair* (New Delhi, 2013), 65–94.
73. Kidwai, *In Freedom's Shade*, 136–38.
74. Kidwai, *In Freedom's Shade*, 196–97.
75. Kidwai, *In Freedom's Shade*, 197.
76. On this question, see Sukeshi Kamra, 'Engaging Traumatic Histories: The 1947 Partition of India in Collective Memory', in Urvashi Butalia (ed.), *Partition: The Long Shadow* (New Delhi, 2015), esp. 170.
77. '"Postmemory" describes the relationship that the "generation after" bears to the personal, collective, and cultural trauma of those who came before – to experiences they "remember" only by means of the stories, images, and behaviors among which they grew up. But these experiences were transmitted to them so deeply and affectively as to seem to constitute memories in their own right. Postmemory's connection to the past is thus actually mediated not by recall but by imaginative investment, projection, and creation. To grow up with overwhelming inherited memories, to be dominated by narratives that preceded one's birth or one's consciousness, is to risk having one's own life stories displaced, even evacuated, by our ancestors. It is to be shaped, however indirectly, by traumatic fragments of events that still defy narrative reconstruction and exceed comprehension'. See Marianne Hirsch at www.postmemory.net (2012). Also see Marianne Hirsch, *Family Frames: Photography, Narrative and Postmemory* (Cambridge, MA, 1997), esp. 22–23.
78. Raza Rumi, *Delhi by Heart: Impressions of a Pakistani Traveller* (New Delhi, 2013).
79. Rumi, *Delhi by Heart*, 12–13. For an extended account of the Shahalmi Gate episode, see Hajari, *Midnight's Furies*, 109–13.
80. Rumi, *Delhi by Heart*, 12–13.
81. Rumi, *Delhi by Heart*, 42–44.
82. Rumi, *Delhi by Heart*, 45.

83. Kavita Panjabi, *Old Maps and New: Legacies of the Partition – A Pakistan Diary* (Calcutta, 2005). Also see Kavita Panjabi, 'A Unique Grace', in Butalia (ed), *Partition: The Long Shadow*, 48–63.
84. For another such second-generation perspective, see Manas Ray's 'Growing Up Refugee', in Anjali Gera Roy and Nandi Bhatia (eds), *Partitioned Lives: Narratives of Home, Displacement and Resettlement* (New Delhi, 2008), 116–45.
85. Panjabi, 'Unique Grace', 48–49. Rita Kothari's often self-referential work has further illuminated the different trajectory faced by Sindhi migrants from a postmemorial point of view, while extending her critical attention to the post-partition situation of Muslim minority groups in the Banni area of Kutch on the Gujarat border. See Rita Kothari, 'From Conclusions to Beginnings: My Journey with "Partition"', in Butalia, (ed.) *Partition: The Long Shadow*, 30–48.
86. Panjabi, 'Unique Grace', 54–63.
87. Also see my discussion of Gurdev Singh Ropana's short story 'Sheesha' (trans. 'The Mirror') in Tarun K. Saint, 'Revisioning and "Restorying" Partition', in Butalia, (ed.) *Partition: The Long Shadow*, 178–99, 182–84.
88. Saint, 'Revisioning and "Restorying" Partition', 191. See also Vishwajyoti Ghosh and Amiya Sen, 'A Good Education', in Butalia, (ed.), *Partition: The Long Shadow*, 64–77. Ananya Jahanara Kabir's work is pertinent in this regard, especially with respect to the afterlife of the partition in the East (compounded by the partition of Pakistan in 1971). See Ananya Jahanara Kabir, *Partition's Post-Amnesias: 1947, 1971 and Modern South Asia* (New Delhi, 2013).

BIBLIOGRAPHY

Memoirs and Fiction

Azad, Maulana Abul Kalam. *India Wins Freedom*. New Delhi: Orient Longman, 2003. First published 1959; complete version 1988.
Bhalla, Alok (ed.). *Stories about the Partition of India*. 3 Vols. New Delhi: Indus, 1994.
Butalia, Urvashi. *The Other Side of Silence: Voices from the Partition of India*. New Delhi: Penguin, 1998.
Ikramullah, Shaista Suhrawardy. *From Purdah to Parliament*. Revised and expanded ed. Karachi: Oxford University Press, 1998; first published 1963.
Kidwai, Anis. *In Freedom's Shade*. Translated by Ayesha Kidwai. New Delhi: Penguin, 2011. Trans. of *Azadi ki Chhaon Mein*, 1974.
Kothari, Rita (ed.). *Unbordered Memories: Sindhi Stories of Partition*. New Delhi: Penguin, 2009.
Lohia, Ram Manohar. *Guilty Men of India's Partition*. New Delhi: Rupa, 1961; reprint 2009.
Manto, Sa'adat Hasan. 'Black Margins', trans. by M. Asaduddin of 'Siyah Hashye', in Muhammad Umar Memon (ed.), *Black Margins: Stories* (New Delhi: Katha, 2001; reprint 2003), 177–87.

Manto, Sa'adat Hasan. 'Jelly', trans. by M. Asaduddin of 'Siyah Hashye', in Muhammad Umar Memon (ed.), *Black Margins: Stories* (New Delhi: Katha, 2001; reprint 2003), 187.

Manto, Sa'adat Hasan. 'A Stroll through the New Pakistan'; 'Bombay During Partition', trans. by Aakar Patel, in *Why I Write: Essays by Sa'adat Hasan Manto* (New Delhi: Tranquebar, 2014), 83–90; 77–82.

Manto, Sa'adat Hasan. 'Toba Tek Singh', trans. by M. Asaduddin, in Muhammad Umar Memon (ed.), *Black Margins: Stories* (New Delhi: Katha, 2001; reprint 2003), 212–20.

Nanda, B.R. *Witness to Partition: A Memoir*. New Delhi: Rupa, 2003; reprint 2006.

Panjabi, Kavita. *Old Maps and New: Legacies of the Partition – A Pakistan Diary*. Calcutta: Seagull, 2005.

Panjabi, Kavita. 'A Unique Grace', in Urvashi Butalia (ed.), *Partition: The Long Shadow* (New Delhi: Zubaan, 2015), 48–63.

Patel, Kamla. *Torn from the Roots: A Partition Memoir*, trans. by Uma Randeria. New Delhi: Women Unlimited, 2006.

Ray, Manas. 'Growing Up Refugee', in Anjali Gera Roy and Nandi Bhatia (eds), *Partitioned Lives: Narratives of Home, Displacement and Resettlement* (New Delhi: Dorling Kindersley, 2008), 116–45.

Rumi, Raza. *Delhi by Heart: Impressions of a Pakistani Traveller*. New Delhi: Harper Collins, 2013.

Shah Nawaz, Mumtaz. *The Heart Divided*. Lahore: ASR Publications, 1990; first published 1957.

Shahnawaz, Jahan Ara. *Father and Daughter: A Political Autobiography*. Karachi: Oxford University Press, 2002.

Taunsvi, Fikr. 'The Sixth River: A Diary of 1947', in Ahmad Salim (ed.), *Lahore 1947* (New Delhi: India Research Press, 2001), 13–28.

Secondary Sources

Brass, Paul R. 'The Partition of India and Retributive Genocide in the Punjab, 1946–47: Means, Methods and Purposes', in Brass (ed.), *Forms of Collective Violence: Riots, Pogroms and Genocide in Modern India* (New Delhi: Three Essays Collective, 2005; reprint 2006), 11–64.

Butalia, Urvashi (ed.). *Partition: The Long Shadow*. New Delhi: Zubaan, 2015.

Das, Veena. *Critical Events: An Anthropological Perspective on Contemporary India*. New Delhi: Oxford University Press, 1996.

Das, Veena. *Life and Words: Violence and the Descent into the Ordinary*. New Delhi: Oxford University Press, 2007.

Devji, Faisal. *The Impossible Indian: Gandhi and the Temptation of Violence*. Cambridge, MA: Harvard University Press, 2012.

Fussell, Paul. *The Great War and Modern Memory*. New York: Oxford University Press, 1977; reprint 2013.

Ghosh, Vishwajyoti, and Amiya Sen. 'A Good Education', in Urvashi Butalia (ed.), *Partition: The Long Shadow* (New Delhi: Zubaan, 2015), 64–77.

Hajari, Nisid. *Midnight's Furies: The Deadly Legacy of India's Partition*. Gurgaon: Viking Penguin, 2015.

Hasan, Mushirul (ed.). *India Partitioned*. 2 Vols. New Delhi: Roli Books, 1997.

Hirsch, Marianne. *Family Frames: Photography, Narrative and Postmemory*. Cambridge, MA: Harvard University Press, 1997.

Hobsbawm, Eric. *The Age of Extremes: A History of the World 1914–1991*. New York: Pantheon, 1994.

Kabir, Ananya Jahanara. *Partition's Post-Amnesias: 1947, 1971 and Modern South Asia*. New Delhi: Women Unlimited, 2013.

Kamra, Sukeshi. 'Engaging Traumatic Histories: The 1947 Partition of India in Collective Memory', in Urvashi Butalia (ed.), *Partition: The Long Shadow* (New Delhi: Zubaan, 2015), 155–77.

Kamtekar, Indivar. 'The Military Ingredient of Communal Violence in the Punjab, 1947', in *Proceedings of the Indian History Congress, 56th session, 1995* (Calcutta: n.p., 1996), 568–72.

Kidwai, Ayesha. Introduction to *In Freedom's Shade*, by Anis Kidwai. New Delhi: Penguin, 2011. Trans. of *Azadi ki Chhaon Mein*, 1974, vii–ix.

Kothari, Rita. 'From Conclusions to Beginnings: My Journey with "Partition"', in Urvashi Butalia (ed.), *Partition: The Long Shadow* (New Delhi: Zubaan, 2015), 30–48.

LaCapra, Dominick. *Writing History, Writing Trauma*. Baltimore, MD: Johns Hopkins University Press, 2001.

Menon, Ritu (ed.). *No Woman's Land: Women from Pakistan, India and Bangladesh Write on the Partition of India*. New Delhi: Women Unlimited, 2004.

Menon, Ritu, and Kamla Bhasin. *Borders and Boundaries: Women in India's Partition*. New Delhi: Kali for Women, 1998.

Nandy, Ashis. 'Coming Home: Religion, Mass Violence, and the Exiled and Secret Selves of a Citizen Killer', in Ashis Nandy, *Regimes of Narcissism, Regimes of Despair* (New Delhi: Oxford University Press, 2013), 65–94.

Pandey, Gyanendra. *Memory, History and the Question of Violence: Reflections on the Reconstruction of Partition*. Calcutta: K.P. Bagchi, 1999.

Pandey, Gyanendra. *Remembering Partition*. Cambridge: Cambridge University Press, 2001.

Saint, Tarun K. 'Exorcizing the Ghosts of Times Past: Partition Memoirs as Testimony', in Amritjit Singh, Nalini Iyer and Rahul K. Gairola (eds), *Revisiting India's Partition: New Essays on Memory, Culture, and Politics* (Lanham, MD: Lexington Press, 2016), 73–90.

Saint, Tarun K. 'Revisioning and "Restorying" Partition', in Urvashi Butalia (ed.), *Partition: The Long Shadow* (New Delhi: Zubaan, 2015), 178–99.

Saint, Tarun K. *Witnessing Partition: Memory, History, Fiction*. New Delhi: Routledge, 2010.

Salim, Ahmad (ed.). *Lahore 1947*. New Delhi: India Research Press, 2001.

Zamindar, Vazira Fazila-Yacoobali. *The Long Partition and the Making of South Asia: Refugees, Boundaries, Histories.* New York: Columbia University Press, 2007.

Tarun K. Saint taught as Associate Professor in the Department of English, Hindu College, University of Delhi. His research looks at the problem of representing in fictional form the traumatic violence during the partition of 1947. He is the author of *Witnessing Partition: Memory, History, Fiction* (New Delhi and London, 2010).

Chapter 11

'To Be Made Over'
Vietnamese-American Re-education Camp Narratives

Subarno Chattarji

For Jon Stallworthy

The fall of Saigon on 30 April 1975 marked the end of US military involvement in Vietnam. For the Vietnamese this was the beginning of another conflict in which the Northern communist victors imposed their will over their defeated Southern countrymen. The post-1975 scenario was a continuation and expression of the complex nature of the Vietnam War, a complexity that many Americans either ignored or were not aware of. As David Chanoff notes: 'For the Vietnamese the war was vastly more complex [than an anti-communist Cold War crusade] – a maelstrom in which the contending tides of colonialism and liberation, communism and nationalism, reform and revolution, Northern revanchism and Southern regionalism clashed violently and mixed treacherously'.[1] Truong Nhu Tang, former member of the National Liberation Front (NLF) and minister in the Provisional Revolutionary Government in South Vietnam, emphasises the fact that people like himself were anti-communist nationalists who desired independence: 'The South Vietnamese found themselves trapped between their loathing of the Thieu dictatorship [propped up by the US] and their fears of communism'.[2] Tang's memoir highlights the fact that this conflict was also a civil war fought among Vietnamese with competing visions of the future of their nation. As the Americans went home, the communists sought to obliterate these contradictions and political schisms in their pursuit of national unity and freedom.³ A significant instrument of political and social control was the re-education camps set up to refashion and reorient Southerners in the ways of communist doctrines.

From 30 April 1975 until well into the 1990s, large numbers of Vietnamese left or were forced to leave their homeland and arrived in the US either as refugees or immigrants. They numbered 172,820 between 1971 and 1980; 280,782 between 1981 and 1990; and 286,145 from 1991 to 2000.⁴ The Vietnamese influx is divided into three 'waves' with the first one immediately following the North Vietnamese victory; the second consisting of 'boat people', largely ethnic Chinese, fleeing after 1978; and the third wave comprising re-education camp survivors and kin of Vietnamese already in the US as well as Amerasian children under the Orderly Departure Program (ODP) (1979) and the Amerasian Homecoming Act (1987) respectively. James Freeman adds a fourth wave of intermittent asylum seekers between 1983 and 1989, and a fifth wave which arrived in countries of first asylum after 14 March 1989.⁵ The experiences of Vietnamese refugees and immigrants in the US now constitute a fairly significant body of literature detailing the lives of a new 'American' cohort.

Media and popular culture narratives of the Vietnamese-American community tend to create and foreground integration and success. The process of Americanisation is represented in linear terms – from the horror of war and escape to the relative peace, stability and prosperity of life in the US. These stories are played out not only within media and popular culture but also in children's literature.⁶ There is a genre of life writing dealing with existence under communism – focusing particularly on re-education camps – that not only highlights the atrocities committed by the government in Vietnam but disrupts the linear progression available in other representations of and by Vietnamese-Americans.⁷ Ideologically, re-education camp memoirs published in the US often serve to justify the war *postfacto* and demonise the communists. What is interesting is that these memoirs and tales were largely ignored by the American political left and there were no protests and little support for hundreds and thousands who were imprisoned, tortured and executed in post-war Vietnam.⁸ This silence is partly explicable in terms of a general amnesia within the US regarding the Vietnam War, a kind of 'strategic forgetting', to use Laurence Kirmayer's phrase.⁹ The relative neglect of re-education camp memoirs in popular and academic discourse could be interpreted as a refusal by those in the US who had protested against the war to fully acknowledge the terror unleashed by the communist regime in Vietnam. For the Vietnamese who suffered and left their homeland, this terrible legacy of the war cannot, however, be easily subsumed within amnesiac frames or Vietnamese-American success narratives.

This chapter focuses on Tran Tri Vu's *Lost Years: My 1,632 days in Vietnamese Reeducation Camps* and Huynh Sanh Thong's edited volume *To Be Made Over: Tales of Socialist Reeducation in Vietnam*. Vu's narrative stresses the act of individual witnessing, the everyday, banal propaganda and cruelty of life in re-education camps which relegated former South Vietnamese 'collaborators' to the status of 'non-people'. The accounts in *To Be Made Over* offer scathing indictments of communist misrule, the dispiriting conformity bred by humourless party functionaries, as well as the horror and boredom of re-education camps. In both texts there is a sense of heroic survival accompanied by a concomitant failure of political and communitarian imagination in post-1975 Vietnam. They narrativise not only extraordinary brutality but quotidian violence and the absence of law and individual rights, thereby providing sharp contrasts with communist propaganda. While the witnessing of atrocity points to the failures of communism and may be compared to European texts by Milan Kundera and Tibor Fischer, the Vietnamese accounts gesture towards a retrospective justification of the war, often erasing or minimising US involvement, which fits nicely with some revisionist histories of the Vietnam War in the US. The texts, therefore, are not just representations of Vietnamese experiences but dovetail into post-war rewritings of the conflict from South Vietnamese as well as American perspectives. This confluence of historical revisionism further consolidates a conservative narrative of the Vietnam War in the US and the 'heroic' participation and survival of their defeated allies, the South Vietnamese.[10]

The trope of heroic survival has an earlier Vietnamese provenance in revolutionary prison memoirs written by communist political prisoners during French occupation. These accounts invested incarceration with great 'symbolic potency', converting 'colonial jails into revolutionary schools'. As Peter Zinoman observes: 'Besides drawing attention to the importance of revolutionary training and political commitment, another tendency of "revolutionary prison memoirs" is to portray communist prisoners as dauntless and heroic figures'.[11] Zinoman argues that these memoirs concealed the elite backgrounds of 'about seventy-five percent of high level party cadres' and constructed the Indochinese Communist Party (ICP) leadership as a proletarian one.[12] In arguably different contexts, re-education memoirs retrieve heroic victim selves while burying individual and collective memories that do not cohere to this template. Across Vietnam and at different historical moments, prison memoirs were conceived as modes of reorienting communal and political frames. These memoirs shape what Kirmayer calls 'landscapes of memory' based not just on personal or socially significant memories, but 'also draw[ing] from meta-memory – implicit models of memory' available to the writers.[13] The re-education memoirs are imbricated within an anxiety of the 'disappearance' of Southern histories, particularly that of the Army of the Republic of Vietnam (ARVN). Lily Dizon, searching for her father, Captain Nguyen Tan Hung, writes: 'In Vietnam, my father and thousands of heroes like him have been dying – and disappearing – again and again for two decades, without memorials, without a tally, with hardly an official ripple. And in the United States, the land of his allies, my father also continues to vanish'.[14] The camp memoirs resist the dissolution and refashioning imposed within communist Vietnam (an echo of their communist forbears in colonial prisons?) but they are equally, as Dizon highlights, addressed to audiences in the United States.

The politicisation of these memoirs is evident in the types of memory work performed by the texts and what is revealing are the kinds of memories retrieved and their contextualisation within frames of autoethnography and witnessing. The Vietnamese memoir as self-inscribed, self-validating ethnographic account privileges an 'authentic' insider perspective translated onto an American landscape that has its own victim-memories and is not always receptive to competing narratives. As with US veteran memoirs, re-education camp memoirs emphasise the retrieval of historical record as if memory were a repository of veridical truth. This, as William Brewer argues, is a common notion: '[...] personal memories are typically accompanied by a belief that they are a veridical record of the originally experienced episode. This does not mean that they are, in fact, veridical, just that they carry with them a very strong belief value'.[15] Because the ideological work of the memoirs is invisibilised within frames of veridical value and read as 'truth' within those frames, the reworking of and retranslation of personal histories is erased. Such memorialisations constitute 'a kind of forgetting, the forgetting that assumes that remembering is finished'[16] precisely because these texts circulate as definitive accounts both for a wider American readership and for the diasporic Vietnamese community. Part of this authenticity, the 'authority' of textual rendition arises, of course, from experiential validation – 'I was there. I lived to tell the tale'. An equally powerful authorial claim rests on absolute, existential moral distinctions drawn between the survivor-narrator and communist rulers/oppressors (and communism per se). Within these frames, 'Because remembering is an action: to bear witness is to oppose'.[17] Telling the tale is not merely a retrieval of memories but a reassertion of agency. As Paul Antze and Michael Lambek argue: 'When memories recall acts of violence against individuals or entire groups, they carry additional burdens – as indictments or confessions, or as emblems of a victimised identity. Here, acts of remembering often take on performative meaning within a charged field of contested moral and political claims'.[18] In creating and preserving a myth of the war, incarceration and Vietnam, these memoirs insert South Vietnamese voices as 'real', heroic and valuable within a field that is either amnesiac or dismissive of former allies.[19] That these memoirs are 'indictments' (of communism, US liberal politics that valorises their 'enemy'), 'confessions' (of hardship, struggle, survival) and 'emblems of a victimized identity' is paradoxical but unsurprising given that they are written from a subject position of disenfranchisement and victimhood, of marginalisation in Vietnam and in the US. The memoirs valorise victimhood within a host culture where victimhood has a 'positive valence'.[20] By retrieving and inserting 'acceptable' memories, re-education camp memoirs bolster a mythography of a war fought for noble ends. Memory and amnesia are conflated, creating memory traces of oppression and heroic survival while jettisoning personal, collective and historical responsibility. The victim-as-hero narrative compensates for loss (in war, of self-esteem, of nation) and re-enters history and ideological space as the bearer of communal memory.[21]

The texts under discussion are akin to some Vietnamese-American oral histories and commentaries which refashion modes of perceiving the new immigrants and their pasts. One avowed purpose of these oral histories is to retrieve South Vietnamese voices and thereby redress political and perceptual bias. As James Freeman writes: 'They [Vietnamese-Americans] were also deeply disturbed by conventional North American interpretations of the Vietnam War, which often omitted the South Vietnamese, either as participants or as victims. Communist views of the war and the post-war Socialist Republic of Vietnam were treated more sympathetically than those of the South Vietnamese government, which was allied with the Americans'.[22] Freeman emphasises the participatory nature of his oral history project, writing that 'refugees were not informants to be questioned, but rather participants who were consulted and who retained powers of editorial discretion and the option to withdraw at any stage of the research and writing'.[23] The attempt to restore agency to the people whose voices are being narrated, rather than speaking for them, represents a significant reorientation. What is not available in the text, however, is whether any of the interviewees actually exercised the option of withdrawal and whether they responded to the ways in which their voices are contained and marked within the book. While Freeman is conscious of an anthropological containment of the subject 'other' through mechanisms of interviews, transcriptions, editing and publishing, his endeavour is not entirely innocent of – indeed cannot be abstracted from – hierarchies of power inherent in refugee–interviewer, interviewee–editor relations and the ways in which these relations are mediated within the politics of post-Vietnam remembrance in the United States.

This is not to imply that Freeman's agenda is simply coercive, for the recently arrived refugee-immigrants were only too willing in most instances to place before the American public their account of the war in contradistinction to the disturbing 'conventional North American interpretations of the Vietnam War'. There is thus a complex interplay at work whereby editorial control and interviewee desire coalesce to create essentially American mediated discourses of life under communism and re-education camps for American audiences. Freeman focuses on the participative as well as the victim frame to restore types of agency denied in dominant popular culture or media representations, and many of these discretionary narratives reinforce a generalised victimhood and further the teleology of fortuitous escape. The participant–victim cusp seems to aver that the primary mode of participative entry into American discourses for the South Vietnamese is as victims and plucky and grateful, if occasionally mordant, survivors in the American landscape. It is not entirely surprising, therefore, that Freeman's narrators contribute to a fairly homogenous memorial template of life under communism. This oral uniformity fits well with dominant US views of communism and binds the nascent Vietnamese-American community, disabling dissent or political opinions that gesture towards a more complex and heterogeneous community of experiences.[24]

Tran Tri Vu was imprisoned from 25 June 1975 to 23 December 1979, one of thousands of former South Vietnamese functionaries interned for no better reason than they were 'collaborators' and needed 're-education': "'You are here to be reeducated and acquire a new personality. [...] The People know everything, the Revolution knows everything'".[25] The all-embracing physical, psychological and ideological reality of the re-education camp is predicated on the imperative to refashion and control those uninitiated in the ways of communist hope and salvation. Within this framework, Vu's counter-narrative written after escaping from Vietnam is a gesture of witnessing and defiance as well as a record of humiliation and pain. Vu cites one Nguyen Van Long, a former lieutenant in the South Vietnamese Rangers: "'We have already suffered humiliation. Is there any greater humiliation than losing the war?'" (3). Vu's memoir amply demonstrates that loss in war was only the beginning of a systematic programme of denigration and degradation.

Many South Vietnamese fled their homes and country before and immediately after Saigon fell. Some were unable to do so despite their best efforts and some stayed back hoping there would be peace and reconciliation. Initial announcements by the communist government indicated that re-education would last for a month and asked Southern government officials to turn themselves in, which most of them did. It was only when the incarceration continued well beyond the thirty-day period that the inmates realised the absolute control desired and exercised by the victorious North. Vu gradually perceives the logic behind the camps:

> Our generation in the South was suddenly charged with wrongdoing because we had not lived in the North, had not been used to the way of reasoning of the Northern people, had not accepted their ideology. Our skin was the same color, we spoke the same language, our ethnic origin and geographic location were the same, and yet we were completely different from them [...]
>
> The position which they adopted for themselves and for us, which they forced us to accept, was that they were the People and we were not [...]. (29)

Vu emphasises a pan-Vietnamese identity which many in both parts of the country would dispute given historical, ethnic and ideological differences between North and South, but his primary purpose is to focus on the type of national unity trumpeted by the communists as well as the nationalists in their struggle against the US, and betrayed by the communists in the way they treated their countrymen after the war. Crucially Vu points to the ways in which the communist party created an absolute dichotomy between 'the People' who 'know everything' and are coterminous with the party, and the non-people. *Nguy* was the term used by the North Vietnamese to designate Southern opponents, which translates as 'traitor' or 'puppet' and 'false, deceptive' in its adjectival form. The communist party fostered divisions deliberately and re-education camps represented an extreme form of institutional discrimination: 'The more we "studied", the more convinced we became that we now constituted a special category of people, discriminated against by the new regime and discarded by the new society' (112). The sense of alienation articulated by Vu was created and thrust upon 'puppet' 'collaborators' and did nothing to foster the nationalistic love of country desired by the communists (and deemed to be absent in nationalists such as Vu).

Part of the politics of the re-education camps was to literally and figuratively segregate people considered a threat to the new regime. Imprisonment was an obvious expression of power relations, a reiteration of the winner–loser paradigm, but it was also a means of discrediting the Vietnamese nationalists who, while opposed to the US presence in Vietnam, were not votaries of communism. By designating all Southerners as 'collaborators', the communists not only obliterated all dissent but flattened a complex political terrain creating in its stead a simplistic us-versus-them framework. The failure of nationalist politics is dwelt on by Va Huy Chan, a former nationalist leader: '"My obscurity is that of nationalists in general. We failed to establish ourselves as a united and disciplined force'" (339). This self-reflexive comment retrieves political histories and failures that look beyond the triumphalism of communist Vietnam. Vu's account stands out in its forensic detailing of the trauma of re-education camp experiences but he also attempts to transcend the immediately personal in his assimilation of reflections by leaders such as Chan. This assimilative context is crucial as Vu perceives his memoir as not merely a framing of the individual self but representative of moments, memories and repressed histories (in post-1975 Vietnam as well as in the US) in its acts and articulations of alternative voices. These representations are politically loaded and the reader has little doubt about Vu's ideological position as a nationalist opposed to the Vietnamese Communist Party, but his rendering fractures the easy oppositions ('puppets' versus 'the People', 'collaborators' versus heroic communist patriots) and one-dimensional narratives created by his captors.

One of these disruptive voices is that of an anonymous old woman who is not allowed to give bananas to prisoners who are being paraded through a village: '"You treat your countrymen worse than the colonialists did!"' (43). Whether apocryphal or not, the woman's outburst rhetorically challenges the carefully constructed and brutal authority set up by the communist victors. Whereas the communists cast the Southerners into a moral and political purgatory, the exclamation serves to invalidate the heroic and indeed moral construction of the communist struggles against French colonialism and US aggression. Quite simply the communists are a type of colonial collaborator in their attitude and actions towards their Southern brethren.

Vu highlights another aspect of communist complicity in his attempt to discredit the communists. He quotes an instructor in one of the camps: '"The Party used the American people to fight the American government, the American press to indict the American leaders, and the US Congress to discourage the US administration. [...] We beat the Americans in America itself"' (57). There is an ironic, and perhaps unconscious, congruence between party propaganda in Vietnam and conservative opinion in the US. Conservative interpretations of the Vietnam War in the US blame the anti-war movement, the liberal media and Congress for the loss of the war, casting these elements as unpatriotic.[26] An ideological underpinning of Vu's memoir is to show up the communists as brutal dictators who did not deserve to win the war and who won primarily because of the pusillanimity of sections of the US body politic. Vu's paradoxical citation of communist party orthodoxy not only reveals connections between two former allies (the Americans and the South Vietnamese) trying to come to terms with defeat, but the ways in which post-war narratives were rewritten to make that loss more palatable.²⁷ Within this frame the 'content is presented as if it were uniformly and objectively available to the remembering subject, as if the narrating "I" and the subject of the narration were identical'.²⁸ The 'objectification' of the relationship between the narrating self and the narrated self translates into memorial templates which acquire the tone and status of veridical truth, a status vital for diasporic consolidation and to address sceptical American readers.²⁹

Vu's account veers from trenchant political critique to self-criticism to occasional sentimentalism about pre-1975 South Vietnam. He emphasises the dislocation from everyday life: 'To a prisoner deprived of the happiness of family life, the long-forgotten sound of a baby's crying seemed to be the sweetest melody in the world' (243). Although prisoners such as Vu were permitted occasional family visits, those merely served to enhance the sense of isolation, the arbitrary and absolute power that ruled their lives, generating hatred and bitterness anew. He points to the utter humourlessness of the *bodoi* (communist soldiers and re-education camp guards): 'The *bodoi* particularly disliked jokes. They seemed to suffer from inferiority complexes and to laugh openly in front of them was an offense that was sometimes severely dealt with' (36). Laughter is a form of rebellion resented for its subversive intent and Vu's account reminds us of the humourlessness and boredom that characterised totalitarian states elsewhere.³⁰

Vu outlines the waste, absurdity and futility of re-educating specialists who could have helped rebuild the war-ravaged country. One inmate says: '"I agree that they [*bodoi*] don't have enough to eat or to wear, but they are squandering *billions*, not just *millions* of dong! Take the specialists – technicians, doctors – who are in reeducation camps. Imagine how much investment our people had put into them! What a waste not using them!"' (256). The squandering of economic, social and technical capital in post-war Vietnam was scandalous and contributed in some measure to its continued poverty.³¹ Long periods of brutal imprisonment and indoctrination also fostered deep-seated bitterness and anger detrimental to future reconciliation and peace. As an old friend tells Vu before his imminent release: '"Try to flee the country. Leave this bloody land of ours. You'll have to go abroad to be able to tell the world the truth"'(375). Vu does escape and his memoir is an act of 'truth' telling, a testament that defies the conformity and silence imposed by the communists. His friend's exhortation, however, characterises the hopelessness of post-war Vietnam, a 'bloody land' where peace leads to vengeance and the continuance of war by other means. The moment of release and escape is also a preparation for separation and exile.³²

While *Lost Years* is primarily one man's account of imprisonment, survival and witness, *To Be Made Over* 'is a collection of memoirs and stories, translated from the Vietnamese, about what the Vietnamese Communists call *cai-taoxa-hoi chu-nghia* (a phrase usually rendered into English as "Socialist reeducation"), especially as it applies to what has occurred in South Vietnam after their victory in 1975'.[33] Huynh Sanh Thong's editorial intent is not to demonise the communists but to show them as human, misguided and fallible: 'The editor avoids stories that revel in vitriol and hatred, preferring tales whose authors speak with a modicum of detachment and objectivity, who depict Communists far less as monsters and agents of some "Evil Empire" than as all too fallible humans, both victimizers and victims, ordinary persons corrupted by power, misled by folly and self-deceit'.[34] While the desire to eschew doctrinaire anti-communism is a welcome change from dedicated anti-communist editors such as James Banerian,[35] it is perhaps unsurprising that the tales collected have little sympathy for communist doctrines and modes of governance (if putting citizens in prison camps can be construed as an act of governance), and they do articulate bitterness and anger. A brief analysis of some of the tales reveals a coherent critique of communist corruption, the hypocrisy of their ideals, an overarching sense of despair and claustrophobia that furthers a collective feeling of internal exile.

Vo Ky Dien's 'The Old Man Who Only Believed What He Saw' presents a transition from naïve belief to disillusion in the ideas of Old Man Seven, a slum neighbourhood blacksmith. Constructed as a series of dialogues between the narrator and the old man, it reveals through idealised modes and criticism the overt propaganda and absurdity of communist doctrine and actions. Old Man Seven compares the revolutionary North to the decadent South in clichéd terms: '[...] what is communism, after all? Communism means justice! In the communist society, there are no millionaires and no paupers, no oppressors on top and no little downtrodden people at the bottom. [...] down here in the South, the rich wallow in luxury while the poor lack the basic necessities of life. Come to think of it, a revolutionist is just like me, a blacksmith'.[36] Once the war is over, the communist utopia turns into a nightmare where Old Man's eldest son is sent to a re-education camp, a second son's transport company is ruined after his buses are confiscated, the youngest son is a party functionary who disowns his father, and the family has to pay a bribe to live in a garage behind their old home. The Old Man's anger and bitterness are summed up by the narrator: 'Throughout his life he had invested all that he held dearest in the Revolution, and that had included his youngest son, his pride and joy. The investment turned out to be a fiasco. The Revolution came, but the good life and happiness were nowhere in sight. All around him he witnessed nothing but hunger and misery, suspicion and hatred.

[...] It had taken Old Man Seven more than twenty years to discover the truth. He had planted and nursed the tree of Revolution with loving care only to reap now its bitter fruits'.[37] The sense of betrayal and futile sacrifice was felt acutely by those who had actively participated and supported the communists, and party policies post-1975 alienated not only 'collaborators' and 'puppets' of the former South Vietnamese regime but also nationalists and less doctrinaire communists.[38] In effect it was the failure of imagination and governance that deepened the sense of a country under siege where the communists continued to wage war through re-education camps and totalitarian diktats.[39]

Chu Quan's 'A Teacher in Ho Chi Minh City' dwells on the dispiriting conformity enforced by party cadres: 'Those who won't gracefully accept historical necessity and who still dream of any other system can only be reactionaries, enemies of the workers and of their Party, which leads them, necessarily. The Party is like a father to his children, the people. Sass Dad and he'll pack you off to "re-education" camp, where he may want to keep you for twenty or thirty years'.[40] Arguably all states exercise a monopoly over violence but the state of fear and retribution created by communist structures is not subject to legal and/or constitutional review. The paternalism of the party is intolerant of dissent and its punishments are entirely arbitrary. Quan's narrator not only points to the hopeless and confined present but also despairs over the future: 'On many mornings, when I wake up at six amidst the hubbub of my neighbourhood, I ask myself: If this situation drags on for another five or ten years, whither will this country go? Whither will Vietnamese men and women go as they founder in a sea of theories, worthless shells that hide pathetic realities inside?'[41] Inevitably this leads to thoughts of his countrymen who have fled the land: '[...] I think of those colleagues who have been lucky enough to escape and go abroad, and I wonder: What are they doing now with their freedom?'[42] While many Vietnamese post-war narratives dwell on exile and longing for home from an immigrant's point of view, Quan perceives the exodus from the perspective of one left behind in the imprisoning reality of home. For a people rooted in the land and in rituals of ancestor worship, the departure for foreign shores and its attendant dangers was often traumatic and exacerbated by the trials of arrival and adaptation within new cultural frameworks. The pursuit of 'freedom' was often obscured by daily struggles for survival and acceptance within the US, but the striving seemed valuable for many new arrivals as they charted hopeful futures that would perhaps distance them in generational and memorial terms from the traumas of separation. Quan's question seems to map these thoughts while holding his exiled countrymen to a possibly higher standard in that their hard-earned freedom must not be wasted in the way in which Vietnam's independence has been squandered.

The oppression of internal exile, of exclusion from the larger community and being under constant surveillance are themes repeated throughout the collection. Three stories in particular dwell on the re-education camp experience from varying perspectives, focusing not only on the oft-repeated themes but also expressing a significant degree of bitterness and anger. Ha Thuc Sinh in 'Welcome to Trang Lon, Reeducation Camp' records the boredom and discomfort of daily living in the camp. Vinh, the prisoner-narrator, sees himself as a 'war reporter' and is driven by the need to witness that animates Tran Vu's memoir: 'On the photographic film of his memory he will diligently and faithfully record all these outlandish scenes of postwar Vietnam'.[43] Memory is perceived as infallible and Vinh has no doubts about the veracity of that record as if it were untouched by the vagaries of time, perspective, prejudice and ideology.[44] As with Vu's memoir, there is a privileging of prisoner narratives as repositories of truth and objectivity, the type of objectivity desired by Huynh Sanh Thong as editor. Such narrative distancing is difficult, especially in the situations in which the narrators find themselves and as is evident in sections of this tale. Vinh describes the convoy that transports prisoners to the camps: 'Long, endless caterpillars, the convoys of trucks are crawling toward one point where they will unload "war criminals" at their first circle of hell'.[45] Echoing Dante Vinh's characterisation of the camp as part of an expanding circle of hell reiterates the idea of the camp and the country as a hellish prison. It is this sense of entrapment that breeds the kind of scorn expressed by a 'young urinator' in the camp: '"Dear schoolmates, is there a single spot left in this land of ours that doesn't deserve to be pissed on?"'[46] While the contempt is comprehensible, the attitude serves to delegitimise the communist struggles for freedom, implying that the land is debased by their victory. Of course the communist party's vengeful reprisals against fellow citizens did not help the cause of solidarity and the nameless, unashamed 'urinator' can express his hate and resentment only through ultimately futile gestures. Tales of re-education repeatedly recall and enact what Lawrence Langer defines as 'humiliated memory' in the context of Holocaust testimonies, whose 'voice represents pure misery, even decades after the events that it narrates'.[47]

Arbitrary mass arrests and internment in camps bred futility and hopelessness. They also evoke comparisons with representations of the Soviet Gulag in Vo Hoang's 'A New Place': 'Cao Son thinks himself such a coward when compared with that Ivan Denisovich in Siberia. [...] he tells himself: "My situation here is more or less the same as what his was in Siberia. It should not be too hard to figure it all out"'.[48] While the protestor in Sinh's story indulges in an act of temporary insubordination, Cao Son is focused on survival: 'Before anything else, the question is to struggle, that is to say, he'll learn how to divide each single day into activities that will keep him alive for the next day and for the next day, until the three-thousand-six-hundred-and-fifty-third day of a prisoner's damned existence like Solzhenitsyn's carpenter [...]'.[49] The evocation of the Gulag in historical and literary terms serves to provide parallels and inspiration as well as indicating a continuum of communist atrocity against their own people. Son portrays himself as a Vietnamese Ivan Denisovich, but one who needs to learn from his literary predecessor the art of maintaining physical and psychic integrity in the face of an oppressive and unreasonable state. It is possible that Hoang and other memoirists of the re-education camps perceived themselves as interpreters and interrogators of their own gulag in much the same way that Solzhenitsyn became a symbol of conscience in Stalinist Russia. Referencing the Gulag serves as a translatable and comprehensible frame for US readers and places Vietnamese narratives within a typology of communist atrocity. Unlike Solzhenitsyn, however, Hoang and other Vietnamese writers of camp experiences have not achieved the same sort of literary or political stature. While many of these memoirs are published by university and prominent trade publishers and have acquired currency in conservative historiography of the Vietnam War, they remain disenfranchised voices, unpleasant reminders of a divisive conflict, memories which even Vietnamese immigrants wish to lay to rest. These narratives offer *post facto* justifications for US involvement yet they co-exist uneasily with memories of atrocity and shame. They cohere neither to an easy teleology of US moral intervention (memoirs such as the one by Quang Pham have a bitter undertow of betrayal) nor to diasporic desires of futurity. Yet these works occupy liminal spaces that are vital in the memories they monumentalise.

Like Vu, Hoang highlights the absurd and all-embracing logic of guilt by association. The narrator Son thinks of his friends and wonders whether his confessions will lead them into trouble: 'Then he thinks of Dien and Hai Khoa, of people in prison and people out of prison. It vaguely dawns on him that everyone who lives in this country is found guilty and sentenced for the crime of living here'.[50] Once again Vietnam is an imprisoning landscape, a type of hell, wherein 'everyone' – not just former South Vietnamese government or military functionaries – is guilty by virtue of being a Southerner and the only path to redemption is through the gates of the re-education camps.

Nguyen Ngoc Thuan in 'The Man Who Dreamed of Spring' reiterates the hellish quality of Vietnamese lives through the elderly prisoner Tinh:

'"War. Death. Prison. I don't know about you, but all my life I've never had any time I could call spring [...] If God does exist, I only wish that he'd let spring come to this land, just once"'. To which his younger interlocutor, Van, replies: '"How could spring ever spring in hell? No leaves and no flowers could stand the fire and blood. That's just one of your pipe dreams, sir" [...] That night Van dreamed that he was crying'.[51] This brief exchange encapsulating wistful hope, angry denial and a dream visioning loss and grief articulates psychological costs and the continuous deferral of renewal and peace. Van's tears are also nostalgic for a pre-war, pre-communist Vietnam because it is the 'pipe dreams' which animate desire and a Machereyan fictive resolution of ideological conflicts. Tinh and Van are nostalgic not for 'the past as it was or even as [they] wish it were; but for the condition of *having been*, with a concomitant integration and completeness lacking in any present'.[52] This rupture marks the memorialisations of Vietnamese history with its seemingly perpetual wars and inability to reconcile. Tinh offers an explanation for Northern hatred and their perpetuation of enmity:

> It's because we [South Vietnamese] were the ones who killed their last hope, the hope they had pinned on us. We bungled our great mission and dashed their dream of a lifetime. They had counted on us to deliver them from slavery. Instead we lost to those bastards in the end and have rotted in prison camps like this ever since [...] everywhere people in the North are abject paupers, living like beasts of burden. For more than thirty years, except those boots on their feet, they have been hungrier, more tattered and more wretched than at any other time. Why shouldn't they hold it against us?[53]

Tinh's psychological thesis is revealing in its combination of self-hatred and self-pity as well as the attribution of salvation inherent in the Southern cause subsequently betrayed in defeat. The locus of hope for the North is the prosperity enjoyed by the South and the purpose of Northern sacrifices was freedom from the shackles of poverty imposed by communism. While the North was more impoverished than the South and communist soldiers were amazed by the consumer goods available in Saigon, Tinh's account ignores poverty in the South as well as the economic disparities created by the influx of American consumer culture. Tinh also obliterates the historical contexts of American bombings in the North, of US policies such as the Strategic Hamlet Programme and Free Fire Zones which led to the influx of rural South Vietnamese into cities, and the zeal with which many Northerners fought the war. Just as the communist party systematically discredited and persecuted Southern nationalists, so too Tinh caricatures Northern motivations implying that economic frustrations have led to their need to exact post-war vengeance. Tinh's contempt for communists is expressed in the tale's opening paragraph:

> If they [party cadres] can believe the most fantastic story like morons, it's because they've been brainwashed and stupefied by the Party and the state. And they've been allowed to parrot such absurdities in front of people they're supposed to re-educate. It's something that deserves pity and compassion, not ridicule. We ought to feel sorry for them because they have misplaced and lost their selves, because thought has been excised from their brains. They lead lifeless lives, having been transformed into Pavlovian dogs to serve a barbaric tyranny built on a barbaric doctrine.[54]

The emphasis on a discerning, vigilant, moral self animates the narrative because narrative is conceived as a mode of retrieving and conserving that Southern self in contrast to the 'misplaced' and 'lost' communist selves. Vu's pan-Vietnamese solidarity is rejected firmly in Thuan's articulation of divisions between a dehumanised and unreflective communist behemoth driven hypocritically by the desire for consumer paradise and a wealthy, self-aware, democratic nationalism sadly defeated in the South. The robotic adherence to party orthodoxy and indeed the transformation of Vietnam into a prison-country is indicative of totalitarian impulses that excise thought and imagination. It is vital, however, that while Thuan and his protagonist offer critical insights into 'the enemy', they do not analyse Southern politics and society prior to 1975 nor do they scrutinise the causes of defeat. Bitterness, anger and contempt are comprehensible within contexts of defeat, humiliation and imprisonment, but they do not reveal the 'modicum of detachment and objectivity' desired by the editor.

Re-education camp memoirs reveal the descent into totalitarian hell after the communist victory in 1975. They are indicative of multiple failures of governance, human rights, law, reconciliation and hope. For a country that had suffered decades of war, 'the Vietnamese Gulag' merely served to perpetuate misery and hatred, leading to thousands of wasted lives and the exodus of millions from their homeland. The memoirs and tales are a testament to a brutally unnecessary post-war history. At the same time these texts participate in the battle for the memory and historicising of the Vietnam War and its aftermath. Vietnamese-American memoirs attempt to create public space for commemoration acceptable to 'split publics', and their divided loyalties and audiences may explain both their liminality and increased visibility.[55]

This brief analysis reveals ways in which divisions between North and South Vietnam are essentialised as if the conflict were only a civil war involving competing ideological and political paradigms. While the civil war aspect is important, the memoirs tend to erase US participation in the war and do not dwell on its effects or analyse the causes for Southern defeat. The South is presented as a defeated but superior and heroic entity. In highlighting communist atrocities and mendacity – a necessary project – Southern histories and complicities are written out, creating a comic book us-versus-them template for the remembrance of the Vietnam War from South Vietnamese perspectives.

NOTES

1. David Chanoff and Doan Van Toai, 'Vietnam': A Portrait of Its People at War (London and New York, 1996), xxi.
2. Truong Nhu Tang, *Journal of a Vietcong* (London, 1986), 192.
3. 'One of the great dramas in the modern history of Vietnam is how that richness and variety [of political opinion, parties, allegiances] were effectively wiped out, and how Ho Chi Minh and the ICP [Indochinese Communist Party] came to dominate what was once an extremely varied terrain.' Patricia M. Pelley, *Postcolonial Vietnam: New Histories of the National Past* (Durham, NC and London, 2002), 198.
4. Joe Ferry, *Vietnamese Immigration* (Philadelphia, 2004), 40.
5. James M. Freeman, *Changing Identities: Vietnamese Americans, 1975–1995* (Boston, 1995), ch. 3.
6. See Susan Auerbach, *Vietnamese Americans* (Vero Beach, FL, 1991); Lori Coleman, *Vietnamese in America* (Minneapolis, MN, 2005); James Haskins, *The New Americans: Vietnamese Boat People* (Hillside, NJ, 1980); Lewis K. Parker, *Why Vietnamese Immigrants Came to America* (New York, 2003); Paul Rutledge, *The Vietnamese in America* (Minneapolis, MN, 1987).
7. See Edward Metzner, Huynh Van Chinh, Tran Van Phuc and Le Nguyen Binh, *Reeducation in Postwar Vietnam: Personal Postscripts to Peace* (College Station, TX, 2001); Kien Nguyen, *The Unwanted: A Memoir* (Boston, New York and London, 2001); Nguyen Long with Harry Kendall, *After Saigon Fell: Daily Life under the Vietnamese Communists* (Berkeley, 1981); The Van Nguyen and David Lynn Hughes, *When Faith Endures: One Man's Courage in the Midst of War* (American Fork, UT, 2004).
8. The indifference of American political and media elites is a point made repeatedly by Doan Van Toai in his memoir, *The Vietnamese Gulag*, trans. by Sylvie Romanowski and Francoise Simon-Miller (New York, 1986). See also James Banerian (ed.), *Losers Are Pirates: A Close Look at the PBS Series 'Vietnam: A Television History'* (Phoenix, AZ, 1985). A letter addressed to Vietnam's observer at the UN, signed by anti-war activists including Daniel Ellsberg, Joan Baez and Daniel and Philip Berrigan, is an instance of post-war protest. 'We voice

our protest in the hope that your Government can avoid the repetition of the tragic historical pattern in which liberators gain power only to impose a new oppression.' Bernard Gwertzman, 'Antiwar Activists Appeal to Hanoi', *New York Times*, 21 December 1976, 4.
9. Laurence J. Kirmayer, 'Landscapes of Memory: Trauma, Narrative, and Dissociation', in Paul Antze and Michael Lambek (eds), *Tense Past: Cultural Essays in Trauma and Memory* (New York and London, 1996), 191.
10. Edward Metzner et al., *Reeducation in Postwar Vietnam* is a perfect instance of collaborative rehabilitation. As Col. Huynh Van Chinh puts it: 'I [...] write for my personal honor as an officer, as well as for the honor of the entire Army of the Republic of Vietnam' (Metzner et al., *Reeducation in Postwar Vietnam*, 43). Along with the rehabilitation of the Army of the Republic of Vietnam (ARVN), the idea of the US as a benign power is continually stressed in these accounts.
11. Peter Zinoman, 'Beyond the Revolutionary Prison Memoir', *The Vietnam Review* 1 (1996), 258.
12. Zinoman, 'Beyond the Revolutionary Prison Memoir', 263. '"Revolutionary prison memoirs" shape the historical record not only through the experiences they repeatedly convey, but by those they continually suppress.' Zinoman, 'Beyond the Revolutionary Prison Memoir', 259.
13. Kirmayer, 'Landscapes of Memory', 175.
14. Lily Dizon, 'Searching for Captain Nguyen Tan Hung', in De Tran, Andrew Lam and Hai Dai Nguyen (eds), *Once Upon a Dream ...the Vietnamese-American Experience* (Kansas City, MI, 1995), 167.
15. William Brewer, 'What Is Autobiographical Memory?' in David C. Rubin (ed.), *Autobiographical Memory* (Cambridge and New York, 1986), 35.
16. Nicola King, *Memory, Narrative, Identity: Remembering the Self* (Edinburgh, 2000), 180.
17. Jay Winter and Emmanuel Sivan (eds), *War and Remembrance in the Twentieth Century* (Cambridge, 1999), 19.
18. Antze and Lambek, *Tense Past*, vii.
19. Myth, as Samuel Hynes notes, 'is not synonym for falsehood; rather, it is a term to identify the simplified, dramatized story that has evolved in our society to contain the meanings of the war that we can tolerate and so make sense of its incoherences and contradictions'. Samuel Hynes, 'Personal Narratives and Commemoration', in Winter and Sivan, *War and Remembrance in the Twentieth Century*, 207. Hynes's observations on First World War memoirs are apt for Vietnamese memoirs.
20. Writing of 'secular pilgrimages' to Holocaust sites in Poland, Jack Kugelmass suggests 'that American society increasingly attributes a positive valence to victimhood and this, at the very least, sets the stage for public displays that in an earlier era would have been scorned or shunned'. Jack Kugelmass, 'Missions to the Past: Poland in Contemporary Jewish Thought and Deed', in Antze and Lambek, *Tense Past*, 205.

21. Quang X. Pham's *A Sense of Duty: My Father, My American Journey* (New York, 2005) is emblematic of memoirs that represent the South Vietnamese as heroic victims.
22. James M. Freeman, *Hearts of Sorrow: Vietnamese-American Lives* (Stanford, CA, 1989), 10. The emphasis on 'perceptual' differences between North Americans and Vietnamese-Americans with regard to South Vietnam and the war is analysed in two essays by Nguyen Manh Hung, 'Refugee Scholars and Vietnamese Studies in the United States, 1975–1982', *Amerasia Journal* 11(1) (1984), 89–99, and '"Vietnam: A Television History": A Case Study in Perceptual Conflict between the American Media and the Vietnamese Expatriates', *World Affairs* 147(2) (1984), 71–84. It is interesting that while liberal America strives towards reconciliation with a former enemy, expatriate Vietnamese rue the loss of the war and home and subsequent invisibility and/or misrepresentation in the US.
23. Freeman, *Hearts of Sorrow*, 22.
24. For an example of diasporic intolerance of dissent, see Kenneth Kim, 'Fired Vietnamese Editor Launches Blog', 27 May 2008, http://news.ncmonline.com/news/view_article.html?article_id=a92925856d7d969bb895f3ab851311e8 (accessed 12 June 2008).
25. Tran Tri Vu, *Lost Years: My 1,632 Days in Vietnamese Reeducation Camps* (Berkeley, 1988), 19. Subsequent page references are indicated in parentheses in the text.
26. See Richard M. Nixon, *No More Vietnams* (London, 1986); and Al Santoli, *To Bear Any Burden: The Vietnam War and Its Aftermath in the Words of Americans and Southeast Asians* (New York, 1985).
27. Vu's narrative strategy is what Wolfgang Schivelbusch calls 'the loser's propaganda [which] will stop at nothing in pressing accusations of injustice and protestations of innocence'. Wolfgang Schivelbusch, *The Culture of Defeat: On National Trauma, Mourning, and Recovery*, trans. by Jefferson Chase (New York, 2001), 18.
28. King, *Memory, Narrative, Identity*, 3.
29. 'As humans we draw on our experience to shape narratives about our lives, but equally, our identity and character are shaped by our narratives.' Antze and Lambek, *Tense Past*, xviii.
30. Tibor Fischer's *Under the Frog: A Black Comedy* (London, 1992) is a brilliant, sardonic portrait of the alternating horror and boredom of living in communist Hungary.
31. The US trade and aid embargo had an equally if not more devastating effect on the post-war economy of Vietnam but is not mentioned in Vietnamese-American memoirs.
32. 'This writing of survival is itself gripped by the shame of not having succumbed, by the shame of still being able to bear witness and by the sadness engendered by being able to speak.' Jean-Francois Lyotard, *Heidegger and 'The Jews'*, trans. by Andreas Michel and Mark S. Roberts (Minneapolis, MN, 1990), 44. Lyotard's analysis of the complex burden of survival, witnessing and speech seems apposite for Vietnamese re-education camp memoirs.

33. Huynh Sanh Thong (ed. and trans.), *To Be Made Over: Tales of Socialist Reeducation in Vietnam* (New Haven, CT, 1988), vii. Subsequent references are indicated by the name of individual authors or the editor.
34. Thong, *To Be Made Over*, xi.
35. James Banerian, editor and translator based in the US, wrote in an editorial note: 'Although the Communists have had an important role in the history of modern Vietnam, no Communist writers will be found in this book. I see no reason to apologize for this conscious omission. [...] Nearly all of the authors included in these pages are victims of Communist repression; it would be ludicrous and illogical to associate the artificial literature of the persecutors with the sincere expressions of the persecuted. Besides, the Moscow-Hanoi partnership employs its own translators so there is no need for me to help them'. James Banerian (ed. and trans.), *Vietnamese Short Stories: An Introduction* (Phoenix, AZ, 1986), 4.
36. Vo KyDien, 'The Old Man Who Only Believed What He Saw', 21.
37. Dien, 'The Old Man', 25.
38. Duong Thu Huong's novels are fine examples of post-war communist disillusionment. See *Paradise of the Blind,* trans. by Phan Huy Duong and Nina McPherson (New York, 1988).
39. Leszek Kolakowski'scharacterisation of totalitarian impulses provides valuable context for the tales: 'The ideology is total [...] Not only does it have all-embracing pretensions, not only is it supposed to be infallible and obligatory; its aim (unobtainable, fortunately) goes beyond dominating and regulating the personal life of every subject to the point where it actually replaces personal life altogether, reducing human beings to replicas of ideological slogans. [...] it annihilates personal life'. Leszek Kolakowski, *My Correct Views on Everything*, ed. by Zbigniew Janowski (South Bend, IN, 2005), 69. Memoirs and tales resist this annihilation of the personal.
40. Chu Quan, 'A Teacher in Ho Chi Minh City', 40.
41. Quan, 'A Teacher in Ho Chi Minh City', 41.
42. Quan, 'A Teacher in Ho Chi Minh City', 42.
43. Ha Thuc Sinh, 'Welcome to Trang Lon, Reeducation Camp', 101.
44. Theorisations of memory posit that memory is not 'time-stamped'. As Laurence Kirmayer argues: 'Memory is anything but a photogenic record of experience; [...] What is registered is highly selective and thoroughly transformed by interpretation and semantic encoding at the time of experience. [...] If memory is much less determinate than a snapshot of the past (as folk theory assumes), then the question of what engenders it is, perhaps, less crucial to its power and authenticity than what authorizes and stabilizes memory so that it becomes *my* memory and *the* memory of an event'. Kirmayer, 'Landscapes of Memory', 177. In Vietnamese re-education camp memoirs, the engendering moments/events along with the authority of survival 'stabilise' those memories and tales as powerful and authentic.
45. Sinh, 'Welcome to Trang Lon', 98.

46. Sinh, 'Welcome to Trang Lon', 99.
47. Lawrence Langer, *Holocaust Testimonials: The Ruins of Memory* (New Haven, CT, 1991), 77.
48. Vo Hoang, 'A New Place', 111.
49. Hoang, 'A New Place', 111.
50. Hoang, 'A New Place', 113.
51. Nguyen Ngoc Thuan, 'The Man Who Dreamed of Spring', 118.
52. Christopher Shaw and Malcolm Chase (eds), *The Imagined Past: History and Nostalgia* (Manchester and New York, 1989), 29. Italics in original.
53. Thuan, 'The Man Who Dreamed of Spring', 116.
54. Thuan, 'The Man Who Dreamed of Spring', 114.
55. 'A public space of trauma provides a consensual reality and collective memory through which the fragments of personal memory can be assembled, reconstructed, and displayed with a tacit assumption of validity.' Kirmayer, 'Landscapes of Memory', 189–90. Kirmayer's argument, albeit in a different context, highlights precisely the drive towards the reconstruction and validation of personal memories in Vietnamese-American memoirs and the problematics of that desire where the 'public space of trauma' is itself contested.

BIBLIOGRAPHY

Memoirs and Novels

Banerian, J. (ed. and trans.). *Vietnamese Short Stories: An Introduction*. Phoenix, AZ: Sphinx Publishing, 1986.

Dizon, L. 'Searching for Captain Nguyen Tan Hung', in D. Tran, A. Lam and H.D. Nguyen (eds), *Once Upon a Dream ... the Vietnamese-American Experience* (Kansas City, MI: Andrews and McMeel, 1995), 158–67.

Doan, V. Toai, and D. Chanoff. *The Vietnamese Gulag*, trans. by S. Romanowski and F. Simon-Miller. New York: Simon and Schuster, 1986.

Duong, T.H. *Paradise of the Blind*, trans. by P.H. Duong and N. McPherson. New York: William Morrow and Company, 1988.

Fischer, T. *Under the Frog: A Black Comedy*. London: Polygon, 1992.

Freeman, J.M. *Hearts of Sorrow: Vietnamese-American Lives*. Stanford, CA: Stanford University Press, 1989.

Nguyen, K. *The Unwanted: A Memoir*. Boston, New York and London: Little, Brown and Company, 2001.

Nguyen, L., with H. Kendall. *After Saigon Fell: Daily Life under the Vietnamese Communists*. Berkeley: University of California, Institute of East Asian Studies, 1981.

Nguyen, T.V., and D.L. Hughes. *When Faith Endures: One Man's Courage in the Midst of War*. American Fork, UT: Covenant Communications, 2004.

Nixon, R.M. *No More Vietnams*. London: W.H. Allen, 1986.

Pham, Q.X. *A Sense of Duty: My Father, My American Journey*. New York: Ballantine Books, 2005.
Santoli, A. *To Bear Any Burden: The Vietnam War and Its Aftermath in the Words of Americans and Southeast Asians*. New York: E.P. Dutton, 1985.
Tran, T.V. *Lost Years: My 1,632 Days in Vietnamese Reeducation Camps*. Berkeley: University of California, 1988.
Truong, N.T. *Journal of a Vietcong*. London: Jonathan Cape, 1986.

Secondary Sources

Antze, P., and M. Lambek (eds). *Tense Past: Cultural Essays in Trauma and Memory*. New York and London: Routledge, 1996.
Auerbach, S. *Vietnamese Americans*. Vero Beach, FL: Rourke Corporation, 1991.
Banerian, J. (ed.). *Losers Are Pirates: A Close Look at the PBS Series 'Vietnam: A Television History'*. Phoenix, AZ: Sphinx Publishing, 1985.
Brewer, W. 'What Is Autobiographical Memory?', in D.C. Rubin (ed.), *Autobiographical Memory* (Cambridge and New York: Cambridge University Press, 1986), 25–49.
Chanoff, D., and Doan V. Toai. *'Vietnam': A Portrait of Its People at War*. London and New York: I.B. Tauris, 1996.
Chu, Q. 'A Teacher in Ho Chi Minh City', in S.T. Huynh (ed.), *To Be Made Over: Tales of Socialist Reeducation in Vietnam* (New Haven, CT: Yale Southeast Asia Studies, 1988), 36–42.
Coleman, L. *Vietnamese in America*. Minneapolis, MN: Lerner Publications Company, 2005.
Ferry, J. *Vietnamese Immigration*. Philadelphia: Mason Crest Publishers, 2004.
Freeman, J.M. *Changing Identities: Vietnamese Americans, 1975–1995*. Boston, London, Toronto, Sydney, Tokyo and Singapore: Allyn and Bacon, 1995.
Gwertzman, B. 'Antiwar Activists Appeal to Hanoi'. *New York Times*, 21 December 1976, 4.
Ha, T.S. 'Welcome to Trang Lon, Reeducation Camp', in S.T. Huynh (ed. and trans.), *To Be Made Over: Tales of Socialist Reeducation in Vietnam* (New Haven, CT: Yale Southeast Asia Studies, 1988), 95–105.
Haskins, J. *The New Americans: Vietnamese Boat People*. Hillside, NJ: Enslow Publishers, 1980.
Huynh, S. T. (ed. and trans.). *To Be Made Over: Tales of Socialist Reeducation in Vietnam*. New Haven, CT: Yale Southeast Asia Studies, 1988.
Hynes, S. 'Personal Narratives and Commemoration', in J. Winter and E. Sivan (eds), *War and Remembrance in the Twentieth Century* (Cambridge: Cambridge University Press, 1999), 205–20.
King, N. *Memory, Narrative, Identity: Remembering the Self*. Edinburgh: Edinburgh University Press, 2000.

Kirmayer, L.J. 'Landscapes of Memory: Trauma, Narrative, and Dissociation', in P. Antze and M. Lambek (eds), *Tense Past: Cultural Essays in Trauma and Memory* (New York and London: Routledge, 1996), 173-98.

Kolakowski, L. *My Correct Views on Everything*, ed. by Z. Janowski. South Bend, IN: St. Augustine's Press, 2005.

Kugelmass, J. 'Missions to the Past: Poland in Contemporary Jewish Thought and Deed', in P. Antze and M. Lambek (eds), *Tense Past: Cultural Essays in Trauma and Memory* (New York and London: Routledge, 1996), 199-214.

Langer, L. *Holocaust Testimonials: The Ruins of Memory*. New Haven, CT: Yale University Press, 1991.

Lyotard, J.-F. *Heidegger and 'The Jews'*, trans. by A. Michel and M.S. Roberts. Minneapolis, MN: University of Minnesota Press, 1990.

Metzner, E.P., V.C. Huynh, V.P. Tran and N.B. Le. *Reeducation in Postwar Vietnam: Personal Postscripts to Peace*. College Station, TX: Texas A & M University Press, 2001.

Nguyen, M.H. 'Refugee Scholars and Vietnamese Studies in the United States, 1975-1982'. *Amerasia Journal* 11(1) (1984), 89-99.

Nguyen, M.H. '"Vietnam: A Television History": A Case Study in Perceptual Conflict between the American Media and the Vietnamese Expatriates'. *World Affairs* 147(2) (1984), 71-84.

Nguyen, N.T. 'The Man Who Dreamed of Spring', in S.T. Huynh (ed. and trans.), *To Be Made Over: Tales of Socialist Reeducation in Vietnam* (New Haven, CT: Yale Southeast Asia Studies, 1988), 114-21.

Parker, L.K. *Why Vietnamese Immigrants Came to America*. New York: Rosen Publishing Group, 2003.

Pelley, P.M. *Postcolonial Vietnam: New Histories of the National Past*. Durham, NC and London: Duke University Press, 2002.

Rutledge, P. *The Vietnamese in America*. Minneapolis, MN: Lerner Publications Company, 1987.

Rutledge, P. *The Vietnamese Experience in America*. Bloomington and Indianapolis: Indiana University Press, 1992.

Schivelbusch, W. *The Culture of Defeat: On National Trauma, Mourning, and Recovery*, trans. by J. Chase. New York: Henry Holt and Company, 2001.

Shaw, C., and M. Chase (eds). *The Imagined Past: History and Nostalgia*. Manchester and New York: Manchester University Press, 1989.

Tran, D., A. Lam and H.D. Nguyen (eds). *Once Upon a Dream...the Vietnamese-American Experience*. Kansas City, MI: Andrews and McMeel, 1995.

Vo, H. 1988. 'A New Place', in S.T. Huynh (ed. and trans.), *To Be Made Over: Tales of Socialist Reeducation in Vietnam* (New Haven, CT: Yale Southeast Asia Studies, 1988), 106-13.

Vo, K.D. 'The Old Man Who Only Believed What He Saw', in S.T. Huynh (ed. and trans.), *To Be Made Over: Tales of Socialist Reeducation in Vietnam* (New Haven, CT: Yale Southeast Asia Studies, 1988), 14-25.

Winter, J., and E. Sivan (eds). *War and Remembrance in the Twentieth Century*. Cambridge: Cambridge University Press, 1999.

Zinoman, P. 'Beyond the Revolutionary Prison Memoir'. *The Vietnam Review* 1 (1996), 256–72.

Subarno Chattarji is Associate Professor in the Department of English at the University of Delhi. His research focuses on literary representations of the Vietnam War. His first book, *Memories of a Lost War: American Poetic Responses to the Vietnam War* (Oxford and New York, 2001), dealt with American poetic responses to the war. He is now working on Vietnamese-American memorialisations of that conflict. He has also written on media and the war on terror as well as the mediatisation of conflict in India and Pakistan, which resulted in *Tracking the Media: Interpretations of Mass Media Discourses in India and Pakistan* (New Delhi and London, 2008); and edited with Sevanti Ninan, *The Hoot Reader: Media Practice in Twenty-First Century India* (New Delhi, 2013). He is also co-author with Suman Gupta, Richard Allen and Supriya Chaudhuri of *Reconsidering English Studies in Indian Higher Education* (London, 2015).

Chapter 12

Memoir Writing as Narrative Therapy
A South African Border War Veteran's Story

Gary Baines

War can be both transformative and traumatic. For Clive Holt, a nineteen-year-old conscript in the South African Defence Force (SADF), it most certainly was. He participated in a protracted campaign in Angola between November 1987 and June 1988 in what were, arguably, the most significant engagements of the twenty-three-year conflict.[1] About fifteen years later, Holt began work on a memoir that was published in 2005 as *At Thy Call We Did Not Falter*.[2] Holt's memoir has the by-line 'a frontline account of the Angolan War, as seen through the eyes of a conscripted soldier'. The blurb on the back cover proclaims it 'a classic account of war, as well as a window into the world of post-traumatic stress disorder'. It fails to live up to the first part of this claim for it is no literary masterpiece. But this is not my concern. Rather, I wish to examine what Holt's story reveals about post-traumatic stress disorder (PTSD) and the psychosocial problems faced by SADF veterans. I also wish to examine whether Holt's story shows the efficacy of narrative therapy. And, finally, I wish to establish whether there is any connection between individual and national healing narratives.

WAR AND THE NARRATION OF TRAUMA

It has become something of a truism that war is a life-altering or transforming experience. Certainly, it can be a catalyst of *inner* change. Samuel Hynes holds that 'no man goes through a war without being changed by it, and in fundamental ways'. He adds that 'though the process will not be explicit in every narrative – not all men are self-conscious or reflective enough for that – it will be there'.[3] Yet change is seldom a straightforward incremental process, nor is the recounting thereof necessarily linear. In fact, personal war narratives are often replete with disturbing events and unsettling episodes, features that signal to the reader the likelihood that the protagonist may be traumatised. According to Yuval Harari, the main task of the twentieth-century military memoirist has been to restore continuity and integrity to the life of the narrator disrupted by war; to weave the story of the soldier's life together again.[4] Adaptive veterans are capable of shaping their narratives into coherent stories or writing memoirs, of developing the cognitive skills to write about their experiences and find a sympathetic audience for their stories, which is important for post-traumatic recovery. Kali Tal stresses the need to bear witness to trauma, and the presence of a community with whom the experience can be shared.[5] Memoir writing and publishing might not equate to clinical therapy but the narrative recovery of trauma is tantamount to treatment.

Psychologist Nigel Hunt propounds a model of narrative analysis developed in conjunction with colleagues working with British war veterans.[6] Hunt's model is an adaptation of grounded narrative analysis and assumes that we order our lives into a story to make meaning of experiences. This model analyses both the form and content of soldiers' stories in order to investigate how veterans reconcile their war experiences with their overall life stories through the development of narrative coherence and social support networks. Here reconciliation implies 'harmony between past, present, and future'.[7] Hunt argues that such an approach holds good for oral testimony and the written word. He suggests that readings of literature (including works of fiction) offer insights into how soldiers cope with their wartime experiences and veterans pursue post-traumatic growth. Somewhat surprisingly, though, Hunt does not have much to say about the value of published autobiographical narratives or memoirs in providing a form of narrative therapy.

Hunt's work exemplifies the 'narrative turn' in psychology. This growing body of research has demonstrated that the experience of trauma disrupts the creation of the life story because it challenges or shatters the long-held assumptions we hold about ourselves and the world. Essentially, traumatic experiences challenge the integrity of the life story; they create an incoherent, disorganised and fragmented narrative. Clinically speaking, the presence of a fragmented narrative existing simultaneously with vivid and emotionally threatening nightmares and/or flashbacks is defined as

PTSD. Thus, treatment should entail the integration of traumatic events into the overall life story thereby increasing coherence and diminishing the disruptive or threatening nature of traumatic memories. Psychologists tend to agree that constructing a coherent story about a traumatic event is essential to recovery. However, Hunt overstates his case when he insists that the development of an *effective* narrative more or less guarantees that a person will experience post-traumatic growth.[8] I would only be prepared to go so far as to say that the narrative approach can contribute to the wellbeing of the subject; it is not a 'cure-all'.

The premise of narrative psychology is that individuals understand themselves through the medium of language, through telling and writing. The construction of a personal narrative is the means by which individuals (re)structure and (re)configure their lives whereas trauma disrupts this coherence. According to Dan McAdams, 'traumatizing events have the capacity to produce 'narrative wreckage' in the life story and ... therapy [is able] to repair such rifts in order to create a greater sense of coherence, continuity and meaning for the individual'.[9]

Similarly, Michele Crossley speaks of trauma as producing a breach or fragmentation in the life story but holds that individuals are constantly engaged in the process of creating themselves through telling and writing their narratives.[10] And Suzette Henke coined the term 'scriptotherapy' by which she means 'the process of writing out and writing through traumatic experience in the mode of therapeutic re-enactment'. Henke champions the ameliorative power of life-writing, which she believes 'has always offered the tantalizing possibility of reinventing the self and reconstructing the subject'.[11] Thus, memoir writing would seem to point to the possibilities of narrative therapy as providing a measure of healing for traumatised war veterans and others suffering from PTSD. For the act of writing represents an attempt by an author to integrate a fractured past, unsettled present and anticipated future into a coherent life story.

The narrative approach challenges assumptions concerning the idea that trauma is unspeakable; that it cannot be narrated or represented by language. Following Chris van der Merwe and Pumla Gobodo-Madikizela,[12] I would argue that trauma can indeed be remembered and communicated. Trauma is defined by these authors as shattered or lost – literally, wounded – life narratives that are often avoided, repressed or drowned in the din of daily life. Thus, they must be addressed via the spoken or written word, although this does not necessarily mean that sufferers attain closure. Literary or personal narrative responses to trauma may not be therapeutic in all cases but at least it affords a means of integrating narratives into a coherent chapter of the life story. And even in instances where they achieve a measure of healing, such narratives do not need to have happy or even resolved endings in order to enable post-traumatic growth. This is borne out by the story of a South African Border War veteran that is the subject of this chapter.

AT THY CALL WE DID NOT FALTER: A WAR MEMOIR

Clive Holt belonged to the cohort of white males conscripted into the SADF. Holt was one of approximately 600,000 able-bodied school leavers who served in the SADF between 1968 and 1993. As a conscript, he had little option other than to heed the call-up and perform national service or *diensplig*. Failure to do so meant harsh penalties.[13] It is evident from the tone of the book's opening chapters that Holt had mixed feelings about national service and went somewhat reluctantly.

When Holt was inducted into the SADF, national service was two years' duration. The period of national service had been gradually extended from nine months to two years as exponential manpower demands were made upon school-leaving white males. The obligations of national servicemen (NSM) continued beyond the initial two-year stints as they were assigned to citizen force or commando units that were liable for periodical training camps. Such camps usually lasted three months and involved deployment in the 'operational areas' from 1974 or stints in the black townships from 1984. Members of 'Dad's army', as the older soldiers were sometimes called, found themselves having to undergo regular (re)training so as to maintain their fighting – as opposed to their physical – fitness. They often served alongside new intakes of NSM. Thus, those belonging to this national service generation were part-time soldiers for much of their adult lives.

NSM were indoctrinated to believe that it was their duty to defend the country against the twin threats of African nationalism and communism, captured by the Afrikaans colloquialisms *rooi/swart gevaar* (literally 'red/black danger').[14] This was in accordance with 'total onslaught' ideology that insisted that a Soviet-orchestrated force, which included Cubans, the armies of the frontline states, guerrilla insurgents as well as revolutionaries within the country, sought to topple the ruling National Party and the minority government. This perceived threat was countered by the creation of a garrison state and the thoroughgoing militarisation of South African society.[15] The process of militarisation was reinforced by social institutions such as the family, education system, mainstream media and the churches. Consequently, national service was widely regarded as a rite of passage and a necessary commitment to preserve white power and privilege.

South Africa's Defence Act was amended in 1976 to sanction the mobilisation of forces beyond its borders if the security of the country was, in the opinion of the State President, under threat.[16] Hence conscripts like Holt were deployed in northern Namibia ostensibly to prevent the infiltration of members of the South West Africa Peoples' Organization (SWAPO) into the territory occupied by the SADF in breach of UN resolutions. But the SADF regularly mounted cross-border operations into Angola that resulted in engagements not only with PLAN (People's Liberation Army of Namibia) guerrillas, but also with the armed forces of Angola and their Cuban allies. The SADF also supported Jonas Savimbi's UNITA (National Union for the Total Independence of Angola) in its insurgency against the MPLA (Popular Movement for the Liberation of Angola) government in Luanda. The term 'Border War' was used by the apartheid state to perpetuate the fiction that SADF troops were protecting South Africa's border and not actually fighting on foreign soil.[17]

The loss of NSM and citizen force members was a politically sensitive issue among South Africa's white electorate. Thus, the Border War was fought extensively by proxy forces in order to minimise casualties among these groups. Indeed, surrogates bore the brunt of the fighting from the 1980s and paid a much higher price for doing so than SADF members.[18] The number of the SADF's own losses was not divulged to the public on account of the strictures placed on the media, which was compelled to rely on official statements for its information about the casualties incurred in the conflict. Under-reporting of war casualties was aimed at preventing the loss of public morale but the circulation of rumours had the opposite result. Confirmation of the exact toll of those killed while on active duty remains unclear and a matter of conjecture.[19]

Some NSM and citizen force soldiers were reluctant to be deployed in Angola, but most would not have passed up the opportunity to 'see action'. They swallowed the line that it was preferable to wage war in neighbouring states than in one's own backyard. Nor did many have misgivings about being assigned to the occupation forces in South-West Africa (SWA)/Namibia, which was effectively treated as a 'fifth province' of the Republic. So by and large, South Africa's citizen soldiers accepted the necessity of military service to defend the country against its enemies as defined by government propaganda. Holt was no exception. Even retrospectively, he remains convinced that he was fighting a serious communist threat although he acknowledges at one point in relation to the SADF's incursion into Angola that it was 'an aggressor in a foreign country'.[20]

At Thy Call is partly based on a diary that Holt kept during the time he was involved in the fighting in Angola. Occasional diary entries punctuate the early part of the narrative and provide the reader with a sense of proximity to the events described in greater detail in the text written some fifteen years later. Diary material was supplemented by information gleaned from the extant military histories and communications from fellow veterans of the campaign. Thus, the book combines first-hand recollections, personal memories and a synthesis of secondary sources. It is by no means a seamless story but is more than a battlefield biography for it does not end with the war. It is not simply a *bildungsroman* or coming of age story. As with most soldier-authors, Holt reflects on how what he did and witnessed as a soldier affected him. And as with so many soldier-authors, he reckons that his first-hand experience of combat (what Harari calls 'flesh witnessing'[21]) qualifies him as a reliable witness of the Angolan or Border War.

Holt's account deals briefly with his training at Bloemfontein before he was assigned to 61 Mechanised Infantry Battalion. His unit was involved in the critical battle of Cuito Cuanavale between the SADF and its surrogate force UNITA on the one hand, and the Angolan army (FAPLA) and its Cuban ally on the other. The author weighs in on the controversy of who won the battle. Holt's version of events in *At Thy Call* corresponds closely with the official SADF version. He cites statistics gleaned from SADF sources and then asks the reader to deduce which side won the engagement.[22] However, Holt holds that he is not in a position to assess the political ramifications of the operations in which he was involved, but is able to comment on the outcome of the battle because 'he was there' (108). As with most military memoirists, he regards his experiential knowledge as authoritative. I have addressed this issue elsewhere.[23] Here I am more interested in Holt's frank disclosures of how memories of this engagement have come to haunt him.

For the sake of providing sufficient contextualisation to appreciate Holt's disclosures about how the fighting affected him, I will provide a brief synopsis of the campaigns in which he was involved. The first phase of the operation that went by the codename Moduler was planned to stop the combined Cuban/FAPLA advance on UNITA's stronghold of Mavinga and, subsequently, its Jamba headquarters. The SADF won a victory against enormous odds at the Lomba River where it halted the advance in its tracks. FAPLA retreated headlong to the Cuito River where it was reinforced by a contingent of Cubans. Operation Moduler segued into Hooper as the SADF launched repeated assaults on well-fortified enemy and mined enemy positions on the Cuito bridgehead. Holt reckons that the SADF's objective was to drive the enemy forces across the Cuito River, destroy the bridge and thus secure the south-eastern Cuanda-Cubango province of Angola for UNITA (88). His description of the assaults suggests that the hard-pressed forces suffered a number of setbacks before withdrawing. Holt discounts the idea that the SADF sought to secure a bridgehead across the Cuito River and capture Cuito Cuanavale.[24]

Holt's unit joined the fray in November 1987 and was soon involved in the thick of battle – what he calls (rather inappropriately) the 'rumble in the jungle' (83). His 61 Mechanised Battalion spearheaded the third assault on the Cuito bridgehead on 25 February 1988, which included some of the fiercest fighting of the campaign. Holt recounts that columns of tanks and infantry assault vehicles (or Ratels) advanced through dense bush and undergrowth on well-fortified and heavily mined enemy positions in the Tumpo triangle. They were subjected to artillery barrages and constant bombardment by MiGs. In the heat of battle, Holt experienced and witnessed some gruesome incidents, one of which unnerved him enough to mark the beginning of 'his nightmare'. The driver of the command Ratel, 'Langes' Geldenhuys, collapsed as a consequence of heat exhaustion and dehydration. This was followed by hysteria in which he cried for his brother whom Holt later learned had been recently killed in a motor vehicle accident. He had reached breaking point (94–95). Adrenalin stimulated by fear kept most of the soldiers functioning but the casualties mounted as they pursued an unrealistic objective of clearing the Tumpo area and destroying the bridge across the Cuito River. The attritional nature of the fighting took a heavy toll on the SADF forces, especially their morale. Confidence was shaken by the enemy's tenacity and some of the troops had reached the end of their tether. Faced with intense life-threatening situations for an extended period, individual soldiers became susceptible to frayed nerves, fitful sleep and frequent bouts of nervous exhaustion – a sure fire recipe for the development of psychological disorders.

The failure of the third assault on the bridgehead forced the SADF to reconsider its strategy in the battle for Cuito Cuanavale.[25] Holt's 61 Mech was withdrawn and replaced by fresh troops after four months of intense fighting. The unit regrouped at a demobilisation camp where they were given a pep talk by General Jannie Geldenhuys and Operation Hooper souvenir t-shirts (114). This was followed by group debriefing sessions in which psychologists were tasked to gauge whether the troops were fit for leave. These debriefings were supposedly designed to detect early warning signals of trauma so as identify and treat those likely to develop PTSD (120). The sessions were actually a farce as they lasted less than half an hour. Holt recollects: 'I felt that I had not even begun to get in touch with the emotional and traumatic impact of what I had been through' (121). However, at the time he was relieved that the psychologist had not bothered to provide more than a perfunctory interview. Neither he nor his comrades were interested in counselling by psychologists of whom they were suspicious. They were much more interested in going home. Holt believed that he would cope with the trauma and return to his life in civvy street without any need of therapy (122). In retrospect, he has come to realise that he was sorely mistaken.

Holt goes to considerable lengths to make the point that the approach of the psychologist was a far cry from the procedure set out in the SADF's debriefing model specifically designed for Angolan war veterans. He cites extensive passages from the notes of a clinical psychologist who headed the Operation Hooper debriefing team to illustrate the gap between theory and practice.[26] Holt calls the chapter in which he describes the process 'Thirty Minutes to Clear the Minefield' (111). This is clearly an ironic take on the short-circuited process that amounted to going through the motions of the debriefing and evaluation session which he and his fellows were obliged to attend. And the analogy of the minefield suggests that the charges were not defused; that the primed mines might lie dormant beneath the soil only to be detonated sometime in the future.

Holt was duly granted leave and during his three-week pass he became aware of his jitteriness and hyper-sensitivity or 'arousal' to aural stimuli. Conversely, he displayed a lack of emotion in relating to death, including that of his own father who had died prior to his going on pass. His inability to relate to his mother and younger brother brought home to him his alienation from his family. This extended to friends and acquaintances as well. Holt was not keen to tell his war stories to people he now regarded as 'outsiders', inasmuch as they had not shared his experiences. He was affronted by people who asked whether he had killed anyone (132). Nor did he wish to have people think he was embellishing stories so as to impress listeners. On the rare occasions that he did relate something about his experiences, he admits to feeling a sense of guilt (129). Otherwise he chose to remain silent. This was partly due to the fact that the South African public was purposefully misinformed about the course of the undeclared war on foreign soil. Government disinformation and censorship bred demoralisation and suspicion. Holt likens himself to a used and discarded prostitute (131).

Meanwhile, the stalemate at Cuito Cuanavale was upset by Fidel Castro assuming personal responsibility for Cuban strategy in south-west Angola.[27] By rebuilding an airstrip at Menongue, Cuban-piloted MiG fighter planes were within range of northern Namibia. The consequent loss of the South African Air Force's air superiority was evident from a sortie that bombed the Calueque dam killing twelve NSM. SADF ground forces had to withdraw or face the prospect of having their escape routes cut off by Cuban forces advancing on the Namibian border and outflanking them. The

SADF then counter-attacked and inflicted casualties on the Cuban/FAPLA forces. However, the overall situation in southern Angola was now far more fluid and gave the Cuban/FAPLA forces the edge. It was the SADF whose teeth had been broken.[28] For the first time ever the Cubans threatened the Namibian border and the SADF appeared vulnerable. The announcement by the Chief of the SADF, General Jannie Geldenhuys, of a massive call-up in mid 1988 attests to this.

Following 61 Mech's redeployment near the Calueque Dam in June 1988, an engagement with Cuban and FAPLA columns resulted in the death of a respected friend, Lieutenant Muller Meiring. Although this incident was not witnessed first-hand, it still caused Holt to reflect anew on his ability to cope with traumatic events. He notes that the standard way of dealing with such doubts was to 'shut up, keep your feelings inside, and carry on with life' (150); in short, to *vasbyt* (persevere). This was in keeping with a military training that stressed that quitting was a sign of weakness and that soldiers never showed emotions. So he 'put on the proverbial brave face, even though he felt sick to the core' (152). Ill equipped to deal with such situations, Holt feared above all that he might 'crack' under the strain and go *bossies*. He defines *bossies* as a 'colloquial term for "bush madness", a condition associated with strange/abnormal behaviour as a result of spending prolonged periods of time in the bush under combat conditions' (191). Anecdotal evidence suggests that such soldiers were stigmatised and ostracised and they invariably became loners and outsiders. For its part, the army often turned a blind eye to the problem but on occasion sent the afflicted troop for psychological evaluation and treatment. This was not so much out of concern for their wellbeing but rather because they were deemed to be unfit for combat. As Holt has it, '[m]ental health was not high on the agenda, and as long as you could perform your assigned function and not succumb to any physical illness or injury, it was assumed that you were okay and fighting fit' (150). Clearly, the SADF had little regard for the wellbeing of its soldiers. Holt has a lingering pride in the performance of his unit and shows an undying loyalty to his fellow soldiers. However, this is offset by a pervasive sense of the futility of war and an indictment of the SADF's treatment of those who put their lives on the line for their country.[29]

If the SADF hierarchy did not take the mental health of its troops seriously, the troops themselves were equally inclined to be blasé about the need for professional intervention. It was common to use disparaging names such as *koptiffies* (head or mental mechanics) to describe psychologists (111). The term implied that the psychologists would mess with one's mind. When Holt notes after his survival of the strike by Cuban MiGs on the Calueque Dam in late June 1988 that he was 'starting to show classic warning signs of something [PTSD] I would not recognize for several more years' (164), he does so with the benefit of hindsight. When he returned home three months later, he experienced nightmares consisting of battle scenes that were repeatedly replayed in his mind. He identifies sleep disorders and drinking problems as tell-tale signs of his condition. After naming his condition and having acquired a working knowledge of the discourse of PTSD, he is able to recognise that his inability to process his traumatic experiences amounted to a 'state of cognitive dissonance' (166). Holt also admits that he resorted to repressing the memories of those events he was unable to process. He reckons that he even contemplated joining the permanent force as he felt totally alienated from civilian life (167). But he decided against such a course of action and *klaared out* of the army (demobilised) in December 1989 soon after his twentieth birthday.

Holt's penultimate chapter, 'Cowboys Do Cry', deals with his readjustment to civilian life. He describes himself as anxious, aggressive and ill tempered, looking for fights and indulging in binge drinking. He also admits to embracing a 'victim mentality' in order to attract the attention and sympathy of his peers (175). Following an incident on New Year's Eve 1989 when he 'snapped', he rejected the suggestion of seeking psychiatric help and, instead, sought solitude in order to reflect on the course of his life. Holt subsequently learned martial arts in order to channel his aggression creatively, and personal motivation so as to regain control of his life by setting himself manageable goals. But his inability to hold down a steady job resulted in him blaming everyone but himself for his (re)lapses; even wallowing in self-pity. But when his then girlfriend lost her brother in a car accident, he was forced once again to confront his inability to deal with loss and pain. However, with his marriage to Alison, Holt found a companion with whom he could share the reliving of his traumas. The birth of a son and the family's migration to Australia are recorded as life-transforming events. Holt reckons that emigration was like 'leaving a haunted house, along with all its ghosts' (183). However, he has since discovered that his ghosts tend to accompany him, as they live in his subconscious.

THE PTSD PARADIGM

In 2002 Holt commenced researching and writing *At Thy Call*. The text attests to the fact that he read literature in the field of PTSD and incorporated certain insights in trying to understand what he had been through. In other words, the project had a therapeutic effect in that it afforded him an opportunity to revisit and engage with his memories, as well as thoughts recorded in his diary. Holt would undoubtedly endorse the statement that 'narration itself becomes therapy and plays its part in reconciling the past with the present and in pacifying the feelings of guilt, pain, disassociation that arise when the unspeakable is confronted'.[30] *At Thy Call* seems to fit into the category of confessional or cathartic literature. Holt, however, sees the book as serving another purpose: to impart his knowledge to others suffering from PTSD. He wishes to illuminate their darkness and to project a path to follow in order to obtain healing. With the enthusiasm of a neophyte, Holt offers veterans suffering from PTSD a chance of a new beginning (187). It is, at least, preferable to promising closure when there can be no guarantee of complete psychosocial healing.

Holt's acute problem of readjustment to civilian life frames his story to a large degree. Because vestiges of the trauma still remain, he cannot seem to escape his nightmares altogether although he has 'learned to live with his memories and understand and control the symptoms' (14). He has obviously improved his capacity to cope with his trauma and developed a degree of resilience as a result of social support from caring family and friends, as well as a sympathetic professional counsellor. Significantly, for Holt the communication of his story seems to have enabled him to find his voice and an appreciative audience.[31] Thus, the writing of his memoir has served as a form of narrative therapy.

Holt's book is one of a number of SADF veterans' memoirs to have been framed by a PTSD paradigm. A former SADF paratrooper, Marius van Niekerk, relates his experiences in *Behind the Lines of the Mind: Healing the Scars of War* (2009) to a psychologist who offers editorial interventions informed by his professional expertise. Consequently, it reads more like a treatise than a memoir.[32] The book has spawned a few other projects.[33] In these, Van Niekerk appears to have been motivated by a mission to facilitate healing and redemption for veterans like himself. Anthony Feinstein's *Battle Scarred: Hidden Costs of the Border War* (2011) relates a number of episodes that reveal the deep emotional and psychological wounds incurred by those with whom the author served and treated in his capacity as a medic.[34] For instance, he tells of the security policeman who, following an ambush in which he failed to overcome his fears, experienced nightmares during which he regressed into a state of childhood. As a psychiatrist who is well versed in the literature of PTSD, Feinstein's observations about the effect of combat are filtered through a professional lens. Unlike Van Niekerk, Feinstein is both participant-witness and observer in his story. And *Battle Scarred* is a rather more accomplished piece of writing with a stronger story line than *Behind the Lines of the Mind*. When read in conjunction with Holt's

At Thy Call, these texts suggest that the discourse of PTSD colours the current crop of Border War narratives.

In the absence of qualitative data, it is difficult to gauge the extent of PTSD among SADF veterans. But anecdotal and quantitative evidence seems to point to it being fairly prevalent. A former *Koevoet*[35] member, John Deegan, related in a documentary programme entitled 'The War Within' how his life became a litany of ills after his tour of duty on the border. His experiences included admission to psychiatric hospitals, the abuse of drugs, run-ins with the law, and broken marriages. Like Holt, he reckoned that he could only begin to deal with his demons once he became aware that others suffered from similar symptoms and that his condition had a name – PTSD.[36] His story resonates with those of some other SADF veterans posted on the internet. Via such sites, these veterans have become aware that PTSD had been declared a diagnostic category by the US medical/psychiatric fraternity in 1980 and their Vietnam counterparts received therapy and counselling. In the absence of a similar state-funded programme in South Africa, a few veterans established their own self-help groups. There are also other sites established for the express purpose of allowing those seeking advice or searching for (cyber)space to tell their stories to do so. For instance, the South African Veterans' Association (SAVA) set up a website that dubs itself 'A Non-Governmental, Non-Profitmaking Veteran Service for Survivors of the 1970s–90s Conflicts'. The website touts the by-line: 'The victims of war are not just those that die, but also those that kill'.[37] This is an indicator that the appropriation of victimhood by SADF veterans is now *de rigueur*, and also suggests that PTSD offers an explanatory framework that provides an alibi for the atrocities of war.[38]

PTSD is obviously not confined to SADF veterans or any other particular sub-set of the South African population. However, there is a relationship between the impact of trauma on individuals and cultures, and even nations; between the individual and collective experience. Notwithstanding Holt's self-imposed exile from his country of birth, his memoir should be understood as a product of specific history and an attempt to negotiate a place in post-conflict South Africa's trauma culture.[39] It connects past, present and future.

TRAUMA IN TRANSITION

The publication of the abovementioned memoirs suggests that any 'taboo' against the writing of life stories by SADF veterans that may have existed has been overturned. The memory work of the Truth and Reconciliation

Commission (TRC) opened a space for ex-conscripts to revisit their experiences. The TRC Report acknowledged the need to 'raise public awareness about the reality and effects of post-traumatic stress disorder' and to encourage former conscripts and soldiers who participated in the conflict 'to share their pain and reflect on their experiences'.[40] Aside from proposing projects aimed at rehabilitating and rebuilding the lives of veterans, the TRC envisaged that they could possibly be 'help[ed] to tell and write their stories'.[41] Although neither Holt nor other SADF memoirists necessarily took their cue from the TRC, they have published their stories against the background of an unsettling political transition. They have either come to terms with the shame and guilt implied in the TRC's naming of the SADF as a 'perpetrator organization',[42] or simply ignored the taint of having been a member of the apartheid army.

Published memoirs have been produced by reasonably articulate and well-adjusted veterans who seek to make sense of their war experiences. A number of these soldier-authors have undoubtedly found their writing cathartic and their style tends to be confessional.[43] In some cases, the narrator confides dark secrets to the reader, who should presumably empathise rather than become judgemental. Other narrators tend to recount their stories in a matter-of-fact way with an uneasy mixture of honesty and self-delusion, candour and scepticism. In his review of Holt's memoir and other publications about the SADF, William Minter notes that '[t]here is neither justification nor critique of the apartheid system ... There are no reflections on guilt or the nature of the South African system, or even acknowledgment that such reflection might be called for [...]'. He adds that all these soldier-authors 'deny that they were fighting for "apartheid", but they are remarkably vague on what they thought they were fighting for'. Minter describes them as living within an 'armoured bubble, isolated from any consideration of the meaning of death and suffering they and their fellows inflicted'. He deduces that the typical NSM was neither a stereotypical patriot nor an Afrikaner nationalist but someone whose loyalty 'appears to have been the military itself' and whose 'cause' 'appears to have been the excitement of war itself'. Minter concludes that '[i]n effect, the military was the "country" they thought they were defending and the social context that defined their reality and protected them from contradictory perspectives'.[44] This seems to amount to an argument that for NSM the war was not at all ideological but a matter of commitment to the institutional culture of the military and a loyalty to brothers in arms. I would concede that this is evident in certain memoirs but that some authors have a slightly more subtle understanding of their roles in the SADF. Notwithstanding the political naïveté of most of these soldier-authors, the elision of guilt and innocence makes for considerable moral ambiguity in these memoirs.

The ambiguity in SADF veterans' discourse about the war is largely a retrospective development. It has been accompanied by a belated recognition by mental health practitioners and clinicians of the existence of combat-related PTSD among former NSM.[45] There is a common belief that PTSD only becomes a major problem for soldiers involved in unjust or unsuccessful wars. As the Border War can – and has – been construed as such, it is tempting to view SADF veterans' trauma symptoms as a consequence of being on the losing side of history. However, this viewpoint cannot be sustained in the light of evidence from other wars of the twentieth century.[46] A related but slightly different argument suggests that the manifestation of PTSD cases was a direct consequence of the political changes that the country has undergone since 1990. A therapist who had provided counselling for former conscripts testified before the TRC that it had been very difficult for them to reconcile themselves with the decriminalisation of their former enemies. She noted:

> Central to most of these testimonies [by ex-conscripts] is the notion that the present has destroyed the foundations of 'meaning' these conscripts adopted to cope with their traumatic experiences. It is easier to cope with having killed someone you believe to be the sub-human agent of forces that wish to destroy everything you hold dear than it is to cope with having killed a normal man, woman or child ... . This crisis is greatly intensified when it is revealed to you that the person you have killed is a 'hero' or 'freedom fighter' or 'innocent civilian'. For some, the contradictions of their experience might prove intolerable.[47]

Thus it was argued that the collapse of the scaffolding of the apartheid system was accompanied by an identity crisis and an increase in psychosocial problems, especially among white males. Although not many conscripts owned up to their part in preserving and benefitting from white power, some did grapple with the extent of their individual responsibility within society at large for the acts committed by perpetrators of human rights abuses. Others found it more comforting to appropriate victimhood. Still, 'questions remain about what constitutes ... a suitable trauma history, and what sentiments can be expressed in the national public sphere'.[48] So there is still an unresolved tension between (white) society's need to know and its wish to deny or ignore what exactly was done in its name.

The work of the TRC occurred in tandem with tumultuous changes in post-apartheid South Africa. National service was phased out following a sequence of events that culminated in the transfer of power from a white minority regime to a democratically elected government. The South African and Cuban withdrawals from Angola, followed by a United Nations supervised settlement in Namibia, paved the way for a relatively peaceful transfer of power whereby the African National Congress (ANC) became the ruling party in South Africa. For some former NSM the transition was fraught with apprehension and misgivings. Many could not understand why they had been asked to sacrifice so much only to surrender power to those whom they had previously regarded as 'the enemy'. It has become a cliché of veterans' discourse to suggest that the SADF 'won all the battles but lost the war'.[49] This sentiment echoes that of some retired SADF generals who have insisted that they defeated the liberation movements and their (communist) allies and thus were in a position to call the shots in negotiations with the ANC. Instead, they were betrayed or 'stabbed in the back' by the politicians who made too many concessions to the ANC when its military wing did not have the capacity to threaten the security of the state or the power of its ruling white minority.[50]

As the apartheid regime's security forces had the most to lose, they were the most recalcitrant in surrendering power. For their part, most SADF veterans remained silent, either out of a sense of loyalty to the old regime and fellow soldiers, or for fear of being held accountable by the ANC government for war crimes or human rights violations. Few testified before the TRC because it was widely believed to be biased against the SADF. Journalist Karen Whitty explains their reluctance to testify in the following terms: 'Bound by a sense of honour to their fellow troops, and the patriarchy still espoused by white South Africa, few men have come forward and spoken about their experiences, however barbaric and mundane, in South Africa's border wars'.[51]

If ex-conscripts were suspicious of the TRC, they were equally wary of public reaction to the divulgence of war crimes and other heinous acts. Accordingly, they seldom made public statements about the conduct of the war. But there have been exceptions. A veteran of the Namibian counter-insurgency campaign called it 'an atrocious war' and admitted that officers turned a blind eye to the offensive conduct of SADF soldiers. Likewise, a former reconnaissance commander acknowledged that he had to constantly restrain his team from going on the rampage in Angola and committing acts of violence against civilians.[52] And there is abundant evidence that *Koevoet* and other units such as 32 Battalion were responsible for torture and other acts of terror. Still, a clique of retired SADF generals refused to acknowledge their role in perpetrating human rights abuses both in and outside of South Africa.[53] Under the circumstances, certain conscripts reported that the lack of public knowledge about the war created suspicion of their stories, while others were summarily dismissed as sympathy seekers or outright liars by the former SADF generals and their apologists.[54] Thus, veterans felt betrayed when the very authorities that they were convinced would defend their actions left them in the lurch. If trauma involves a betrayal of trust and the abuse of relations of power,[55] then it is not surprising that many veterans elected to remain silent for fear of being victimised.

NSM have generally protested their innocence when confronted with the charge of defending the apartheid system. The perception that they were mere cogs in the wheel of a large conscript army allowed them to appear in their own eyes as passive victims of circumstance. Thus, TRC amnesty applications were primarily from the ranks of the liberation armies or non-statutory forces. 'Of the 256 members of the apartheid era security forces that applied for amnesty ... only 31 had served in the SADF. In contrast, there were close to 1,000 applications for amnesty from members of the various armed structures aligned to the ANC'.[56] Relatively few ex-combatants made statements as victims, choosing not to represent themselves in this way. Conversely, a former End Conscription Campaign (ECC) organiser, Laurie Nathan, explained to the TRC that he believed SADF conscripts were 'both victims and perpetrators'.[57] The TRC characterised a special hearing on conscription as 'neither an attempt to look for perpetrators, nor a process that will lead to the awarding of victim status'.[58] In spite of its good intentions, the TRC 'left the experiences of "ordinary" soldiers largely invisible – not merely forgotten but "wished away"', as a report of the Centre for the Study of Violence and Reconciliation (CSVR) declares.[59] Their own perception of marginalisation has encouraged SADF veterans, as well as those of the non-statutory forces, to embrace victimhood.

The trope of 'soldier-as-victim' has become a cliché in the representations of war. Kali Tal has highlighted the tendency to collapse the distinction between victims and perpetrators among American Vietnam veterans. She notes that they were:

> exposed to combat or other life-threatening events, and ... exposed to the carnage resulting from combat were traumatized. But combat soldiers, though subordinate to their military superiors and frequently at the mercy of their enemies, still possess a life-or-death power over other people ... These soldiers carry guns, they point them at people and shoot to kill ... Much recent literature – popular, clinical and academic – places the combat soldier simply in the victim's role, helpless in the face of war, and then helpless to readjust from the war experience upon his return home ... The soldier in combat is both victim and victimizer; dealing death as well as risking it.[60]

Gillian Eagle, too, has expressed concern about this trend. She noted that the '[o]pening [of] the door to the employment of PTSD as a diagnostic justification for the enactment of violence conceivably provides the basis for blurring the boundaries between victims and victimisers'.[61] This makes for an undifferentiated 'victim culture' which is by no means unique to South Africa. Peter Novick's work on the Holocaust has suggested that the appropriation of 'vicarious victimhood' for the sake of moral capital reflects a wider cultural shift in the late twentieth century.[62] Indeed, there is an unseemly competition for victimhood among ethnic, gender, religious and other self-identified social interest groups reckoned to be marginalised.[63] Victim culture is ubiquitous among war veterans.[64] And memoirists like Holt tap into this groundswell of sympathy, projecting themselves as hapless victims rather than warriors – or, their South African equivalent, *grensvegters* (literally 'border fighters').

CONCLUSION

Following a period of about fifteen years of relative neglect and repression of combat-related trauma, Clive Holt produced *At Thy Call*. The retelling and rewriting of his Border War story enabled Holt to work through his self-diagnosed PTSD. This was obviously personally therapeutic but not necessarily a panacea for his condition. Still, Holt is clearly a survivor and his experience suggests that narrative therapy can be beneficial for individuals afflicted by PTSD.

Might narrative therapy have a wider application? Might it be a means to treat the wounds of the body politic in post-conflict societies? According to Teresa Phelps, storytelling provides a measure of healing and reconciliation in societies undergoing transition to democracy.[65] The TRC certainly embraced this laudable vision. But despite the TRC's attempt to construct a constitutive history for the emerging nation, there has not emerged a singular, uncontested narrative about the past. In other words, there has been no 'buy-in' to a master narrative by large sectors of the population and so a plethora of voices are still competing to be heard in post-apartheid South Africa. This is not necessarily an unhealthy situation. But individual stories of healing are unlikely to translate into collective 'cure'. Inasmuch as the Angolan countryside is despoiled by the detritus of the war in which Holt fought, the road of healing and reconciliation that traverses the South African landscape is littered with considerable narrative wreckage. His memoir – and others like it – would suggest that trauma culture is the default state of the nation.

NOTES

1. Leopold Scholtz, *The SADF in the Border War, 1966–1989* (Cape Town, 2013).
2. Clive Holt, *At Thy Call We Did Not Falter* (Cape Town, 2005). First published in Australia by Paradigm Media Trust in 2004. I have referenced the South African edition.
3. Samuel Hynes, *The Soldier's Tale: Bearing Witness to Modern War* (London, 1998), 3.
4. Yuval N. Harari, 'Martial Illusions: War and Disillusionment in Twentieth-Century and Renaissance Military Memoirs', *Journal of Military History* 69(1) (2005), 68.
5. Kali Tal, *Worlds of Hurt: Reading the Literature of Trauma* (New York, 1996), 21.
6. Karen J. Burnell, Nigel Hunt and Peter G. Coleman, 'Developing a Model of Narrative Analysis to Investigate the Role of Social Support in Coping with Traumatic War Memories', *Narrative Inquiry* 19(1) (2009), 91–105. This article is reworked as chapter 9 in Nigel C. Hunt, *Memory, War and Trauma* (Cambridge, 2010).
7. G. Coleman, 'Creating a Life Story: The Task of Reconciliation', *The Gerontologist* 39(2) (1999), 134, cited in Burnell et al, 'A Model of Narrative Analysis', 92.
8. Hunt, *Memory, War and Trauma*, 117.
9. Dan P. McAdams, *The Stories We Live By: Personal Myths and the Making of Self* (New York, 1993), 67–68.
10. Michele L. Crossley, *Introducing Narrative Psychology: Self, Trauma and the Construction of Meaning* (Buckingham, 2000), 10.
11. Suzette A. Henke, *Shattered Subjects: Trauma and Testimony in Women's Life-Writing* (New York, 2000), xii, xv.
12. Chris van der Merwe and Pumla Gobodo-Madikizela, *Narrating our Healing* (Newcastle, 2007).
13. The alternatives were to object on conscientious – actually religious pacifist – grounds and face a six-year jail sentence, or flee the country.
14. Willem Steenkamp, 'The Citizen Soldier in the Border War', *Journal for Contemporary History* 31(3) (December 2006), 13.
15. The most extensive treatment is to be found in Jacklyn Cock and Laurie Nathan (eds), *War and Society: The Militarisation of South Africa* (Claremont, 1989).
16. Kathy Satchwell, 'The Power to Defend: An Analysis of Various Aspects of the Defence Act', in Cock and Nathan, *War and Society*, 49–50.
17. David Williams, *On the Border: The White South African Military Experience 1965–1990* (Cape Town, 2008), 117.
18. For instance, San or Bushmen trackers and guerrilla irregulars from Daniel Chipenda's faction of the National Front for the Liberation of Angola (FNLA) forces recruited to units such as 32 Battalion have been displaced and marginalised in post-apartheid South Africa. In the case of 32 Battalion veterans, their difficulties include deprivation, an uncertain future as a refugee community shuttled from camp to camp within some of the most desolate areas of the

country, and unsympathetic treatment by the ANC government, all of which makes them easy prey for mercenary recruiters. A brief summary of their conditions can be found at 'Pomfret: Mercenary Town?, Mail & Guardian (online), 1 October 2007, http://mg.co.za/article/2007-10-01-pomfret-mercenary-town. See also Jan Breytenbach, *Buffalo Soldiers: The Story of South Africa's 32 Battalion 1975–1993* (Alberton, 2003). For the plight of the Bushmen, see David Robbins, *On the Bridge of Goodbye* (Cape Town, 2007).

19. In a statement to Parliament in 1982, the then Minister of Defence Magnus Malan reckoned that the SADF had a casualty rate of 0.012% (or 12 in every 100,000) of the average daily strength of its armed forces in South-West Africa. It is not clear whether this figure is for those killed in active service or includes casualties from accidents and suicides but it is a gross underestimate of the actual situation. Interested parties have published rolls of honour but none can be described as definitive. Willem Steenkamp's estimate of 715 SADF personnel killed in action between 1974 and 1988 is clearly too low. See his 'The Citizen Soldier in the Border War', 20. John Dovey's roll of honour lists 1,986 SADF members killed on active duty over the period 1964–94 (but has no data for 1980 and 1981). See http://www.justdone.co.za/ROH/main.php?page=main. Peter Stiff's roll of honour is based on the names listed at the Fort Klapperkop memorial supplemented by his own research. See Steven Webb, *Ops Medic: A National Serviceman's Border War* (Alberton, 2008), 249–86.

20. Holt, *At Thy Call*, 150. Subsequent page references are given in parentheses in the text.

21. Y.N. Harari, *The Ultimate Experience: Battlefield Revelations and the Making of Modern War Culture, 1450–2000* (Basingstoke, 2008).

22. On page 109 Holt reproduces the official SADF statistics for losses of men and materiel in Angola between September 1978 and March 1988 (Operations Hooper and Moduler). According to these figures gleaned from the SADF mouthpiece *Paratus* in March 1989, 14, the SADF lost 31 whereas FAPLA lost 4,768 soldiers. No mention is made of UNITA's casualties. Elsewhere, Holt is aware of the discrepancies between official statements about the war in Angola and what he saw with his own eyes. See Gary Baines, *South Africa's Border War: Conflicting Narratives and Contested Memories* (London, 2014), 105–19, for a fuller discussion of the outcome of the battle of Cuito Cuanavale.

23. Baines, *South Africa's Border War*, 14–18.

24. Holt's version is in line with the claims of SADF generals and the then Minister of Defence Magnus Malan that it was never the SADF's intention to occupy Cuito Cuanavale. This has been rejected by those who see the battle as a turning point in the defeat of the apartheid army. See, for instance, Ronnie Kasrils, 'Historic Turning Point at Cuito Cuanavale', Address to Public Forum 'Historic Turning Point at Cuito Cuanavale', Rhodes University, 28 May 2008, http://www.pmpsa.gov.za/FILES/pdfs/Kasrils.pdf (accessed 5 November 2010).

25. Edward George, *The Cuban Intervention in Angola, 1965–1991: From Che Guevara to Cuito Cuanavale* (London, 2005), 227.

26. Barry Fowler, *Grensvegter? South African Army Psychologist* (Halifax, 1996), 123–27, reproduced in Holt, *At Thy Call*, 116–20.
27. Edgar Dosman, 'Countdown to Cuito Cuanavale: Cuba's Angolan Campaign' in Gary Baines and Peter Vale (eds), *Beyond the Border War: New Perspectives on Southern Africa's Late-Cold War Conflicts* (Pretoria, 2010), 207–28; Piero Gleijeses, 'Moscow's Proxy? Cuba and Africa 1975–1988', *Journal of Cold War Studies* 8(2) (2006), 3–51 and 'Cuba and the Independence of Namibia', *Cold War History* 7(2) (2007), 285–303.
28. This description borrows from Castro's metaphor. See Dosman, 'Countdown to Cuito Cuanavale', 219, 223. The boxing analogy suggests that the Cubans parried the SADF at Cuito with a left jab and then countered with a right thrust towards the Namibian border. Ironically, such a strategy amounted to a variation on Soviet conventional battle tactics of which Castro was highly critical.
29. K. Whitty, Review of Clive Holt, *At Thy Call We Did Not Falter*, iafrica.com, 22 August 2005, http://entertainment.iafrica.com/books/nonfiction/69246.html.
30. Sharon Ouditt, 'Myths, Memories, and Monuments: Reimagining the Great War', in Vincent Sherry (ed.), *The Cambridge Companion to the Literature of the First World War* (Cambridge, 2005), 256.
31. Telephone conversation with Clive Holt, 8 February 2006.
32. Van Niekerk relates his story to Peter Tucker. See *Behind the Lines of the Mind: Healing the Scars of War: The Story of a South African Parabat* (Self-published, 2007).
33. Van Niekerk's projects include the co-production of two films, *Nomansland* (1995) and *My Heart of Darkness* (2007). The first is a docudrama that depicts his attempts to come to terms with PTSD and is shot entirely in the confined space of a room in Stockholm. The second documents Van Niekerk's journey to Angola, which he undertakes in order to reclaim his life and lost innocence. The voice-over narration invokes 'the horror' à la Marlon Brando in an atmospheric setting that owes as much to *Apocalyse Now* as to the Angolan landscape. Van Niekerk engages with his erstwhile enemies whose forgiveness he seeks and obtains by way of a ritualistic cleansing ceremony. An extract from the film is available at http://www.youtube.com/watch?v=WOEuF6m9vns (accessed 3 November 2010). Most of the comments on the site were negative. Some veterans took exception to Van Niekerk's presumption to speak on behalf of all SADF soldiers. Others were angered by this advocacy of the need for atonement; they believe they owe no-one apologies as they, too, were victims of the war.
34. Anthony Feinstein, *Battle Scarred: Hidden Costs of the Border War* (Cape Town, 2011). An earlier version was published as *In Conflict* (Windhoek, 1998).
35. *Koevoet* was a counter-insurgency unit formed by the South African Police that operated in Namibia. Its name is derived from the Afrikaans word for 'crowbar'.

36. Transcript of 'The War Within', broadcast on M-Net, 10 June 2001, http://www.carteblanche.co.za/display/displayPrint.asp?ID=1750 (accessed 19 January 2006).
37. http://www.saveterans.org.za/ (accessed 12 November 2008). The site has since become defunct.
38. I elaborate on this in *South Africa's Border War*, 81–84.
39. L. Meskell, 'Trauma Culture: Remembering and Forgetting in the New South Africa', in Duncan Bell (ed.), *Memory, Trauma and World Politics* (Basingstoke, 2006), 157–75.
40. *Truth and Reconciliation Commission Report (TRC Report)*, v. 4 (Cape Town, 1998), 221.
41. *TRC Report*, v. 4, 242.
42. Mahmood Mamdani, 'Amnesty or Impunity? A Preliminary Critique of the Report of the Truth and Reconciliation Commission of South Africa', *Diacritics* 32(3–4) (2002), 35.
43. Those not mentioned in this chapter include Rick Andrew's *Buried in the Sky* (Johannesburg, 2001), Frank Nunes' *Altered States* (Durban, 2008), Granger Korff's *19 with a Bullet: A South African Paratrooper in Angola* (Johannesburg, 2009) and Tim Ramsden's *Border-Line Insanity: A National Serviceman's Story* (Alberton, 2009). This list does not include a number of volumes of oral history in which authors have collated conscripts' reminiscences and arranged them thematically. Examples are Barry Fowler's *Pro Patria* (Halifax, 1995, 2008), J.H. Thompson's *An Unpopular War: Voices of South African National Servicemen* (Cape Town, 2006) and Cameron Blake's *Troepie: From Call-Up to Camps* (Cape Town, 2009) and *From Soldier to Civvy: Reflections on National Service* (Cape Town, 2010). I have discussed this literature in *South Africa's Border War*, 18–22.
44. William Minter, 'The Armored Bubble: Military Memoirs from Apartheid's Warriors', *African Studies Review* 50(3) (2007), 150–51.
45. See, for example, Gary Koen, 'Understanding and Treating Combat-Related Post-Traumatic Stress Disorder: A Soldier's Story', unpublished MA thesis, Rhodes University, 1991. For a pithy review of the extent and nature of post-conflict trauma and other psychosocial problems among veterans from the ranks of the statutory and non-statutory forces, see Sasha Gear, 'The Road Back: Psycho-social Strains of Transition for South Africa's Ex-Combatants' in Baines and Vale, *Beyond the Border War*, 245–66.
46. Van Niekerk and Tucker, *Behind the Lines of the Mind*, 36.
47. *TRC Report*, v. 5, 360.
48. Meskell, 'Trauma Culture', 164.
49. Webb, *Ops Medic*, 93.
50. Jannie Geldenhuys, *Dié Wat Wen:'n Generaal se Storie uit 'n era van Oorlog en Vrede* (Pretoria, 1993) makes this argument most baldly. The English translation dispensed with the assertive title and provided a more neutral one. It was published as *A General's Story: From an Era of War and Peace* (Johannesburg, 1994).

It has since been revised and published under the title *At the Front: A General's Account of South Africa's Border War* (Johannesburg, 2009).
51. Whitty, Review of Clive Holt, *At Thy Call We Did Not Falter*.
52. Van Niekerk and Tucker, *Behind the Lines of the Mind*, 66.
53. They made a submission to the TRC that was co-ordinated by General Dirk Marais, former Deputy Chief of the Army, on behalf of his peers. It was entitled 'The Military in a Political Arena: The SADF and the TRC'. See Hilton Hamann, *Days of the Generals* (Cape Town, 2001), 130.
54. For instance, the testimony of conscript Kevin Hall has been carefully scrutinised and rebutted by Hamann, *Days of the Generals*, 221–23 and Magnus Malan, *My Lewe Saam met die SA Weermag* (Pretoria, 2006), 474–76.
55. Jenny Edkins, *Trauma and the Memory of Politics* (Cambridge, 2003), 4.
56. D. Foster, P. Haupt and M. de Beer, *The Theatre of Violence: Narratives of Protagonists in the South African Conflict* (Cape Town, 2005), 15–16.
57. TRC Special Submission, cited in Daniel Conway, '"Somewhere on the Border – of Credibility": The Cultural Construction and Contestation of "the Border" in White South African Society', in Baines and Vale, *Beyond the Border War*, 92.
58. *TRC Report*, vol. 4, 221.
59. Sasha Gear, *Wishing Us Away: Challenges Facing Ex-combatants in the 'New' South Africa* (Johannesburg, 2002).
60. Tal, *Worlds of Hurt*, 10.
61. Gillian Eagle, 'The Political Conundrums of Post-Traumatic Stress Disorder', in D. Hook and G. Eagle (eds), *Psychopathology and Social Prejudice* (Cape Town, 2002), 87.
62. Peter Novick, *The Holocaust and Collective Memory: The American Experience* (London, 1999), 8.
63. Margaret Macmillan, *The Use and Abuses of History* (London, 2009), 59.
64. I have elaborated upon this in *South Africa's Border War*, 84–87.
65. Teresa Godwin Phelps, *Shattered Voices: Language, Violence and the Work of Truth Commissions* (Philadelphia, 2004), 8.

BIBLIOGRAPHY

Memoirs and Oral Histories

Andrew, Rick. *Buried in the Sky*. Johannesburg: Penguin Books, 2001.
Blake, Cameron. *From Soldier to Civvy: Reflections on National Service*. Cape Town: Zebra Press, 2010.
Blake, Cameron. *Troepie: From Call-Up to Camps*. Cape Town: Zebra Press, 2009.
Breytenbach, Jan. *Buffalo Soldiers: The Story of South Africa's 32 Battalion 1975–1993*. Alberton: Galago, 2003.
Feinstein, Anthony. *Battle Scarred: Hidden Costs of the Border War*. Cape Town: Tafelberg, 2011.

Fowler, Barry. *Grensvegter? South African Army Psychologist*. Halifax: Sentinel Projects, 1996.
Fowler, Barry. *Pro Patria*. Halifax: Sentinel Projects, 1995, 2008.
Geldenhuys, Jannie. *Dié Wat Wen:'n Generaal se Storie uit 'n era van Oorlog en Vrede*. Pretoria: Van Schaik Publishers, 1993. Translated into English as *A General's Story: From an Era of War and Peace*. Johannesburg: Jonathan Ball Publishers, 1994; and *At the Front: A General's Account of South Africa's Border War*. Johannesburg: Jonathan Ball Publishers, 2009.
Holt, Clive. *At Thy Call We Did Not Falter*. Cape Town: Zebra Press, 2005.
Korff, Granger. *19 With a Bullet: A South African Paratrooper in Angola*. Johannesburg: 30° South Publishers.
Malan, Magnus. *My Lewe Saam met die SA Weermag*. Pretoria: Proteaboekhuis, 2006.
Nunes, Frank. *Altered States*. Durban: Just Done Publishing, 2008.
Ramsden, Tim. *Border-Line Insanity: A National Serviceman's Story*. Alberton: Galago, 2009.
Robbins, David. *On the Bridge of Goodbye*. Cape Town: Jonathan Ball, 2007.
Thompson, J.H. *An Unpopular War: Voices of South African National Servicemen*. Cape Town: Zebra Press, 2006.
Van Niekerk, Marius, and Peter Tucker. *Behind the Lines of the Mind: Healing the Scars of War: The Story of a South African Parabat*. Self-published, 2007.
Webb, Steven. *Ops Medic: A National Serviceman's Border War*. Alberton: Galago, 2008.

Secondary Sources

Baines, Gary. *South Africa's Border War: Conflicting Narratives and Contested Memories*. London: Bloomsbury Press, 2014.
Baines, Gary, and Peter Vale (eds). *Beyond the Border War: New Perspectives on Southern Africa's Late-Cold War Conflicts*. Pretoria: Unisa Press, 2008.
Burnell, Karen J., Nigel Hunt and Peter G. Coleman. 'Developing a Model of Narrative Analysis to Investigate the Role of Social Support in Coping with Traumatic War Memories'. *Narrative Inquiry* 19(1) (2009), 91–105.
Cock, Jacklyn, and Laurie Nathan (eds). *War and Society: The Militarisation of South Africa*. Claremont: David Philip, 1989.
Conway, Daniel. '"Somewhere on the Border – of Credibility": The Cultural Construction and Contestation of "the Border" in White South African Society', in Gary Baines and Peter Vale (eds), *Beyond the Border War: New Perspectives on Southern Africa's Late-Cold War Conflicts* (Pretoria: Unisa Press, 2008, 75–93.
Crossley, Michele L. *Introducing Narrative Psychology: Self, Trauma and the Construction of Meaning*. Buckingham: Open University Press, 2000.
Dosman, Edgar. 'Countdown to Cuito Cuanavale: Cuba's Angolan Campaign', in Gary Baines and Peter Vale (eds), *Beyond the Border War: New Perspectives on Southern Africa's Late-Cold War Conflicts* (Pretoria: Unisa Press, 2008, 207–28.

Eagle, Gillian. 'The Political Conundrums of Post-Traumatic Stress Disorder', in D. Hook and G. Eagle (eds), *Psychopathology and Social Prejudice* (Cape Town: University of Cape Town Press, 2002), 75–91.

Edkins, Jenny. *Trauma and the Memory of Politics*. Cambridge: Cambridge University Press, 2003.

Foster, D., P. Haupt and M. de Beer. *The Theatre of Violence: Narratives of Protagonists in the South African Conflict*. Cape Town: Institute for Justice and Reconciliation, 2005.

Gear, Sasha. 'The Road Back: Psycho-social Strains of Transition for South Africa's Ex-combatants', in Gary Baines and Peter Vale (eds), *Beyond the Border War: New Perspectives on Southern Africa's Late-Cold War Conflicts* (Pretoria: Unisa Press, 2008, 245–66.

Gear, Sasha. *Wishing Us Away: Challenges Facing Ex-combatants in the 'New' South Africa*. Johannesburg: Centre for the Study of Violence and Reconciliation, 2002.

George, Edward. *The Cuban Intervention in Angola, 1965–1991: From Che Guevara to Cuito Cuanavale*. London: Frank Cass, 2005.

Gleijeses, Piero. 'Cuba and the Independence of Namibia'. *Cold War History* 7(2) (2007), 285–303.

Gleijeses, Piero. 'Moscow's Proxy? Cuba and Africa 1975–1988'. *Journal of Cold War Studies* 8(2) (2006), 3–51.

Hamann, Hilton. *Days of the Generals*. Cape Town: Zebra Press, 2001.

Harari, Yuval Noah. 'Martial Illusions: War and Disillusionment in Twentieth-Century and Renaissance Military Memoirs'. *Journal of Military History* 69(1) (2005), 43–72.

Harari, Yuval Noah. *The Ultimate Experience: Battlefield Revelations and the Making of Modern War Culture, 1450–2000*. Basingstoke: Palgrave Macmillan, 2008.

Henke, Suzette A. *Shattered Subjects: Trauma and Testimony in Women's Life-Writing*. New York: St Martin's Press, 2000.

Hunt, Nigel C. *Memory, War and Trauma*. Cambridge: Cambridge University Press, 2010.

Hynes, Samuel. *The Soldier's Tale: Bearing Witness to Modern War*. London: Pimlico, 1998.

Kasrils, Ronnie. 'Historic Turning Point at Cuito Cuanavale'. Address to Public Forum 'Historic Turning Point at Cuito Cuanavale', Rhodes University, 28 May 2008. http://www.pmpsa.gov.za/FILES/pdfs/Kasrils.pdf (accessed 5 November 2010).

Macmillan, Margaret. *The Use and Abuses of History*. London: Profile Books, 2009.

Mamdani, Mahmood. 'Amnesty or Impunity? A Preliminary Critique of the Report of the Truth and Reconciliation Commission of South Africa'. *Diacritics* 32(3–4) (2002), 33–59.

McAdams, Dan P. *The Stories We Live By: Personal Myths and the Making of Self*. New York: Guildford Press, 1993.

Merwe, Chris van der, and Pumla Gobodo-Madikizela. *Narrating our Healing*. Newcastle: Cambridge Scholars Publishing, 2007.

Meskell, L. 'Trauma Culture: Remembering and Forgetting in the New South Africa', in Duncan Bell (ed.), *Memory, Trauma and World Politics* (Basingstoke: Palgrave Macmillan, 2006), 157–175.

Minter, William. 'The Armored Bubble: Military Memoirs from Apartheid's Warriors'. *African Studies Review* 50(3) (2007), 147–152.

Novick, Peter. *The Holocaust and Collective Memory: The American Experience*. London: Bloomsbury, 1999.

Ouditt, Sharon. 'Myths, Memories, and Monuments: Reimagining the Great War', in Vincent Sherry (ed.), *The Cambridge Companion to the Literature of the First World War* (Cambridge: Cambridge University Press, 2005), 245–60.

Phelps, Teresa Godwin. *Shattered Voices: Language, Violence and the Work of Truth Commissions*. Philadelphia: University of Pennsylvania Press, 2004.

Satchwell, Kathy. 'The Power to Defend: An Analysis of Various Aspects of the Defence Act', in Jacklyn Cock and Laurie Nathan (eds), *War and Society: The Militarisation of South Africa* (Claremont: David Philip, 1989), 40–50.

Scholtz, Leopold. *The SADF in the Border War, 1966–1989*. Cape Town: Tafelberg, 2013.

Steenkamp, Willem. 'The Citizen Soldier in the Border War', *Journal for Contemporary History* 31(3) (2006), 1–22.

Tal, Kali. *Worlds of Hurt: Reading the Literature of Trauma*. New York: Cambridge University Press, 1996.

Williams, David. *On the Border: The White South African Military Experience 1965–1990*. Cape Town: Tafelberg, 2008.

Gary Baines is Professor in the History Department at Rhodes University, Grahamstown, South Africa. He has published extensively on the history of Port Elizabeth, public history, memory studies and the apocalyptic imagination. He co-edited with Peter Vale, *Beyond the Border War: New Perspectives on Southern Africa's Late-Cold War Conflicts* (Unisa Press, 2008). He is also the author of *South Africa's 'Border War': Contested Narratives and Conflicting Memories* (Bloomsbury, 2014).

Chapter 13

Pugnacity, Pain and Professionalism
British Combat Memoirs from Afghanistan, 2006–14

Joanna Bourke

What does it feel like to kill other human beings? That was the first question asked of a young Apache pilot immediately after firing rockets into Taliban positions. There was really only one answer:

> I hadn't given it a moment's thought until now – it all seemed so natural after almost two years of training ... I'm glad we did what we did. On a professional level, I'm happy; I know I have passed the test. I didn't crumble under the pressure of the real thing, didn't decide I couldn't pull the trigger ... Now I'm a killer.

This response comes near the middle of this pilot's memoir, but the incident is clearly so important that it is mentioned a number of times. This first 'kill' is even used to introduce the memoir. In the book's first pages, readers are told that the crew of the Apache attack helicopter had just spotted three 'leakers' (that is, suspected Taliban moving away from a position the Apache has just bombed). 'My fingers close around the cold trigger', the memoirist recounted, adding:

> I pause for a split second to think about the gunfire I am about to spray across the battlefield. At that moment, I realize that I have no choice but to be good at my job. There are people relying on me.

These themes appear regularly in memoirs written by British warfighters who served in combat in Afghanistan: the heady emotions linked to killing, the centrality of professionalism, and the unquestioned obligation to defend one's comrades are at the heart of what writers of this genre of war memoirs view as the British warrior tradition. The only thing that differentiates this memoirist from her fellow war-scribblers is that she is a woman.

Charlotte Madison is not only Britain's first female Apache pilot, she is also the first British female pilot to kill in an Apache. She was proud to be in control of technologies that could 'punch holes in everything they touch' and described watching 'with satisfaction' as her weapons wreaked havoc on flesh and fields alike. After her first 'kill', she had moral scruples, but admitted that she felt 'on top of the world and [I] have a big grin plastered all over my face'. Back at base, her squadron's intelligence sergeant pinched his nose and screwed up his face as soon as he saw her, claiming that 'he can tell whether the returning crews have killed anyone just by smelling their breath'. She clearly had 'kill-breath'. For Madison, killing meant proving that she was 'just as good as one of the boys': 'after today', she said with pride, 'I'll no longer be the new girl'.[1]

In recent history, the involvement of British warfighters (a neologism that has become more prominent since 9/11) in Afghanistan began in October 2001, when Britain joined the US in conducting air strikes against Afghanistan during Operation Enduring Freedom. British troops 'on the ground', however, became significant from January 2006 when Britain took over leadership of the International Security Force in the Helmand province. In April that year, the Defence Secretary John Reid visited the province, announcing, 'We're in the south to help and protect the Afghan people to reconstruct their economy and democracy. We would be perfectly happy to leave in three years time [sic] without firing one shot'.[2]

These hopes were in vain. Between June and August, British soldiers expended around 450,000 rounds of small arms fire and 750 mortar rounds in 498 individual engagements with the enemy.[3] During the thirteen years of the campaign, 9,500 British troops served in 137 bases in the Helmand province; 453 were killed. During the entire campaign in Afghanistan, it is estimated that 92,000 Afghans were killed, 26,000 of whom were civilians. Nearly 100,000 more Afghans were wounded.[4] British involvement ended in October 2014, when the Union Jack was lowered at Camp Bastion.

This chapter asks: what can combat memoirs written by British servicemen and women who served in Afghanistan between 2006 and 2014 tell us about contemporary war memoirs, killing in the 'new wars' of the twenty-first century, and what military personnel and publishers sought to convey about the war in Afghanistan? As we will see, these memoirs differ significantly from those published after the First and Second World Wars. What they share, however, is the role of memoir as memory-making. In particular, the ironic register of innocence shattered and disillusionment is present, but is significantly muted. Instead, there is a glorification of technology, professionalism and pain (both inflicted and experienced).

This chapter is based on all the British combat memoirs that have been published so far concerning the conflict in Afghanistan between 2006 and 2014. The selection has used Yuval Noah Harari's definition of a memoir as a 'synthetic narrative text' dealing with a long time span; they are 'written retrospectively' and largely from personal memory; and, crucially, 'the authors appear as protagonist'.[5] In addition, I have only looked at *combat* memoirs; that is, memoirs written by protagonists who are active combatants. This means that I have excluded works that are largely political or strategic (for example, the autobiography of General Sir Richard Dannatt, Chief of the General Staff from 2006).[6] I have also excluded compilations of reminiscences and, perhaps more crucially, milblogging or online military blogs. These genres deserve an independent, extended analysis.

BRITISH COMBAT MEMOIRS FROM AFGHANISTAN

British involvement in the Helmand province was only in its first year when the first combat memoirs began to be published. They were extremely popular; some even became bestsellers. Their authors served in a range of positions, including snipers, reconnaissance soldiers, paratroopers, Marines and naval fighter pilots. None of the experiences and emotions they recount are representative of the thousands who were deployed to Afghanistan. Most are written by men who served in elite units or won medals. They are disproportionately the reminiscences of officers. The lives of warfighters who were killed or, in the aftermath of their military service, became homeless or committed suicide are absent. There is also the problem of censorship since the Ministry of Defence curtailed what could be published.[7]

Nevertheless, these memoirs share a lot in common. They have a similar layout. Nearly all are prefaced with maps of Afghanistan, especially the Helmand province, as well as sketches of the main operations and the layout of the bases. Most include glossaries – or, as one put it, lists on 'How to Speak Bootneck'[8] – which not only translate expert terms and acronyms, but also provide guidance in pronunciation (for example, one memoirist found it necessary to tell readers that the 30 mm High Explosive Dual Purpose round known as HEDP is 'pronounced "Hedpee"').[9] As if to impress upon readers their status as 'set apart' from civilian society, all introduce photographic snapshots of themselves and their comrades. These photographic mementoes are highly individualised. They show everyday life in base camp and beyond, with a strong emphasis on adventure, camaraderie and tomfoolery.

Furthermore, while these authors repeatedly insist on this separateness from their readers, they also loudly proclaim their ties to family back home. In other words, these warfighters present themselves as 'set apart' and yet intimately in touch with girlfriends, wives and children; there is nothing in between, such as ties to community or nation. In other words, loyalty to their unit was unshakable, but there was little sense of a larger identity. Nationalist proclamations are rare. The photographs inserted mid-volume testify to individual 'characters', engaged in an adventure that was (and was expected to be) transformative.

Unlike previous war memoirs, these ones are unembarrassed by the minutiae of everyday life, including nudity, sexual intercourse and defecation. Private lives are public. In addition, they are extremely frank about their relationships to family members, particularly girlfriends (and, for Madison, her boyfriend), wives and children. Earlier memoirists were much more reticent in discussing their 'private lives'. In contrast, it was *de rigueur* for these memoirists to talk about love, sex, domestic quarrels, pregnancy, the birth of their children, and what some called AIDS (that is, 'Apache Induced Divorce Syndrome').[10] Indeed, *not* to have done so would have signalled a loner and led to questions about sexual orientation.

Stylistically, the memoirs also share many characteristics. They are all written in an active style, or what can be called 'combat gothic'. They employ the first person, and their texts are strewn with direct speech, staccato sentences, unusual juxtapositions, colloquial vernacular and robust slang. Some list co-authors, who helped frame the text in more literary ways, but others probably received significant editorial help. Like memoirists from the two world wars, these writers routinely claim that the process of writing was an attempt to come to terms with their experiences of extreme violence.[11] Writing was a form of self-fashioning: it was 'an important therapeutic outlet'[12] and 'an emotional and cathartic experience'.[13]

Unlike the canonical war memoirs of the two world wars, memoirs written in the context of the 'new military' of the twenty-first century praise, rather than abhor, the industrial might of the pre-eminent military powers. Every author is captivated by the technological sophistication of Allied forces and they often devote a significant proportion of their text to gloating over their unit's technical wizardry.[14] Mark Hammond's *Immediate Response* and both of Ed Macy's memoirs, *Apache* and *Hell Fire*, even include extremely detailed technical diagrams of the 'Apache AH Mk1' and the 'Boeing Vertal Chinook HC Mk1'. These diagrams point out every detail of the weapon, including each vent, sensor, fan, hub, antenna, electronics bay, wheel, gearbox, seat, exhaust, panel, fuselage, shaft, blade, compartment and so on.[15]

This forensic attention to detail is partly a consequence of what Anthony King has called the 'new military' of post-9/11 society. Unlike previous mass armies, which emphasised normative values like comradeship and nationalism in order to motivate the soldiers, twenty-first-century forces emphasise professionalism. The professional soldier is 'a result of prolonged training', through which he 'acquires the skills which enable him to render a specialized service'. Professionalism 'has become the status honour of the armed forces today; it is the normative standard by which members of the group judge themselves and others, and enforce appropriate conduct to each other'.[16] These twenty-first-century warfighters were neither conscripts nor generalist 'grunts', but men and women who volunteered for service in extraordinarily skilled positions. Of course, not all serving personnel were specialists, but those who wrote memoirs were. These pilots, navigators of Apaches or Chinooks, snipers, paratroopers and reconnaissance officers were charged with maintaining and engaging technologies that gave them post-human powers of destruction. The fact that they were volunteers who had embraced the warrior profession with gusto, fully cognisant of the risks and challenges, enabled them to adopt the language of heroism and valour un-self-consciously. Most had been born into families with a long history of military service, and those who weren't claimed to be obsessed with everything military from childhood. As Doug Beattie put it, he was 'born in barracks'. When he was old enough to enlist, the men he was serving with 'seemed like family. Of course, some of them were'.[17] As a result, the trope of disillusionment that is so prevalent in First World War memoirs is largely absent – or, more accurately, disillusionment was part of what it meant to be a warfighter in the twenty-first century. In his classic *The Great War in Modern Memory*, Paul Fussell claimed that 'Every war is ironic because every war is worse than expected'.[18] This is only partially correct for the memoirists writing from Afghanistan. War itself *was* ironic. They expected nothing less.

The established trope of a breach between expectation and reality that featured so strongly in autobiographies from the two world wars (not to mention the memoirs and films of the Vietnam War period) is also not present in the lengthy accounts of military training. These authors expected military training to be one of the greatest tests of their lives; they knew it would be humiliating and painful; and, importantly, these were grounds for celebration. The 'baptism of fire' made the warfighter.[19]

In memoir after memoir, authors boast about their ability to endure the toughest military training. They brag about being 'bullied by all and sundry', enduring 'sadistic games', suffering sleep deprivation, being 'thrashed' and 'covered from head to toe in shit', and undergoing punitive discipline regimes.[20] As Patrick Hennessy of the Grenadier Guards recalled, they were 'beasted and beasted and beasted until we hated the world and the only way to stop the pain was to give in completely to all the screaming and aggression'. It made him go 'mad with horrible big fuck-off knives'.[21] The violence was visceral. Macy was proud that, when he was a 'crow' (that is, a junior paratrooper), he 'got one hell of a kicking'. In his training, he suffered a 'bust nose, dislocated jaw, three broken ribs and [a] split testicle', but once they had healed, he 'fell in love with life as a paratrooper'.[22] They all accepted the message that 'Pain is weakness leaving the body', as one poster at the Infantry Battle School put it.[23] Through undertaking a series of ordeals, 'boys' symbolically died, initiating the process by which warrior men were born. It was a position that the one female memoirist also accepted.

Rather than remonstrating against or becoming disillusioned by hazing and brutal training regimes, these apprentice warfighters believed that such practices were necessary to 'turn us from stinking civvie students into soldiers'.[24] The 'gravel belly' Marine, Mark Ormrod, admitted that 'we were threaders and thought it was shit, but it bonded the troop'. By 'forcing us to work as a unit to avoid the beastings', he insisted, the instructors were 'starting to turn us into Royal Marines'.[25] This was what Hennessy meant when he recalled that, once all the pain was over, 'I looked across at the boys and felt a surge of warmth, a previously unknown kinship with these men, these strangers'.[26]

Blood and wounds were badges of courage.[27] They were a source of pride. In Hennessy's words, 'there was nothing the platoons liked better than getting thrashed and comparing horror stories afterwards: whose platoon sergeant was the most ferocious, who had crawled the most punishment miles and slept the fewest hours'. He observed that the 'Sovereign's Banner' was awarded to the best platoon of the year, but Hennessy and his mates exclaimed: 'Screw the Sovereign's Banner!' Instead, what they really cared about was 'the post-exercise punditry and one-upmanship and who had lost and broken the most men'.[28] Violence not only created a sense of belonging for individual members, it also forged a strong, shared identity that would enable the group to act cohesively in combat. Inter-unit violence was meaningfully violent: pain maketh the man.

COMBAT

If proving oneself tough enough to undergo every humiliation and physical trial that instructors could inflict was a powerful rite of passage for these memoirists, actual combat was the pinnacle of a warfighter's identity. To be a man (or woman) of war *required* battlefield action.[29] This theme is not unique to these twenty-first-century memoirs; it has a long tradition in war writing. One of the most evocative examples of the emphasis on combat can be found in Patrick Bury's memoir of service in Afghanistan, entitled *Callsign Hades*. He lauded the 'infantry mission', which was 'To close with and kill the enemy, in all weather conditions, in all terrain by day or by night'. In case his readers did not fully grasp what he was referring to, he informed them that 'We relish that word, kill. KILL. We are the sharp end. We are the warriors. We are proud of our role. Who the fuck are the rest of the army? What the fuck do they do? We fight. We kill. We are the infantry. The warriors. The God of fucking war ... Destruction. It feels good'.[30]

As was typical in these combatant memoirs, Bury insisted that 'No one with the warrior calling joined the army to be a logistician, administrator or educator'.[31] Hennessy agreed. He noted that warfighters in Afghanistan resented the title of 'Operational Training and Advisory Group' or 'OPTAG'. Outsiders might think that their job was to 'mentor' and 'liaise' with the Afghan National Army, he fretted. It sounded too much 'like holding hands and building bridges'. Hennessy reminded readers that 'If we'd wanted to build bridges, we'd have joined the Engineers'. Instead, 'we were combat soldiers, teeth arm [sic], and our culture demanded more. If they'd called the task OBFET (Operational Blow the Fuck out of Everything Team), then every battlegroup in the Army would have been creaming for it'.[32] Indeed, some of the memoirists had served in noncombat roles. Ormrod, for instance, had been in motor transport, but was thrilled when he was 'deployed as a gravel belly [infantryman] at last'. He had found stories of 'Bootnecks' going into battle with 'fixed bayonets ... electrifying'; he rejoiced when he was finally able to join the elite club of active combatants.[33]

From their first day in Afghanistan, the chief question on everyone's minds was 'were we going to be shooting people?' and 'would we get into trouble if we did?' To their great relief, the answers were 'yes' and 'no', respectively.[34] The men were 'chomping at the bit', Apache pilot Macy recalled. Even being sent out on particularly risky missions 'didn't temper our excitement – it added to it'.[35]

Part of the reason for this excitement was the recognition that to be a true warfighter there were actually *two* initiation rites: as we have seen, the first was military training; the second was combat. All the memoirists confessed to being apprehensive. As Beattie recalled in *An Ordinary Soldier*, prior to going into battle he realised that 'we were about to be confronted by something exceptional'. It was 'going to be one hell of a test', but he was not afraid of the enemy so much as 'letting the side down, of not being up to the job'.[36] Ormrod and Bury made similar comments. Ormrod knew he was 'a pretty good Marine on exercise but no man can predict how he or his mates will behave under fire'. He observed that 'It was going to be the ultimate test ... would I be any good at it?'[37] Bury also noted that he had sought 'war's experience to prove to myself that I was a man'. When first coming under fire, his thoughts were 'this is it. Combat. The experience I have sought all my life. Now I will know if I have what it takes. Now I will know if I can do it'.[38] They all wanted to show that they were 'up for it'.[39] They only felt like they were a 'proper soldier' after the first confirmed 'kill'.[40]

Given this fixation with battle, it is hardly surprising that they pitied or despised service personnel who did not see actual combat. A sniper team who had 'seen little or no action' were considered to have bad luck: 'I was feeling a little sorry for them', observed their attack controller.[41] A fighter pilot who was unlucky enough not to have been given an appropriate target was taunted: was he a 'pacifist, or a war-dodger'?[42] Gender also mattered: Madison was teased for being a '"peace-loving" female' since she was the last of her unit to kill.[43] Those in support roles recognised their inferior status. On the rare occasions when they were allowed to watch the less gory sections of 'Kill TV' (that is, recordings of the attacks), it was a major 'morale booster'. 'Groundies' were quick to point out: 'Yes! I loaded that Hellfire!'[44] Men and women further behind the lines were nothing more than 'Rear. Echelon. Mother. Fuckers'[45] or 'Lungi Fungi'.[46]

KILLING

How did they subsequently narrate their acts of killing? In contrast to memoirs published by British soldiers serving during the two world wars of the twentieth century, these twenty-first-century 'warfighters' not only recognised that their identity and status *depended upon* murderous aggression, they actually revelled in their ability to inflict extreme violence on other human beings. Indeed, the importance of killing was signalled by the fact that many memoirs began with a graphic description of combat.[47] And the closer they got to the goriness, the better. As Hennessy remarked, there was something 'iconic' about the bayonet. It was at the 'top of the hierarchy' since 'everyone understands' that status lies in 'how close you get to the enemy'.[48] Warfighters who missed that face-to-face moment went to considerable effort to visit the scene of death afterwards. This was what Jake Scott was referring to when he sought permission to conduct a 'clearance patrol' after a major fight. He wanted to look at the bodies of the two men he had killed, admitting that it was 'sick ... but also fully satisfying'.[49] This emphasis on closeness includes not only *physical* proximity but technological as well, as the crew of Apaches testified.

Furthermore, every memoir used the language of 'adrenaline' in their descriptions of battle. They found it 'intoxicating'.[50] It provided a 'rush' that was 'off the scale'.[51] When Hennessy realised that he was going into battle for the first time, he admitted that he 'whoop[ed] with delight'. In breathless prose, he described how he and his comrades jumped 'gleefully from the vehicles' and started 'firing, actually firing real bullets, at the invisible and unperturbed enemy. Actually firing our weapons in glorious and chaotic anger. Actually firing'.[52] Direct hits led to 'whoops of delight'.[53] They would cheer, as though at a sports game.[54] Others would cry out 'Yee-hah, 'ave some of that!' while firing mortar rounds into enemy positions.[55] Some would scream, 'Hoofing! WHOOOHOOO! YESSSS! HOOFIN' DON'T MESS WITH THE BULL-DOGS, YOU BASTARDS!' as they punched the air.[56] One sniper described how he would give his fellow sniper a 'thumbs up' and shout, 'Good shit man, you rock!'[57]

Sexual metaphors were common. The first engagement with the enemy was described as 'popping your cherry': it warranted 'congratulations'.[58] Although the bayonet was a 'nasty weapon', it gave 'the army a hard-on'.[59] Fixing bayonets was 'pure infantry porn'.[60] Hennessy reflected that battle 'ramps the heartbeat up so high and pumps adrenaline and euphoria through the veins', adding that it could only be compared to 'the winning goal scoring punch, the first kiss, the triumphant knicker-peeling moment'. He wondered whether it was 'sexually charged because it's the ultimate affirmation of being alive'.[61] Attack aircraft were named after famous porn stars ('a suitable tribute to the lifeblood of deployed armies').[62] These killing machines were called 'Heather Brook, Tabitha Cash, Lolo Ferrari, Jenna Jameson, Tera Patrick, Taylor Rain, and Sylvia Saint', which allowed pilots and crew to say things like 'I've just spent three hours inside Lolo Ferrari, and she goes like a belt-fed Wombat'.[63] As a concession to 'Groundies' (some of whom were women) and 'to show the Army Air Corps wasn't sexist', they called the Apache XZ204 'Ron Jeremy' after 'the fastest dick in Hollywood'.[64] They were all killers in bed.

Excess was pleasurable. Their aim was not simply to wound or kill the enemy, but to eradicate them from the face of the earth. In fact, the formidable power of the weaponry available to these warfighters rendered 'excess' inevitable. As Madison bragged when she described bringing down a tower where the Taliban were sheltering, the 'destructive power' of the Hellfire air-to-surface missile was 'terrifying. It can defeat all known armour. So tanks, cars, houses, compounds – you name it; it can blow it up with the squeeze of a finger ... It's awesome; the tower simply vaporizes before my eyes'.[65] Numerous memoirs repeated Madison's mantra that their 'job' was deemed a success if the enemy was 'vaporised' or 'turned to dust'.[66] Although some memoirists wrote about legal understandings of proportionality (that is, that the degree of destruction had to be proportionate to the risk), others blandly reported dropping 500 pounds of high explosive on a small hut with one enemy combatant inside,[67] or firing a 40-mm high explosive against an insurgent when a 5.56 mm single-shot would have been sufficient.[68] In any case, after battle a good mood pervaded each unit. Men returning from battle were 'clearly jubilant', Docherty observed, especially since 'after two weeks of tedium in the filthy dust, they've finally fired their guns'.[69] Despite the risks, British warfighters recognised that combat was 'one of the most intense experiences of their lives so far ... It holds a tragic allure'.[70] Not surprisingly, those who missed the battle were 'gutted'.[71]

This pride that 'warfighters' took in extreme aggression made them frustrated in their dealings with the 'top brass'. For example, Macy simply could not understand the generals and politicians who were 'sensitive about classifying the Apache as a killing machine'. He complained that senior personnel 'didn't really like us to talk' about the purpose of the attack helicopter. 'God knows what they thought we were going to do when we go there', he jeered.[72] The authors of these combat memoirs were resentful of the restraints imposed by the Rules of Engagement.[73] Time and again, they railed against rules dictating that they could only fire at the enemy if they had been fired at first. Macy noted that Apache pilots and crew were 'expected to perform flawlessly – with our arms tied behind our backs. And if I put so much as a foot wrong, because I didn't have crystal balls and couldn't read the enemy's mind, I'd find myself court-martialled for not knowing whether the enemy had hostile intent'.[74] Memoirists believed that the Rules of Engagement were 'nonsense', having been drafted by lawyers and 'pen-pusher[s]' from Whitehall who had no appreciation of the realities of life in the front lines in Afghanistan.[75] They were bitter about the fact that 'Kill TV' leaked to the press and uploaded onto YouTube 'could make us look like war criminals'.[76] Some even complained that the politicians were being kinder to the enemy and to enemy prisoners-of-war than to their own men. As Ormrod grumbled, 'most of the lads thought HQ were being a bit too picky'.[77]

Even worse, they claimed that the Taliban were using the Rules of Engagement to evade attack – and even to taunt them. For example, from live camera feed inside the Apache, Macy described following a 'scruffy bloke with a beard, dressed from head to toe in black ... flapping his dishdash [*sic*] as he went to show us he wasn't armed'. He had 'got the message we were onto him. Cunning sod. He knew we couldn't engage him ... I didn't see his face, but I knew he'd have a grin plastered right across it'.[78] Ormrod agreed. The stringent Rules of Engagement, he argued, 'encouraged the Taliban[,] knowing we were cautious about opening fire. It was frustrating because every lad in every sanger [temporary fortified position] knew exactly what he was looking at, but the HQ always seemed to come own on the side of caution'. He recognised that it would simply prolong and intensify the conflict if errors were made and too many civilians were killed, but added that 'If you're just going to let the Taliban carry on as normal, you might as well go home'.[79]

Their resentment was fuelled by the realisation that the enemy had no compunction about breaking every rule of 'civilised' warfare. Rules of Engagement that had been appropriate for Northern Ireland were simply never going to work against this lawless enemy.[80] In Macy's words, 'Our enemy in southern Afghanistan couldn't give a stuff what mandate we'd come under. If they got their hands on us, a quick death would be the very best we could hope for'.[81] The 'powers that be' needed to 'dispense with the myth that Helmand was a tree-hugging mission'[82] or, as Bury sarcastically noted, that warfighters should act 'like the soft, moral, Geneva-bound men we are'.[83]

Because the Taliban never adhered to the rules, responses to them had to be uncompromising. In Ormrod's memoir entitled *Man Down*, he recounted an incident when an Afghan family came to their perimeter to plead for medical help for their badly scalded baby. He recalled not trusting them, fearing they would launch a suicide attack. 'In any other country', he admitted, he would have been thinking how to help the baby, but 'this is Afghanistan and we were living in a different reality. Out here, compassion might be a stupid and dangerous reaction. The Taliban would pour a pot of boiling water over a baby in a heartbeat if they thought it would get a suicide bomber inside our perimeter'.[84] When Bury was reflecting on collateral damage or the anguish of giving an order that meant that civilians were killed, he also asked, 'what could you do? It was the situation's fault. Afghanistan's fault. Anyone's but your own fault. The whole thing was a swirling, multi-coloured sandstorm viewed from a spinning Wurlitzer, which left you sick and never sure of anything and still needed you to make life-and-death decisions in an instant. A second ago'.[85]

It was 'Afghanistan's fault' that bloody dismemberment of the enemy was the ultimate aim. None of the memoirists attempted to mask this fact, a characteristic that further distinguishes these memoirs from many of their predecessors during the First and Second World Wars. In contrast to the 'top brass', Macy and his co-fighters celebrated the murderous potential of this combat helicopter. 'To me', he commented, 'it was breathtakingly simple'. Attack pilots

> didn't deliver soup. We didn't help old ladies across the road, and we didn't shoot out lollipops. Our main battle function was to close with the enemy and kill them. Snipers and Apache pilots were the only two combatants to get a detailed look at the face of the man they were about to kill. Nine times out of ten, we'd watch them in close-up on a five-inch-square screen before we pulled the trigger. It was no different to a sniper fixing his quarry in the sights of his bolt action rifle until the optimum moment to engage. We shared the same mindset: the mindset of a professional assassin.[86]

This way of thinking about combat made killing a very *personal* act. I mean this in three senses: it was carried out by individuals who possessed unique skills; the aggressors were emotionally invested in the violence; and the descriptions of it were visceral. For example, Beattie devoted an entire page to an almost pornographic account of stabbing an enemy soldier to ensure that he was truly dead. He claimed that his 'sharpened blade' easily slid into the man. He

> heard the metal slice through the flesh, felt it break bone and cut gristle as it glided further in, right up to the hilt. Did I hear a small gasp from the man? I don't know, perhaps it was the devil inside me playing with my imagination. When it could go no further, I twisted the bayonet to increase the damage. Just as we'd been taught ... I didn't give it a second thought. Just as we had been taught.[87]

Similarly, in his memoir *Blood Clot* (2008), Scott exulted in the fact that the .50 cartridge 'could cut through men like a knife through warm butter'. He also observed that the 7.62 belt-fed machine gun (a 'widow-maker' that fired 1,000 rounds per minute) would 'tear you apart literally'. He added: 'I loved this weapon'.[88]

However, the outlook of a 'professional assassin' encouraged another, very different way of writing about the infliction of violence: that is, a detached, ironic, macho language. One example can be seen in the memoir of an Apache pilot where, after killing some insurgents who had been sheltering in a village, he coolly quipped that the 'freshly painted wall' of one of the houses 'got one final coat – toffee brown [blood] – but on the flip side, the washing was still clean'.[89]

This way of writing about killing often led to the trivialisation of weapons and their effects on human flesh. When 'Bommer' Grahame released flechettes (that is, five-inch-long Tungsten darts that shred human flesh) into enemy positions, he joked that 'I was no Carol Vorderman, but that was going to rasp'.[90] Flechettes were described as 'jinking through the air' before they 'blossomed' into their human and material targets.[91] Formidable weapons were 'delivered' on human targets, as if they were flowers.[92] Bombs were 'fireworks' and pilots had a 'grandstand view'.[93] Weapons caused a 'splash'.[94] Hellfire air-to-surface missiles were 'puppies.[95] Bright red blood was 'poetic and eerily beautiful'.[96] A sniper described his rounds as creating 'a small plume of pink mist'.[97] Killing was aestheticised.

The beguiling aesthetics of violence was partly conditioned by these men's exposure to the cinema of war. In all wars in the modern period, cinema has been influential in giving meaning to martial violence.[98] The war in Afghanistan is no exception although, as we will see, with a twist. All of the memoirs coming out of the British experience in Afghanistan make reference to films, some with great frequency. War films were important in these writers' childhoods and from the beginning of military training. Hennessy even maintained that films were used in at least two-thirds of their classes. He claimed that by the end of their time at Sandhurst, most soldiers would have watched all of *Band of Brothers*, most of *Gladiator* and *Saving Private Ryan*, as well as large parts of *Full Metal Jacket*, *A Bridge Too Far* and ('for reasons which escape me') *Heat*.[99] It was not surprising, then, that Bury concluded that his final exercise at Sandhurst was like 'being part of your own war movie, in which we direct and star ... Our own interactive *Saving Private Ryan* paid for by the British taxpayer'.[100]

This emphasis on film continued once these warfighters were deployed in Afghanistan. A great deal of time in camp was spent 'watching noisy Hollywood violence',[101] making it seem natural to view combat through the lens of *Apocalypse Now*,[102] *Black Hawk Down*,[103] *Platoon*,[104] *Full Metal Jacket*[105] or *Saving Private Ryan*,[106] and to see themselves as a 'band of brothers'.[107] Numerous memoirists claimed to be in 'Top Gun mode' or 'living out *Top Gun* fantasies'.[108] Even Beattie (who admitted that, given his relative maturity, he 'should have known better') was captivated by the 'romantic notion' of war inspired by Lawrence of Arabia and his Second World War hero Blair Mayne. In the field, Beattie admitted, 'It was just like *Top Gun*, me playing the Tom Cruise character Maverick, Chipper taking on Anthony Edwards' role as Goose, my wingman, the faithful number two'.[109] Under fire, 'reality seemed suspended', Beattie mused; he felt as if he was 'both a film star on the cinema screen, and the guy in the audience watching the movie'.[110]

There was a difference, though, in the way warfighters in Afghanistan viewed combat through the lens of film. Twenty-first-century service personnel had been influenced by the ironic, disillusioned cinema (and, indeed, literature, although that is mentioned much less frequently) of the post-Vietnam War period. These films not only reflected on the men's brutal realisation that war was not a movie – a frequent theme of First and Second World War cinema and literature – but they also self-consciously echoed the belief that war was full of ironic episodes, incongruous juxtapositions and inescapable disillusionment. When warfighters in Afghanistan drew on cinematic representations of combat, they imbibed the inevitability of irony and disillusionment. In other words, there is a defiant 'knowingness' in these memoirs, which reverses earlier tropes of innocence turning bitter with disillusionment. In effect, these warfighters fused the ironic, filmic and literary trope with a heroic, twenty-first-century 'professional military' one.

The cinematic imaginary was not the only lens through which killing was framed. At another extreme was the use of the science of ballistics. This was particularly fortunate since it was both a way of educating readers and of reminding readers of their superior knowledge of the science of war. We have already seen examples of this in the memoirist's love of acronyms and specialised terms. It appears in accounts of the effects of weapons on human bodies as well. For example, Macy informed readers that artillery shells, each of which contained eighty flechettes, were effective in attacking 'multiple personnel in the open'. He explained that these darts were capable of 'shredding everything within a fifty-metre spread. Each dart's intense supersonic speed created a huge vacuum behind it. If it hit a man in the chest, that vacuum would suck away everything in its path, and was powerful enough to tear flesh and muscle from a human target if it passed within four inches of one'.[111] Ormrod also described the devastating impact of cavitation on material and human bodies. In his words, 'My tracer was impacting right where I wanted it and I knew for certain I was hitting my man. Fire one 7.62mm round at a dustbin full of water and it doesn't just blow the lid off, the shockwave around the bullet will punch all the water out of it as well'. In case readers weren't sufficiently clear of the analogy between a 'dustbin full of water' and the human body, he reminded them that the weapon's effect at close range 'would be like putting a man through a meat grinder'.[112] In effect, both authors were describing the process of cavitation, whereby once missiles exceed a certain velocity, the severe shockwave creates a temporary cavity that wreaks terrible havoc.

THE AFGHANS

It was possible to write about weapons that turned humans into minced meat or simply 'vapourised' them because of dismissive attitudes towards Afghan civilians, police and army. There are some exceptions (most notably in the memoir of the linguist Docherty, who was actually able to talk directly to Afghan people),[113] but many of the memoirists seem to have despised the people they were supposed to be defending. They believed that Afghan communities 'hadn't changed for a thousand years',[114] and the Afghan people were dirty, left excrement in the streets and mistreated their women.[115] As Bury raged, 'I hate the locals ... For not returning our smiles. For not being human. For hating us. For watching us walk over IEDs'.[116]

Attitudes towards the Afghan army and police were more ambiguous. These locals could show considerable stoicism when wounded[117] and they had 'balls'.[118] However, as Hennessy complained, they

> couldn't shape their berets. They didn't get up early and they stopped everything for meals, for prayer, for a snooze. They had no discipline. They smoked strong hashish and mild opium. They couldn't map-read. They had no tanks, no planes, no order to the chaos of their stores. Their weapons weren't accounted for. Their barracks weren't healthy and safety compliant.[119]

The Afghan National Police (ANP) were corrupt and 'little better than a bunch of bandits'.[120] Others criticised their Afghan allies for being 'lunatics' who couldn't 'read a map, they don't understand grid references, they have no command-and-control structure, and no idea what we are trying to achieve'.[121] They were cowards.[122] They engaged in sexual activity with animals, young boys and men,[123] or as Grahame put it, they were 'as straight as a bloody roundabout'.[124]

Ambivalence also characterised their response to the Taliban enemy. There was a grudging respect for their tradition of 'fighting prowess'.[125] Macy (who routinely dehumanised the enemy) could admit that many were 'strong, well armed, well trained and ferocious'.[126] Ormrod was also complementary. He observed that the Taliban were 'ferocious and fanatical'. They also displayed traits that were respected by British warfighters. In other words,

> Unlike the Iraqi insurgents, they loved a scrap and were prepared to stand and fight like a proper enemy. They weren't idiots either. Some of our blokes had been well impressed watching them fire and manoeuvre during contacts. The enemy had received decent infantry training and wasn't afraid to put it to use. You had to respect the fact that they were prepared to go toe to toe with us.

These warrior traits simply made him even more keen to kill them. In his words, 'I couldn't wait to have a crack at them'.[127]

They never let their respect go too far, however. After all, British warfighters were there to kill. Grahame complained that the enemy had a 'sneaky-beaky' mode of operating. He complained that the Taliban fired from hiding places so the men didn't 'have a clue where the shot was coming from' (this was hardly a fair criticism since Grahame was responsible for directing fire strikes from Apaches high in the air).[128] The enemy, though, was expendable and scarcely human. A man who was running away after battle was a 'leaker' who had to be stopped.[129] Or, as one Apache pilot was told, 'If they're fighting-age males leaving the area of the fort, I'm happy they're leakers'.[130] Unlike British warfighters who exemplified 'training, professionalism and, above all, courage', the Taliban were 'like rats up a drainpipe'.[131] They were 'trapped rats ... a truly pathetic sight'[132] and Apache pilots played the game of 'bat-a-rat'.[133] They were 'quarry'.[134] In contrast, non-human animals were treated with immense concern and love. The title of Pen Farthing's memoir tells it all: *One Dog at a Time. Saving the Strays of Helmand. An Inspiring True Story* (2009).[135]

Indeed, the enemy did not really even feel pain. In Macy's words, 'If you shot a Taliban warrior, one 5.56-mm bullet wouldn't do. You'd have to put two or three in him'. In part, he believed that this was because the Taliban 'barely did first aid', so the men had nothing to lose. It was also because 'a lot of them were so smacked out [on drugs] they didn't even feel the rounds'.[136] Cartwright echoed this belief in his memoir *Sniper in Helmand* (2011). He noted that one Afghan soldier had been shot three times yet still managed to stumble away. 'It was widely rumoured at the time', Cartwright noted, 'that quite a few of the Taliban were high on heroin, which would have helped numb the pain'.[137] In Grahame's words, a Taliban fighter was 'high as a kite' and so was incapable of 'registering the bullets as they tore into him'.[138] It was a belief that may have helped alleviate some of the guilt of killing. This was what Ormrod reflected on when he admitted that killing the Taliban gave him neither pleasure nor pain. He 'didn't give them a second thought. The fact they must have been off their tits on opium to take on Marines in well-defended sangars, with no cover and no heavy weapons, made me feel no sympathy for them at all'.[139]

Ormrod's ethical detachment in killing was typical. These memoirists tended to eschew trauma narratives associated with slaughter. This does not mean they were emotionally neutral. As we have seen, they often expressed exhilaration in battle. They also often mused reflectively on the distress they were inflicting on other sentient human beings. What distinguished them from earlier war memoirs (especially those from the wars in Korea or

Vietnam) is their pragmatism. They needed to 'get on with the job' and sensibly 'come to terms with' the inevitable emotional turmoil of war. Even in those memoirs that were literally about dismemberment – notably Martyn Compton and Michelle Compton's *Home from War* – the tone is relentlessly upbeat and practical. As Martyn and Michelle Compton declare on the last page, 'Life's in your face all the time, and you can't back down. Tomorrow will keep coming, whether you like it or not – so you might as well face it'.[140] It is not that problems such as post-traumatic stress disorder, loneliness and alienation from civilian society are not mentioned – they are – but the response is pragmatic and professional rather than being couched in the language of trauma. Of course, this may be due to the fact that these men were writing their memoirs while still serving in the forces or only shortly after leaving. They do not want to be seen as traumatised soldiers, but as tough survivors. But it may also be because they are not bearing witness to atrocity in the self-conscious way that memoirists from the Vietnam War memoirs were doing. Rather, most accept that atrocities both inflicted and experienced were inevitable. Warfighters were professionals, with incredible practical skills, who simply 'did their best' in the cauldron of war.

CONCLUSION

Combat memoirs are examples of what Samuel Hynes called 'The Soldiers' Tale'.[141] Although I started this chapter with Charlotte Madison, Britain's first female Apache pilot, these 'soldiers' tales' were predominantly heterosexual and male. Male was the norm.[142] The word 'cunt' was used in a derogatory fashion[143] and university-educated soldiers or those who were temporarily frightened were 'gay' or 'fucking HOMO'.[144] Within the combat forces, there was considerable ambivalence about women. If they were tough, could 'muck in', 'had no problems with pulling the trigger' and 'hadn't sacrificed one ounce of femininity in the process', they might earn grudging admiration.[145] But they could never compete with the 'God of fucking war ... Destruction'.[146] As Beattie put it, 'I was completely devoted to my wife. Except I wasn't. Yes, I was in love, head over heels, but not just with her. The army was my mistress. And she knew how to captivate me. Whenever things were going stale, whenever I thought of ending it, she offered up a new challenge, a new temptation, a new inspiration'.[147]

Such passionate devotion to the 'mistress' of war characterised all these twenty-first-century memoirists. Their loyalty was to those men and women immediately around them, as well as their families back home, but the key emphasis was on their professional skills. Patriotism and ideology are remarkably muted. Except for a few brief sentences about 9/11 and vague talk of protecting society from terrorism, there is remarkably little about the 'why' of combat and a great deal about the 'how'. This makes it difficult to see these memoirs as witnessing the horrors of war. Rather, they pay homage to the inevitability of war without end and without borders. Traditional traits – such as heroism, honour and courage – were highly respected, even while they were being recast in an aggressive, affective bravado that their predecessors probably would not have understood or would have regarded as childish. Furthermore, rather than responding to the 'diminished status of war in public consciousness', as Elisabeth Piedmont-Marton argued in relation to Gulf War memoirs, these memoirs emerge from a young, male society steeped in the language, performance and practice of war, as imbibed in war films and First Person Shooter computer games.[148] They invite their readers to participate in the pleasure of violence, albeit from a safe distance.

NOTES

1. Charlotte Madison, *Dressed to Kill* (London, 2010), 3, 100–2 and 114–15.
2. 'A Shot in Afghanistan?', Channel 4 News, 14 July 2009, http://www.channel4.com/news/articles/uk/factcheck+a+shot+in+afghanistan/3266362.html.
3. Tim Ripley, *16 Air Assault Brigade: Britain's Rapid Reaction Force* (Barnsley, 2008), 257.
4. 'Costs of War. Afghan Civilians', http://watson.brown.edu/costsofwar (accessed 21 November 2015).
5. Yuval Noah Harari, *Renaissance Military Memoirs. War, History, and Identity, 1450–1600* (Woodbridge, 2004), 17; and Harari, 'Military Memoirs: A Historical Overview of the Genre from the Middle Ages to the Late Modern Era', *War and History* 14(3) (2007), 290.
6. General Sir Richard Dannatt, *Leading from the Front. The Autobiography* (London, 2010).
7. See Leo Docherty, *Desert of Death. A Soldier's Journey from Iraq to Afghanistan* (London, 2007).
8. Mark Ormrod, *Man Down* (London, 2009).
9. Ed Macy, *Hell Fire* (London, 2009), 106.
10. Ed Macy, *Apache* (London, 2008), 37; and Macy, *Hell Fire*, 140.
11. Doug Beattie with Philip Gomm, *An Ordinary Soldier. Afghanistan: A Ferocious Enemy. A Blood Conflict. One Man's Impossible Mission* (London, 2008), 296.
12. Patrick Hennessy, *The Junior Officers' Reading Club. Killing Time and Fighting Wars* (London, 2009), 328.
13. Colonel Stuart Tootal, *Danger Close. Commanding 3 PARA in Afghanistan* (London, 2009), xiv.

14. Macy, *Hell Fire*, 106–11.
15. Major Mark Hammond as told to Clare Macnaughton, *Immediate Response* (London, 2009), frontispiece; Macy, *Apache*, xxi–xiv; Macy, *Hell Fire*. Also see Commander Ade Orchard, *Joint Force Harrier* (London, 2008).
16. Anthony King, *The Combat Soldier: Infantry Tactics and Cohesion in the Twentieth and Twenty-First Centuries* (Oxford, 2013), 63 and 363.
17. Beattie, *An Ordinary Soldier*, 37.
18. Paul Fussell, *The Great War and Modern Memory* (New York and London, 1975), 7.
19. Orchard, *Joint Force Harrier*, 32.
20. Patrick Bury, *Callsign Hades* (London, 2010), 5 and 26; James Cartwright, *Sniper in Helmand* (Barnsley, 2011), 2–6; Hammond, *Immediate Response*, 19; Hennessy, *The Junior Officers' Reading Club*, 37 and 42–45; Ormrod, *Man Down*, 113 and 116; Tootal, *Danger Close*, 12; Martyn Compton and Michelle Compton, with Marnie Summerfield Smith, *Home from War. How Love Conquered the Horrors of a Soldier's Afghan Nightmare* (Edinburgh, 2009), 62; Madison, *Dressed to Kill*, 23–34.
21. Hennessy, *The Junior Officers' Reading Club*, 73.
22. Macy, *Apache*, 26.
23. Hennessy, *The Junior Officers' Reading Club*, 98.
24. Hennessy, *The Junior Officers' Reading Club*, 37.
25. Ormrod, *Man Down*, 117.
26. Hennessy, *The Junior Officers' Reading Club*, 54.
27. Ormrod, *Man Down*, 128.
28. Hennessy, *The Junior Officers' Reading Club*, 70.
29. The exception is Compton and Compton, *Home from War*, most of which deals with surviving horrific wounds.
30. Bury, *Callsign Hades*, 44–46.
31. Bury, *Callsign Hades*, 33.
32. Hennessy, *The Junior Officers' Reading Club*, 14.
33. Ormrod, *Man Down*, 20–21.
34. Hennessy, *The Junior Officers' Reading Club*, 9.
35. Macy, *Apache*, 198–99.
36. Beattie, *An Ordinary Soldier*, 75. Also see Hammond, *Immediate Response*, 49; and Tootal, *Danger Close*, 143.
37. Ormrod, *Man Down*, 21.
38. Bury, *Callsign Hades*, 8 and 20.
39. Docherty, *Desert of Death*, 103.
40. Cartwright, *Sniper in Helmand*, 64.
41. Sergeant Paul 'Bommer' Grahame and Damien Lewis, *Fire Strike 7/9* (London, 2009), 40. Also see Hammond, *Immediate Response*, 60; and Tootal, *Danger Close*, 22.
42. Orchard, *Joint Force Harrier*, 138. Also see 189.
43. Madison, *Dressed to Kill*, 114.
44. Macy, *Apache*, 90.
45. Bury, *Callsign Hades*, 221.

46. Tootal, *Danger Close*, 128.
47. Grahame and Lewis, *Fire Strike 7/9*, 1.
48. Hennessy, *The Junior Officers' Reading Club*, 73.
49. Jake Scott, *Blood Clot. In Combat with the Patrols Platoon, 3 Para, Afghanistan 2006* (Solihull, 2008), 114.
50. Docherty, *Desert of Death*, 103.
51. Ormrod, *Man Down*, 42.
52. Hennessy, *The Junior Officers' Reading Club*, 4. The only time 'whooping' was mentioned in a disapproving way was by Madison, who thought it was 'unprofessional' (*Dressed to Kill*, 102).
53. Macy, *Apache*, 125.
54. Scott, *Blood Clot*, 133.
55. Ormrod, *Man Down*, 91 and 176.
56. Bury, *Callsign Hades*, 78. Also see Hammond, *Immediate Response*, 133.
57. Cartwright, *Sniper in Helmand*, 61–62.
58. Macy, *Apache*, 81.
59. Hennessy, *The Junior Officers' Reading Club*, 73.
60. Hennessy, *The Junior Officers' Reading Club*, 288.
61. Hennessy, *The Junior Officers' Reading Club*, 210–11.
62. Macy, *Apache*, 98.
63. Macy, *Apache*, 98.
64. Macy, *Apache*, 98–99.
65. Madison, *Dressed to Kill*, 113–14.
66. Macy, *Apache*, 165 and 213; Ormrod, *Man Down*, 89; Beattie, *An Ordinary Soldier*, 117; Scott, *Blood Clot*, 133; Grahame and Lewis, *Fire Strike 7/9*, 132.
67. Beattie, *An Ordinary Soldier*, 188.
68. Ormrod, *Man Down*, 99.
69. Docherty, *Desert of Death*, 160. Also see Tootal, *Danger Close*, 192.
70. Docherty, *Desert of Death*, 176–77.
71. Docherty, *Desert of Death*, 176.
72. Macy, *Apache*, 38.
73. Macy, *Apache*, 80.
74. Macy, *Hell Fire*, 168.
75. Macy, *Hell Fire*, 167. Also see Grahame and Lewis, *Fire Strike 7/9*, 72; Orchard, *Joint Force Harrier*, 215–18; Tootal, *Danger Close*, 88.
76. Macy, *Apache*, 43.
77. Ormrod, *Man Down*, 58–59.
78. Macy, *Apache*, 73 and 76. Also see Beattie, *An Ordinary Soldier*, 202–3; and Bury, *Callsign Hades*, 131; Grahame and Lewis, *Fire Strike 7/9*, 118; Docherty, *Desert of Death*, 103.
79. Ormrod, *Man Down*, 58–59.
80. Macy, *Apache*, 95.
81. Macy, *Apache*, 8.
82. Macy, *Apache*, 95.

83. Bury, *Callsign Hades*, 218.
84. Ormrod, *Man Down*, 54.
85. Bury, *Callsign Hades*, 91.
86. Macy, *Apache*, 38–39.
87. Beattie, *An Ordinary Soldier*, 124.
88. Scott, *Blood Clot*, 31 and 33. Also see Tootal, *Danger Close*, 3.
89. Macy, *Apache*, 165.
90. Grahame and Lewis, *Fire Strike 7/9*, 127.
91. Macy, *Apache*, 223.
92. Hammond, *Immediate Response*, 50; and Orchard, *Joint Force Harrier*, 194 and 256.
93. Macy, *Apache*, 121.
94. Macy, *Apache*, 230.
95. Macy, *Apache*, 259.
96. Hennessy, *The Junior Officers' Reading Club*, 302.
97. Cartwright, *Sniper in Helmand*, 62.
98. See my *An Intimate History of Killing: Face-to-Face Killing in Twentieth-Century Warfare* (London, 1999).
99. Hennessy, *The Junior Officers' Reading Club*, 55–56.
100. Bury, *Callsign Hades*, 38.
101. Docherty, *Desert of Death*, 61.
102. Bury, *Callsign Hades*, 190.
103. Macy, *Hell Fire*, 182; and Scott, *Blood Clot*, 57.
104. Hennessy, *The Junior Officers' Reading Club*, 55–56.
105. Cartwright, *Sniper in Helmand*, 4. Also see 59 and 89.
106. Grahame and Lewis, *Fire Strike 7/9*, 236.
107. Tootal, *Danger Close*, xiv.
108. Macy, *Apache*, 121; and Hennessy, *The Junior Officers' Reading Club*, 121. Also see Hammond, *Immediate Response*, 49 and 132; Orchard, *Joint Force Harrier*, 33; Pen Farthing, *One Dog at a Time. Saving the Strays of Helmand. An Inspiring True Story* (London, 2009), 19 and 22; Madison, *Dressed to Kill*, 80.
109. Beattie, *An Ordinary Soldier*, 80–81 and 88. Also see Macy, *Apache*, 17 and 35.
110. Beattie, *An Ordinary Soldier*, 95.
111. Macy, *Apache*, 76.
112. Ormrod, *Man Down*, 42.
113. Docherty, *Desert of Death*.
114. Ormrod, *Man Down*, 32 and 81. Also see Beattie, *An Ordinary Soldier*, 110.
115. Scott, *Blood Clot*, 61 and throughout; and Farthing, *One Dog at a Time*, 17.
116. Bury, *Callsign Hades*, 219.
117. Scott, *Blood Clot*, 124.
118. Hennessy, *The Junior Officers' Reading Club*, 17.
119. Hennessy, *The Junior Officers' Reading Club*, 17.
120. Tootal, *Danger Close*, 49.
121. Beattie, *An Ordinary Soldier*, 94. Also see 103.

122. Grahame and Lewis, *Fire Strike 7/9*, 90.
123. Ormrod, *Man Down*, 51; Beattie, *An Ordinary Soldier*, 137 and 223; Bury, *Callsign Hades*, 102 and 129; Docherty, *Desert of Death*, 93; Hennessy, *The Junior Officers' Reading Club*, 17; Tootal, *Danger Close*, 57.
124. Grahame and Lewis, *Fire Strike 7/9*, 84, 92 and 95; Hennessy, *The Junior Officers' Reading Club*, 222.
125. Tootal, *Danger Close*, 41; and Hennessy, *The Junior Officers' Reading Club*, 17.
126. Macy, *Apache*, 150.
127. Ormrod, *Man Down*, 21.
128. Grahame and Lewis, *Fire Strike 7/9*, 90.
129. Macy, *Apache*, 216.
130. Madison, *Dressed to Kill*, 2.
131. Macy, *Apache*, 118 and 120.
132. Macy, *Apache*, 229.
133. Madison, *Dressed to Kill*, 75.
134. Macy, *Apache*, 213.
135. Farthing, *One Dog at a Time*.
136. Macy, *Apache*, 85.
137. Cartwright, *Sniper in Helmand*, 40.
138. Grahame and Lewis, *Fire Strike 7/9*, 147.
139. Ormrod, *Man Down*, 43. Also see Bury, *Callsign Hades*, 115; and Grahame and Lewis, *Fire Strike 7/9*, 136–37 and 147.
140. Compton and Compton, *Home from War*, 304.
141. Samuel Hynes, *The Soldiers' Tale: Bearing Witness to Modern War* (London, 1997).
142. Orchard, *Joint Force Harrier*, 243 and 245.
143. Hennessy, *The Junior Officers' Reading Club*, 61 and 245.
144. Hennessy, *The Junior Officers' Reading Club*, 143 and 226.
145. Macy, *Apache*, 93 and 97–98. In contrast, see Orchard, *Joint Force Harrier*, 39.
146. Bury, *Callsign Hades*, 44–46.
147. Beattie, *An Ordinary Soldier*, 49.
148. Elisabeth Piedmont-Marton, 'Writing against the Vietnam War in Two Gulf War Memoirs. Anthony Swofford's *Jarhead* and Joel Turnipsee's *Baghdad Express*', in Alex Vernon (ed.), *Arms and the Self. War, the Military, and Autobiographical Writing* (Kent, OH, 2005), 257.

BIBLIOGRAPHY

Memoirs

Beattie, Doug, with Philip Gomm. *An Ordinary Soldier. Afghanistan: A Ferocious Enemy. A Blood Conflict. One Man's Impossible Mission.* London: Simon & Schuster, 2008.
Bury, Patrick. *Callsign Hades.* London: Simon & Schuster, 2010.
Cartwright, James. *Sniper in Helmand.* Barnsley: Pen & Sword, 2011.

Compton, Martyn, and Michelle Compton, with Marnie Summerfield Smith. *Home from War. How Love Conquered the Horrors of a Soldier's Afghan Nightmare.* Edinburgh: Mainstream Publishing, 2009.

Dannatt, General Sir Richard. *Leading from the Front. The Autobiography.* London: Corgi, 2010.

Docherty, Leo. *Desert of Death. A Soldier's Journey from Iraq to Afghanistan.* London: Faber & Faber, 2007.

Farthing, Pen. *One Dog at a Time. Saving the Strays of Helmand. An Inspiring True Story.* London: Ebury Press, 2009.

Grahame, Sergeant Paul 'Bommer', and Damien Lewis. *Fire Strike 7/9.* London: Ebury Press, 2009.

Hammond, Mark, with Clare Macnaughton. *Immediate Response.* London: Penguin Books, 2009.

Hennessy, Patrick. *The Junior Officers' Reading Club. Killing Time and Fighting Wars.* London: Penguin, 2009.

Macy, Ed. *Apache.* London: Harper Perennial, 2008.

Macy, Ed. *Hell Fire.* London: Harper Perennial, 2009.

Madison, Charlotte. *Dressed to Kill.* London: Headline Review, 2010.

Orchard, Commander Ade. *Joint Force Harrier.* London: Penguin, 2008.

Ormrod, Mark. *Man Down.* London: Corgi, 2009.

Ripley, Tim. *16 Air Assault Brigade: Britain's Rapid Reaction Force.* Barnsley: Pen & Sword, 2008.

Scott, Jake. *Blood Clot. In Combat with the Patrols Platoon, 3 Para, Afghanistan 2006.* Solihull: Helion and Co. Ltd., 2008.

Tootal, Colonel Stuart. *Danger Close. Commanding 3 PARA in Afghanistan.* London: John Murray, 2009.

Secondary Sources

Bourke, Joanna. *An Intimate History of Killing: Face-to-Face Killing in Twentieth-Century Warfare.* London: Granta, 1999.

Bourke, Joanna. *The Story of Pain: from Prayer to Painkillers.* Oxford: Oxford University Press, 2014.

Bourke, Joanna. *Wounding the World. How the Military and War Games Invade Our Lives.* London: Virago, 2015.

Fussell, Paul. *The Great War and Modern Memory.* New York and London: Oxford University Press, 1975.

Harari, Yuval Noah. *Renaissance Military Memoirs: War, History, and Identity, 1450–1600.* Woodbridge: Boydell, 2004.

Harari, Yuval N. 'Military Memoirs: A Historical Overview of the Genre from the Middle Ages to the Late Modern Era'. *War in History* 14(3) (2007), 289–309.

Hynes, Samuel. *The Soldiers' Tale: Bearing Witness to Modern War.* London: Pimlico, 1997.

King, Anthony. *The Combat Soldier: Infantry Tactics and Cohesion in the Twentieth and Twenty-First Centuries*. Oxford: Oxford University Press, 2013.

Piedmont-Marton, Elisabeth. 'Writing against the Vietnam War in Two Gulf War Memoirs. Anthony Swofford's *Jarhead* and Joel Turnipsee's *Baghdad Express*', in Alex Vernon (ed.), *Arms and the Self. War, the Military, and Autobiographical Writing* (Kent, OH: The Kent State University Press, 2005), 257–72.

Joanna Bourke is Professor of History in the School of History, Classics and Archaeology at Birkbeck, University of London, where she has taught since 1992. Her work has ranged from the social and economic history of Ireland in the late nineteenth and early twentieth centuries, to social histories of the British working classes between 1860 and the 1960s, to cultural histories of military conflict between the Anglo-Boer war and the present. In recent years, she has been researching the history of the emotions, particularly fear and hatred. She has also been exploring the history of sexual violence. She is the author of more than ten books, including *Dismembering the Male: Men's Bodies, Britain, and the Great War* (London, 1996); *An Intimate History of Killing: Face-to-Face Killing in Twentieth Century Warfare* (London, 1999); *Fear: A Cultural History* (London, 2005); and *Rape: A History from 1860s to the Present* (London, 2007). Her latest work is *The Story of Pain: From Prayer to Painkillers* (Oxford, 2014).

Index

Aaron, Daniel 73
Abu Lughod, Lila 195, 202
Abu Sitta, Salman 202
accuracy or 'authenticity' of memoirs 6, 8, 100, 143–4, 177, 232, 247n44
Afghanistan 5, 277–94
   Afghan National Police (ANP) 291
   Afghans, attitudes towards 287–8, 291–3
   'Apache Induced Divorce Syndrome' ('AIDS') 280
   Apache (Macy, E.) 281
   battlefield action 283–4
   Blood Clot (Scott, J.) 288
   British combat memoirs (2006-14) 277–94
   Callsign Hades (Bury, P.) 283
   Camp Bastion 278
   casualties in 278
   cinema of war, influence of 289–90
   combatant memoirs from 279–82
   endurance 282
   everyday life, minutiae of 280
   excess, pleasure in 284–5
   expectation and reality, trope of breach between 281–2
   forensic attention to detail 281
   Hell Fire (Macy, E.) 281
   Helmand, International Security Force in 278
   High Explosive Dual Purpose (HEDP) rounds 279–80
   Home from War (Compton, M. and Compton, M.) 293
   Immediate Response (Hammond, M.) 280–81
   industrial might of military powers, praise for 280–81
   killing in, experiences of 277, 278, 284–90
   loyalty to units 280
   Man Down (Ormrod, M.) 287
   memoirs of warfare in, themes of 278, 280–81
   non-combat personnel, attitude to 284
   One Dog at a Time. Saving the Strays of Helmand. An Inspiring True Story (Farthing, P.) 292
   Operation Enduring Freedom 278
   'Operational Training and Advisory Group' ('OPTAG') 283
   An Ordinary Soldier (Beattie, D.) 284
   peaceful reconstruction, hopes for 278
   post-9/11 military (and society) 281
   post-exercise punditry, one-upmanship and 282
   professionalism 278, 279, 281, 292
   Rules of Engagement 286–7

sexual metaphors, use of 284
Sniper in Helmand (Cartwright, J.) 292
style of memoirs 280
technical wizardry, pride in 280–81
top brass', dealings with 286
training regimes 282
warfighting 278, 279, 280, 281–2, 285–7, 290, 291–2
  initiation to 283–4
  passionate devotion to 293–4
African National Congress (ANC) 266, 267
Akimichi, Takano 125
Akira, Murai 123
Ali, Aruna Asaf 209
All Quiet on the Western Front (Remarque, E.M.) 2, 3, 11, 41
All That Remains (Khalidi, W.) 200
Allenby, Field Marshall Edmund 98
American Revolutionary War (1775-83) 51
American War of Independence (1775-83) 1, 15n3
Andrews, William L. 98, 102
Angola 266, 268, 270n22, 271n33, 299–60
  deployment of conscripts to 256–7
  National Front for the Liberation of Angola (FNLA) 269–70n18
  protracted South African Border War in 252
Antze, Paul 232–3
Anvayer, Sofya 156–8
'Apache Induced Divorce Syndrome' ('AIDS') 280
Apache (Macy, E.) 281
Appomattox 89
Arab political memoirs 196
archives
  Arab archives, absence of 195
  Israel,1948 War memoirs in 194, 196, 199–200, 201–2, 203n4

  Japanese memoirs of total war in 113–14, 115, 116, 117, 118, 119
  lacunae in 29–30
  military archives in Japan 118, 119
  National Archives in Paris 30
  reconstruction of Indian archives on Partition 216–17
  Soviet archives of Great Patriotic War 159
  United Nations archives 198
  Zionist archives 195
Ariès, Philippe 16n18
Armistice, silence of 35
Army Life in a Black Regiment (Higginson, T.W.) 87
Arnold, Benedict 76
Aruma, Shirō 116
Asahi News 116
Assmann, Jan 17n23
At Thy Call We Did Not Falter (Holt, C.) 252, 255–61, 261–3, 268
atonement in blood 148–50
Attlee, Clement 211
Augé, Marc 28
Auschwitz 30, 33
Austen, Jane 62
Austin, J.L. 27, 29, 34–5
Azad, Maulana 214, 220
Azuma Shirō Diary (Aruma, S.) 116

Banerian, James 238
Barbusse, Henri 39, 40, 41, 43
Barefoot Gen (Nakazawa, K.) 128
Barker, Pat 36, 40
Barkin, Kenneth D. 16n20
Barrell, John 56
Bartov, Omer 172
Battle Scarred: Hidden Costs of the Border War (Feinstein, A.) 262–3
battlefield action in Afghanistan 283–4
battlefield atrocities 116
battlefield experiences 112–13, 119–20, 130

of American Civil War 78–9, 86, 94–5, 100–101, 102
of Great War 94–5, 97–8, 102–3
battlefield feats, glorification of 10
battlefield gothic 10–11
battlefield silence 34–5
battlefield wounds 78–9
Beattie, Doug 281, 284, 288, 289, 293
Behind the Lines of the Mind: Healing the Scars of War (van Niekerk, M.) 262–3
Bells of Nagasaki (Takashi, N.) 122
Ben-Gurion, David 196
Ben Ze'ev, Efrat 33, 202
Bereaved Families Association *(Izokukai)* in Japan 114
Bhalla, Alok 209
Bhasin, Kamla 216
Bildung experience 48, 60, 63
Bildungsroman
  narrative therapy, memoir writing as 257
  remembering, war memoirs and culture of 2
'biographical illusion,' Bourdieu's perspective on 13–14
'Black Margins' (Manto, S.H.) 214
The Black Phalanx (Wilson, J.T.) 87
Blackwood's Edinburgh Magazine 58
Blanchot, Maurice 44
Blaser, Bernard 98
Bleeds My Memory (Anvayer, S.) 156–7
Blight, David 83
Bloch, Maurice 21n66
Blood Clot (Scott, J.) 288
blood-letting in 'civil' society 208–9
Blunden, Edmund 8–9, 96, 97, 102–3
Bogacheva, Irina 159
Bombay during partition 216
Božović, Saša 171, 174–5, 176, 182–3
Borba 173
Border War in South Africa, narrative therapy and 252–68
Born on the Fourth of July (Kovic, R.) 3
Borroughs, George 52

Bott, Alan 98
Bourdieu, Pierre 13
Bourke, Joanna 10, 11, 14, 277–300
Bragg, General Braxton 80
Brass, Paul 208
Bray, Norman 97
Brecht, Bertolt 43
Brewer, William 232
Brezhnev, Leonid 144, 155
Bristow, James 51
British combat memoirs (2006-14) in Afghanistan 277–94
British memoirs and memories of Great War 94–105
  battlefield experiences 94–5, 97–8, 102–3
  catalogue of war books, breadth of 99
  citizen-soldiers 99, 103, 105
  Dardanelles campaign 97–8
  dedications and forewords 101–2
  demoralisation 104
  There's a Devil in the Drum (Lucy, J.) 98
  eyewitness accounts 100
  Fire-Eater: Memoirs of a V.C. (Pollard, A.L.) 95–6
  global scale of war, change in literature in face of 98–9
  Good-bye to All That (Graves, R.) 97
  interwar war memoirs 95–6
  junior officers, writings of 98, 99
  life-altering events 103–4
  literary historiography, state of 95
  memoirs of war 96–9
  memorists of war 99–105
  Middle East 97–8
  non-fiction war books 96–7
  novels, memoirs contrasted with 100
  prisoner of war (POW) narratives 98
  process of writing 100–101
  Royal Flying Corps (RFC) 98
  shared experiences 101
  social meaning, war and 95–6

Testament of Youth (Brittain, V.) 104
transformation, narrative of 102–3
traumatic memories 100–101
'truth,' idea of 100
Vain Glory (Chapman, G.) 100
War Books (Falls, C.) 94
war memoirs, geographical concentrations of 97
The Weary Road (Douie, C.) 104
western front 96, 97–8, 101, 104
British retreat to Lisbon (1810) 57
Brittain, Vera 40, 96, 104
Britten, Benjamin 31
Burns, Ken 81
Bury, Patrick 283, 284, 287, 289, 291
Butalia, Urvashi 216
Byron, George Gordon, Lord 56, 60

Julius Caesar 1, 49
Cage, John 28
Callsign Hades (Bury, P.) 283
Calueque Dam 260–61
Calvin, John 34
Camp Bastion 278
campaigns, synopsis of Holt's involvement in 257–9
Carmel, General Moshe 197–8
Carrard, Philippe 18n29
Carrington, Charles 33, 97, 103, 104
Cartwright, James 292
Castro, Fidel 259
casualties
 in Afghanistan 278
 of Border War in South Africa 256, 258, 260, 270n19, 270n22
 of war 53
Catton, Bruce 74
Celan, Paul 32
Céline, Louis-Ferdinand 42
Centre for the Study of Violence and Reconciliation (CSVR) in South Africa 267
Chan Va Huy 235–6
Chanoff, David 229

Chapman, Guy 97, 100, 101–2, 104
Chiba, Japan, history museum in 113
Chickamauga 85–6, 90n14
Child, Lydia Maria 83–4
Chiran Special Attack Pilot Museum in Japan 114–15
Chizuko, Fushimi 125
Chrysanthemums and Nagasaki (Michiko, I.) 128
Chughtai, Ismat 210
cinema of war 289–90
 silent films 36–7
citizen-soldiers 2
 British memoirs and memories of Great War 99, 103, 105
The Civil War (Ken Burns documentary, PBS) 81
civilian life
 readjustment to 261
 war in contrast to luxuries of 61
civilian memoirs of total war 121–5, 129
Cleese, John 38
Co. Aytch (Watkins, S.R.) 78–82
Cohen, General Shmuel Mula 198
Čolaković, Rodoljub 172, 178
Cold Harbor 74
Coleridge, Samuel Taylor 57, 62
collaboration 168–9
 interpretation of 177–9
 resistance and, Partizan Epic and 169–71, 176–7, 177–9, 180–81
 Russian Free Army (ROA) and 151, 153–4
 sexual collaboration 156
collective memory 111, 112, 129, 202–3, 248n55
 international collective memory 196
 Palestinian collective memory 193, 201
 subversion of 197
 of war, soldiers' memoirs and 117–19, 129
collective violence in India 208

Collingwood, Robin George 201
combatant memoirs from Afghanistan 279–82
communities and total war, narratives and responsibilities 128–31
Compton, Martyn and Michelle 293
Confederate literature, nostalgia in 83–4
Confederate social order, defence of 76
Confederate Veteran 80, 87
Congress in India 211–12. 213, 214, 220–21n1, 222n28, 223n47
constative silences 34–8
Conyngham, David Power 77–8
The Crazy Iris (Masuji, I.) 122
Crimean War 5
'critical self-reflection' *(hansei)* 116
Crossley, Michele 254
Cruise, Tom 289
Cuito Cuanavale 257–8, 259–60, 270n22, 270n24, 271n27, 271n28
cultural memories, war memoirs and 48

The Danger Tree (Macfarlane, A.) 41
Dannatt, General Sir Richard 279
Dapčević, Peko 172–3
Dardanelles campaign 97–8
Darrow, Margaret H. 19n39
Das, Veena 216
Davidson, Basil 181
Davis, Jefferson 76
de Man, Paul 33
death, Holt's lack of emotion in relating to 259
debriefings 258–9
decolonisation, wars of 5
dedications, forewords and 101–2
Deegan, John 263
Defence Act in South Africa, amendments to (1976) 256
Delany, Paul 15n2
Delhi by Heart: Impressions of a Pakistani Traveller (Rumi, R.) 218–19

democratisation of war memoirs 2
demoralisation, war memoirs and 104
Denby, David J. 16n8
There's a Devil in the Drum (Lucy, J.) 98
Devji, Faisal 208, 212, 213
diaries, memoirs in 100, 113, 115, 117, 118–19, 122, 130, 131–2n6, 171, 203n5
   remembering, war memoirs and culture of 2, 8, 13, 16n12, 17n22, 17n25
Dien Vo Ky 238
disillusionment narrative 11
distrust, 'syndrome' of 152–3
Dizon, Lily 232
Djilas, Milovan 171, 176–7, 178, 179–80, 183, 184
Djordjevic, Dimitrije 183–4
Djuretić, Veselin 178–9
Docherty, Leo 286, 291
Dodd, William E. 87
Dostoyevsky, Fyodor 213
Douie, Charles 97, 104
Dulić, Tomislav 170, 184
Durova, Nadezhda 18n37

Eagle, Gillian 268
Early, Jubal A. 74–7, 84, 88–9
East Punjab, predatory attacks on Muslims in 212
Eclectic Review 56
Edwards, Anthony 289
Eksteins, Modris 20n60
emotional intensity in memoirs 50–51
End Conscription Campaign (ECC) in South Africa 267
The End of the Imperial Navy (Toyoda, S.) 118
To the End of the Land (Grossman, D.) 35
endurance 60, 282
   stoical endurance 61
English Civil War (1642-51) 1
English Review 51
essentialist silences 33, 40, 43–4

euphemisms 38–9, 41, 43, 44
Evans, A.J. 98
everyday life, minutiae of 280
excess, pleasure in 284–5
expectation and reality, trope of breach between 281–2
expulsion of Palestinians Isreal,1948 War memoirs 197–8
eyewitness accounts 78–9, 100, 146, 172, 186n12
   in romantic military memoirs 52–3
Eyre, Giles 98

fact and fiction in memoirs 3, 143–4
   fictionalisation 8–9, 19n51, 117, 122
   reality and fiction, blurring of line between 12
Falls, Cyril 94–5, 104–5
family silences 40–41
Farthing, Pen 292
Faulkner, William 74
Fawlty Towers (BBC TV) 38
Feinstein, Anthony 262–3
Fell, Alison S. 19n40
Felman, Shoshana 33–4
Le feu (Barbusse, H.) 39, 41, 42, 43
Fire-Eater: Memoirs of a V.C. (Pollard, A.L.) 95–6
firebombing in Tokyo 113, 114, 122–3, 124–5
Fireflies (Yōko, O.) 122
Fires on the Plain (Shōhei, Ō.) 117
First World War 2, 3, 7, 9, 147–8, 168, 213, 245n19, 279, 281, 288
   British memoirs and memories of 94–105
   cinema of war 37, 289–90
   literature on 17n25
   silence in war, witnesses to 33, 36, 37, 43
Fischer, Tibor 231
A Visit to Flanders, in July, 1815 (Simpson, J.) 52
Floyd, Thomas Hope 101

The Forest Chronicles (Sen, A.) 220
Fothergill, Robert A. 17n22
Fowler, Edward 16n13
France 5, 18n28, 30, 51, 54, 59, 170
French Revolutionary and Napoleonic Wars (1792-1815) 1, 3
Franco, Francisco 32
Franco-Prussian War (1870-71) 5
In Freedom's Shade (Kidwai, A.) 209, 216–18
Freeman, James 230, 233–4
Freud, Sigmund 36
Frey, Anne 49
Fukushima Prefectural Museum 113
Fumio, Noguchi 118
Fussell, Paul 38, 39, 95, 209, 281

Gallagher, Gary W. 76
Commentaries on the Gallic Wars (Caesar, J.) 1, 49
Gance, Abel 37
Gandhi, Mohandas Karamchand 209, 210, 212–13, 214, 217
Garapon, Jean 15n1
Garzon, Judge Balthazar 29, 32
Gaza, Israeli assault on 201
Geldenhuys, General Jannie 258, 260
Genesis 1948 (Kurzman, D.) 193, 199
Gentleman's Magazine 54
Germany 5, 18n28, 98, 150, 153, 156
   War of Unification 5
Gerster, Robin 19n42
Gettysburg 74, 77, 86, 87
Ghosh, Vishwajyoti 220
Gilbert, Vivian 97–8
Gildea, Robert 171–2
Gilpin, William 54–5
Girardet, Raoul 15–16n7
Gleig, George 49, 53–4, 57–9, 60, 61–3
global scale of war, change in literature in face of 98–9
Gobodo-Madikizela, Pumla 254
Golan, General Nahum 198
Good-bye to All That (Graves, R.)

British memoirs and memories of Great War 97
silence, war memoirs and witness to 42
'A Good Education' (Ghosh, V. and Sen, A.) 220
Gorbachev, Mikhail 144, 150
Gordon, Caroline 74
Gordon, John B. 84–7, 88–9
Graham, Stephen 98
Grahame, Sergeant Paul 'Bommer' 289, 291, 292
Grant, Ulysses S. 81–3, 85
Graves, Robert 3, 13, 40, 42
British memoirs and memories of Great War 96, 97, 98, 101
The Great War in Modern Memory (Fussell, P.) 281
Griffith, Wyn 100–101, 103
Grossman, David 35
Gujral, Satish 209

Haffner, Sebastian 20n54
Hagana Book 201
Haig, Field Marshall Douglad 43
Hajari, Nisid 211
Hammond, Mark 280–81
Harari, Yuval 253
Harari, Yuval Noah 48–9, 50, 60, 171, 279
Hardy, Jocelyn 98
Hasan, Mushirul 209
The Heart Divided (Nawaz, M.S.) 209
Heidegger, Martin 32
Hell Fire (Macy, E.) 281
Helmand, International Security Force in 278
Helmet for My Pillow (Leckie, R.) 2–3
Hemingway, Ernest 2
Henke, Suzette 254
Hennessy, Patrick 282, 284, 285, 289, 291
heroic-patriotic narrative 144, 150, 158
Herrs, Michael 13
Herzog, Tobey C. 20n52

Hewitson, Mark 171
A Hidden Biography (Veselovsky, B.) 150–51
Higginson, Thomas Wentworth 87
High Explosive Dual Purpose (HEDP) rounds 279–80
Hindu Mahasabha 211
Hiromitsu, Iwatani 118
Hiroshima Diary (Michihiko, H.) 122
Hirsch, Marianne 218
Hisako, Yoshizawa 122
Hisao, Kimura 118
history
  advent of alternative approaches to 5
  Israeli historical narrative 193–4
  memoirs as historical sources, scholarly distrust of 144
  oral histories 200, 201, 233
  positivist history 200–201
  'self-histories' *(jibunshi)* 115
  war, history and memoir writing 6–10
Hoang Vo 240–41
Hocke, Gustav René 17n22
Hoffman, Bettina 16n14
Holmes, Oliver Wendell 42–3
Holt, Clive 252, 255–61, 261–3, 264, 268
Home from War (Compton, M. and Compton, M.) 293
Hopkin, David M. 15–16n7
How To Do Things With Words (Austin, J.L.) 29
Howard, John 9
Howell, John 53
human bondage, southern perceptions on 75
humanisation of war 160
Hung, Captain Nguyen Tan 232
Hunt, Nigel 253–4
al-Husayani, Haj Amin 195
Hynes, Samuel 10, 21n68, 39, 95, 252–3, 293

Ichirō, Tomiyama 129
Immediate Response (Hammond, M.)
    280–81
India 5
    Great Calcutta Killing 211
    Hindu Mahasabha 211
    transfer of power in 208
India Partitioned (Hasan, M.) 209
India Wins Freedom (Azad, M.) 214
industrial might of military powers,
    praise for 280–81
'I-novels' *(shishōsetsu)* in Japan 117
interwar war memoirs 95–6
Intifadas in Israel 201
Iraq 5, 10, 291
The Irish Brigade and Its Campaigns
    (Conyngham, D.P.) 77–8
Isamu, Kogura 118
Israel 5, 12, 18n27, 20–21n64, 33
    Defence Forces Archives (IDFA)
        200, 201
    historical narrative from perspective
        of 193–4
    Palestinian conflict, roots of 200
    Zionist archives in 195
Israel, 1948 War memoirs
    Acre, poisoning of water supply into
        199
    All That Remains (Khalidi, W.) 200
    Arab archives, absence of 195
    Arab political memoirs 196
    archives, descriptions in 200
    collective memory, subversion of
        197
    dichotomous historiographical
        perspectives 193–4
    expulsion of Palestinians 197–8
    future research, suggestions for
        202–3
    Gaza 201
    Genesis 1948 (Kurzman, D.) 193, 199
    Hagana Book 201
    hegemonic narrative 195–6
        challenges to 197–8

Intifadas 201
Israel Defence Forces Archives
    (IDFA) 200, 201
Israeli and Zionist archives 195
Israeli historical narrative 193–4
Israeli-Palestinian conflict, roots of
    200
joint narrative of the victims and the
    victimisers 198
Lebanon, Israeli wars in 201
memorial industry in Israel 196
oral history 200, 201
The Palestinian Catastrophe (Palumbo,
    M.) 199
Palestinian collective memory
    193–4
Palestinian *Nakbah* (catastrophe)
    193, 194–5
Palestinian perspective 198–202
Palestinian war memoirs 194–5
personal memories 197
positivist history 200–201
sources, qualities and potential of
    198
Tantura, massacre at 201
veteran war memories 196
victims' view 198–202
Zionist narrative 195–6
Israel,1948 War memoirs 193–203
Italian War of Unification 5
Iwate Servicemen's War Records in Japan
    114

'J'Accuse' (Abel Gance film) 37
Janney, Caroline E. 81
Japan
    Bereaved Families Association
        (Izokukai) 114
    Chiba, history museum in 113
    Chiran Special Attack Pilot Museum
        114–15
    firebombing in Tokyo 113, 114,
        122–3, 124–5
    Fukushima Prefectural Museum 113

'I-novels' *(shishōsetsu)* in 117
Iwate Servicemen's War Records 114
Kitakami, Iwate Prefecture 113
Kōchi, 'Grassroots Museum' in 114
National Institute of Defence Studies (NIDS) 113
organisations, post-war and social, importance of 112–16
Osaka International Peace Museum ('Peace Osaka') 114
'Peace Movement' in 111, 114, 116
Ritsumeikan University's International Peace Center 114, 116
Sendai, history museum in 113
Shizuoka Peace Museum 114
Wadatsumi-kai 114
Women's National Defence Association *(Kokub? fujinkai)* 129
Yasukuni Shrine 115
Yūshūkan Museum 114, 116, 127
see also total war, Japanese memoirs of

Jarrhead (Swafford, A.) 10
'Jelly' (Manto, S.H.) *216*
Jinnah, Mohammed Ali 210, 211, 212, 213, 215, 216
Jones, E.H. 98
Jones, James 3
Jones, Major William 181
Journal of a Soldier of the Seventy-First (Howell, J., Ed.) 53
A Journal of the Operations of the Queen's Rangers, from the End of the Year 1777, to the Conclusion of the Late American War (Simcoe, J.) 51
journals, memoirs in 8, 13, 17n22, 80, 89n1, 156, 161n15
Journals of Major Robert Rogers (1765) 51
Jünger, Ernst 42

Kahan, Claudine 21n71
Kamtekar, Indivar 213
Khalidi, Walid 198–9, 200

Khrushchev, Nikita 144
Kidwai, Anis 209, 210, 216–18, 220
Kihachirō, Sugehara 121
King, Anthony 281
King James Bible 31
Kirmayer, Laurence 230, 231–2
Kitakami, Iwate Prefecture in Japan 113
Kiyo, Watanabe 129
Kiyoko, Kameda (nee Kanemaru) 123–4
Knott, Sarah 16n9
Kōchi, 'Grassroots Museum' in Japan 114
Koevoet paramilitary organization 263, 266, 271n35
Kōhei, Watanabe 122
Kondrat'yev, Vyacheslav 146
Köpp, Gabriele 11, 20n62
Korean memoirs of total war 114, 127–8, 130–31, 136–7n58, 136n57
Korean War 5
Kothari, Rita 210
Kovačević, Sava 177
Kovic, Ron 3, 4
kulaks, Stalin's war on 147
Kumao, Harada 117
Kundera, Milan 231
Kurzman, Dan 193, 199

Lahore, life in (1946) 211
Lahore 1947 (Salim, A.) 209
Lambek, Michael 232–3
Langer, Lawrence 240
Lawrence, T.E. 97, 289
Lawson-Peebles, Robert 15n3, 51
Lebanon 35
   Israeli wars in 201
Leckie, Robert 3
Lee, General Robert E. 74–5, 76, 82
Lengel, Edward G. 16n12
Lessing, Doris 40
Letters from Portugal and Spain (Ker Porter, R.) 52

Levi, Primo 33
Lewis, C.S. 102
Lewis, Patrick A. 80
life-altering events 103–4
Lincoln, President Abraham 77
literary historiography, state of 95
literary interlocutors, role of 117–18
liturgical silences 30–31, 43–4
Locke, John 50
Loftus, Elizabeth 34
Lomonosov, Dmitry 143
  distrust, 'syndrome' of 152–3
Lomsky-Feder, Edna 18n27
London Review 52
Lonely Girls with Burning Eyes (Novak, M.) 3
Long Nguyen Van 234
Lost Cause, mythology of 75, 77, 78, 80–81, 83, 84–5, 87
'lost youth,' voice of 125–6, 129
loyalty to units in Afghanistan 280
Lucy, John 98
Ludendorff, General Erich 43

McAdams, Dan 254
McClellan, Major General George B. 86
Macfarlane, Alan 41
Mackenzie, Compton 98
McKinley, President William 83–4
Macy, Ed 281, 282, 283, 286–7, 288, 290, 291, 292
Madison, Charlotte 277–8, 280, 284, 285–6, 293
Mailer, Norman 3
Maimonides 31
Malihabadi, Josh 209
Man Down (Ormrod, M.) 287
Manning, Frederick 2, 100
Manto, Sa'adat Hasan 214–16, 218, 220
Marc, Franz 40
Mares'ov, Aleksey 152
Margalit, Avishai 42
Marjanovic, Vladislav 184

Markwick, Roger 14, 143–67
Masalha, Nur 196
'massacre of the innocents' 146–8
Masuji, Ibuse 122
Matar, Dina 195
Mayne, Blair 289
meaning, changing frameworks of 14
Meiring, Lieutenant Muller 260
A Memoir of the Last Year of the War for Independence (Early, J,A.) 75
Memoirs of the Late War in Asia (1788) 51
memorialisation 97, 130–31, 232, 242
  interwar memories 9–10
  memorial industry in Israel 196
  memories filtered by time 13–14
  memorists of war 99–105
  memory, Augé's perspective on 28
  postmemorial consciousness 218–20
  process in Japan 111–12
Mendelsohn, Felix 31
Menon, Ritu 210, 216
mental health of troops 260–61
Menzies, Robert 9
Mexican War (1846-48) 5
Michihiko, Hachiya 122
Michiko, Ishimure 128
Middle East 97–8, 196
The Middle Parts of Fortune (Manning, F.) 2
Mihailović, Dragoljub (Draža) 168–9, 178
Milburne, H. 53
The New and Enlarged Military Dictionary (1802) 49
Minter, William 264
Mitchell, Margaret 74, 79
Mitrović, Mitra 173, 174, 179, 181–2
Mitsuru, Yoshida 117
Molotov, Vyacheslav M. 151
Montesquiou-Fezensac, Raymond de 2
Monthly Review 62
Theory of Moral Sentiment (Smith, A.) 50
Moro, Aldo 201
Morris, Benny 199–200

Mortimer, Geoffrey 16n16
Mottram, R.H. 97, 100
Motzkin, Gabriel 17n21
Müller, Herta 44
Muslim League 211–12. 213, 223n47
  National Guard 211, 213
mutual culpability, notion of 219–20

The Naked and the Dead (Mailer, N.) 3
Namibia 259–60, 266, 271n28, 271n35
  deployment of conscripts to 256
  treatment by South Africa 256
namya 145–6, 156
Nanda, B.R. 210–14, 220
My Nanjing Platoon (Aruma, S.) 116
Naoe, Endō 122–3
Napoleon Bonaparte 85
  retreat from Moscow 2
narrative analysis, Hunt's model of 253–4
Narrative of the Sufferings of James Bristow, Belonging to the Bengal Artillery, During Ten Years Captivity with Hyder Ally and Tippoo Saheb (Bristow, J.) 51
narrative psychology 254
narrative therapy, memoir writing as 252–68
  African National Congress (ANC) 266, 267
  Angola, deployment of conscripts to 256–7
  Battle Scarred: Hidden Costs of the Border War (Feinstein, A.) 262–3
  Behind the Lines of the Mind: Healing the Scars of War (van Niekerk, M.) 262–3
  Bildungsroman 257
  Border War in South Africa, narrative therapy and 252–68
  Calueque Dam 260–61
  campaigns, synopsis of Holt's involvement in 257–9
  civilian life, readjustment to 261
  Cuito Cuanavale, Battle of 257–8, 259–60, 270n22, 270n24, 271n27, 271n28
  death, Holt's lack of emotion in relating to 259
  debriefings 258–9
  Koevoet paramilitary organization 263, 266, 271n35
  mental health of troops 260–61
  Namibia, deployment of conscripts to 256
  narrative analysis, Hunt's model of 253–4
  narrative psychology 254
  national servicemen (NSM) in South Africa 267
  loss of, political sensitivity of 256
  obligations of 255
  National Union for the Total Independence of Angola (UNITA) 256, 257
  paradigm of post-traumatic stress disorder (PTSD) 261–3
  People's Armed Forces of Liberation of Angola (FAPLA) 257, 260
  People's Liberation Army of Namibia (PLAN) 256
  post-traumatic stress disorder (PTSD) 252, 253–4, 258, 261–3, 265, 268, 271n33
    extent among SADF veterans of 263
  South African Veterans' Association (SAVA) 263
  South West Africa Peoples' Organization (SWAPO) 256
  At Thy Call We Did Not Falter (Holt, C.) 252, 255–61, 261–3, 268
  trauma
    challenge to assumptions of unspeakableness of 254–5
    in transition 263–8
  war and narration of 252–5

Truth and Reconciliation Commission (TRC) 263–4, 265–6, 267, 268
'The War Within' (documentary) 263
see also South Africa
Nathan, Laurie 267
National Institute of Defence Studies (NIDS) in Japan 113
national myths, war memoirs and 7–8
national servicemen (NSM) in South Africa 255–6, 259, 264–6, 267
National Union for the Total Independence of Angola (UNITA) 256, 257
Nawaz, Mumtaz Shah 209
Neale, Adam 55
Nedić, Milan 178
'negro equality,' anxieties about 76–7
Nehru, Jawaharlal 212, 214
Nets-Zehngut, Rafi 196
New York Times 77, 87
No Woman's Land (Menon, R.) 210
Noakhali killings (1946) 211
Noël, Colonel Jean-Nicolas-Auguste 3, 16n15
non-fiction war books 96–7
non-Japanese memoirs of total war 126–8, 129
'normal life,' war as rupture to 3
Novak, Marian Faye 3, 18n35
novelists, memoirists and 8–9
novels, memoirs contrasted with 100

O'Brien, Tim 27, 42
O'Connor, Flannery 74
Old Maps and New: Legacies of the Partition - A Pakistan Diary (Panjabi, K.) 219
One Dog at a Time. Saving the Strays of Helmand. An Inspiring True Story (Farthing, P.) 292
Operation Enduring Freedom 278
'Operational Training and Advisory Group' ('OPTAG') 283

An Account of the Operations of the British Army (Ormsby, J.) 52
oral histories 5, 136n54, 216–17, 233, 272n43
  Isreal and 1948 War memoirs 199–200, 201
  Palestinian oral history 197
An Ordinary Soldier (Beattie, D.) 284
Ormrod, Mark 282, 284, 286, 287, 290, 291–2
Ormsby, James 52, 55
Osaka International Peace Museum ('Peace Osaka') 114
Owen, Wilfred 35, 41, 44

Pakistan 5–6
  partition of India and 208–9, 211–19, 221n3, 223n47
Palestine 12, 97
  collective memory 193–4
  expulsion from Israel of Palestinians 197–8
  oral history of 197
  Palestinian *Nakbah* (catastrophe) 193, 194–5
  perspective on Israeli 1948 War memoirs 198–202
  politics of 195
  victims' view, 1948 in Israel 198–202
  war memoirs from perspective of 194–5
The Palestinian Catastrophe (Palumbo, M.) 199
Palumbo, Michael 199
Pandey, Gyanendra 216
Panjabi, Kavita 219
Pappe, Ilan 20–21n64, 193–205
Paris Revisited, in 1815, by Way of Brussels (Scott, J.) 52
Partition of India, memories of 208–20
  'Black Margins' (Manto, S.H.) 214
  blood-letting in 'civil' society 208–9
  Bombay during partition 216
  collective violence 208

Congress 211–12. 213, 214, 220–21n1, 222n28, 223n47
Delhi by Heart: Impressions of a Pakistani Traveller (Rumi, R.) 218–19
East Punjab, predatory attacks on Muslims in 212
The Forest Chronicles (Sen, A.) 220
In Freedom's Shade (Kidwai, A.) 209, 216–18
Gandhi, Mohandas Karamchand 209, 210, 212–13, 214, 217
'A Good Education' (Ghosh, V. and Sen, A.) 220
Great Calcutta Killing 211
The Heart Divided (Nawaz, M.S.) 209
Hindu Mahasabha 211
India Partitioned (Hasan, M.) 209
India Wins Freedom (Azad, M.) 214
'Jelly' (Manto, S.H.) 216
Jinnah, Mohammed Ali 210, 211, 212, 213, 215, 216
Lahore, life in (1946) 211
Lahore 1947 (Salim, A.) 209
memoirs and post-memoirs 209–10
Muslim League 211–12. 213, 223n47
National Guard 211, 213
mutual culpability, notion of 219–20
Nehru, Jawaharlal 212, 214
No Woman's Land (Menon, R.) 210
Noakhali killings (1946) 211
Old Maps and New: Legacies of the Partition - A Pakistan Diary (Panjabi, K.) 219
postmemorial consciousness 218–20
Punjab, catastrophe in 210–12
Rashtriya Swayam Sevak Sangh (RSSS) 211, 213
Rawalpindi and Multan, anarchy in 211
'retributive genocide' 208
self-reflexity in recent memoirs 218, 220

'A Stroll through the New Pakistan' (Manto, S.H.) 214–15
'Toba Tek Singh' (Manto, S.H.) 216
Torn from the Roots (Patel, K.) 216–17
Train to Pakistan (Singh, K.) 218
transfer of power 208
Unbordered Memories (Kothari, R.) 210
Witness to Partition: A Memoir (Nanda, B.R.) 210–14
Patel, Kamla 209, 210, 214, 216–17
Patriotic War
atonement in blood 148–50
legitimating state narrative of 144–5
patriotic conservatism 144
Soviet archives of Great Patriotic War 159
see also Russian post-Soviet memoirs of Great Patriotic War
Pavelić, Ante 177–8
Pavlowitch, Stevan K. 184
'Peace Movement' in Japan 111, 114, 116
Peninsular War (1808-14) 52–4
war interest fuelled by 52–3
Pennington, Reina 18n8
People's Armed Forces of Liberation of Angola (FAPLA) 257, 260
People's Commissariat of Internal Affairs (NKVD) 153
People's Liberation Army of Namibia (PLAN) 256
perestroika 145–6
performative speech act theory 27, 29
Personal Memoirs, 1885-86 (Grant, U.S.) 82–3, 85
personal memories 89, 95, 118, 197, 216, 232, 248n55, 257, 279
Peru, truth and reconciliation commission in 20n63
Petiteau, Natalie 15–16n7
Pham Quang 241
picturesque, utilisation of 54–9, 60–61

Three Essays: on Picturesque Beauty; on Picturesque Travel; and on Sketching Landscape (Gilpin, W.) 54–5
Piedmont-Marton, Elisabeth 294
political silences 29–30, 32, 38, 43–4
politics 32, 55, 88–9, 183
  of memoir production and preservation 116–28
  memory and responsibility, relationship between 129
  Palestinian politics 195
  politics-from-above narrative 195
  of post-Vietnam remembrance in US 233
  US liberal politics 233
  of Vietnamese-American re-education camps 235–6
  of war memoirs 10–11
  Yugoslav politics 187n28
Pollard, A.L. 95–6
Portelli, Alessandro 21n65, 201
Porter, Robert Ker 52, 60
positivist history 200–201
post-9/11 military (and society) 281
post-exercise punditry, one-upmanship and 282
post-traumatic stress disorder (PTSD) 252, 253–4, 258, 265, 268, 271n33
  extent among SADF veterans of 263
  paradigm of 261–3
postmemorial consciousness 218–20
POW Memoir (Shōhei, Ō.) 117
Pravda 144
prisoner-of-war (POW) narratives
  British memoirs and memories of Great War 98
  remembering, war memoirs and culture of 7, 37
Pritam, Amrita 210
privations of war, virtues of 61–2
professionalism in Afghanistan 278, 279, 281, 292
Proust, Marcel 213
Punjab, catastrophe in 210–12

Putin, Vladimir 144–5, 160

Quan Chu 239–40
Quarterly Review 53

Rabin, Yitzhak 199
race and slavery in Confederate veterans' memoirs 73–89
  Appomattox 89
  Army Life in a Black Regiment (Higginson, T.W.) 87
  The Black Phalanx (Wilson, J.T.) 87
  black soldiers 79–80
  Chickamauga 85–6, 90n14
  The Civil War (Ken Burns documentary, PBS) 81
  Co. Aytch (Watkins, S.R.) 78–82
  Cold Harbor 74
  Confederate Veteran 80, 87
  emancipation, warnings on consequences of 75–6
  Gettysburg 74, 77, 86, 87
  human bondage, southern perceptions on 75
  The Irish Brigade and Its Campaigns (Conyngham, D.P.) 77–8
  Lost Cause, mythology of 75, 77, 78, 80–81, 83, 84–5, 87
  A Memoir of the Last Year of the War for Independence (Early, J.A.) 75
  'negro equality,' anxieties about 76–7
  northern memoirs 81–3
  Personal Memoirs, 1885-86 (Grant, U.S.) 82–3, 85
  racism 76, 78, 79–80, 81, 82, 90n9
  remembrances of war
    public appetite for 73, 74
    scholarly attitudes to 73–4
  Reminiscences of the Civil War (Gordon, J.B.) 84–7
  Shiloh 74, 86
  slavery 74, 75–7, 78, 79, 80–82, 83, 84–5, 86–8

southern literature, nostalgia in 83–4
southern memoirists' address on race and memory of slavery 74
southern social order, defence of 76
Stone's River 74
United Confederate Veterans (UCV) association 84
The Unwritten War (Aaron, D.) 73
veterans' memoirs, importance of 74, 88–9
white supremacy, socio-political conflicts on 77, 80–81
racism 76, 78, 79–80, 81, 82, 90n9
Radcliffe, Cyril 212
Rashtriya Swayam Sevak Sangh (RSSS) 211, 213
Ravel, Maurice 31
Rawalpindi and Multan, anarchy in 211
reading war memoirs 12–15
Recollections of the Peninsula (Sherer, M.) 49, 56–7
Red Army
  leadership of, Shelkov's view of 147–8
  Main Political Directorate (GPU) of 158
  punishment company *(Shtrafrot)* 148–9
  women POWs, accusations of treason against 155
Reid, John 278
Remarque, Erich Maria 2, 3, 41
remembering, war memoirs and culture of 1–15
  accuracy or 'authenticity' of memoirs 6
  All Quiet on the Western Front (Remarque, E.M.) 2, 3, 11, 41
  Bildungsroman 2
  'biographical illusion,' Bourdieu's perspective on 13–14
  Born on the Fourth of July (Kovic, R.) 3

cathartic experience of writing 4
citizen soldiers 2
decolonisation, wars of 5
democratisation of war memoirs 2
diaries, memoirs in 8
disillusionment narrative 11
fictionalisation 8–9
future research, suggestions for 14–15
Helmet for My Pillow (Leckie, R.) 2–3
history, advent of alternative approaches to 5
intellectual exercise, writing as 13
Jarrhead (Swafford, A.) 10
journals, memoirs in 8
literature, growth of 5
Lonely Girls with Burning Eyes (Novak, M.) 3
meaning, changing frameworks of 14
memories filtered by time 13–14
memory between wars 9–10
The Middle Parts of Fortune (Manning, F.) 2
The Naked and the Dead (Mailer, N.) 3
Napoleon's retreat from Moscow 2
national myths, war memoirs and 7–8
'normal life,' war as rupture to 3
novelists, memoirists and 8–9
With the Old Breed: At Peleliu and Okinawa (Sledge, E.B.) 3
politics of war memoirs 10–11
prisoner-of-war (POW) narratives 7, 37, 98
reading war memoirs 12–15
reality and fiction, blurring of line between 12
reasons for writing 4
remembering, pain of 11
retrospective memory 13–14
The Thin Red Line (Jones, J.) 3
twentyfirst-century war memoirs 11
Undertones of War (Blunden, E.) 8–9

war, history and memoir writing 6–10
war memoirs
  history and 6
  male predomination in writing of 6–7
  Vietnam and change in mould of 3
  writing process 12–13
  writing to remember (and forget) 1–4
remembrances of war
  public appetite for 73, 74
  scholarly attitudes to 73–4
  see also memorialisation; war memoirs
Reminiscences of the Civil War (Gordon, J.B.) 84–7
Rendall, Steven 17n22
Repina, Lorina 143
Requiem for the Battleship Yamato (Mitsuru, Y.) 117
research, suggestions for
  Isreal,1948 War memoirs 202–3
  remembering, war memoirs and culture of 14–15
A Narrative of the Retreat of the British Army from Burgos (Borroughs, G.) 52
'retributive genocide' 208
retrospective memory 13–14
Richards, Frank 98
Rinnosuke, Senta 120
Ritsumeikan University's International Peace Center 114, 116
The Roads We Choose (Bogacheva, I.) 159
romantic authorship, *Bildung* of war and 59–63
romantic military memoirs 48–63
  Bildung experience 48, 60, 63
  British retreat to Lisbon (1810) 57
  civilian life, war in contrast to luxuries of 61
  cultural memories, war memoirs and 48

emotional intensity 50–51
eyewitness accounts of war 52–3
A Visit to Flanders, in July, 1815 (Simpson, J.) 52
Journal of a Soldier of the Seventy-First (Howell, J., Ed.) 53
A Journal of the Operations of the Queen's Rangers, from the End of the Year 1777, to the Conclusion of the Late American War (Simcoe, J.) 51
Journals of Major Robert Rogers (1765) 51
Letters from Portugal and Spain (Ker Porter, R.) 52
Memoirs of the Late War in Asia (1788) 51
The New and Enlarged Military Dictionary (1802) 49
Theory of Moral Sentiment (Smith, A.) 50
Narrative of the Sufferings of James Bristow, Belonging to the Bengal Artillery, During Ten Years Captivity with Hyder Ally and Tippoo Saheb (Bristow, J.) 51
An Account of the Operations of the British Army (Ormsby, J.) 52
Paris Revisited, in 1815, by Way of Brussels (Scott, J.) 52
Peninsular War (1808-14), war interest fuelled by 52–3
picturesque, utilisation of 54–9, 60–61
Three Essays: on Picturesque Beauty; on Picturesque Travel; and on Sketching Landscape (Gilpin, W.) 54–5
privations of war, virtues of 61–2
Recollections of the Peninsula (Sherer, M.) 49, 56–7
A Narrative of the Retreat of the British Army from Burgos (Borroughs, G.) 52
romantic authorship and *Bildung* of war 59–63

romanticism, sentimentalism and 48–9
sentimentalism
  sentimental military memoirs 49–54
  sentimentalism effects of 50
  State Romanticism of British literary culture 49, 62
The Subaltern (Gleig, G.) 49, 53–4, 57–9, 62
suffering in memoirs 51–2
A Room of One's Own (Woolf, V.) 40
Royal Flying Corps (RFC) 98
Rozhkova, N.E. 144
Rules of Engagement in Afghanistan 286–7
Rumi, Raza 218–19
Russian Free Army (ROA) 151, 153–4
Russian post-Soviet memoirs of Great Patriotic War 143–60
  atonement in blood 148–50
  Bleeds My Memory (Anvayer, S.) 156–7
  collaboration, Russian Free Army (ROA) and 153–4
  distrust, 'syndrome' of 152–3
  fact and fiction in memoirs 143–4
  heroic-patriotic narrative 144
  A Hidden Biography (Veselovsky, B.) 150–51
  humanisation of war 160
  kulaks, Stalin's war on 147
  'massacre of the innocents' 146–8
  memoirs as historical sources, scholarly distrust of 144
  patriotic conservatism 144
  Patriotic War, legitimating state narrative of 144–5
  People's Commissariat of Internal Affairs (NKVD) 153
  perestroika 145–6
  Red Army
    leadership of, Shelkov's view of 147–8
  Main Political Directorate (GPU) of 158
  punishment company *(Shtrafrot)* 148–9
  women POWs, accusations of treason against 155
  The Roads We Choose (Bogacheva, I.) 159
  Russian Free Army (ROA) 151, 153–4
  soldiers' memoirs, dearth of 145–6
  Soviet prisoners of war (POWs) 145, 146, 150–52, 156–7, 158, 160
    distrust of, syndrome of 152–3
    Red Army women POWs, accusations of treason against 155
  Stalin, Josef 144, 147, 152, 154, 157
    Order 227 from (concerning retreat) 147–8
    Order 270 from (concerning those taken prisoner) 150, 162n34
  Stalingrad 147–8, 154
  state-sanctified depiction of war 144
  suspicion, 'indelible stain' of 156–8
  taboo themes 158–9
  'traitors' 150–52
  women at war 154–6
  Young Woman with a Sniper's Rifle (Zhukova, Y.) 155
  Znamya 145–6, 156
Ryūza, Endō 125
Rzhevskaya, Yelena 145–6

Sa'di, Ahmad 195, 202
Sahgal, Lakshmi 209
Salim, Ahmad 209
Sassoon, Siegfried 3, 13, 100
Savimbi, Jonas 256
Savoskina, Yefrosiya 159
Scott, Jake 285, 288
Scott, John 52
Scott, Sir Walter 62

Second World War 2–3, 7, 9–10, 11, 169, 177, 178–9, 182, 279, 288
  cinema of war 289–90
  literature on 17n25
  Partition of India and 208, 210, 213, 220–21n1
  post-Soviet Russian memoirs of 143–60
'self-histories' *(jibunshi)* 115
self-reflexity 218, 220
Sen, Amiya 220
Sendai, history museum in 113
sentimentalism 62–3, 64n11, 64n12, 65n15
  about pre-1975 South Vietnam 237
  effects of 50
  Romanticism and 48
  sentimental military memoirs 49–54
Seven Years' War (1757-63) 51
sexual metaphors, use of 284
shared experiences 101
Shelkov, Mikhail 146–8
  blood, atonement in 148–50
Sherer, Moyle 49, 53–4, 55–7, 58, 59, 60–63
Shigeyoshi, Special Attack Pilot Hamazono 120
Shiloh 74, 86
Shizuoka Peace Museum 114
Shlaim, Avi 195
Shōhei, Ōoka 117
al-Shuqairi, Ahmad 195
silence, war memoirs and witness to 27–44
  Armistice, silence of 35
  Auschwitz 30, 33
  constative silences 34–8
  The Danger Tree (Macfarlane, A.) 41
  To the End of the Land (Grossman, D.) 35
  essentialist silences 33, 40, 43–4
  euphemisms 38–9, 41, 43, 44
  family silences 40–41
  Fawlty Towers (BBC TV) 38
  Le feu (Barbusse, H.) 39, 41, 42, 43
  Good-bye to All That (Graves, R.) 42
  How To Do Things With Words (Austin, J.L.) 29
  'J'Accuse' (Abel Gance film) 37
  lacunae in archives 29–30
  liturgical silences 30–31, 43–4
  memory, Augé's perspective on 28
  performative speech act theory of J.L. Austin 27, 29
  political silences 29–30, 32, 38, 43–4
  A Room of One's Own (Woolf, V.) 40
  silence
    forgetting and 29
    in music, power of 31
    performative nature of 28, 38–41
  silent films 36–7
  social construction of silence 31–2
  speech, remembrance and 29
  spiritualism 37
  In Stahlgewittern (Jünger, E.) 42
  traumatic silence 30, 35–6
  'truth' about war, memories and contested terrain of 41–3
  Voyage au bout de la nuit (Céline, L.-F.) 42
  witnesses, moral and immoral 41–3
  women's war memories 39–40
Simcoe, John 51
Simonov, Konstantin 146
Simpson, James 52
Singh, Khushwant 210, 218
Sinh Ha Thuc 240–41
slavery
  Confederate veterans' memoirs and 74, 75–7, 78, 79, 80–82, 83, 84–5, 86–8
  emancipation, warnings on consequences of 75–6
Sledge, Eugene Bondurant 3
Smith, Adam 50
Sniper in Helmand (Cartwright, J.) 292
social construction of silence 31–2
social meaning, war and 95–6

social organizations, memoirs and 112–16, 117, 124, 128–9
soldiers' memoirs
  collective memory of war and 117–19, 129
  dearth of Soviet memoirs 145–6
  see also memoirs of war
Solzhenitsyn, Alexander 241
Sommers, Cecil 98
South Africa
  Border War in, narrative therapy and 252–68
  Centre for the Study of Violence and Reconciliation (CSVR) 267
  Defence Act, amendments to (1976) 256
  Defence Force (SADF) 252, 255–8, 259–60, 262–3, 263–5, 266–7
  End Conscription Campaign (ECC) 267
  Namibia, treatment by 256
  Veterans' Association (SAVA) 263
South West Africa Peoples' Organization (SWAPO) 256
Southey, Robert 56
Soviet prisoners of war (POWs) 145, 146, 150–52, 156–7, 158, 160
  distrust of, syndrome of 152–3
  Red Army women POWs, accusations of treason against 155
Soviet Russia 7, 17n23, 173
  Gulag 240–41
  Korean soldiers captured by Soviet forces 127–8
  Manchurian border 116
  see also Russian post-Soviet memoirs of Great Patriotic War
Spanish Civil War 5
speech, remembrance and 29
spirtiualism 37
In Stahlgewittern (Jünger, E.) 42
Stalin, Josef 173

Order 227 from (concerning retreat) 147–8
Order 270 from (concerning those taken prisoner) 150, 162n34
post-Soviet memoirs of Great Patriotic War 144, 147, 152, 154, 157
Stalingrad 147–8, 154
State Romanticism of British literary culture 49, 62
state-sanctified depiction of war 144
Stone's River 74
'A Stroll through the New Pakistan' (Manto, S.H.) 214–15
The Subaltern (Gleig, G.) 49, 53–4, 57–9, 62
suffering 2, 8, 11, 33, 37, 48–9, 120–21, 159, 176, 264, 282
  British memoirs and memories of Great War 94, 95–6, 97, 98, 102–3, 104
  civilian suffering in Japan 122–3, 124–5, 128
  confrontation with forms of 53–4
  displacement of 65n26
  loss and, lack of moral purpose and 76
  personal suffering, hardship and 55
  Proust on 213
  romantic military memoirs and visions of 49–50, 51–2, 57, 59–60
  sacrifice and, stories of 173
  sentimental suffering 62–3
  stoical endurance of 61
  victimisation and 120–21
Suleiman, Susan Rubin 18n30
Suleri, Sara 210
'Summer Flower' (Tamiki, H.) 122
suspicion, 'indelible stain' of 156–8
Swafford, Anthony 10
Sweets, John 170

taboo themes in Soviet Russia 158–9

Taiwan, Japanese period (1895-1945) in 125–6
Takashi, Nagai 122
Tal, Kali 253, 267
Tamiki, Hara 122
Tang Truong Nhu 229–30
Tantura, massacre at 201
Tate, Allen 74
Taunsvi, Fikr 209
technical wizardry, pride in 280–81
Tennant, John 98
Testament of Youth (Brittain, V.) 104
Thieu Nguyen Van 229
The Thin Red Line (Jones, J.) 3
Thirty Years War (1618-48) 1, 10
Thuan Nguyen Ngoc 241–3
Timofeyeva-Yegorova, Anna 155–6
Tito, Josip Broz 168, 170, 172, 175–6, 179–80, 182
'Toba Tek Singh' (Manto, S.H.) 216
'top brass,' dealings with 286
Torn from the Roots (Patel, K.) 216–17
Toshio, Shimao 117
total war, Japanese memoirs of 111–31
  archives 113–14, 115, 116, 117, 118, 119
  Azuma Shirō Diary (Aruma, S.) 116
  Barefoot Gen (Nakazawa, K.) 128
  Bells of Nagasaki (Takashi, N.) 122
  Bereaved Families Association *(Izokukai)* 114
  Chiran Special Attack Pilot Museum 114–15
  Chrysanthemums and Nagasaki (Michiko, I.) 128
  civilian memoirs 121–5, 129
  collective memory of war, soldiers' memoirs and 117–19, 129
  communities, narratives and responsibilities 128–31
  The Crazy Iris (Masuji, I.) 122
  'critical self-reflection' *(hansei)* 116
  The End of the Imperial Navy (Toyoda, S.) 118
  firebombing in Tokyo 113, 114, 122–3, 124–5
  Fireflies (Yōko, O.) 122
  Fires on the Plain (Shōhei, Ō.) 117
  Hiroshima Diary (Michihiko, H.) 122
  Iwate Servicemen's War Records 114
  Korean memoirs 114, 127–8, 130–31, 136–7n58, 136n57
  literary interlocutors, role of 117–18
  'lost youth,' voice of 125–6, 129
  mass media, role of 115
  memorialisation process 111–12
  military archives 118, 119
  My Nanjing Platoon (Aruma, S.) 116
  National Institute of Defence Studies (NIDS), Tokyo 113
  non-Japanese memoirs 126–8, 129
  organisations, post-war and social, importance of 112–16
  politics of memoir production and preservation 116–28
  POW Memoir (Shōhei, Ō.) 117
  production of memoirs, state and 113
  Requiem for the Battleship Yamato (Mitsuru, Y.) 117
  'self-histories' *(jibunshi)* 115
  Shigeyoshi, Special Attack Pilot Hamazono 120
  social organizations, memoirs and 112–16, 117, 124, 128–9
  soldiers' memoirs, collective memory of war and 117–19, 129
  suffering, victimisation and 120–21
  'Summer Flower' (Tamiki, H.) 122
  Taiwan, Japanese period (1895-1945) in 125–6
  veterans' groups *(sen'yūkai)* 116
  war memoirs, mass-production of 114–15
  wartime discourse, tenacity of 119–20, 130
  wartime experiences
    'Peace Movement' and textualised

'memory' of 114
veterans' memoirs and 'truth' of 118–19
wartime propaganda, censorship and 112–13
wartime records, post-war reflection on 119
Yasukuni Shrine 115
Yūshūkan Museum 114, 116, 127
Toyoda, Soemu 118
Train to Pakistan (Singh, K.) 218
'traitors,' Soviet Russian perspective on 150–52
transformation, narrative of 102–3
trauma
challenge to assumptions of unspeakableness of 254–5
in transition 263–8
traumatic memories 100–101
traumatic silence 30, 35–6
war and narration of 252–5
Travers, Tim 49
'truth'
about war, memories and contested terrain of 41–3
idea of 100
Truth and Reconciliation Commission (TRC) in South Africa 263–4, 265–6, 267, 268

Unbordered Memories (Kothari, R.) 210
Undertones of War (Blunden, E.) 8–9
United Confederate Veterans (UCV) association 84
United States Literary Gazette 57
The Unwritten War (Aaron, D.) 73

Vain Glory (Chapman, G.) 100
van der Merwe, Chris 254
van Niekerk, Marius 262–3
Vernon, Alex 18n33
Veselovsky, Boris 150–52
veterans' groups *(sen'yūkai)* in Japan 116

victims of war 8, 14, 32, 34, 39, 50, 125, 126, 128, 144, 263, 271n33
joint narrative of the victims and the victimisers 198
Palestinian victims of Nakbah 198–9
suffering, victimisation and 120–21
'victim mentality,' embrace of 261
'victim' narrative, adoption of 123, 127, 130
victimised identity, emblems of 132–3
victims' view, 1948 in Israel 198–202
Vietnam 229–30
Army of the Republic of Vietnam (ARVN) 232
future of, competing visions of 229–30
Indochinese Communist Party (ICP) 231
National Liberation Front (NLF) in 229
Orderly Departure Program (ODP) 230
pan-Vietnamese identity 235
Vietnam War 3–4, 5, 7, 9–10, 229, 230, 231, 233, 234, 236, 241, 243–4
Afghanistan, influences on troops in 281–2, 290, 293
Vietnamese-American re-education camp narratives 229–44
agency, restoration of 233
American mediation of discourses 234
To Be Made Over: Tales of Socialist Reeducation in Vietnam (Thong H.S.) 231, 237–8
'boat people,' flight of 230
'collaborators' as 'non-people' 231, 234, 235–6
communist misrule, indictments of 231
disenfranchisement, victimhood and 233
experiential validation 232

heroic survival, trope of 231
historical revisionism 231
internment, hopelessness and 240–41
Lost Years: My 1,632 days in Vietnamese Reeducation Camps (Vu T.T.) 231, 234–7
'The Man Who Dreamed of Spring' (Thuan N.N.) 241–3
media and popular culture narratives of Vietnamese-American community 230
'A New Place' (Hoang V.) 240–41
'The Old Man Who Only Believed What He Saw' (Dien V.K.) 238
oral histories 233
Orderly Departure Program (ODP) 230
performative remembrance 232–3
prison memoirs 231–2
Provisional Revolutionary Government in South Vietnam 229
re-education, institutional discrimination 234–5
re-education camp memoirs
  disappearances and 232
  politicisation of 232–3, 235–6
  relative neglect of 230
  revelations from 243
re-education camp survivors 230
Saigon, fall of (April 1975) 229
'A Teacher in Ho Chi Minh City' (Quan C.) 239–40
Thong Huynh Sanh 231, 238, 240
US, Vietnamese influx into 230
Vu Tran Tri 231, 234–7, 240, 241, 243
'Welcome to Trang Lon, Reeducation Camp' (Sinh H.T.) 240–41
Vladimirov, Yury 153–4
Vlasov, General Andrey 151, 154
Vorderman, Carol 289

Voyage au bout de la nuit (Céline, L.-F.) 42

Wadatsumi-kai 114
Wagner-Jauregg, Julius 36
Wang Jingwei regime in China 123
War Books (Falls, C.) 94
war memoirs
  Confederate veterans' memoirs, importance of 74, 88–9
  cultural memories and 48
  democratisation of 2
  demoralisation and 104
  by foreign volunteers 17n26
  geographical concentrations of 97
  as historical sources, scholarly distrust of 144
  interwar war memoirs 95–6
  mass-production of 114–15
  memoirs and post-memoirs 209–10
  national myths and 7–8
  reading war memoirs 12–15
  remembering, war memoirs and culture of
    history and 6
    male predominance in writing of 6–7
    Vietnam and change in mould of 3
  twentyfirst-century memoirs 11
  veteran memories from 1948 War in Israel 196
  warfare in Afghanistan, themes of 278, 280–81
  see also British memoirs and memories of Great War
  see also diaries, memoirs in
'The War Within' (documentary) 263
warfighting in Afghanistan 278, 279, 280, 281–2, 285–7, 290, 291–2
  initiation to 283–4
  passionate devotion to 293–4
wartime discourse in Japan, tenacity of 119–20, 130
wartime experiences

'Peace Movement' and textualised 'memory' of 114
veterans' memoirs and 'truth' of 118–19
wartime propaganda, censorship and 112–13
wartime records, post-war reflection on 119
Waterloo 52–3
Watkins, Frederick H. 80
Watkins, Sam R. 78–82, 87, 88–9
Wayne, John 10
The Weary Road (Douie, C.) 104
West, Rebecca 40
West Bank 35, 195
western front 96, 97–8, 101, 104
white supremacy, socio-political conflicts on 77, 80–81
Whitmarsh, Andrew 20n55
Whitty, Karen 266
Wilson, Edmond 41
Wilson, Joseph T. 87
Winter, Jay 11, 17n24, 27–47
With the Old Breed: At Peleliu and Okinawa (Sledge, E.B.) 3
Witness to Partition: A Memoir (Nanda, B.R.) 210–14
witnesses, moral and immoral 41–3
Wittgenstein, Paul 31
women at war 7, 14–15, 146, 154–6, 171, 173–4
    in Afghanistan 277, 278–9, 281, 284–5, 293
    'comfort' women 126
    war memories of 39–40, 202
Women's National Defence Association *(Kokubō fujinkai)* in Japan 129
Woolf, Virginia 40
Wordsworth, William 62
writing
    cathartic experience of 4
    as intellectual exercise 13
    process of 12–13, 100–101
    reasons for 4
    to remember (and forget) 1–4
    war, history and memoir writing 6–10
Wu Jinchuan 126
Wuthenow, Ralph-Rainer 15n6

Xiao Jinhai 125

Yamashita, Samuel 122
Yasukuni Shrine 115
    Yūshūkan Museum 114, 116, 127
Yōko, Ota 122
Yoshiaki, Fukuma 114
Young, Hubert 97
Young Woman with a Sniper's Rifle (Zhukova, Y.) 155
Yugoslavia 5, 168–85, 197
    absolutes, war of 169–71
    The Allies and the Yugoslav War Drama (Djuretić, V.) 178–9
    Borba (Communist Party organ) 173
    Bosnia-Herzegovina, Partisan detachments in 172
    'brotherhood and unity,' foundation stone of 169–70
    Chetniks 168–9, 170, 178–9, 184
    collaboration
        interpretations of 177–9
        propagandistic assessment of 178–9
    Croatia 177–8
    'ego documents,' stimulation of interest in 171–2
    emotional beings, Partizans as 174–5
    establishment of state of 168
    fallen hero, Tito toppled 179–80
    gender blindness of Partizan Epic 180–83
    Kingdom of 170, 176, 187n28
    memoir literature 171–5
    moral probity, images of 174
    National Salvation, Government of (1941-44) 177–8

Neretva River 174–5
The New Class (Djilas, M.) 176–7
official historiography of war in 168–9, 170–71, 175–6, 177, 180–81, 184–5
order out of chaos, claims of creation of 176–7
ordinary people, roles of 174
Partizan culture, components of 176
Partizan Epic
   creation of 170
   distortions in memoirs of 175–83
   reimagination of 168–85
People's Liberation of Yugoslavia (AVNOJ) 173
politics of 187n28
resistance, demythologisation of 170–71
revolution and war, entanglement of 173
Serbian ultra-nationalism 178

Special Operations Executive (SOE) 181
suffering, sacrifice and hardship in Partisan warfare 173
Tebi, moja Dolores (Božović, S.) 171
Tito and Communist Party, leadership of 172–3
'truth' in memories 172
Twelve Months with Tito's Partisans (Jones, W.) 181
Ustaše in Croatia 177–8
violence of 'Balkan man' 177
Wartime (Djilas, M.) 171, 176–7
Winning Freedom (Čolaković, R.) 172
women in resistance 180–83
Yukiko, Yoshihara 124–5

Zhukov, Marshal Georgy 145
Zhukova, Yulya 155
Zinoman, Peter 231
Zionist narrative 195–6

www.ingramcontent.com/pod-product-compliance
Lightning Source LLC
Chambersburg PA
CBHW072144100526
44589CB00015B/2078